JOURNAL FOR THE STUDY OF THE OLD TESTAMENT
SUPPLEMENT SERIES
331

Sheffield Academic Press

Studies in the Archaeology of the Iron Age in Israel and Jordan

edited by
Amihai Mazar

with the assistance of
Ginny Mathias

Journal for the Study of the Old Testament
Supplement Series 331

Copyright © 2001 Sheffield Academic Press

Published by
Sheffield Academic Press Ltd
Mansion House
19 Kingfield Road
Sheffield S11 9AS
England

Typeset by Sheffield Academic Press
and
Printed on acid-free paper in Great Britain
by Bookcraft Ltd
Midsomer Norton, Bath

British Library Cataloguing-in-Publication Data

A catalogue record for this book is available
from the British Library

ISBN 1-84127-203-5

CONTENTS

PREFACE

The present volume is the outcome of a colloquium initiated and organized by the Institute of Jewish Studies, University College London, 16–17 April 1996. Professor Mark Geller was the initiator of the conference, and I helped in academic and professional matters. The colloquium took place in the Institute of Archaeology, UCL and was an opportunity for Israeli, British and other European scholars to meet and discuss matters relating to the Iron Age of Israel and Jordan. Out of the 18 lectures given during the colloquium, 13 lectures were submitted for publication.

The papers in this volume deal with various aspects of the Iron Age. The first four papers deal with spatial archaeology and settlement patterns. This subject has been extensively developed in Israel thanks to surface surveys carried out in the country since the early 1960s. Changes in settlement patterns are now recognized as a crucial tool for the study of changes in ancient societies; in Israel and Jordan they have a special significance for historical studies as well. The four papers in this section demonstrate the power of this tool. All of them are based on extensive field work carried out by A. Zertal in Samaria, A. Ofer in Judah, G. Lehman in the Akko Plain, and S. Gibson in various areas in the hill country of Israel.

The six papers in the second section deal with religion and iconography. The only two Iron Age temples known today in Israel, those of Dan and Arad, are discussed by A. Biran and Z. Herzog. Herzog's paper on Arad is revolutionary in relation to earlier conclusions presented by Y. Aharoni and by the author himself. R. Kletter and K. Prag discuss aspects of clay figurines and other cult objects; T. Ornan identifies the Assyrian goddess Ištar on a number of seals and on a silver pendant at Tel Miqne, and suggests relations to the biblical 'Queen of Heaven'; N. Franklin examines the iconography and meaning of the wall relief in Room V at Sargon's palace in Khorsabad.

The last section comprises three studies related to specific sites. M. Steiner presents her views on the controversial question of the urban development of Jerusalem during Iron Age II; A. Mazar presents the data concerning Iron Age II at Tel Beth Shean, and publishes Hebrew ostraca from that site. Finally, P. Bienkowski and L. Sedman discuss several finds from Busayra, the capital of Edom, and their relation to finds from Horvat Qitmit and 'En Haṣeva in Israel.

The present volume is published at a time when many questions relating to the Iron Age of Israel are under scrutiny. The controversial subjects are the relative and absolute chronology of the twelfth to ninth centuries, the nature and development of the Israelite states, and the role of archaeology in examining the validity of the biblical text. Though these questions are hardly discussed in the present volume, I hope that nevertheless the volume will contribute to the dynamic and ever-expanding subject to which the colloquium was dedicated.

I thank Professor Mark Geller and the Institute of Jewish Studies, University College London, and Professor Philip Davies and Sheffield Academic Press for making this publication possible. I also thank Miss Ginny Mathias from the Institute of Jewish Studies for her efforts in copy-editing and preparing the papers to go to press.

Amihai Mazar
The Hebrew University of Jerusalem

ABBREVIATIONS

AASOR	Annual of the American Schools of Oriental Research
ABD	David Noel Freedman (ed.), *The Anchor Bible Dictionary* (New York: Doubleday, 1992)
ADAJ	*Annual of the Department of Antiquities of Jordan*
AJA	*American Journal of Archaeology*
AN	*Archaeological News* (Jerusalem: Israel Antiquities Authority; Hebrew)
ANET	J.B. Pritchard (ed.), *Ancient Near Eastern Texts Relating to the Old Testament* (Princeton: Princeton University Press, 3rd edn, 1969)
AnOr	Analecta orientalia
AOAT	Alter Orient und Altes Testament
AOS	American Oriental Series
BA	*Biblical Archaeologist*
BAR	British Archaeological Reports, International Series
BARev	*Biblical Archaeology Review*
BASOR	*Bulletin of the American Schools of Oriental Research*
BBB	Bonner biblische Beiträge
BHS	*Biblia hebraica stuttgartensia*
BN	*Biblische Notizen*
BO	*Bibliotheca orientalis*
BWANT	Beitrage zur Wissenschaft vom Alten und Neuen Testament
BZ	*Biblische Zeitschrift*
BZAW	Beihefte zur *ZAW*
CTA	A. Herdner (ed.), *Corpus des tablettes en cunéiformes alphabétiques découvertes à Ras Shamra-Ugarit de 1929 à 1939* (Paris: Imprimerie nationale Geuthner, 1963)
EB	N. Tur-Sinai, S. Yeivin and B. Mazar (eds.), *Encyclopaedia Biblica* (Jerusalem, 1958–1976; Hebrew)
EI	*Eretz-Israel* (Jerusalem: Israel Exploration Society)
HAR	*Hebrew Annual Review*
HSM	Harvard Semitic Monographs
HTR	*Harvard Theological Review*
IEJ	*Israel Exploration Journal*
JAOS	*Journal of the American Oriental Society*
JBL	*Journal of Biblical Literature*

JNES	*Journal of Near Eastern Studies*
JNSL	*Journal of Northwest Semitic Languages*
JSOT	*Journal for the Study of the Old Testament*
JSOTSup	*Journal for the Study of the Old Testament*, Supplement Series
JSR	Z. Ehrlich and Y. Eshel (eds.), *Judaea and Samaria Research Studies, Proceedings of the Tenth Annual Meeting* (Kedumim-Ariel; Hebrew)
JSS	*Journal of Semitic Studies*
NEAEHL	E. Stern (ed.), *The New Encyclopaedia of Archaeological Excavations in the Holy Land* (4 vols.; Jerusalem, 1993).
OBO	Orbis biblicus et orientalis
PEFA	*Palestine Exploration Fund Annual*
PEFQS	*Palestine Exploration Fund, Quarterly Statement*
PEQ	*Palestine Exploration Quarterly*
PJ	*Palästina-Jahrbuch*
RB	*Revue Biblique*
RSV	Revised Standard Version
SBL	Society of Biblical Literature
SBLDS	SBL Dissertation Series
SJOT	*Scandinavian Journal of the Old Testament*
UF	*Ugarit-Forschungen*
VT	*Vetus Testamentum*
VTSup	*Vetus Testamentum*, Supplements
ZAW	*Zeitschrift für die alttestamentliche Wissenschaft*
ZDMG	*Zeitschrift der deutschen morgenländischen Gesellschaft*
ZDPV	*Zeitschrift des deutschen Palästina-Vereins*

LIST OF CONTRIBUTORS

AVRAHAM BIRAN
Nelson Glueck School of Biblical Archaeology, Hebrew Union College, Jerusalem, Israel

PIOTR BIENKOWSKI
National Museums and Galleries on Merseyside, Liverpool Museum, UK

NORMA FRANKLIN
Department of Archaeology, Tel Aviv University, Israel

SHIMON GIBSON
W.F. Albright Institute of Archaeological Research, Jerusalem, Israel

ZE'EV HERZOG
Tel Aviv University, Israel

RAZ KLETTER
Land of Israel Studies Department, University of Haifa, Israel

GUNNAR LEHMANN
Ben-Gurion University of the Negev, Israel

AMIHAI MAZAR
The Institute of Archaeology, The Hebrew University of Jerusalem, Israel

AVI OFER
Judaean Highland Project, Israel

TALLAY ORNAN
The Israel Museum, Jerusalem

KAY PRAG
The Manchester Museum, The University of Manchester, UK

LEONIE SEDMAN
School of Archaeology, Classics and Oriental Studies, University of Liverpool, UK

MARGREET L. STEINER
Leiden, Holland

ADAM ZERTAL
Department of Archaeology, Haifa University, Israel

Part I

SETTLEMENT PATTERNS AND LANDSCAPE ARCHAEOLOGY

1

THE MONARCHIC PERIOD IN THE JUDAEAN HIGHLAND: A SPATIAL OVERVIEW*

Avi Ofer

The Judaean Highland project was conducted by me, with the assistance of Gideon Suleimani and partially also Raz Kletter, from 1982 onwards. The research was conducted on behalf of the Israel Exploration Society, the Nadler Institute of Archaeology in Tel-Aviv University and the Israel Ministry of Science. I would like to thank especially Professor Kochavi, who gave me access to the material from his important rescue survey in the same region (1968; see Kochavi 1972), and helped us in many other ways.[1]

In the first part of this paper I will describe the region, the survey and the methods of evaluation. In the second half I will present some of the results concerning the Iron Age phases[2]—especially those of Iron Age 2, which is usually taken (rightly, as will be seen later) as the period of the Monarchy.

The Highland of Judah is the whole region south of Jerusalem, not including the city itself.[3] The area is around 800 sq. km.

*   The original lecture is reproduced here with detailed apparatus and minor changes (including the title). It is based on my dissertation (Ofer 1993), which was carried out under the supervision of Professors Moshe Kochavi and Nadav Na'aman. I would like to dedicate the article to the memory of Ilana, Na'aman's late wife, who passed away a few days before the original lecture was presented in the conference. All biblical references are according to the BHS; all English translations of biblical texts are taken from the RSV, unless otherwise stated.

1.   For a full list of institutions and individuals who helped us, see Ofer 1993: 2*-3*.

2.   For the ceramic sub-division of the Iron Age in Judah see Appendix 1A.

3.   In this I follow the biblical concept, cf. Josh. 15.8, 18.16. For some other purposes the Highland of Hebron may be a better unit to analyse, which includes

It is divided into six sub-regions:

1. The South[4]: dry, moderate topography.
2. The Southern Desert Fringe.
3. The 'Southern Springs': a mid-region between the South and the Central Highland, with some major perennial springs.
4. The Central Highland: characterized by fertile high valleys, the real heart of the Judaean Highland. Here is found the Tel of ancient Hebron, the natural centre of the Judaean Highland.
5. The Northern Highland: a narrow mountainous region in the north.
6. The Northern Desert Fringe.

All in all, 334 dated sites were surveyed in the Judaean Highland, from all ceramic periods. To evaluate this mass of data, a new method was developed.[5]

The crucial problem, once we have surveyed a site and identified the pottery, is estimating its size in each period in which it existed. For this, we use the percentages of identified sherds, in relation to the estimated maximum inhabited area of the site. Calculating the sherds' percentages is, in principle, a simple task—but one has to take care not to oversimplify it. First, we have to identify the pottery-rims which are indicative for each period, existing *only* then. We call those the unique sherds of each period.[6]

An example is a pottery analysis of Khirbet Karmil[7] (Table 1.1, Fig. 1.1). Note the typical distribution of unique sherds, as compared to those common to two following sub-periods, and to those common to the whole period of Iron Age 2. At first sight one may think that

---

only the first four sub-regions described below.

4. In Hebrew I call it Negev Ha'har, the Negev (southern and dry region) of the Highland, following Achsah, daughter of Caleb: 'כי ארץ הנגב נתתני' ('since you have set me in the land of the Negeb'), Josh. 15.19 = Judg. 1.15.

5. For the theoretic base and the practical evolution of this method see Ofer 1993: Part 2, 143-79 (excursi 2/A-2/B), English summary pp. 26*-28*.

6. Or *fossiles directeurs*. Although not fashionable, the *fossiles directeurs* are still highly important in ceramic analysis and dating of survey material.

7. Kh. Karmil, site no. (16-09) 321/32/1; see Ofer 1993: II, Appendix 2/A, 44, and pl. 50e(ה). The exact length of periods may, of course, be disputable. However, as in any case of quantification, one has to decide, and the figures here represent what I think is the best approximation. They are generally rounded to units of half a century, or 25 years in the very short stages of the Iron Age 2.

	Raw sherd–counting	Unweighted percentages	Weighted count	Count-weighted percentages	Period length (centuries)	Time-weighted percentages
OTTOMAN	1	1	1.0	1	4	0
MEDIAEVAL	1	1	1.1	1	8	0
Byz-Med	1	1				
BYZANTINE	15	13	24.2	20	3	13
Rom.-Byz.	11	9				
ROMAN 2	5	4	10.6	9	3	6
1-2	4	3				
ROMAN 1	2	2	5.1	4	1	9
Hel.-Rom.1	5	4				
HELLENISTIC	3	3	6.0	5	2.5	4
PERSIAN	2	2	3.3	3	2.5	2
3-Persian	4	3				
IRON 3	4	3	10.6	9	1.25	14
2c-3	4	3				
IRON 2C	6	5	15.5	13	1.25	21
2b-2c	5	4				
IRON 2B	2	2	5.2	4	1.25	7
2a-2b	2	2				
IRON 2A	3	3	5.4	5	1.25	7
Iron Age 2 (undivided)	8	7				
MB 2-3 ('2a-b')	26	22	26.0	22	3	14
EB 1	4	3	4.0	3	3.5	2
Unidentified	16					
Total	134					

Table 1.1. *Kh. Karmil—pottery reading and weighting (database for the following graphs). For the Iron Age phases see Appendix 1A.*

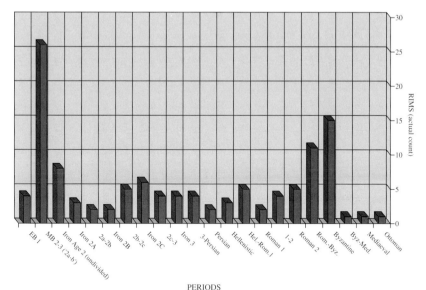

PERIODS

Fig. 1.1. *Kh. Karmil: unweighted sherd-count*

Middle Bronze Age and Byzantine Period are dominant in the site, while the Iron Age is not.

However, we have many sherds which can be identified, but not so accurately as the previous ones: they may belong to two or three consecutive periods. They have to be distributed among the identified periods according to the percentage of their proved sherds—the unique ones.[8] After such calculation, the graphs change; in our example the MB and Byzantine ages still higher, but Iron Age 2 phases are now much more significant (Fig. 1.2).

The next step refers to the different length of each period. The same number of people, living in the same inhabited area, during a period double in length, will leave us double number of sherds. We have to weight this factor. This can be done by dividing our sherd counting by the length of each period, then recalculating the percentage. This procedure changes the results to a large extent. Thus, the simplified counting of sherds was misleading. Iron Age 2c-3 phases, much shorter than the undivided MB or Byzantine ages, appear only now as they really are: the most significant phases of occupation in the site (Fig. 1.3).

8.   However, when we have such intermediate sherds but only one of their possible periods is clearly attested in the site, all of them will be attributed to that period only.

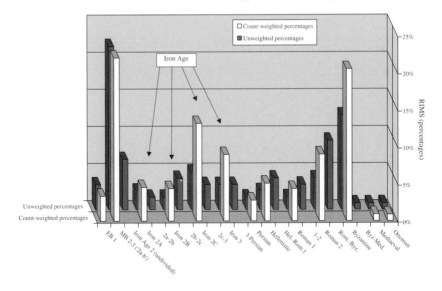

Fig. 1.2. *Kh. Karmil: weighted count*

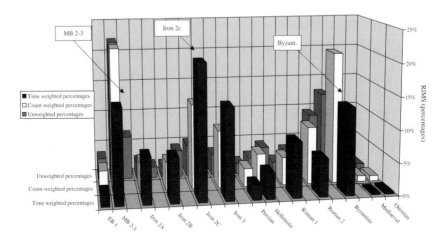

Fig. 1.3. *Kh. Karmil: weighted percentages*

Thus, the estimation of the size of settlement for each stage seems to be clear: the *maximum* weighted percentage is that of the period covering the *maximum* area. The settlement size of each other stage is proportional to its weighted percentage. Finally, a small correction is applied for those ancient periods covered by later ones (although in the eroded Highland this problem is not so crucial).

It is now possible to draw the settlement graphs and maps of each identifiable period, and follow the settlement development in the given region: here, the Highland of Judah.

Figure 1.4 presents the summary of the history of the region, in terms of inhabited dunams (1 dunam = $^1/_{10}$ hectar). Note the low figures in the Bronze Ages, the three cycles of Bronze Age settlement: EB1, EB3, MB—and the declines following them. A fourth wave of settlement appears in the Iron Age 1,[9] but this time it continues to the Iron Age 2a[10] and onwards. In the Iron Age 2 the Judaean Highland is no longer a fringe area, but an integral part of the settled land. Note also the two peaks of inhabited area: one in Iron 2c,[11] toward the end of the eighth century BCE; the other—much higher—in the Byzantine period.

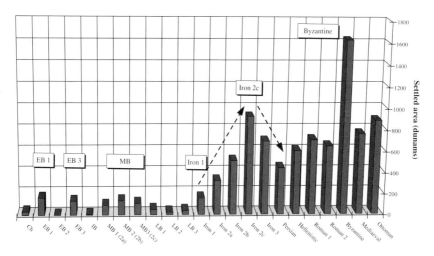

Fig. 1.4. *Settled area in the Judaean highland*

But is the settled area the best indication for population size? The conventional factor of 20–25 inhabitants per settled dunam is but a mean.[12] The actual figures range between less than 10 to more than 40

9.   c. twelfth to mid-eleventh century BCE.
10.   c. mid-eleventh to tenth century BCE.
11.   c. eighth century BCE; stratigraphically ending at 701 BCE, ceramically ending some decades later.
12.   Archaeologists of the Land of Israel tend to use the coefficient of 25 inhabitants per settled dunam (i.e. Broshi and Gophna 1984: 42), and regard it as even somewhat high (Finkelstein 1988: 331-32, and n. 37 there).

inhabitants per settled dunam,[13] Here, recording the intensity of sherds in every site, for example in terms of sherds per one hour survey by one surveyor, gives a better indication of the amount of human activity.[14] The graph of the ceramic intensity during the various periods is the greatest surprise of all (Fig. 1.5).

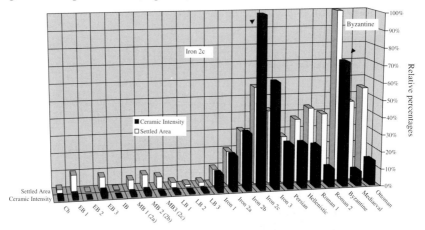

Fig. 1.5. *Ceramic intensity*

Comparing the two kinds of data: settled area, versus ceramic activity, note that the Byzantine period has the largest settled area of all, but the sites are not so densely populated. The ceramic activity, so maybe the proportional amount of population, seems to be much higher in Iron 2c.[15]

13.   The latest research in the population of traditional society (Arab villages) in this land is that of Biger and Grossman (1990, 1992). This research shows that the density of population may vary as much as 6–100 (!) inhabitants per settled dunam, and in many cases it varies between 10–40/50 (Biger and Grossman 1992: Table 1). Although in their examined period the density in the Judaean Highland was only 14.5, it is clear that in different conditions the figures could be much different (as in the contemporanous nearby Shephelah: 28.1, Table 3 [Biger and Grossman 1992]).

14.   In our survey we recorded systematically the time spent sherd-collecting and the number of surveyors. We also estimated the effectiveness of the surveyors according to three categories: professionals, students with some training, others. Hence, we have a reasonable estimation for this factor. However, using a simple scale of five or even three categories of sherd intensity at the site may be enough (many, moderate, few), and this data can be deduced from most published surveys.

15.   These results lead to the conclusion that for the Iron Age we should use a higher coefficient per dunam, especially for phase 2c. If the mean coefficient is 20–22 inhabitants per settled dunam, I tend to conclude that for most phases of the Iron

However, most of the following evaluations are still based on the conservative settled area factor. These further evaluations form the basis of the overview of the Iron age in the Judaean Highland (below).

We may calculate the land use, still per settled dunam: on the one hand *rendzina* soils, best fitted for winter crops and grazing—namely, for a more pastoral society; on the other the *terra-rossa* soils, less abundant but better for horticulture (see Fig. 1.6).[16]

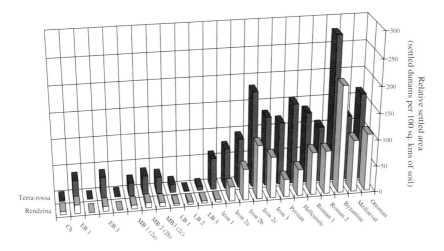

Fig. 1.6. *Relative land uses*

We can also compare their relative relationships—this is a disinterested evidence for the pastoral or settled background of the settlers, not dependent upon our historical premises, not to say pre-judgments. Note in the graph in Figure 1.7,[17] Early Bronze, Middle Bronze, Late Bronze, and the surprising Iron 1: most horticultural of all, this period does not seem to reflect any desert-fringe pastoralism, it seems! The latter occurs, with growing use of *rendzina* soils, in Iron 2a, and Iron

Age we should use at least 25, and for Iron 2c we should use 30; even those figures may be somewhat low.

16. This graph shows the average settled area per 100 square kms of each of the two main types of soils (namely, the settlements which mainly use one of the two types). Hence, it shows the preferences of the population in relative terms.

17. Fig. 1.7 just emphasizes the preferences shown in Fig. 1.6—the results of dividing the relative settled areas of *terra-rossa* by those of *rendzina*.

2b. Then, in Iron 2c, the process reaches its peak and the society stabilizes. Only with the impoverishment of the South following the end of the Iron Age, horticulture regains priority for a while, during the Persian-Hellenistic Period.

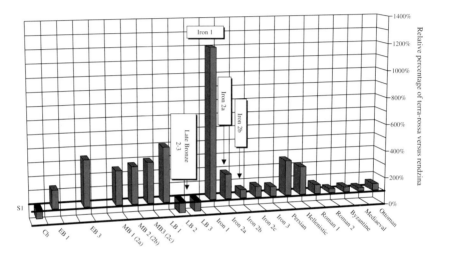

Fig. 1.7. *Comparative land use*

We may follow the distribution of settlements, according to their size —a rank-size analysis, common in geography.[18] This may indicate social units, their centres, and their measure of inner integration.

18. Rank-size analyses were intoduced into humanities and social sciences by Zipf (1941; 1949, esp. pp. 324 onwards). Hagget (1965), Berry and Horton (1970) and others applied these analyses to geography. Soon afterward, they were incorporated into spatial archaeology, for example by Vapnarsky (1969), Hodder and Orton (1976), and most remarkably by Johnson (1977, 1980, 1981, 1987). In brief, the analyses are based on the fact that empiric data from various societies show that in a well-integrated socio-economic unit, the second site (according to its size or other factors of human activity) is 1/2 of the 1st site (the greatest site), the third is 1/3 of the first, and so on: the n site is $1/n$ of the first. This is true for sites above some minimal size (5–10 dunams or more). This distribution appears as a diagonal on a logarithmic scale, which is hence the best representation of that analysis. A concave logarithmic distribution (a primate distribution) represents a system dominated by a primate-city, much larger than usual (Smith 1982a, b). It may be only a part of the whole unit (including its capital), or a very large unit composed of some integrated sub-units, with a larger capital.

One has to put these distributions on a logarithmic scale,[19] and calculate a certain index to express its shape and nature.[20] A diagonal curve,
in Figure 1.8, indicates one well-integrated social unit in the region,
such as Early Bronze Age 3, third millennium BCE: an integrated unit
under dominant Ras-Tawra (60 dunams).

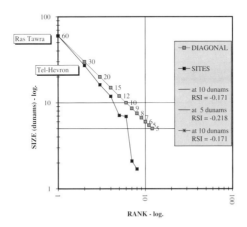

Fig. 1.8. *Early Bronze 3: rank-size distribution*

The Middle Bronze Age, under Tel-Hevron, fits well with the administrative tablet which we found there (Ofer 1989; Anbar and Na'aman
1987) (Fig. 1.9).

19. If the graphs are not logarithmic on both axes they are *always* concave,
although in different degrees, and a visual comparison is effectively very hard.
Thus, Gophna and Portugali (1988) published detailed non-logarithmic graphs
(their Figs. 10-11), all concaves of course, so that they could deduce from them but
few meaningful conclusions.
20. Among the different indices which were offered (El-Shakhs 1972; Malecki
1975), that of Johnson (1980, 1987) is still the best, although not without problems.
Johnson's Rank Size Index (RSI) is zero (0) for a perfect diagonal, positive (up to
1) for a convex logarithmic graph, and negative (down to minus–infinity) for a
concave one. In the future I hope to introduce an improved index; meanwhile, any
comparison has to consider the difference between the positive and the negative
ranges. The RSI is calculated for those sites bigger than the minimum indicated
above (n. 18), which is called 'RSI cut point' (Johnson 1987: 109). In the following
distributions two different cut points are examined and calculated (5 and 10
dunams); however, any comparison is to be made with the same cut-point for all
the distributions examined.

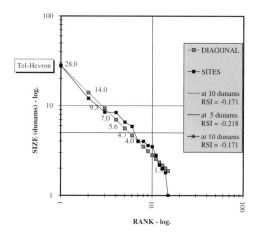

Fig. 1.9. *Middle Bronze 1 (2a): rank-size distribution*

Once the curve becomes convex, in a relatively small region like this, it indicates that we are dealing with just a part of a unit, not including its centre.[21] In the Highland of Judah it happens for the first time, and from then on, in Iron Age 2a—around 1000 BCE (Fig. 1.10).

When adding the closest dominant site *outside* our region ('Site J'), we see a quite well-integrated unit (Fig. 1.11), under the dominance of this site, which should be therefore the capital of this unit.[22]

The rank size index (RSI) of different periods can also be compared to analyse this aspect of the region's history (Fig. 1.12).

21. The convex distribution was much discussed from the 1980s onwards, i.e. by Johnson in his articles (above, n. 18), Kowalewsky (1982), Paynter in an essential article including many references (1983), and Bunimovitz (1989: 57-70; see also 1994) for Canaan during the second millenium BCE. Sometimes it may represent the existence of more than one unit in the analysed area, but that only in very large regions. In relatively small regions it represents generally a part of a wider unit, and one has to look around the region to find the rest of the unit, including its centre.

22. 'Site J' is of course the archaeological site of Jerusalem. Its area before Iron 2c is hard to estimate, but there are pure archaeological reasons to ascribe to it about 150 dunams at that period (Ofer 1993, part 2: 203-204). The conventional estimation is also about 160 dunams, but that relies mainly on the interpretation of the biblical sources.

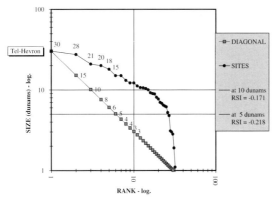

Fig. 1.10. *Iron 2a: rank-size distribution*

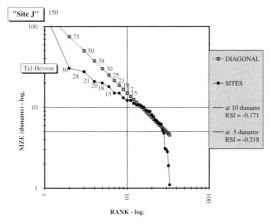

Fig. 1.11. *Iron 2a—including 'site J': rank-size distribution*

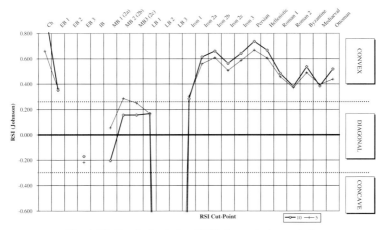

Fig. 1.12. *Rank size index (RSI) through the periods*

General Overview and Conclusions [23]

The Late Bronze Age in the Judaean Highland is a void.

Iron Age 1,[24] twelfth to mid-eleventh century BCE: new settlers; nothing in the wide pasture areas in the east, almost nothing in the south; no one clear capital. Hebron, Jerusalem and Tell es-Safi seem to be the principal sites in Judah. Who are these apparently non-pastoral settlers? In Jerusalem, we know, they are Jebusites, most probably of Anatolian origin.[25] In Tel es-Safi (Gath), they are Philistines (Rainey 1975; Singer 1994, esp. 305-306, 315-18, 324-25). Perhaps this is the time when the so-called 'Hittites' arrive to Hebron, mentioned later in the biblical traditions? (cf. Na'aman 1994: 239-40). *'Yelidei ha'anaq'* who are mentioned in the Caleb traditions as the predecessors of the Calebites in Hebron and Debir, may also be a group which emerged at that time.[26]

Iron 2a, mid-eleventh to tenth century BCE, marks the beginning of settlement in the pasture areas. There is a major change in the site of Hebron. It seems that the beginning of this stage is the time of the

23. For estimations of settled area and population in the various stages of the Iron Age, see Appendix 1B.

24. For a more detailed review of that period in the Judaean Highland see Ofer 1994.

25. As were probably most of the 'seven peoples of Canaan'—cf. Mendenhall 1973: 144-63, Na'aman 1994: 239-43.

26. The problem of *'Yelidei ha'anaq'* is complicated (for my detailed discussion see Ofer 1993: Part 1, 10-11). In brief, they may be West-Semitic (Lipinski 1974, esp. pp. 41-44), of northern 'Hittite' origin (Na'aman 1994: 263-64), or a combination of Semitic and northern elements (Ofer 1993, above). Ahiman and Talmai may be West-Semitic names (Zadok, oral communication) although the latter may also be Hurrian (Zadok, cf. de Vaux 1948), Sheshay is not indicative (being an onomatopeic name), while 'Anaq itself is clearly West-Semitic (Noth 1966: 105); the suggestion of a Greek origin by Maclaurin (1965) seems to be impossible, ignoring the clearly Semitic 'Ayin in the name, and his discussion is highly speculative and oversimplified. Most probably *'Yelidei ha'anaq'* was a tribal unit, maybe with three chieftains. The theory of L'Heureux (1976), following Willesen (1958) and adopted by Na'aman (above), that *yelidim* are members of a 'cultic association of warriors', seems to me too speculative to build a super-structure upon it. For the Caleb traditions see n. 27.

Calebites' arrival, conquering not a Bronze Age city, but an Iron Age 1 site in Hebron, populated by '*Yelidei ha'anaq*' and/or the 'Hittites'.[27]

At the beginning of this stage we have also the first inhabitation of desert fringe sites such as Teqoa', ha-Qain, Ma'on, and our Kh. Karmil/ Carmel.

But probably the most important archaeological fact is, as discussed above, that the socio-economic and political structure of Judah at that period is that of a well-integrated unit, most probably a kingdom, most probably subject to the site of Jerusalem. This may be highly important in view of the new trend which doubts the existence of a real monarchy in tenth-century Judah.[28] Realistically, the biblico-historical evidence cannot prove or disprove that. But the spatial analysis, which ignores any prejudgment, seems to support the existence of such a kingdom. However, this kingdom still follows the geographical boundaries of the old city-state of Bronze Age Jerusalem.

An analysis of the material published from Benjamin seems to confirm these conclusions.[29] As concerns the Shephelah, Yehuda Dagan's survey shows that it only began to be populated at that stage.[30]

27. About the Calebites and the Caleb traditions I rely on my detailed analysis, Ofer 1993: Part 1, 5-11 (summarized in Ofer 1994: 110-12); see also the dissertations of Beltz (1974) and Pace (1976), and the important contributions by Noth (1966: 101-12), Auld (1976: esp. 210-20) and especially Mittman (1975: 34-64).

For the late arrival of the Calebites, and the other southern pastoral elements in Judah and Israel, there is an important argument that has not been sufficiently noted. This is the dominance of their traditions in the Bible, which is itself a hint to their relatively late arrival as the last important element to influence and shape the biblical account and traditions.

28. This school is well attested in the works of scholars such as Thompson 1994 and Davies 1992.

29. Finkelstein and Magen 1993. As there are no spatial analyses nor overall discussions about the Highland of Benjamin in this important publication, I analysed the published data according to my own methods.

30. Dagan 1992: 252-55 (English summary p. VII). This work is highly important, although in my opinion the results have to be calibrated before they can be properly used. However, Iron 2a is very weak according to Dagan himself. Taking into account that even the identified 'tenth century' settlements were mostly paralleled to Lachish Stratum V, which we know now is ceramically equal to Stratum IV and both are defined as Iron 2b (see Appendix 1A), the Iron 2a in the Shephelah may be even sparser.

Iron 2b, the ninth century, which is so hard to identify, is now more identifiable through Orna Zimhoni's important work on Lachish Strata V and IV.[31]

The settlement process in the east and the south still continues. This evidence, as well as the biblical evidence, sheds new light on the common definition of the Settlement Age and its customary chronological frame. Instead of twelfth–eleventh centuries BCE as the date of the age of settlement and sedentarization, we probably should take a much wider and more complex range. The settlement age in Judah seems to last no less than 400 years, from the twelfth to ninth centuries BCE. Its first stage, up to the mid-eleventh century, seems to have mainly a horticultural basis. The second and third stages, mainly sedentarization of desert-fringe pastorals, overlap the first half of the Monarchy period.

Iron 2c: in the eighth century the process stabilizes, with an impressive growth of settlement numbers, settlement size and human activity (as indicated by ceramics), but now in the whole area. Judah reaches its zenith; only by now, when the sedentarization of pastorals is completed, is it crystallizing into an homogenous unit. It seems that the historical analysis also confirms this. In the Shephelah and Benjamin the situation is the same, and these regions overshadow the Judaean Highland[32]—but not for long.

31. Zimhoni 1997; see again Appendix 1A below.

32. In Benjamin (see n. 29 above) the archaeological situation is unequivocal, as the surveyors did not separate the different phases of Iron 2. However, most archaeological evidence shows that as in the Judaean Highland, phase 2c was the zenith of Iron 2 settlements, including most of the undivided Iron 2 sites—and their number and overall settled area are higher than in the much larger Judaean Highland. In the Shephelah, Dagan (1992: 256-58, English p. VIII) attributed to this phase more than 4000 settled dunams (and more 4000 dunams for the unsurveyed area!), but this is when taking the maximal area of the sites, which is not identical with the maximal settled area (including unsettled slopes of the tels, and so on). These figures may be important by themselves, but what we are looking for here is the maximal *settled* area, which is generally only 60 per cent of Dagan's maximal area. Moreover, it is clear that in many sites even this maximum was reached during periods other than the Iron Age. All in all, a detailed analysis of Dagan's highly important survey leads me to an estimate of about 2500 settled dunams (including the gaps in our knowledge)—which is still the highest figure in Judah. A biblical analysis also shows the supremacy of Benjamin and the Shephelah at that time—Ofer 1993: Part 1, excursus 1/B, esp. pp. 52-53.

The massive destruction by Sennacherib at the end of this stage affected the whole country, as confirmed by all the surveys and excavations, and no region shows a full recovery from it.

However, in the next stage, Iron 3, the northern highland of Judah, and apparently also Benjamin, recover much more than the Shephelah.[33] Here begins a long-term process, whose results are clear in the subsequent period.

In the Persian period, the northern Judaean Highland flourish as never before, while from Hebron southward the settlements become more and more impoverished.[34] The cycle of the Monarchy period is now completed. The wide socio-political unit of greater Judah disappears, and a lesser Judah replaces it—the northern highland and Benjamin. Actually, its borders are quite similar to those of the Iron 2a Judah, and even earlier, to those of the Bronze Age kingdom of Jerusalem.[35]

In *longue durée* terms, greater Judah of the mid-monarchic period was but an episode. However, greater or lesser, later-monarchic and post-exilic Judah was the main arena for the emergence of Judaism. The

33. The archaeological situation in Benjamin is even more unequivocal than the previous stage. In the Shephelah the surveyor estimates that the number of settlements was reduced to about 14 per cent of the previous stage and their total settled area to 24 per cent (Dagan 1992: 259, English p. IX); my estimates are rather higher (up to 40 per cent for the settled area).

34. Here we have an ideal agreement between the historical sources, which put the southern border of Yehud around Beth-Zur, and the archaeological picture which is changing dramatically south of this site.

35. The discussion about the size and influence of the Canaanite kingdom of Jerusalem was renewed recently. Finkelstein (1990) argued that it was one of the two main powers in the central highland of Canaan (following Kallai and Tadmor 1969), while Na'aman (1992) maintained that the periphery and influence of this kingdom was much more limited (following Alt 1925a, b). That the highland of Benjamin was dominated by Jerusalem is, however, generally accepted (cf. Na'aman 1986). It is well attested that during the Amarna period Jerusalem had strong influence in the inner Shephelah, around Keilah. The region of the Hebron-Debir highland was almost devoid of population, and should also be under the influence of Jerusalem and/or the Shephelah kingdoms, most probably manouvering between them as Keilah did. In any case, the maximal periphery of Late Bronze Age Jerusalem should include the highlands of Benjamin and Hebron, as well as the fringes of the Shephelah. This seems to be very similar to the borders of early Judah, as well as those of Persian Yehud (which even has loose control in the southern highland).

archaeological evidence provides us with the settlement background of this process.

Here ends our spatial overview of the region. But the Highland of Judah, and Hebron, are not merely one more region to be explored and analysed. Our civilization has deep roots there. While walking through the length and breadth of this land, in these troubled years, I could not avoid thinking about both past and present of the region. Hebron, el-Halil, is today (the 1990s) a main centre of fundamentalist hate and terror. Let us hope that despite all the difficulties, peace will return to this tormented area. Let us hope that new contributions to human civilization, and a new cultural synthesis, will again emerge here, in peace.

Appendix 1A: Preliminary Notes about the Ceramic Sub-Division of the Judaean Iron Age

The ceramic sub-division of the Iron Age in Judah which is used in this article deserves some explanation (for detailed discussion see for the time being in my thesis, Ofer 1993, vol. I, part 2: 15-51, chapter 2.B; I intend to publish a special article based on it). The old divisions, important as they were, are no longer valid: cf. Garstang *et al.* 1922; Albright 1949: 112. The new subdivision of the 'Israelite' period, offered by Aharoni and Amiran (1958), is hard to implement in Judah, as stated by Amiran herself (1969: 191). The *Old Encyclopedia of Archaeological Excavations* (Avi-Yonah and Stern 1995–98) adopted a hybrid system in which Iron 2c included both eighth and seventh/sixth centuries BCE which are absolutely different (cf. Lachish Strata III versus II), while Iron 2b was practically unidentifiable. In the new edition (Stern 1993) Iron 2c was limited to the distinctive seventh/sixth century (=Lachish Stratum II), but Iron 2b was enlarged to include now both eighth and ninth centuries BCE, which are again absolutely different (Lachish Strata III versus IV, see below). Archaeologists began then to use an *absolute* chronological terminology for the essentially *relative* phasing of the Iron Age, which may be very misleading. To the best of my recognition we have to return to the relative nomenclature of phasing, and there are five—and only five—distinctive ceramic phases in Iron Age Judah:

- Iron 1: c. twelfth to mid-eleventh century BCE (round figures: c. 1200–1050 BCE).
  This is what is called generally 'Iron 1' or 'Early Iron 1': i.e. Izbet Zarta III, Ebal 2-1, Giloh.
- Iron 2a: c. mid-eleventh to tenth century BCE (round figures: c. 1050–925 BCE).
  Generally known as 'tenth century BCE', this phase includes strata such as Tel Qasileh XI–IX, Izbet-Zartah II–I, 'Beer-Sheba' VIII–VI (and at least some of the

material from IX and V), Tel Esdar III–II, Arad XII–XI. In most sites this stage can be divided into two stratigraphic assemblages (and even more), taken generally as late eleventh (or just eleventh) and tenth centuries BCE, accordingly. However, the ceramic assemblages consist in my opinion of a single identifiable ceramic stage, which cannot be further separated in the survey or other non-stratigraphic context. To some extent this phase is close to that of Holladay (1990), although his dating seems to me untenable (see Ofer 1993: Part 2, 21-23). To sum up: we have here but *one* ceramic stage, generally dated to c. mid-eleventh to tenth century BCE.

- Iron 2b: c. ninth century BCE (round figures: c. 925–800 BCE).

  This stage was absolutely unidentifiable in Judah till recently. However, Stratum IV in Lachish was successfully separated and analysed through Orna Zimhoni's work on the pottery from this key-site of Iron Age 2 Judah (Zimhoni 1997). The pottery of Lachish IV and the identical pottery of Stratum V now defines this ceramic stage. It differs absolutely from the pottery of Lachish III (Iron 2c), and is separate from Iron 2a assemblages although (in my opinion) close to them.

- Iron 2c: c. eighth century BCE (round figures: c. 800–675 BCE). Stratigraphically it surely ended at 701 BCE, ceramically maybe some decades later (our division here is the ceramic one).

  Lachish III and parallel strata in Judah. Here is a typical case of the old confusion between ceramic versus stratigraphic phases (cf. the bitter dispute about Samaria, Hazor and Megiddo: Aharoni and Amiran 1958: 178 ff, Tufnell 1959: 94 ff, Kenyon 1964: 145 ff and table on p. 148). As the ceramic assemblages of the 701 destructions define this ceramic stage, we have to assume by definition that it lasted at least some more few decades following these destructions.

- Iron 3: c. seventh to mid-sixth century BCE (round figures: c. 675–550 BCE).

  Lachish II and parallel strata in Judah. Here again, the assemblages are defined by the 587/6 destructions and the ceramic phase should last then some more decades, including probably most of the 'Babylonian' phase.

  The Persian Period is dated in Judah to 538–332 BCE (round figures: 550–350 BCE).

Appendix 1B: Estimations of Settled Area and Population in Iron Age Judah

These estimations are based on my material from the Judaean Highland, a preliminary analysis of mine for the surveys in Benjamin (Finkelstein and Magen 1993) and the Shephelah (Dagan 1992), and more data from the various regions of Judah. The analyses and figures are preliminary, but I hope that they give a reasonable impression about this important topic (see also Ofer 1993: Part 2, 216-21, excursus 2/D, and the table there). All figures are rounded.

	Raw sherd–counting	Unweighted percentages	Weighted count	Count-weighted percentages	Period length (centuries)	Time-weighted percentages
OTTOMAN	1	1	1.0	1	4	0
MEDIAEVAL	1	1	1.1	1	8	0
Byz-Med	1	1				
BYZANTINE	15	13	24.2	20	3	13
Rom.-Byz.	11	9				
ROMAN 2	5	4	10.6	9	3	6
1-2	4	3				
ROMAN 1	2	2	5.1	4	1	9
Hel.-Rom.1	5	4				
HELLENISTIC	3	3	6.0	5	2.5	4
PERSIAN	2	2	3.3	3	2.5	2
3-Persian	4	3				
IRON 3	4	3	10.6	9	1.25	14
2c-3	4	3				
IRON 2C	6	5	15.5	13	1.25	21
2b-2c	5	4				
IRON 2B	2	2	5.2	4	1.25	7
2a-2b	2	2				
IRON 2A	3	3	5.4	5	1.25	7
Iron Age 2 (undivided)	8	7				
MB 2-3 ('2a-b')	26	22	26.0	22	3	14
EB 1	4	3	4.0	3	3.5	2
Unidentified	16					
Total	134					

Table 1.1. Kh. Karmil—pottery reading and weighting (database for the following graphs). For the Iron Age phases see Appendix 1A.

Bibliography

Aharoni, Y., and R. Amiran
    1958   'A New Scheme for the Sub-Division of the Iron Age in Palestine', *IEJ* 8: 171-84.

Albright, W.F.
    1949   *The Archaeology of Palestine* (Harmondsworth: Penguin Books).

Alt, A.
    1925a   'Die Landnahme der Israeliten in Palästina', *Reformationprogramm der Universität Leipzig* (Leipzig) Reprinted with addenda, and cited from Alt 1953.
    1925b   'Jerusalem Aufstieg', *ZDMG* 79: 1-19. Cited from Alt 1959.
    1953   *Kleine Schriften zur Geschichte des Volkes Israel*, I (Munich: Beck'sche): 89-125.
    1959   *Kleine Schriften zur Geschichte des Volkes Israel*, III (Munich: Beck'sche): 243-57.

Amiran, R.
    1969   *Ancient Pottery of the Holy Land* (Jerusalem: Massada Press) Ramat Gan.

Anbar, M., and N. Na'aman
    1987   'An Account Tablet of Sheep from Ancient Hebron', *Tel Aviv* 13-14: 3-12.

Auld, A.G.
    1976   *Studies in Joshua: Text and Literary Relations* (PhD thesis printed by the British Library Document Supply Centre, Edinburgh).

Avi-Yonah, M., and E. Stern (eds.)
    1975–78   *Encyclopaedia of Archaeological Excavations in the Holy Land* (4 vols.; London: Oxford University Press; Jerusalem: Israel Exploration Society and Massada Press).

Beltz, W.
    1974   *Die Kaleb Traditionen im Alten Testament* (Ph.D. Diss., BWANT 98; Stuttgart: W. Kohlhammer).

Berry, B.J.L., and F.W. Horton
    1970   *Geographic Perspectives on Urban Systems* (Englewood Cliffs, NJ: Prentice–Hall).

Biger, G., and D. Grossmann
    1990   'Village Population in Palestine During the 1930s–1940s and their Relevance to Ethnoarchaeology', *The 2nd International Congress on Biblical Archaeology* (1990) Jerusalem. (*Abstracts*: pp. 7-8; does not appear in the *Proceedings of the Congress*).
    1992   'Population Density in the Traditional Village of Palestine', *Cathedra* 63: 108-21 (Hebrew).

Broshi, M., and R. Gophna
    1984   'The Settlements and Population of Palestine in the Early Bronze Age II–III', *BASOR* 253: 41-53.

Bunimovitz, S.
    1989   *The Land of Israel in the Late Bronze Age: A Case Study of Socio-Cultural Change in a Complex Society* (PhD thesis, Tel Aviv University;

Hebrew, with English contents and summary, English edition in preparation).

1994   'Socio-Political Transformations in the Central Hill Country in the Late Bronze–Iron I Transition', in Finkelstein and Na'aman 1994: 179-202.

Dagan, Y.

1992   *The Shephelah During the Period of the Monarchy in Light of Archaeological Excavations and Survey* (unpublished MA thesis, Tel Aviv University; Hebrew, with English contents and summary).

Davies, P.R.

1992   *In Search of 'Ancient Israel'* (Sheffield: JSOT Press).

El-Shakhs, S.

1972   'Development, Primacy, and Systems of Cities', *Journal of Developing Areas* 7: 11-35.

Finkelstein, I.

1988   *The Archaeology of the Israelite Settlement* (Jerusalem: Israel Exploration Society).

1990   "Dimorphic Chiefdoms" in the Hill Country of Israel During the Middle and Late Bronze Ages', *The Second International Congress on Biblical Archaeology* (Jerusalem: Israel Exploration Society and The Israel Academy of Sciences and Humanities). (*Abstracts*: p. 24; does not appear in the *Proceedings of the Congress*).

Finkelstein, I., and Y. Magen

1993   *Archaeological Survey of the Hill Country of Benjamin* (Jerusalem: Israel Antiquities Authority Publications; Hebrew, with English section including a full list of sites and their pottery).

Finkelstein, I., and N. Na'aman (eds.)

1994   *From Nomadism to Monarchy: Archaeological and Historical Aspects of Early Israel* (Jerusalem: Yad Izhak Ben-Zvi and Israel Exploration Society; Washington: Biblical Archaeology Society).

Garstang, J., L. Vincent, W.F. Albright and W.J. Phythian-Adams

1922   'A New Chronological Classification of Palestinian Archaeology', *BASOR* 7: 9.

Gophna, R., and J. Portugali

1988   'Settlement and Demographic Processes in Israel's Coastal Plain from the Chalcolithic to the Middle Bronze Age', *BASOR* 269: 11-28.

Hagget, P.

1965   *Locational Analysis in Human Geography* (London).

Hodder, I., and C. Orton

1976   *Spatial Analysis in Archaeology* (Cambridge: Cambridge University Press).

Holladay, J.S. Jr

1990   'Red Slip, Burnish, and the Solomonic Gateway at Gezer', *BASOR* 277/8: 23-70.

Johnson, G.A.

1977   'Aspects of Regional Analysis in Archaeology', *Annual Review of Anthropology* 6: 479-508.

1980   'Rank-Size Convexity and System Integration: A View from Archaeology', *Economic Geography* 56: 234-47.

1981   'Monitoring Complex System Integration and Boundary Phenomena with
           Settlement Size Data', in S.E. van der Leeuw (ed.), *Archaeological
           Approaches to the Study of Complexity* (Amsterdam: Universiteit von
           Amsterdam): 144-87.
1987   'The Changing Organisation of Uruk Administration on the Susiana
           Plain', in F. Hole (ed.), *The Archaeology of Western Iran* (Washington
           DC): 107-39.

Kallai, Z., and H. Tadmor
1969   'Bit Ninurta = Beit Horon: On the History of the Kingdom of Jerusalem
           in the Amarna Period', *EI* 9: 138-47 (Hebrew).

Kenyon, K.M.
1964   'Megiddo, Hazor, Samaria and Chronology', *Bulletin of the Institute of
           Archaeology, University of London* 4: 143-56.

Kochavi, M.
1972   'The Land of Judah', in M. Kochavi (ed.), *Judea, Samaria and the Golan:
           Archaeological Survey 1967–1968* (Jerusalem: The Archaeological
           Survey of Israel and Carta; Hebrew, with English title, content and site
           indices).

Kowalewsky, S.A.
1982   'The Evolution of Primate Regional Systems', *Comparative Urban
           Research* IX(1): 60-78.

L'Heureux, C.E.
1976   'The *yelide harapa*': A Cultic Association of Warriors', *BASOR* 221: 83-
           85.

Lipinski, E.
1974   ''Anaq-Kiryat 'Arba-Hébron et ses sanctuaires tribaux', *VT* 24: 41-55.

Maclaurin, E.C.B.
1965   'ANAK/'ANAΞ', *VT* 15: 468-74.

Malecki, E.J.
1975   'Examining Change in Rank-Size Systems of Cities', *The Professional
           Geographer* 27(1): 43-47.

Mendenhall, G.E.
1973   *The Tenth Generation: The Origins of the Biblical Tradition* (Baltimore:
           The Johns Hopkins University Press).

Mittmann, S.
1975   *Deuteronomium 1$_1$-6$_3$: literarkritisch und traditiongeschichtlich
           untersucht* (BZAW, 139; Berlin: W. de Gruyter).

Na'aman, N.
1986   'The Canaanite City States in the Late Bronze Age and the Inheritances of
           the Israelite Tribes', *Tarbiz* 55: 463-88 (Hebrew).
1992   'Canaanite Jerusalem and its central hill country neighbours in the second
           millennium BCE', *Ugarit-Forschungen* 24: 275-91.
1994   'The "Conquest of Canaan" in the Book of Joshua and in History', in
           Finkelstein and Na'aman 1994: 218-81.

Noth, M.
1966   *Numbers* (Das Alte Testament Deutsch 7/ OTL). ET J.D. Martin (London:
           SCM Press, 1980 [1968]).

Ofer, A.
    1989   'Excavations at Biblical Hebron', *Qadmoniot* 22/3-4: 88-93 (Hebrew).
    1993   *The Highland of Judah During the Biblical Period* (PhD thesis; 2 vols.;
                Tel Aviv University; Hebrew, with English detailed contents and
                summary).
    1994   '"All the Hill Country of Judah": From a Settlement Fringe to a
                Prosperous Monarchy', in Finkelstein and Na'aman 1994: 92-121.

Pace, J.R.
    1976   *The Caleb Traditions and the Role of the Calebites in the History of
                Israel* (Ph.D dissertation; Emory).

Paynter, R.W.
    1983   'Expanding the Scope of Settlement Analysis', in J.A. Moore and A.S.
                Keene (eds.), *Archaeological Hammers and Theories* (New York:
                Academic Press).

Rainey, A.F.
    1975   'The Identification of Philistine Gath: A Problem in Source Analysis for
                Historical Geography', *EI* 12: 63*-76*.

Singer, I.
    1994   'Egyptians, Canaanites, and Philistines in the Period of the Emergence of
                Israel', in Finkelstein and Na'aman 1994: 282-338.

Smith, C.A.
    1982a   'Placing Formal Geographical Models into Cultural Contexts: The
                Anthropological Study of Urban Systems', *Comparative Urban Research*
                IX(1): 50-59.
    1982b   'Modern and Premodern Urban Primacy', *Comparative Urban Research*
                IX(1): 79-96.

Stern, E. (ed.)
    1993   *New Encyclopedia of Archaeological Excavations in the Holy Land* (4
                vols.; Jerusalem: Israel Exploration Society and Carta).

Thompson, T.L.
    1994   *Early History of the Israelite People from the Written and Archaeological
                Sources* (Leiden: E.J. Brill).

Tufnell, O.
    1959   'Hazor, Samaria and Lachish', *PEQ* 91: 90-105.

Vapnarsky, C.A.
    1969   'On Rank-Size Distributions of Cities: An Ecological Approach',
                Economic Development and Culture Change 17: 584-95.

de Vaux, R.
    1948   'Les Patriarches hébreux et les découvertes modernes (suite)', *RB* 55:
                321-47.

Willesen, F.
    1958   'The Yalid in Hebrew Society', *Studia Theologica* 12: 192-210.

Zimhoni, O.
    1997   'Lachish Levels V and IV: comments on the Material Culture of Judah in
                the Iron Age II in the Light of the Lachish Pottery Repertoire' (MA thesis
                presented to Tel Aviv University, 1995 [trans. A. Paris; ed. L. Singer-
                Avitz and D. Ussishkin]), in *Studies in the Iron Age Pottery of Israel:*

Typological, Archaeological and Chronological Aspects (Tel-Aviv University): 57-178 (ch. 3).

Zipf, G.W.

    1941   *National Unity and Disunity* (Bloomington, IL: The Principia Press).

    1949   *Human Behavior and the Principle of Least Effort* (repr. 1972; New York: Hafner).

2

THE HEART OF THE MONARCHY: PATTERN OF SETTLEMENT AND HISTORICAL CONSIDERATIONS OF THE ISRAELITE KINGDOM OF SAMARIA

Adam Zertal

Introduction

The central part of the northern Israelite kingdom and its nucleus, that is, the area around the capital Samaria, has not had the benefit of much information either in the biblical sources or from in-depth archaeological research. Despite general attempts to evaluate the history of the kingdom and special events in it (Whitley 1952; Yadin 1955; Haran 1967; Cody 1970; Lipinski 1972; Soggin 1984: 205; Sader 1984: 270-72; Reinhold 1989: 125-52; Mazar 1990: 406-16; Lemaire 1991, 1993), less effort was invested in estimating the population of the region (Zertal 1989a, and later Broshi and Finkelstein 1992) and its pattern of settlement had not had enough 'hard' information available for research. The first three volumes of the Manasseh hill-country survey (Zertal 1992a, 1996, 2000), covering some 50 per cent of the area, and the additional unpublished information covering more than 30 per cent of the rest, has opened new sources for the study of the region.

With this detailed data one can assess an important field of historical-archaeological research: the pattern of settlement, a valuable tool for historical studies. However, the complicated nature of the human settlement process, with its components and nuances, calls for a prudent sense of balance in evaluating the various factors and painting the historical picture.

The goal of this paper is to use the new data to create a picture of an area of c. 2500 sq. km, of the hill-country of Manasseh. This region includes most of the Middle-Eastern landscapes, excluding sea-shores: Mediterranean hill-country, fertile inner valleys, wide wadi-beds, desert fringes and the Jordan valley. The location of the area between the Mediterranean coast on one side and the Transjordanian plateau on the other, makes it most appropriate for an examination of the interrelationship between the two regions and their influence on the geography, economy and history of the Israelite kingdom.

We shall begin with some general problems. An interesting historical phenomenon is that all four capitals of the Northern Kingdom were located in the tribal territory of Manasseh: Shechem (1 Kgs 12.25), Penuel in Transjordan (1 Kgs 12.25), Tirzah (Tell el-Far'ah North: 1 Kgs 14.17) and Samaria (1 Kgs 16.23-24). To these, perhaps, should be added the 'second capital', Jezreel.

This fact stands in some contradiction to the biblical narratives, according to which it was the Ephraimite tribal territory which grew in power during the 200 years of the history of the Northern Kingdom. In the books of 1–2 Kings and the eighth century prophets the Northern Kingdom is regularly called 'The Kingdom of Ephraim', indicating the so-called late Ephraimite superiority.

We have, therefore, a historical problem: while in the Bible Ephraim is superior in the time of the late Northern Kingdom, it was Samaria and the Manassite territory which remained the formal and the actual centres of the kingdom. What could have been the reasons for such a situation? Why, for example, did the capital not 'move' later into Ephraim? (Shiloh, with its cultic traditions, could have been a good candidate.)

In a series of papers (Sellin 1917; Albright 1931; Lemaire 1972, 1978, 1985; Zertal 1988: 343-57, 1991: 42-48, 1992a: 55, 1994: 66-69) the possibility was already discussed that Manasseh played a central role in the early history of Israel. In these papers it was suggested that Manasseh was the nucleus of the early Josephite territory and the core of the crystallization of early Israel. This interpretation may explain to some degree the important role that the Manassite tribal allotment continued to play in the intertribal relationships, if not its influence on the location of the Israelite capitals.

Alt (1913) and Mazar (1935) tried to solve the Manasseh–Ephraim problem by analysing the list of the Solomonic districts in 1 Kgs 4.7-20, a document preserving some political conflicts between the tribes and the kingdom. Alt claimed that according to the list the first district, the hill country of Ephraim (1 Kgs 4.8) has stretched north and 'swallowed' the old Manassite tribal territory, considered to be the third district (1 Kgs 4.9). This, according to him, is evidence of the early superiority of Ephraim vis-à-vis Manasseh. But later research (Zertal 1984, 1992b, c) has shown that Arubboth, the capital of the third district, and Hepher (1 Kgs 4.9) are both located in the old Manassite territory. This means that the third district kept the boundaries of tribal Manasseh, and the possible explanation should be sought in the process of the editing of the Bible, which is beyond our scope here.

Alt (1966b) has also shown the different chararcter of the Northern Kingdom vis-à-vis Judah: a 'moving' capital with changing dynasties in the north, much like the contemporary Assyrian and Babylonian models (Grayson 1992: 750), as against the 'personal union' of the Davidic dynasty in Jerusalem.

Dating and Terminology
The Iron Age II period begins, according to most scholars, with the United Monarchy. The tenth century BCE still seems a good starting point for the research. As for the end of the period, 721 BCE (the fall of Israelite Samaria and the foundation of the Assyrian province of Samaria) and 586 BCE were both kept as 'fixed dates' for the end of the period. In the survey, we based the interpretation of our finds mainly on the dated pottery of the excavations of Samaria (Kenyon 1957), Tell Balatah/Shechem (Holladay 1966) and Tell el-Far'ah North (Chambon 1984). These three provided us with relatively accurate tools for dating the pottery of the Iron Age II sites.

The subdivision of Iron Age II has been a focus of debate. Without entering to this debate here, we find the period from 1000 to 586 BCE, namely Iron Age II, to be too long for the chronological scheme of the Northern Kingdom, characterized by rapid and stormy political changes. We will therefore temporarily use the term Iron Age III for the period from the fall of Samaria in 722/1 BCE to the fall of Jerusalem in 586/7 BCE (Zertal 1996: 84-86). In these 150 years Samaria was the capital of the Assyrian province of northern Palestine, and its material culture can be easily distinguished from that of Judah (Holladay 1966: 547-54; Zertal 1989b).

General Characteristics
From the archaeological data the Northern Kingdom of Israel emerges as a well-organized state, rich in agricultural resources and well protected. Its capital Samaria controlled the main roads which crossed it: the international 'Via Maris' from the coast to the valley of Jezreel

(Aharoni 1979: 52-53), the main road of the hill-country from Hebron to Beth-Haggan (Aharoni 1979: 57-58) and the crossing road from the coast to Transjordan (Aharoni 1979: 60). By means of this control, and its political and military power, this state played a central role in the history of Palestine in the ninth–eighth centuries BCE. Apart from the evidence of economic prosperity, remarkable efforts were invested by the kingdom in fortifying its borders, in its roads and in the capital itself. These are clearly evinced in the military investments in general, and in the length of the siege by the Assyrian army of Samaria in particular (*contra* Na'aman 1990).

In addition to settlements and military posts, cult places may have been present too, although these tend not to have survived unless located in the desert fringes.

Statistics

The Manasseh survey has revealed so far more than 300 sites with Iron Age II pottery, 80 per cent of which were previously unknown. Of these, only 262 have so far been entered into the computer and processed according to our method.[1] The Iron Age II is one of the peaks of settlement density in all periods, with only the Byzantine period being more populous.

The number of sites in the same territory was double that of the Iron Age I period (c. 1250–1000 BCE), the pottery of which was found at 135 sites. Iron Age II sites spread throughout almost all the territory, with only a few areas left unsettled. To draw the pattern of settlement, various factors were checked. These were divided into two groups:

A. The inner division and distribution of Iron Age II sites in the surveyed area and the relationships between Iron Age II and sites of other periods (Fig. 2.1); and

B. The relationship between Iron Age II sites and the environmental factors. This part is not included in this paper.

For group A, comparisons were made in three consecutive periods: Late Bronze Age (49 sites), Iron Age I (135) and Iron Age II (262 sites). For the sake of statistical convenience enclosures, cave sites, fortresses and camps were put temporarily under their size-groups.

---

1. For our method of processing see Zertal and Greenberg 1983. All the computer data for this article was processed by Mrs Viki Ben-Ari, to whom I am deeply indebted.

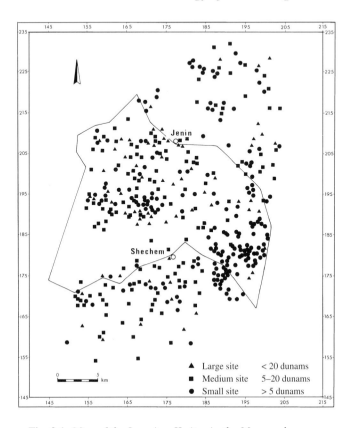

Fig. 2.1. *Map of the Iron Age II sites in the Manasseh survey*

A. *The Inner Division and Distribution of Iron Age II Sites*

Foundation and Continuity

Sixty-five per cent of the Iron Age II sites (171 in number) are newly founded, compared with 75 per cent in Iron Age I (102 sites) and 16 per cent in the Late Bronze Age (8 sites). This settlement 'peak' in the region can be explained by two factors: the economic prosperity in the kingdom (mainly during the eighth century) and the high rate of foundation of new sites in the desert fringes. This is indeed the first time that the 500 sq. km of the desert fringes and Jordan valley are almost entirely settled, mainly by family farms.

Was this development simply an organic and natural process, or was it also a deliberate effort to settle the borders of the kingdom? We assume that some of the kings of the ninth–eighth centuries undertook major projects of settling people on formerly underpopulated territories. This view is supported by the speedy settlement on the desert fringes, where the number of sites was doubled within less than 100 years. One can probably find hints to this process in the Bible and other sources, where kings are fortifying the borders and developing new terriories. Ahab is distinguished by 'all the cities that he built' (1 Kgs 22.39). Mesha the king of Moab praises himself for building projects (*ANET* 320-21). In two cases—Uzziah and Hezekiah of Judah—there are descriptions of agricultural projects: 'Also he [Uzziah] built towers in the desert, and digged many wells, both in the low countries and in the plains; husbandmen also, and vinedressers in the mountains, and in Carmel; for he loved husbandry' (2 Chron. 26.1). Although these descriptions are missing for Israel, this is most certainly due to the fact that biblical information regarding the latter's history is rare, laconic and sometimes hostile.

Single- and Multi-Period Sites

Here again the special character of the Iron Age II prosperity is indicated. Sixty-two per cent (161 sites) of the Iron Age II are single-period, namely they were founded and ceased to exist between the ninth to the seventh centuries BCE, and existed mainly during the eighth century. This is compared to 47 per cent (64 single-period sites) of the Iron Age I and 12 per cent (6 single-period sites) of the Late Bronze Age. The opposite is true for multi-period sites: during the Late Bronze Age long-lived, multi-period tells are the main group (88 per cent of the total); in Iron Age I half of the sites are of this category,[2] and in Iron Age II only 38 per cent are multi-period sites.

Reasons for Prosperity and Cessation of Settlement

Since no indications exist for changes in the natural conditions during the Iron Age II period (Lipschitz and Weisel 1987: 253) the question arises what caused the prosperity and how did it come to an end. Though more research is needed to establish accurately the reasons for

---

2.   The fact that 50 per cent of the Iron Age I sites are multi-period (mostly tells) can be explained by the Canaanite-Israelite relationships in the Manassite territory, when Iron Age I populations (mainly Israelites) merged with the existing societies by way of trade, intermarriage (see Gen. 34) or adoption. Alt (1966a) indicated the special character of Manasseh in this respect, and see also Aharoni 1979: 211.

the prosperity, two sets of economic and political factors may be suggested: the close relationship of Israel with Phoenicia, which developed international trade; and the stability and power of the Omri-Ahab dynasty and later, which were translated into population density, security and development. In spite of consecutive attacks on the Israelite kingdom by Aram, in addition to other wars (Miller 1967, 1996; Lipinski 1979; Lemaire 1993) the northern state seemed not only to survive but to prosper, evidence supported by our finds.

Circumstances for the end of the Iron Age II sites are clearer. The area under research was a focus of the Neo-Assyrian policy of population exchange in 722/1 BCE onwards (and see also Oded 1979), and the influence of the Assyrian conquest and deportations was crucial. In another paper I wrote:

> The Assyrian conquest of 722/1 BCE seems to have emptied large parts of the country. The 27,290 persons deported from Samaria by Sargon II (*ANET*: 284) represented about half of the estimated eighth-century population (nearly 50,000).[3] The main regions which suffered were the eastern valleys, for reasons still unknown (Zertal 1989a: 14-15).

It can be suggested that the time of the Israelite kingdom (Iron Age II) was a short and rare period of settlement expansion under optimal political and economic conditions. This came to an abrupt end owing to the Assyrian occupation, which seems to have destroyed most of the eastern part of the Samaria region. It was brought about by the deportation of population and the resettlement, in their stead and to a much lesser degree, of new deportees from Mesopotamia and Arabia (Oded 1979).

These results run somewhat counter to the biblical description of the Babylonian deportation in Judah following the fall of Jerusalem in 586 BCE, when Nebuzaradan left in the country just the 'vinedressers and husbandmen' (2 Kgs 25.12; Jer. 52.16). In Samaria the Assyrians seem to have depopulated entire regions and to have settled newcomers there. A piece of archaeological evidence for this process may be the distribution of the wedge-shaped decorated bowl over the territory. This special decoration can now be used as an indicator for the period between 722 BCE and the end of the seventh century (Zertal 1989b).

---

3.   The estimated population according to the survey results until 1989 was 50,000, while in the last seven years of survey an estimated 20,000–25,000 people were added. Secondly, it is the desert fringes which have been explored during these years, so that most of the new additions came from there.

Size and Types of Sites

a. *Farms*. One half (131 sites) of the Iron Age II settlements are small in size (about half a hectare in area). Most of them were defined by their plans as family farmsteads, comprising a house or houses for the family and its associated structures and courtyard(s) for the animals. Many of these have been explored and drawn during the survey (Fig. 2.2). Their excavation and detailed research is a goal for the future, as they provide us with the basic information about the social structure of the family and its economy.

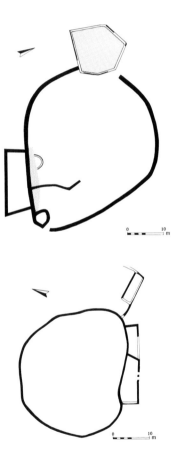

Fig. 2.2. *Plans of two Iron Age II family farms in Manasseh:*
Abu Sha'ara (top) and Wadi Ras el-Kharubeh (bottom)

Stager (1985), who explored the archaeology of the family in the Iron Age I period, concentrated on the private household within a village. The Iron Age II, though, was the period when the isolated family farms flourished. The farm is an ideal means for exploiting small, remote or infertile pieces of land. Their high proportion in the Iron Age II society again indicates prosperity and the search for the formerly underrated lands. Their especially high rate of occurrence in the desert fringes is additional evidence for this phenomenon (Fig. 2.3). A similar picture of farm distribution was presented from the western fringes of the Ephraimite territory during the Iron Age II (Dar 1982, 1986; Finkelstein 1981; Faust 1995).

The distribution of farms indicates the basic social structure of Israelite society, where small independent peasants played a central role in quantity and quality. It is well attested by the biblical sources, where independent farming appears as the ideal way of life (e.g. 1 Kgs 5.5; 2 Kgs 18.31; Isa. 36.16; Mic. 4.4).

Unlike Iron Age II Judah, where this phenomenon is well known (Stager 1976, 1977; Meitliss 1989, 1992; Amit 1992), no farm has been excavated so far in the Kingdom of Israel, but the farm economy can be initially traced through the works of Eitam (1992, 1996: 695-99) and others (Bornstein 1992). In Eitam's research, installations for the production of wine, olive-oil and other products, dated to the Iron Age II period, were discovered in the desert fringes of Manasseh. Eitam's finds form additional support for the suggestion that Iron Age II is the period of expansion into this region and that the settlers' economy was mostly based on sedentary agriculture. The beginnings of this sedentary agriculture only in the Iron Age II may indicate the semi-nomadic character of their predecessors, the Iron Age I early Israelites, who presumably lived on the same territory with an economy based on sheep husbandry (Zertal 1998a).

Farmsteads are mentioned in the Bible in various terms: the words are *bayit* (house), *tira* (translated wrongly as 'castle'—Gen. 25.16; Num. 31.10; Ezek. 25.4), *hatzer* (a house with a courtyard—Lowenstahm 1958) and probably *hava* (translated as 'small town'—Num. 32.41). The latter appear only in connection with Jair in Transjordanian Manasseh, which means it is not a common term (Schmitz 1992).

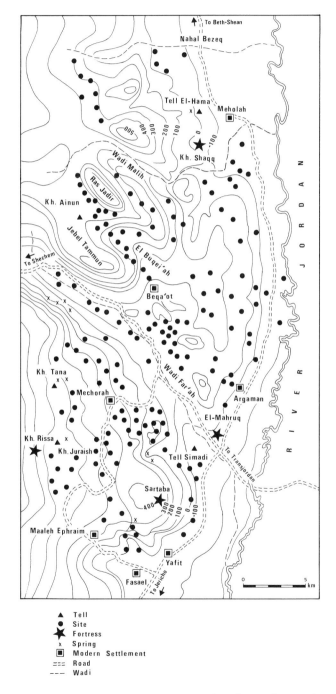

Fig. 2.3. *The Desert Fringes of the Northern Kingdom during the Iron Age II period*

b. *Villages*. Nearly one-third (82 sites, 31 per cent of the total) of the Iron Age II sites are villages, 1–5 acres in size and presumably with 200–250 inhabitants on average.[4] Judging by the survey, the villages—as well as the farms—were unfortified, a fact indicating the relative security provided by the kingdom and the fortified towns, used as refuges in times of war or disturbance.

Two excavated villages from the Iron Age I–II period, Tell 'Amal in the Beth Shean valley (Levy and Edelstein 1972; Edelstein and Feig 1993) and Tell Qiri in the Jezreel valley (Ben-Tor 1987, 1993) may be used as an example of this type in the Mediterranean region of Manasseh. Although only a small part of Tell Qiri was excavated, it is evident that the place (estimated at some 1–1.5 hectares in area) was unfortified (Ben-Tor 1993: 1229) and its inhabitants were occupied mainly, or even solely, with agriculture. The excavator presumes that a cultic place stood there (Ben-Tor 1993: 1229). Indications of the village economy, evidently similar to those found in our survey, are as follows:

1. Bones of sheep, cattle and other domesticated animals, pointing to an economy based on animal husbandry, were found (Davis 1987). Some small-scale hunting was recorded as well.
2. Grinding stones and sickle blades indicating wheat and barley agriculture (Ben-Tor 1987: 236-43; Rosen 1987).
3. Oil-presses, cup-marks, olive-stones and other botanical finds (Lipschitz and Weisel 1987) attesting to growing of olives, other fruits (pomegranates), vegetables (peas, vetch) and wheat.
4. Many silos again indicate large-scale grain growing.

It is thus suggested that the traditional Mediterranean agriculture did not change during Iron Age II, persisting as the basic economy of the region (Eitam 1980; Zertal 1988: 329-40).

It seems that the main economic focus at the village of Tell 'Amal were the workshops for weaving and dyeing (Edelstein and Feig 1993: 1448), judging by the loomweights of different sizes and other semi-industrial installations. It adds an additional angle to the activities of the village, though it is hard to ascertain whether this activity belonged to private persons or to the kingdom.

---

4.   For recent population estimates see Ofer 1993: 153-86. We still believe that the average of 25 inhabitants per 1000 sq. m of a built-up area may be a balanced figure for population statistics.

The village is regularly called in the Bible *'ir* ('town'). The Aramaic and Arabic term *kefar* ('village' as opposed to *'ir:* 'town') is mentioned only twice (Song 7.21; 1 Chron. 27.25).

c. *Towns and Cities.* The remaining 18 per cent of the sites were defined as towns (more than 2 hectares in area—altogether 49 sites). Additional definitions for towns, apart from size, were fortification, location and shape: most of the towns are located upon hilltops, are fortified and are elliptical or round in shape. The inner design and architecture of Israelite towns has been the focus of various studies (Lampl 1968; Shiloh 1978; Breamer 1982; de-Geus 1984, 1993; Fritz 1990) and deserve a separate paper. Here we say only that in the area under analysis there was one metropolis—Samaria, all other cases being average towns (2–4 hectares in size). The estimated area of Iron Age II Samaria according to Kenyon (Avigad 1993: 1302), is 70 hectares, with an estimated population of 17,000. Samaria had developed into a large central capital, larger than Jerusalem in the same period.

Our knowledge of the medium-size towns comes from a series of excavations at sites like Megiddo, Beth-Shean, Hazor, Tell el-Far'ah (N), and probably Tell en-Nasbeh. All these were enclosed by wide city-walls with towers and a city-gate complex, their interior was occupied by administrative buildings, and only a small living area was left for the population. The fortified towns should be considered as fortresses and administrative centres rather than dwelling places. Most of the people lived in the smaller settlements—farms and villages. The population density map (Fig. 2.4), shows the interrelationship between the capital Samaria, the centre, and the area around it populated by villages and farms. The central town was also used as shelter for the population in times of war.

A town is called *'ir* (town) or *'ir mivtzar* (fortified town, and note the first millennium terms *'al šarruti*—kingdom city, and *'al dannuti*—fortified city (Ikada 1979).

From the map (Fig. 2.1) it seems that fortified towns of the medium-size group are dispersed equally over the territory. Such a division of towns is found not only in the Mediterranean region but also in the eastern valleys and the desert fringes of Manasseh, where fortified towns are situated 5–10 km apart: in the valleys of Zebabdeh these are the tells Tilfit, Zebabdeh and Kh. Salhab; in Tubas valley are Kh. 'Ainun and Kh. Fuqaha; in Wadi Malih are Kh. Mhallal and Tell Hilu; in Wadi Far'ah are Tell el-Far'ah, Tell Miski, Beit Farr (A), Tell Za'annuni, Mrah el-'Anab etc, (see Zertal 1996: 81-84).

This pattern may be interpreted either as the result of natural development and growth and/or as a deliberate effort by the kingdom to fortify its remote areas, prepare a shelter for the growing population of the farms and villages and create a tax-collecting network.[5] Only further research may elaborate on this interesting problem.

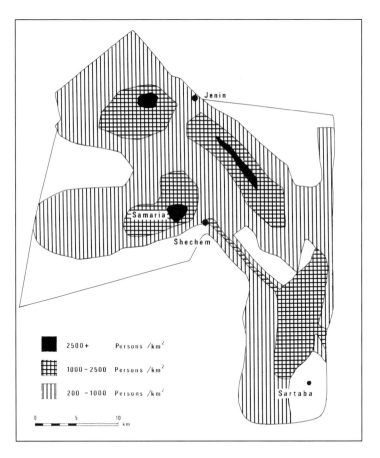

Fig. 2.4. *Population density in Iron Age II Manasseh (1998). Some of the sites on the desert fringes were discovered later and do not show on this map*

5.   Without entering here into the matter of the Samaria ostraca, it should be added that we were not able to distinguish in the field any evidence of large-area estates, owned either by the king or by rich viziers (Lemaire 1977: 23-85).

d. *Enclosures and Seasonal Sites in the Desert Fringes and the Jordan Valley: Semi-Nomads and Transhumance*. These two regions constitute a special phenomenon: seasonal sites of shepherds and semi-nomads, living in permanent transhumance. These sites, already prominent in the Iron Age I period, can be subdivided into two types: enclosures and cave sites.

Enclosures, oval or round and built of large stones, typify the Iron Age I–II sites in these two regions. Their average diameter is 20–30 m, so they can enclose up to 100 head of sheep. In some cases they are surrounded by buildings (as in Tullul el-Beidha in the Jordan valley), where it seems that the enclosure was the centre of a village. In other cases just the enclosure is discernable; here it may be presumed that the animals were kept inside, while the people lived around and outside, probably in tents.

A problem that arises is the presence in some cases of large quantities of potsherds inside the enclosures, indicating that people were living inside.

This conclusion is arrived at from the similarity in pottery distribution between these and the permanent sites. It might be suggested that some of the enclosures were used as fortified camps for some temporary groups of population (shepherds, caravaneers, soldiers and so on—Figs. 2.5–2.6).

Cave sites are a special feature of the Jordan valley. These are natural caves with courtyards in front. Caves are good shelters in summer or winter, and the courtyards are used to enlarge the defended space. According to the finds, cave sites were used since the Chalcolithic period, with Iron Age II pottery present as well. Some are in use up to our own time.

Enclosures are called *gedera* (e.g. Num. 32.16, 36; Isa. 24.4) and *hazera* (*-im*) (e.g. Josh. 15.45; 21.12). The desert fringes are called *naveh* in the Bible, a name which can also be applied to the sites mentioned above. This is where the sheep are found (2 Sam. 7.8): 'the habitation of shepherds causing their flocks to lie down' (Jer. 33.12), and it is a word repeated by Amos (1.2) and others.

e. *Fortresses, Towers and Camps*. The 20 sites defined as such show that the Northern Kingdom was well protected by at least three kinds of fortified sites (apart from the towns), or combination of the three: lookout points, road fortresses (which include the special group of fortresses around Samaria) and military camps.

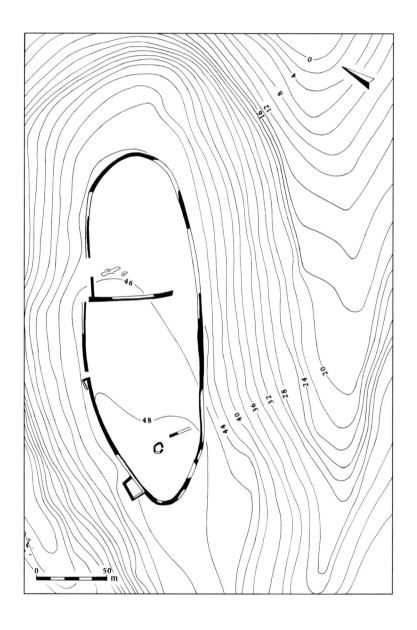

Fig. 2.5. *Plan of the possible* gilgal *(fortified enclosure) at el-'Unuq near Wadi Far'ah, built in the Iron Age I period and continuing in existence until Iron Age II*

Fig. 2.6. *An aerial photograph of el-'Unuq*

1) *Lookout points*: these are small sites located on high hilltops with especially good visibility. Umm ej-Jurein (Zertal 1996: 474-75, site 200) is an example: it is located on a hill high above Wadi Far'ah, and its architecture comprises a simple building with two rooms (Fig. 2.7). Although its function is uncertain, the location can hardly be interpreted other than as a lookout. Another example is Umm Hallal on the Sartaba massif (Israel grid 1917/1696, to be published in Vol. 4 of the survey), where a circular pile of stones may indicate a lookout point. Its location at the highest point on a bare rocky mountain also points in this direction. A third example is Abu Ghazi near Samaria (see below).

2) *Road fortresses*: Two types of these could be discerned among the fortified sites built to protect roads: the courtyard type and the circular 'towers' of the Jordan valley.

To the first type belong the fortress el-Bird (Wadi Malih), most of the fortresses around Samaria, and one discovered on the Sartaba massif (Kh. Abu Daraj, Israel grid 1912/1698).

The first, el-Bird (Zertal 1996: site 91, 273-76), is located near Wadi Malih, on top of a large site of the Middle Bronze Age I period (Intermediate Bronze). It consists of a rectangular court with rooms around, but the site has not been excavated. Kh. Abu Daraj is located on a steep saddle on the north-western Sartaba massif. At this point the road ascending from Wadi Far'ah to the south-west crosses the saddle near the 'Ain Abu Daraj spring, and a road from the Roman period was discovered nearby. The fortress itself consists of a large courtyard surrounded by a wall of big stones, with a square tower at the highest point.

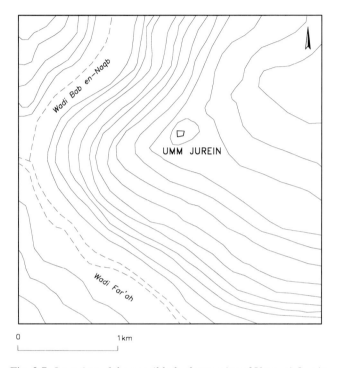

Fig. 2.7. *Location of the possible lookout point of Umm ej-Jurein*

The pottery includes Iron Age II and Roman period; thus, though part of the architecture may be of the Roman period, it appears that an Iron Age fortress was already located at this place.

A fortress of the same type was excavated at Kh. Abu Tuwein in Judah, where a central courtyard is surrounded by rooms (Mazar 1993a). Some of the Iron Age Negev fortresses are of the same type.

Circular towers were found in three locations near the Jordan valley, where the main roads run from the valley westwards into the heart of the kingdom. They have been published in detail (Yeivin 1974, 1992, 1993; Zertal 1995), so only a brief description is given here.

In all three (Kh. esh-Shaqq in Wadi Malih, Kh. el-Mahruq in Wadi Far'ah and Rujum Abu Muheir south of Sartaba) circular towers 19– 21 m in diameter and consisting of three concentric circles were discerned (Fig. 2.8). In two cases (Shaqq and Mahruq) there was a rectangular building associated with the tower, and in one case (Shaqq) what seems to be the remains of a casemate wall which enclosed the fortress.

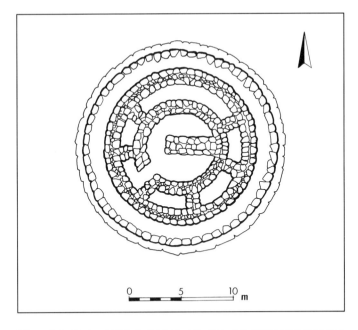

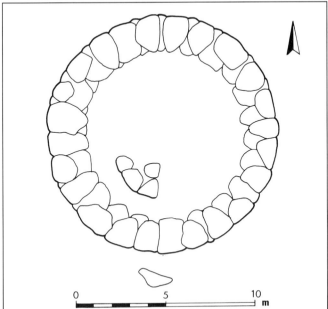

Fig. 2.8. *Plans of the circular towers of Kh. esh-Shaqq in Wadi Malih (top)*
and el-Mahruq in Wadi Far'ah (bottom)

The dating of the fortresses is not certain. Yeivin (1993: 931), who excavated Kh. el-Mahruq, dated its foundation to the tenth–ninth centuries BCE. No certain date was given to Rujum Abu Muheir, also excavated by Yeivin. It has been suggested that these towers could have been the forerunners of the Ammonite round towers, considered to be the most typical Ammonite architectural feature. (Zertal 1995: 269-72). A different possibility is that they represent an Ammonite influence on eastern Israel during the ninth–eighth centuries or even an invasion, probably echoed by Amos (1.13) as a part of his prophecy on Ammon.

3) *Network of fortresses around Samaria*: Some 14 fortified sites, located on the roads leading to Samaria from the north and the east, were located during the survey. They are distributed along the roads crossing the high hilly range north of Samaria with Jebel Abu Yazid at the centre, and on the hilly region east of Samaria. It is here suggested that the 14 sites, all bearing Iron Age II pottery exclusively, or extending into the Iron Age III/Persian periods, were built and used as part of an organized network of defensive sites around the capital (Zertal 1998b and Fig. 2.9).

Apart from two (nos. 1 and 4), all of them are courtyard-type fortresses. The following is a list of these sites, from north to south and from west to east (the site numbering and pages are from Zertal 1992a):

A. Sites on the roads leading from the north (Dothan valley) to Samaria:

1. The fortified Tell es-Sirtassa (site 137: 296-98, probably to be identified with biblical Abi'ezer—Zertal 1992a: 71);
2. The lookout fortress of Abu Ghazi, overlooking Samaria from the north (site 139: 300-301);
3-4. The fortress Qasr Abub'r (site 141: 302-303) and the courtyard fortress of Dabth el-'Afarith (site 142: 304-305). Both on the pass through Jebel Dabrun;
5. Kh. en-Naqb (site 143: 306-307), on the pass through Jaba;

B. Sites on the roads leading from the east (Tell el-Far'ah/Tirzah) to Samaria:

6. el-Mizan (site 216: 408);
7. Khirbet Mujrabin (site 227: 421-22);
8. Karm el-Qasqas (site 224: 418);
9-10. Dhahrat en-Nisnas (A-B): sites 237-38: 434-36;
11. Dhahrat es-Senobar (site 239: 436-37);

12. Qasr ez-Zoreh (site 240: 437-38);
13. Khirbet el-Isyar (site 250: 452-53);
C. Sites on the road leading from the south:
14. Maqtal Bil'aish (site 246: 447-48).

The elements which led us to see these as road and lookout fortresses are the similar location and architecture and the common pottery dating, but until large-scale research and excavations are undertaken the whole concept should remain a suggestion.

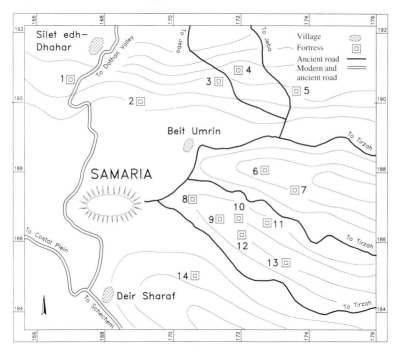

Fig. 2.9. *Map showing the fortresses around Samaria*
(numbers are according to the text)

f. *Military Camps and Bases.* I suggest identifying two Iron Age II sites as camps and/or military bases.

1) el-Qa'adeh, published in the survey (Zertal 1992a: site 56, 323-25), and in a special article (Zertal 1993b), is a fortified enclosure dated to the Iron Age II and the Persian periods, located c. 10 km north-east of Samaria, near the Sanur valley. It consists of a large square, c. 70 m long on each side, surrounded by a stone-wall 6–7 m wide with rooms or constructions inside the wall. The square enclosure is empty of archi-

tecture apart from two rows of rooms, and a gate-complex at the eastern side. The very unusual architectural features (including a large cistern and a special 'service' area outside), and the similarity to Assyrian military camps depicted in the ninth/eighth centuries BCE reliefs, point to the likelihood of its being an Assyrian military camp, probably erected in connection with the siege of Samaria. In fact, hardly any other explanation can be given concerning the site, but in the absence of known archaeological parallels for fortified Assyrian sites, the grounds for our identification are the similarity to the reliefs (Unger 1912; King 1915; Gadd 1936: pl. 29(a); Ussishkin 1982: 118 and Fig. 73) and the process of elimination of other possiblities. Twenty-five per cent of the pottery at the site was dated to Iron Age II–III and 75 per cent to the Persian period, which means a prolonged use of the base. Some pieces of thin grey 'Assyrian' carinated bowls are of special interest (Kenyon 1957: 12, 15, 17, Fig. 11; Chambon 1984: 1-11, pl. 61).

2) Khirbet Za'atarah (Zertal 1992a: site 156, 162-63), is located in the north-eastern part of Manasseh, c. 3 km south of Jenin. The site is a large, square enclosure comprising a courtyard surrounded by walls each 60 m long and 4–5 m wide. The site is cultivated now, so the location of the gate and other elements inside the courtyard are not clear.

A camp is the biblical *mahaneh*, meaning, for our purpose, a military camp (*EB* IV, 801-805), like in Judg. 7.21; 2 Kgs 7.7 and others.

g. *Cultic Sites.* Cultic sites are commonly mentioned by the eighth-century Israelite prophets (places like Beth-El and the *gilgalim* in Amos 4.4; 5.5; Hos. 4.15; 9.15 and so on), but only a few of them survive. Apart from large-scale temples excavated inside Iron Age II towns (Dan, Arad, Beer-Sheba), only relatively undisturbed sites, which show a distinctive cultic architecture, can be traced during surveys. An example of an outside temple is the Edomite shrine at Kh. Qitmit in the Beer-Sheba valley (Beit-Arieh 1993). In this respect, two sites on our desert fringes might be suggested as cultic installations: Jebel el-Mahjara 2 and Merah 'Arrar.

Jebel el-Mahjara 2 is located on a very prominent hilltop (378 m above sea-level) on the north-western side of the Sartaba massif. It overlooks the Mechora valley, the eastern high range of Jebel el-Kebir and the region of Wadi Zeit to the north. The site consists of a large oval enclosure, 120 × 150 m in diameter (c. 1.5 hectares in area), surrounding a rocky hilltop. At the centre there is a square building with two small round enclosures 10–15 m in diameter, one above the other (Fig. 2.10). An entrance (?) is located on the northern side. All the pottery is dated to the eighth century, but many of the potsherds belong to types unknown to us.

Merah 'Arrar is located not far from Jebel Mahjara. Its large 'temenos' wall, c. 100 m in diameter, surrounds a very rocky hilltop close to the large site of Kh. Tana et-Tahta. At the centre of the enclosure there is a square construction with an entrance on the northern side. The pottery is similar to that of Jebel el-Mahjara 2 and differs from the regular Iron Age II inventory.

The location and the extraordinary size of these enclosures, as well as the elimination of other possibilities, indicate that they are probably cultic places. They might be the continuation of the Iron Age I Israelite tradition of high places upon high mountains, which consist of an enclosure with a cultic place in the middle.

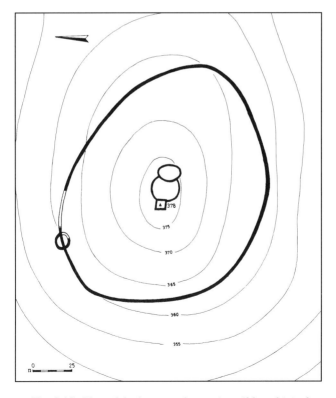

Fig. 2.10. *Plan of the large enclosure (possibly cultic) of*
el-Mahjara 2 on the Sartaba Massif

Conclusions

The territory of Manasseh, the geographical centre of the Northern Kingdom of Israel, was explored by a full survey. The results indicated a high degree of prosperity in the economy and pattern of settlement in the ninth and (mainly) the eighth centuries BCE. The natural development of the population and of agriculture were presumably accompanied by deliberate efforts on the part of the central government to settle the desert fringes and to fortify the roads and the borders.

The nearly 300 Iron Age II settlements explored were divided into groups by size and other characteristics. Most of the population dwelt in farmsteads and villages and some in the fortified towns, considered to be administrative and fortified 'castles' rather than dwelling-sites. The farms and villages were the main means of the kingdom to settle free peasants in formerly unsettled areas, by giving them land and security. The capital Samaria was a prominent metropolis thanks to its size and status as a centre for the whole region. The survey, together with information provided by excavations and biblical accounts, presents a picture of the social and economic structure of the Northern Kingdom until its fall to the Assyrians in the end of the eighth century BCE.

Bibliography

Aharoni, Y.
    1979   *The Land of the Bible: A Historical Geography* (Philadelphia: Westminster Press).
Albright, W.F.
    1931   'The Site of Tirzah and the Topography of Western Manasseh', *JPOS* 11, 241-51.
Alt, A.
    1913   'Israels Gaue unter Salomo', *BWAT* 13: 1-39.
    1966a   'The Settlement of the Israelites in Palestine', *Essays on Old Testament History and Religion:* 133-71 (Oxford: Basil Blackwell).
    1966b   'The Monarchy in Israel and Judah', *Essays on Old Testament History and Religion*: 239-61 (Oxford: Basil Blackwell).
Amit, D.
    1992   'A Survey of Farms in North Judaea', *AN* 97: 77-78 (Hebrew).
Avigad, N.
    1993   'Samaria (City)', *NEAEHL* 4: 1300-10.
Beit-Arieh, I.
    1993   'Qitmit, Horvat', *NEAEHL* 4: 1230-33.
Ben-Tor, A.
    1987   *Tell Qiri, A Village in the Jezreel Valley, Report of the Archaeological Excavations 1975–1977* (Qedem, 24; Jerusalem: Hebrew University).

1993	'Qiri, Tell', *NEAEHL* 4: 1228-29.

Bornstein, A.
1992	'The Economy of the Manassite Territory in light of the Samaria Ostraca', *JSR*, Proceedings of the 1st Annual Meeting, 1991: 61-122.

Breamer, F.
1982	*L'architecture domestique de l'age du fer* (Paris: Editions Recherches sur les Civilisations).

Broshi, M., and I. Finkelstein
1992	'The Population of Palestine in the Iron Age II', *BASOR* 287: 47-60.

Chambon, A.
1984	*Tell el-Far'ah 1: L'age du fer* (Paris: Editions Recherches sur les Civilisations).

Cody, A.
1970	'A New Inscription from Tell el-Rimah and King Jehoash of Israel', *CBQ* 32: 325-40.

Dar, S.
1982	'Ancient Agricultural Farms in Nahal Beit Arif', *Nofim* 16 (Hebrew).
1986	'The Agricultural Countryside of the Land of Samaria from the First Temple to the Byzantine Period', *Nofim* 18–19 (Hebrew).

Davis, S.
1987	'The Faunal Remains', in Ben-Tor 1987: 249-52.

Edelstein, G., and N. Feig
1993	'Tel 'Amal', *NEAEHL* 4: 1448-50.

Eitam, D.
1980	'The Production of Oil and Wine in Mt. Ephraim in the Iron Age', MA thesis presented to Tel Aviv University (Hebrew).
1992	'Khirbet Haddash: Royal Industry Village in Ancient Israel', *JSR*, Proceedings of the 1st Annual Meeting, 1991: 161-85 (Hebrew).
1996	'The Survey of the Agricultural Installations', in Zertal 1996: 681-739.

Faust, A.
1995	'Settlement on the Western Slopes of Samaria at the End of the Iron Age', *JSR*, Proceedings of the 4th Annual Meeting, 1994: 23-31 (Hebrew).

Finkelstein, I.
1981	'Israelite and Hellenistic Farms in the Foothills and in the Yarkon Basin', *EI* 15 (Aharoni Volume): 331-49 (Hebrew).

Fritz, V.
1990	*Die Stadt im alten Israel* (Munich: Beck Publishers).

Gadd, C.J.
1936	*The Stones of Assyria: The Surviving Remains of Assyrian Sculpture, their Recovery and their Original Positions* (London: Chatto & Windus).

de-Geus, C.H.J.
1984	*De Israelitische Stad* (Kampen).
1993	'Of Tribes and Towns: The Historical Development of the Israelite City', *EI* 24 (Malamat Volume): 70*-76*.

Grayson, A.K.
1992	'Mesopotamia, History of (Assyria)', *ABD* 4: 732-55.

Haran, M.
1967	'The Rise and Decline of the Empire of Jeroboam ben Joash', *VT* 17: 266.

Holladay, J.S.
1966   *The Pottery of Northern Palestine in the Ninth and Eighth Centuries BC*, (PhD thesis presented to Harvard University, Cambridge, MA).

Ikada, Y.
1979   'Royal Cities and Fortified Cities', *IRAQ* 41: 75-87.

Kenyon, K.
1957   'Pottery: Early Bronze and Israelite', in J.W. Crowfoot, G.M. Crowfoot and K.M. Kenyon (eds.), *The Objects of Samaria: Samaria-Sebaste 3* (London: Dawsons of Pall Mall for Palestine Exploration Fund): 90-216.

King, L.W.
1915   *Bronze Reliefs from the Gates of Shalmaneser* (London: The British Museum).

Lampl, P.
1968   *Cities and Planning in the Ancient Near East* (New York: Braziller).

Lemaire, A.
1972   'Le "pays de Hepher" et les "filles de Zelophehad" à la lumière des ostraca de Samarie', *Semitica* 2: 13-20.
1977   *Inscriptions Hebraiques I: Les ostraca* (Paris: Cerf).
1978   'Les Bene Jacob', *RB* 85: 321-37.
1985   'La haute Mesopotamie et l'origine de Bene Jacob', *VT* 34: 95-101.
1991   'Hazael de Damas, roi d'Aram', in D. Charpin and F. Joannes (eds.), *Marchands, diplomates et empereurs. Etudes sur la civilisation mesopotamiennes offerts à P. Garelli* (Paris: Editions Recherches sur les Civilisations): 91-108.
1993   'Joas de Samarie, Barhadad de Damas, Zakkur de Hamat, La Syrie-Palestine vers 800 av. J.-C.', *EI* 24 (Malamat Volume): 148*-57*.

Levy, S., and G. Edelstein
1972   'Fouilles de Tel-'Amal (Nir David)', *RB* 79, 325-65.

Lipinski, E.
1972   'Le Ben-Hadad II de la Bible et l'histoire', *Proceedings of the Fifth World Congress of Jewish Studies* (Jerusalem: Hebrew University): 157-73.
1979   'Aram et Israel du Xe au VIII siecle av. J.-C.', *Acta Antiqua* 27: 49-102.

Lipschitz, N., and O. Weisel
1987   'Analysis of the Botanical Material of the 1975–79 Seasons', in Ben-Tor 1987: 252-57.

Lowenstahm, S.
1958   'Hatzer, Hatzerim', *EB* 3: 273-74 (Hebrew).

Mazar, A.
1990   *Archaeology of the Land of the Bible, 10,000–586 BCE* (New York: Doubleday).
1993a   'Abu Tuwein, Khirbet', *NEAEHL* 1: 15-16.

Mazar, B.
1935   'Die westliche Linie des Meerweges', *ZDPV* 58: 79-84.

Meitliss, Y.
1989   'Agricultural Settlement Near Jerusalem in the End of the Iron Age' (MA thesis presented to the Hebrew University, Jerusalem; Hebrew).

1992 'The Agricultural Farms around Jerusalem at the End of the First Temple Period', in *The Twelfth Meeting of the Department for Eretz Israel Studies* (Ramat Gan: Bar-Ilan University; Hebrew).

Miller, J.M.
1967 'The Fall of the House of Achab', *VT* 17: 307-24.
1996 'The Elisha Cycles and the Accounts of the Omride Wars', *JBL* 85: 441-54.

Na'aman, N.
1990 'The Historical Background to the Conquest of Samaria', *Biblica* 71: 206-25.

Oded, B.
1979 *Mass Deportations and Deportees in the Neo-Assyrian Empire* (Wiesbaden: Reichert-Verlag).

Ofer, A.
1993 *The Highland of Judah during the Biblical Period*, Part II (PhD thesis presented to Tel-Aviv University, Tel Aviv; Hebrew).

Reinhold, G.G.
1989 *Die Beziehungen Altisraels zu den aramaischen Staaten in der israelitisch-Judaischen Konigszeit* (Frankfurt: Peter Lang).

Rosen, S.A.
1987 'The Lithic Assemblage of the Iron Age Strata', in Ben-Tor 1987: 246-49.

Sader, H.
1984 Les états araméens de Syrie depuis leur fondation jusqu'à leur transformation en provinces assyriennes (Tübingen: Franz Steiner Verlag).

Schmitz, P.C.
1992 'Havoth-Jair', *ABD* 3: 82-83.

Sellin, E.
1917 *Gilgal* (Leipzig: A. Deichert).

Shiloh, Y.
1978 'Elements in the Development of Town-Planning in the Israelite City', *IEJ* 27: 36-51.

Soggin, J.A.
1984 *A History of Israel* (Philadelphia: Westminster Press).

Stager, L.E.
1976 'Farming in the Judaean Desert in the Iron Age', *BASOR* 221: 145-48.
1977 'Ancient Farming in the Judaean Wilderness', *BARev* 3/3: 43-46.
1985 'The Archaeology of the Family in Ancient Israel', *BASOR* 260: 1-34.

Unger, E.
1912 *Zum Bronzetor von Balawat* (Leipzig: Metzger & Wittig).

Ussishkin, D.
1982 *The Conquest of Lachish by Sennacherib* (Tel Aviv: Tel Aviv University).

Whitley, C.F.
1952 'The Deuteronomistic Presentation of the House of Omri', *VT* 2: 137-52.

Yadin, Y.
1955 'Some Aspects on the Strategy of Achab and David', *Biblica* 36: 332-51.

Yeivin, Z.
    1974   'Israelite Towers at Khirbet Mahruq', *Qadmoniyot* 7(27-28): 102-104 (Hebrew).
    1992   'Two Watchtowers in the Jordan Valley', *EI* 23: 155-74 (Hebrew).
    1993   'el-Mahruq, Khirbeh', *NEAEHL* 3: 929-31.

Zertal, A.
    1984   Arruboth, Hepher and the Third Solomonic District: A Monograph on Biblical Geography (Tel Aviv: Sifriat Poalim; Hebrew).
    1988   *The Israelite Settlement in the Hill-Country of Manasseh* (Haifa: Haifa University; Hebrew).
    1989a   'The Pahwah of Samaria (Northern Israel) during the Persian Period: Types of Settlement, Economy, History and New Discoveries', *Transeuphratène* 2: 9-30.
    1989b   'The Wedge-Shaped Decorated Bowl and the Origin of the Samaritans', *BASOR* 276: 77-84.
    1991   'Israel enters Canaan: Following the Pottery Trail', *BARev* 17.5: 28-50.
    1992a   *The Survey of the Hill-Country of Manasseh*. I. *The Syncline of Shechem* (Tel Aviv: IDF Publishing House and Haifa University; Hebrew).
    1992b   'Arubboth', *ABD* 1: 465-67.
    1992c   'Hepher', *ABD* 3: 138-39.
    1993a   'The Mount Manasseh (Northern Samaria Hills) Survey', *NEAEHL* 4: 1311-12.
    1993b   'A Fortified Camp from the Iron Age Near Samaria', *JSR*, Proceedings of the 2nd Annual Meeting, 1992, (Qedumin-Ariel; Hebrew): 147-69.
    1994   '"To the Land of the Perizzites and the Giants": On the Israelite Settlement in the Hill-Country of Manasseh', in N. Na'aman and I. Finkelstein (eds.), *From Nomadism to Monarchy* (Jerusalem and Washington: Yad Yitzhak Ben Zvi, Israel Exploration Society and Biblical Archaeological Society): 37-70.
    1995   'Three Iron Age Fortresses in the Jordan Valley and the Origin of the Ammonite Circular Towers', *IEJ* 45: 253-73.
    1996   *The Survey of the Hill-Country of Manasseh*. II. *The Eastern Valleys and the Fringes of the Desert* (Tel Aviv: IDF Publishing House and Haifa University; Hebrew).
    1998a   'The Iron Age I Culture in the Hill-Country of Canaan: A Manassite Look', in S. Gitin, A. Mazar and E. Stern (eds.), *Mediterranean Peoples in Transition, Thirteenth to Early Tenth Centuries BCE* (Jerusalem: Israel Exploration Society): 238-51.
    1998b   'An Iron Age Fortresses Network around Samaria', *JSR*, Proceedings of the Eighth Meeting, 1998 (Kedumim-Ariel; Hebrew).

Zertal, A., and M. Greenberg
    1983   'Methods of Archaeological Surveys and Data Processing', *Proceedings of the Tenth Archaeological Congress in Israel* (Jerusalem: Israel Exploration Society; Hebrew): 5.

Zertal, A., and N. Mirkam
    2000   *The Survey of the Hill-Country of Manasseh*. III. *From Nahal Iron to Nahal Shechem* (Tel Aviv: IDF Publishing House and Haifa University; Hebrew).

3

PHOENICIANS IN WESTERN GALILEE: FIRST RESULTS OF AN ARCHAEOLOGICAL SURVEY IN THE HINTERLAND OF AKKO[*]

Gunnar Lehmann

Palestine was never a country of just one ethnicity, one language, religion or culture. Its differentiated topography favoured a heterogeneous population. During the Bronze and Iron Ages different groups of population with distinct patterns of economic and social capacities developed in their geopolitical setting, in the rich coastal plains and wide valleys and in the less wealthy highlands, steppe or desert.

The study of ethnicity and ethnic identifications in the ancient Near East based on the archaeological or historical record is under new scrutiny (cf. Kamp and Yoffee 1980). For a long time concepts of ancient Near Eastern ethnicity were overshadowed by common prejudices which eventually have been attacked as 'orientalism' (Said 1978) and as a projection of modern, anachronistic understanding of nationalism and the character of national states being forced upon the archaeological and historical record (see for example the study of Anderson 1991). Much of the reconstructed traditions based on ethnic differentiations turned out to be in fact invented traditions, created by modern scholars in the context of western society (see also the discussion in

[*] The Akko-Survey, conducted in 1993–96, was sponsored by the Evangelische Kirche Deutschlands. During most of this period the author was the acting director of the German Protestant Institute of Archaeology in Jerusalem. In a crucial phase 1994–95 the project was continued with the financial support of the German Embassy in Tel Aviv. It was later continued during 1995–96 on behalf of the Freie Universität Berlin. The final research and the preparation of the publication was made possible by a research grant of the Deutsche Archäologische Institut in Berlin, Germany. I am in particular grateful for the support of Dr Susanne Wasum-Rainer, Professor Ricardo Eichmann and Professor H.J. Nissen.

Hobsbawm and Ranger 1983). Such approaches may have encouraged historians to deconstruct the traditional concepts of 'Canaanites' or 'Ancient Israel' (Lemche 1991 and Davies 1992); attempts which themselves were challenged in an ongoing debate (see Rainey 1996 and Lemche's reply 1998).

Kamp and Yoffee (1980: 99) warned us that 'pure cultures' never existed in the ancient Near East and that 'hybrid cultures' were in fact the norm. However, both authors conclude that one organizational principle in this plurality in fact is that of ethnicity (among the vast literature on ethnicity see, e.g., Alonso 1994; Banks 1996; Brett 1996; or Jones 1996). In this paper I will address to the question of Phoenicians and their impact on northern Palestine during the Iron Age. While in modern research the Phoenicians are ranked prominently among the peoples of the ancient Near East, there are only a few studies which are concerned with the question of who these people actually were. And even fewer will go beyond a mere description, trying to explain the development of the term 'Phoenician' in its socio-cultural context.

According to Davies there are three dimensions of an ancient ethnicity such as the Phoenicians (in his context 'Ancient Israel'): one is the literary (the Bible, Phoenician, Egyptian, Assyrian, Greek and other sources), another is the historical (the inhabitants of the Lebanese and Syrian coast during the Iron Age) and the third is what modern scholars have constructed out of the other two (Davies 1992: 11). From my point of view Davies, being a biblical scholar, neglected to some extent the potential of archaeology in this context. In fact there is an abundant literature today, often under the label of 'pots and people', dealing with the question of how to identify ethnicity with archaeological evidence, i.e. the material record (see now Jones 1996). While identification of Hurrians, Philistines and Israelites was discussed (Kramer 1977; Bunimovitz 1996; Finkelstein 1997; Dever 1995), apparently there are no problems in identifying Phoenicians. This is at least the impression given, since there is almost no one working on the topic (except for i.e. Pastor-Borgoñon 1988–90 and especially Winter 1995).

Apparently, the Phoenicians never formed a united political entity or national state 'Phoenicia'. They were organized in a number of city states along the Lebanese and Syrian coast. Often competing with each other, these small states seem to be a 'geopolitical left-over' of the Bronze Age, protected to some extent by their geographical setting and promoted by a lack of imperialist activities by Mesopotamian and Egyptian empires during the beginning of the Iron Age (Stieglitz 1990).

Until recently, Phoenicians in northern Israel were a phenomenon studied only on the basis of excavations. Sites such as Dor, Tell Abu Hawam, Akko, Tell Keisan, Rosh Zayit or Achziv are examples for this approach (Stern 1990, 1991, 1994: 101; Herrera Gonzalez 1990; Briend and Humbert 1980; Gal 1992: 47-53). In this paper I would like to complement these researches with a spatial analysis of survey results in the hinterland of Akko. In particular, I would like to address the question of whether it is possible to identify the Phoenicians as agents in the transformation processes of the settlement patterns and the landscape of the hinterland of Akko.

The Akko Plain

Since the mediaeval period European travellers and pilgrims have visited Akko and its hinterland. Scientific literature on the region, its history and its geography is abundant. It was thus surprising that no archaeological survey had been conducted in Akko's immediate hinterland. When the writer, then acting director of the German Protestant Institute of Archaeology in Jerusalem, started such an investigation together with Martin Peilstöcker, Israel Antiquities Authority, as part of the *Archaeological Survey of Israel* we had no great hopes of finding a lot of still undetected evidence.

To our surprise, as a result of our research the number of ancient settlements were more than doubled. This is also due to new methods of prospecting. The *Akko Survey* was designed to search not just for settlements but to include a study of ancient landscape elements. While there were 17 ancient settlements registered when we started fieldwork there are now in the final stages of our research some 50 settlements on the map (see Fig. 3.1 and the list in Appendix 3A; Lehmann 1994b). In addition, we registered hundreds of ancient terraces, agricultural installations, cisterns and wells in the area (for approaches of landscape archaeology see for example Gibson 1995; Wilkinson and Tucker 1995).

In an attempt to study all remains of past human activities in the area, we took into consideration all cultural activities from the Paleolithic until the year 1948. This paper will present some first results of this survey, dealing only with a structural analysis of the Late Bronze and

Iron Age settlement history. To complement our results I will also include the results of surveys in the neighbouring areas of the Akko plain conducted by other archaeologists (Fig. 3.2).

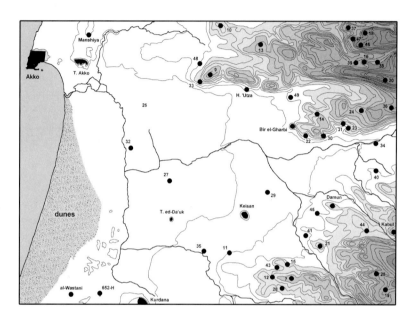

Fig. 3.1. *Sites of the Akko-Survey (Lehmann and Peilstöcker, 1993–96)*

The Akko plain extends from Ras an-Naqura (Hebrew Rosh ha-Niqra), the 'Tyrian Ladder' in antiquity, in the north to the Karmel in the south. To the west the Mediterranean forms a natural border while in the east the plain passes into a hill country which soon rises into the Galilean mountains. In the north-east these mountains form Upper Galilee with summits at a height of 500 m to more than 1000 m; in the south-east, Lower Galilee, mountains rise up to approximately 300 m.

Deep alluvial soils characterize the Akko plain. The soil was washed down from the limestone mountains east of the plain. All along the coast there are dunes between Haifa and the area north of Achziv. The soils in the hill country consist of brown Mediterranean forest soils. In the mountains there are predominantly terra-rossa soils. Sufficient rainfall makes dry-farming possible all over the area; in addition there are several springs.

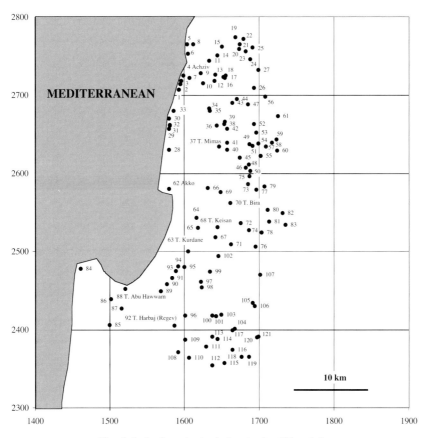

Fig. 3.2. *Archaeological sites in the Akko plain*
(Late Bronze Age, Iron Age and Persian period)

In the flat, gently sloping plain we find a number of large tells. At a height of 40 m the first limestone rocks come out of the alluvial soils. Here the plain passes into the hill country. After only a few kilometers the area becomes mountainous with elevations of 200–400 m. Above elevations of 40 m there are no more tells. The typical form of ruin in the hill and mountain areas is the *khirbe*, with stone as the predominant building material, which is still visible on the surface. However, since antiquity, stones of these ruins were robbed and reused in nearby villages, causing continual damage to the ancient settlement remains.

Thus, the Akko plain is a typical Mediterranean plain. It was Fernand Braudel who pointed out the historical and geographical importance of these plains for the development of the Mediterranean culture (Braudel 1972: 60-84). The coastal plains have fertile soils and favourable conditions for transport and traffic—if one manages to drain the plain. Under natural conditions there are frequently swamps and marshland at the foot of the hills in the very flat alluvium. In addition there are the dunes along the coast of the Akko plain which hold back the water. The result is stagnant water and malaria. Draining and maintaining the eventually gained agricultural areas demands investments and political administration.

As a result most premodern settlements in the plain were situated at the transition between the alluvium and the hills on the first rock formations rising from the plain. Even those sites which were in the alluvial area are in most cases on elevations and small rock formations. Only a very few sites, generally very small, are founded immediately on the alluvial soils. These observations are important for the question as to how many archaeological sites in the plain may have been covered by alluvium, therefore invisible to the surveyor. The survey results should be checked against the settlement pattern of the nineteenth and the early twentieth century. On the maps of the *Survey of Western Palestine* there are two sites occupied on alluvial soils. These small settlements, characterized as 'huts', are the sites al-Wastani and no. 32 on Fig. 3.1. Although these sites existed only about 100 years ago, nothing is visible of their huts today. During the British Mandate conditions were most favourable for traditional agriculture in the plain. The alluvium was drained but still the settlements remained on the heights and hills. Villages such as Damun, Ruways or Tamra maintained their grain and vegetable fields in the plain from their elevated positions. In the dry month the farmers came down to their fields and erected small huts there. The large tells such as Tell al-Fukhkhar (Akko), Tell Keisan or Tell Kurdana (Tel Aphek) are all situated on natural hills. These large tells were occupied until the Hellenistic period. During the third century BCE most tells were abandoned.

The traditional settlement patterns in this Mediterranean coastal plain existed until about 1948. Usually the political power was centralized in the plain, often in one of the harbour cities, in this case in Akko. To what extent the hill and mountain areas were integrated in this settlement pattern and administrative system depends on the centre's political and economic capacity to act. In times when integration was lacking the mountain areas quickly gained an increasing political independence and it was difficult to re-establish political control from the coast. Two hundred years ago, in the eighteenth century CE, one example of this process was the rise and fall of Sheikh Dhahir al-'Umar. This local Galilean ruler established a small territorial state in the centre of Galilee and eventually succeeded in gaining control over the coastal plain. He moved his capital to Akko and was finally liquidated by an Ottoman expedition led by Ahmad al-Jazzar, who conquered Akko and defeated Sheikh Dhahir. These very well-recorded events are an extraordinary source of information for the scale of political and social operations, and the accessibility and geopolitical conditions in premodern Galilee (see now Niemann 1997: 265-67).

Economically the plain and the highlands are dependent on each other. Timber and other raw materials and products of the mountains are an important part of the Mediterranean exchange system. Milk and meat products as well as wine and olives from the highlands are consumed in the plains. Grain and vegetables grown in the lowlands as well as manufactured craft products from the urban centres in the plain are needed in the highlands.

Surveys and Excavations

In this analysis, I will use mainly the archaeological record in addition to the few historical sources of the Late Bronze and Iron Age in order to reconstruct the historical geography of the Akko plain during these periods. Among the excavations are Achziv (Fig. 3.1: site 4), Khirbat 'Abda (18), as-Sumayriya (Tell ar-Ras, Giv'at Yasif) (28), Tel Kabri (35), Tell Mimas (Beth ha-'Emeq) (37), Akko (Tell al-Fukhkhar) (62), Tell Keisan (68), Khirbat 'Ayyadiya (Horvat 'Utza) (69), Tell Bir al-Gharbi (Tel Bira) (70), Ras az-Zaytun (Rosh Zayyit) (81), Tell Abu Hawam (88), Tell al-Harbaj (92), Tell al-Far (96), Khirbat Abu Mudawwar (107) and Tell al-'Amr (108).[1]

Although this is an impressive number of excavations the history of settlement in the hinterland of Akko becomes apparent only with the help of the archaeological surveys conducted there (see for example the

---

1.   For Tell Abu Hawam, Achziv, Akko (Tell al-Fukhkhar), Tel Kabri, Beth ha-'Emeq (Tell Mimas), Tel Bira (Tell Bir al-Gharbi), Tell Keisan, Tel Ma'amer (Tell al-'Amr), Tel Regev (Tell al-Harbaj), Rosh Zayyit (Ras az-Zaytun) see the articles and bibliography in *NEAEHL*. See also Khirbat 'Abda (Prausnitz 1973: 219-23), Khirbat 'Ayyadiya (Horvat 'Utza) (Ben-Tor 1966; Getzov 1993), Tell al-Far (personal communication from Dr Zvi Gal), Khirbat Abu Mudawwar (Tel Mador) (Gal 1992: 36-43), as-Sumayriya (Tell ar-Ras, Giv'at Yasif) (Messika 1996).

study of the Persian period by Briend 1990 using only excavations). The northern part of the plain was surveyed by Rafael Frankel in his *Survey of Western Galilee* (Frankel 1986, 1994; Frankel and Getzov 1997). The centre of the plain, the immediate hinterland of Akko, was investigated by the writer and Martin Peilstöcker in their *Akko-Survey* (Fig. 3.1; see Lehmann 1994b, 1995). The south-western part was studied by Avraham Ronen and Yaacov Olami (Kloner and Olami 1980; Ronen and Olami 1983; Olami 1974 and more unpublished reports in the archives of the Israel Antiquities Authorities). The southern hill and mountain areas were surveyed by Avner Raban (1982) and Zvi Gal (1992). The survey by Zvi Gal in the south-eastern part is still not completed. Thus, final reports are still missing and problems arise as to the exact date and size of some sites.

The modern survey techniques applied in the above-mentioned projects enable us to cautiously estimate the settlement sizes of each site in its respective periods of occupation. Several techniques were used during the *Akko-Survey* to collect this information: one of them was the time and cost intensive so-called 'Portugali-Method' outlined by Tel Aviv geographer Yuval Portugali (1982). This method included the opening (i.e. digging) of the top soil and the total retrieval of all diagnostic pottery in the sample areas. This paper will be limited to the Late Bronze Age (c. 1550–1200 BCE), the Iron Age I (c. 1200–1000 BCE), Iron Age II (c. 1000–586 BCE) and the Babylonian and Persian periods (586–332 BCE). Since there is a renewed discussion on the dates of Iron Age I, especially the 'Philistine' pottery, and the tenth-century BCE chronology (cf. Finkelstein 1995 and 1996), we may have to expect some future changes in the pottery dating. However, for this preliminary presentation I will use the traditional dates.

For the spatial analysis I will use five categories of settlement sizes, using the Palestinian 'dunam' unit (10 dunam = 1 hectare): sites of less than 20 dunam size are considered 'small settlements' including hamlets and small villages. Settlements of between 21 and 30 dunam are 'medium-sized settlements' and settlements between 31 and 50 dunam are 'large settlements'. Any site between 50 and 100 dunam is called a 'very large settlement' and sites of more than 100 dunam are considered 'urban centres'.

Another criterion was the topographical position and especially the elevation of each site. As already mentioned, limestone rock formations emerge from the alluvium at a height of approximately 40 m above sea level. The survey area below 40 m above sea level is thus called 'plain', the area between a height of 40 and 200 m above sea level is considered to be hill country and any areas above 200 m sea level will be referred to as mountainous.

About 100 settlements existed in the plain at some point during the Late Bronze Age, the Iron Age and the Persian period. These settlements consist of urban centres, villages, hamlets and fortified sites. The spatial analysis presented in this paper required several data: the names and coordinates of each site, the period of settlement, the size of each site in its respective period and its topographical setting.

For most of the sites there is sufficient and reliable data as to when they were settled. However, as already pointed out, for a number of sites in the northern and southern parts of the plain there are still some problems of dating and estimating the settlement sizes. Fifteen sites, more than 10 per cent of all sites, are so far dated only to the Iron Age without any further information as to whether they were settled in the Iron Age I or II. Most of these sites are situated in the hill and mountain area. They are all smaller than 20 dunam—with the exception of Khirbat Ga'atun (25 dunam), and 10 out of these 15 sites were occupied only during the Iron Age. This group thus forms a significant part of our data, with considerable impact on the results of the analysis. To include this information I had to work with 'minimal' and 'maximal' values in this analysis. As 'minimum' I understand all data without the 15 sites, whereas the 'maximum' includes all 15 sites in both phases, Iron Age I and II. The real historical values will be somewhere in between these two extremes.

Only future fieldwork and final publications will provide the exact data for these 15 Iron Age sites. However, the settlement pattern which became apparent from surveys in other areas of the hinterland of Akko such as the *Akko-Survey* and the survey conducted by Avner Raban (1982) lead to the assumption that the minimum value might be close to the reality of Iron Age I and the maximum value applicable to Iron Age II. Israel Finkelstein comes to similar results, estimating some 878 dunam overall settlement size in the Iron Age II Akko plain (Finkelstein 1993). This is approximately my maximum value for Iron Age II, a period in which settlement flourished in the plain.

Another problem arises from surveys conducted before the Second World War, especially the researches of Aapeli Saarisalo (1929). In both the *Akko-Survey* and the *Survey of Western Galilee* some of the results differ from those of Saarisalo. In particular, Saarisalo's Late Bronze Age dates were not confirmed by the modern surveys. In the area of the *Akko-Survey* Saarisalo noted Late Bronze Age pottery at sites such as Tell Da'uk, Khirbat 'Ayytawiya und Khirbat Tirat Tamra (Saarisalo 1929: 38-39). During our intensive investigations at these sites we did not find any Late Bronze Age pottery. Unfortunately, Saarisalo did not publish his pottery or his dating criteria and I don't know on what evidence his conclusions are based. As a result of our fieldwork I decided not to use Saarisalo's Late Bronze Age dates where they contradict my or Frankel's evidence. On other sites I will add a question mark to these dates.

The Size of Settlement Area

The spatial analysis of the overall settlement size in the hinterland of Akko demonstrates that between the Late Bronze Age and the Persian period (c. 1550–330 BCE) the majority of the population was living in the plain (Table 3.1). In Table 3.1, I included both the above-mentioned 'minimum' and 'maximum' numbers for the Iron Age. Both figures demonstrate that the plain's share of the overall settlement size was almost always about 50 per cent or more. The only exception was Iron Age I, which is very different from the Late Bronze Age. Most significantly, the settlement in the hill country and the mountains is clearly increasing during the Iron Age. In the Persian period the settlement areas in the mountains are shrinking. Thus, the figures indicate a clear break in the settlement pattern between the Late Bronze Age and Iron Age I. The settlement size was then significantly enlarged during Iron Age II, while continuity characterizes the transition between Iron Age II and the Persian period.

Table 3.1. *Settlement size*

	Plain		Hill country		Mountains		Total
	Dunam	%	Dunam	%	Dunam	%	Dunam
Late Bronze Age	478	70.3	181	26.6	21	3.1	680
Iron Age I	246	45.9	214	40.0	76	14.2	536
	(284)	(43.1)	(253)	(38.4)	(122)	(18.5)	(659)
Iron Age II	503	53.3	335	35.5	105	11.2	943
	(541)	(50.8)	(374)	(35.0)	(151)	(14.2)	(1066)
Persian Period	560	55.4	366	36.3	84	8.3	1010

Note: Without parentheses, 'minimum'; with parentheses, 'maximum'.

The Impact of Topography

Clear trends of development in the settlement system emerge also in an analysis of the number and size of the sites in relation to their topographical setting, that is. whether they are situated in the plain, the hill country or in the mountains (Table 3.2). Unfortunately, again we have to work with the minimum and maximum numbers for Iron Age sites. During the Late Bronze Age the population in the study area clearly preferred settlements and agriculture in the plain. There are almost no villages in the mountains. Recent and still unpublished surveys in Upper Galilee by Avi'am, Getzov and Frankel as well as by Lehmann and Niemann confirm this observation (see also Thompson 1979). Large settlements with an area of 31–100 dunam were situated exclusively in the plain. Only a few small villages were inhabited in the hill country. These villages were all smaller than 14 dunam—among the few exceptions is Tell Mimas (Bet ha-'Emeq). This site probably had an area of 40 dunam. Even beyond the Akko plain there were only very few small villages further east in Upper Galilee during the Late Bronze Age (Thompson 1979; Gal 1988).

This pattern is in sharp contrast to that of the Iron Age I. Most small villages with a size of less than 30 dunam were now in the hill country, with a few larger villages of up to 50 dunam. The mountains are now increasingly more important for settlement and agriculture. However, the sites are all very small: none of them is larger than 30 dunam. Sites with an area of more than 50 dunam are situated almost exclusively in the plain.

The distribution pattern of settlements during Iron Age II is similar to that of Iron Age I. Most small villages are again in the hill country or in the mountains. The importance of the mountain area is further increasing. Again all sites of more than 50 dunam are situated in the plain, with the possible exception of Tell Mimas (Bet ha-'Emeq). This site may have been as large as 50 dunam and was probably a regional centre on the junction between the plain and the hill country. Apparently, the hinterland of Akko was densely settled during Iron Age II. This would be in accord with the settlement patterns in most areas of Palestine during this period. Iron Age II was a first climax in the settlement history of the country after what seems to be centuries of decline during the Late Bronze Age.

Table 3.2. *Distribution of settlements according to size and topographical situation*

Size (dunam)	1–20	21–30	31–50	51–100	100+	Total
Late Bronze Age						
Plain	16	2	4		1	23
Hill country	12	1	1			14
Mountains	4					4
Total sites						41
Iron Age (without further details)						
Plain	3					3
Hill country	5					5
Mountains	6	1				7
Total sites						15
Iron Age I						
Plain	7	3	3			13
Hill country	9	3	1			13
Mountains	12					12
Total sites						38
Iron Age II						
Plain	10	3	4	1	1	19
Hill country	19	2		1		22
Mountains	12	1				13
Total sites						54
Persian Period						
Plain	18	3	4		1	26
Hill country	29		1	1		31
Mountains	14					14
Total sites						71

The development of the hill country and the mountains for settlement and agriculture is the most important trend in the hinterland of Akko during the Iron Age. As already stated, most villages were situated here above the 100 m elevation line. Thus, apparently a significant part of the population in the hinterland of Akko specialized in growing wine and olives in the hill country and the mountains. They were also herding sheep and goats. In contrast, grain was the typical crop of the plain. This pattern points to an early agricultural specialization and an economic use of manpower in cultivating the plain during Iron Age II. The wine and the olive products especially were most probably grown for export. All these developments would require an efficient administration in Iron Age II.

During the Persian period the overall number of settlements and the area of occupation is slightly increasing. The settlement pattern is still very similar to that of Iron Age II. Still the hill country and the mountains are densely occupied. There are two distinct categories of villages in the hinterland of Akko: small ones up to 30 dunam and larger ones of up to 50 dunam. Again Tell Mimas (Bet ha-'Emeq) seems to have been an important regional centre, being the only site in the hill country of more than 50 dunam. The only urban centre of this period was Akko with its important harbour.

Rank-Size Analysis

The size of the Late Bronze Age sites was more differentiated than during Iron Age I. During the Late Bronze Age there were three distinct categories:

- villages up to 30 dunam;
- sub-centres between 30 and 50 dunam; and
- Akko as an urban centre with more than 100 dunam.

In contrast to this pattern, the Iron Age I is less differentiated and characterized by mostly small villages with an area between 10 or 20 dunam (Fig. 3.3). There are only five settlements larger than 30 dunam, Akko (the overall size of the site is 117 dunam, but it remains unclear how much of this was occupied during Iron Age I), Achziv (31 dunam), Tell Abu Hawam (31 dunam), Tell Keisan (38 dunam) and Tell Mimas (Bet ha-'Emeq) (40 dunam). These five villages were apparently the modest centres of the area during Iron Age I.

The number of larger settlements increased in Iron Age II. Three sites have an area of more than 50 dunam: Akko (117 dunam), Bir al-Gharbi (70 dunam) and Tell Mimas (Bet ha-'Emeq) (68 dunam). Most settlements, however, have an area of 10–40 dunam. The patterns of the Persian period are similar to that of Iron Age II, but note the increase of small villages with an area of 10–20 dunam (Fig. 3.3). The settlement pattern of the Persian period is thus slightly more differentiated than in the preceeding Iron Age II.

In Near Eastern archaeology rank-size analyses have been used already in several cases to study early settlement systems. In rank-size graphs contemporary settlements within a region are arranged in descending order of site size. The sites are plotted on double logarithmic paper and may form a concave or convex curve; linear results are rather rare. The interpretation of these curves continues to be debated (Johnson 1981). Usually a linear result is supposed to represent a hierarchical, well-integrated settlement system with one major centre. Convex curves result when the medium-sized settlements in the system are still larger than the linear rank-size values predict. The settlement system is less well integrated. Medium-sized sites compete with each other and challenge the centre. Concave curves indicate the existence of a prime centre that overshadows all other in size (Wilkinson and Tucker 1995: 79-80). In Israel/Palestine rank-size analyses have been used in Bunimovitz' study of the Late Bronze Age (1989) and Ofer's spatial analysis of the Judaean mountains (1993a, b, 1994).

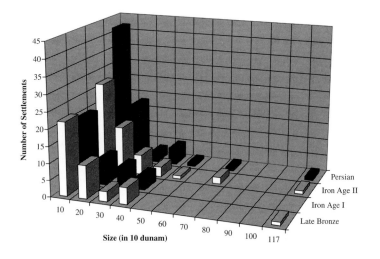

Fig. 3.3. *Settlement size classification*

The rank-size curves in this paper are all convex (Fig. 3.4). Figure 3.4a illustrates the settlement system of the Late Bronze Age. The curve is close to the linear log-normal curve. This indicates a well integrated settlement system with Akko as its centre: a clear representation of a Late Bronze Age city-state with its hierarchical structures. The arching convex curve of the Iron Age I demonstrates a different pattern (Fig. 3.4b). In this system there is almost no integration. Several medium-sized sites compete with each other. There is no indication of a hier-archical, centralized system in the area. In fact, the curve illustrates a complete break with the preceding Late Bronze Age system.

(a)

(b)

(c)

(d)

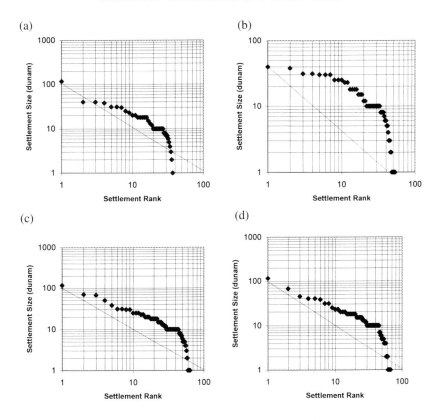

Fig. 3.4. *Rank-size graphs: (a) Late Bronze Age; (b) Iron Age I;*
(c) Iron Age II; (d) Persian period

Again a fundamental change took place in the transition between Iron Age I and II. In Iron Age II (Fig. 3.4c) and during the Persian period (Fig. 3.4d) the settlement system returned to the pattern of the Late Bronze Age. The area is well integrated under one city centre, Akko. The hinterland of Akko appears to be well organized into a centralized, hierarchical structure. The curves of the Iron Age II and of the Persian period are almost identical, indicating a continuity in the settlement system between the two periods.

Continuity and Disruptions in the Settlement History

An analysis of the continuities and breaks in the settlement traditions in the hinterland of Akko reveals distinct developments and trends (Table 3.3). In this analysis I used all available reliable data without maximum

Table 3.3a. *Settlement continuity*

	1 Cont. LB/IA I	2 Discont. LB/IA I	3 Begin IA I	4 Cont. IA I/ IA II	5 Discont. IA I/IA II	6 Begin IA II	7 Cont. IA II/ Persian	8 Discont. IA II/ Persian	9 Begin Persian
Plain									
Small	6	10		5	2	6	10		10
Medium	1	1	1	3		1	3		
Large	4			3		1	3	1	1
Very large	1						1		
Centre									
Total	12	11	1	11	2	8	18	1	11
Hill country									
Small	1	11	9	2	7	17	14	5	13
Medium	1		1	2	1			2	
Large	1			1					1
Very large									
Centre							1		
Total	3	11	10	5	8	17	15	7	14
Mountains									
Small	3	1	9	5	7	7	7	5	6
Medium	3					1		1	
Large									
Very large									
Centre									
Total	3	1	9	5	7	8	7	6	6
Total	18	23	20	21	17	33	40	14	31

Table 3.3b. *Settlement continuity of 15 sites which are dated only 'Iron Age'*
without further differentiation into sub-phases

	Cont. LB/'IA'	Begin in 'IA'	Cont. 'IA'/Persian
Small settlements	3	9	2
Medium settlements		1	
Large settlements			
Very large settlements			
Centres			
Total	3	10	2

Notes:
Settlement size:
Small   = 1–20 dunam
Medium   = 21–30 dunam
Large   = 31–50 dunam
Very large = 51–100 dunam
Centre   = 100 dunam and more

The combination LB/'Iron Age' is considered to be continuity.
The combination Iron Age I/'Iron Age' or 'Iron Age'/Iron Age II is ignored.
The combination 'Iron Age'/Persian Period is considered to be continuity.

and minimum numbers. The analysis demonstrates that the most dramatic changes concerned the small and medium-sized villages. In the large
settlements—mostly the tells of the plain—occupation usually continued, even if on a smaller scale. Only very few of these large sites were
abandoned between the Late Bronze Age and the Persian period. Since
excavations were conducted usually on the large sites, these excavations failed to demonstrate the developments in the settlement system of
the hinterland of Akko. The excavation data suggested predominantly
continuous developments. Only the modern archaeological surveys
demonstrated the real continuities and breaks in this settlement system.

The Plain
Continuity is most distinct in the plain. More than 50 per cent of the
settlements were never abandoned. However the transition from the
Late Bronze Age to Iron Age I is marked by a considerable rupture.
Almost half of the settlements were abandoned, most of them small
villages. Only one new village was founded in the plain (Tell al-'Idham
1577.2458). Most of the Iron Age I settlements in the plain were
already occupied during the Late Bronze Age. Thus, the settlement sys-

tem shrank. Eighty-five per cent of the Iron Age I settlements continue in Iron Age II, only 15.4 per cent were abandoned, and eight villages were newly founded (i.e. 42 per cent of all Iron Age II settlements). The settlement system thus developed with few disruptions. In the plain almost all Iron Age II settlements continue into the Persian period.

The Hill Country

The developments in the hill country are in sharp contrast to the developments in the plain. Most of the settlements, 78.6 per cent, were abandoned in the transition between Late Bronze Age-Iron Age I. Just 21.4 per cent continued to be occupied. This disruption is even further emphasized by the fact that 76.9 per cent of all Iron Age I sites in the hill country were newly founded. The transition from Iron Age I to Iron Age II is again marked by a disruption. Some 61.5 per cent of the settlements were abandoned, only 38.5 per cent continued and 77.3 per cent of all Iron Age II sites were new foundations. Finally, the transition between Iron Age II and the Persian period is characterized by continuation: 68.2 per cent of the settlements continued, 31.8 per cent were abandoned and 48.3 per cent of the settlements of the Persian period in the hill country were new founded. While the settlement system continued to be relatively stable from Iron Age II to the Persian period, in comparison to the plain there is markedly less continuity in the hill country.

The Mountains

The settlement history in the mountains is generally similar to the processes in the hill country. However, most sites were not abandoned in the transition from Late Bronze Age to Iron Age I. Three settlements continued and only one was abandoned. Nine new villages in the mountains in Iron Age I indicate a growth of the population here as in the hill country. Again there is also a disruption between Iron Age I and Iron Age II. In only five of the twelve settlements of Iron Age I did occupation continue. The seven remaining settlements were abandoned. We find continuity only in the transition from Iron Age II to the Persian period. Seven of the Iron Age II sites continued, six were abandoned, but there were also six new foundations. This development corresponds in detail to that in the hill country.

As already pointed out, there are 15 sites which were dated only 'Iron Age' without further differentiation as to whether they were inhabited in either Iron Age I or II or both. Almost all of these sites are situated in the hill country and in the mountains. Twelve of the 15 sites were founded at some point in Iron Age I or II, only three were already occupied during the Late Bronze Age and none of them continued into the Persian period (Table 3.3b). Without further, more detailed, dating these sites are of no use for an analysis of the settlement continuity in the hinterland of Akko.

Reconstructing the Settlement History

Against the background of modern settlement archaeology, that is, archaeological surveys and spatial analysis, we are able to write a new kind of regional history of the Akko plain. This kind of history is not supposed to be a history of events. With the few available written historical sources this would anyway be a short, eclectic and random list of names and dates. In fact one wonders to what extent correct identifications of Bronze and Iron Age place-names would actually add significant data to our analysis. The history emerging from modern settlement archaeology reflects the *longue durée* of Fernand Braudel, it is mainly his *histoire conjoncturelle* in combination with some elements of his *histoire structurale* (Braudel 1972; cf. Burke 1992: 151-52); in other words, an attempt to reconstruct the economic and political systems of the societies living in the Akko plain in the context of their environment.

There are only a few additional historical data and this paper is not the place to discuss them in detail (for some discussions see Kuschke 1971; Kallai 1986; Na'aman 1986; Thompson *et al.* 1988; Briend 1990; Lemaire 1991; Lipinski 1991). I will deal with these questions in a forthcoming study.

The city state of Akko dominates in the settlement pattern of the Late Bronze Age (see Fig. 3.5). This political entity appeared in Late Bronze Age texts (cf. Amarna texts: Moran 1992: index; papyrus Anastasi I: Fischer-Elfert 1986: 176). During the fifteenth and the fourteenth century BCE the Eygptian hegemony over Palestine had caused some consolidation in the politics of Palestine (Bunimovitz 1989: 6*). Following Renfrew, Bunimovitz explains the Late Bronze Age system of city states with the help of the so-called *Early State Module* (Bunimovitz 1989: 7*; Renfrew and Bahn 1991: 334-35). The city state of Akko encompassed an urban centre, Akko, then still Tell al-

Fukhkhar, and a territory of some 15 km radius around it. This hinterland did not extend beyond much more than a day's journey to its periphery and back to the centre (Bunimovitz 1989: 8*).

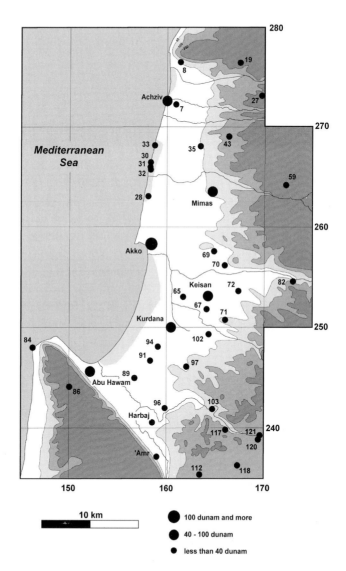

Fig. 3.5. *Sites of the Late Bronze Age*

Sub-centres were Tell Kurdana (Tel Aphek, Fig. 3.2: no. 63), Tell Keisan (no. 68), Tell Mimas (Beth ha-'Emeq, no. 37) and Tel Achziv (no. 4). In the north the Late Bronze Age city state of Akko bordered on Ras an-Naqura (Rosh ha-Niqra); in the east there were only very few villages in the mountains. The territory of Akko most probably did not extend much beyond the 200 m elevation line. To the south the borders are less clear. Here was the harbour of Tell Abu Hawam, today within modern Haifa. A second port within the city state's territory, even remote on its very periphery does not seem to be very probable. Hence, Bunimovitz draws the border of the Akko city state in the Late Bronze Age immediately south of Tell Kurdana (Tel Aphek). According to locational analysis this seems to be the best solution. It is in accord with the *Early State Module*, and fits with its dimensions and its central place structure.

Late Bronze Age texts mention the independent city of Achshaph (Akshapa) in the vicinity of Akko (cf. Amarna texts: Moran 1992: 366,23; 367,1; papyrus Anastasi I: Fischer-Elfert 1986: 177). This city is also mentioned in the Bible and is situated within the area of the tribe of Asher.[2] According to the papyrus Anastasi I, Achshaph seems to have been immediately south of Akko. Since both Tell Keisan and Tell Kurdana (Aphek) were apparently part of the city-state of Akko it is difficult to identify them with Achshaph. Benjamin Mazar and Yohanan Aharoni located Achshaph at Tell Harbaj (no. 92) (Mazar 1950; Aharoni 1979). Lipinski looks for this site in the immediate hinterland of Tell Abu Hawam, at Tell an-Nakhl (no. 89) or in its vicinity (Lipinski 1991: 158-59, cf. this article also for references on Achshaph). Both Tell Harbaj (25 dunam) and Tell an-Nakhl (14 dunam) seem to be rather small even for a tiny Late Bronze Age city-state, but there are no other larger tells in the southern Akko plain. However, if one assumes with Mazar, Aharoni, Bunimovitz and Lipinski that Achshaph was at the southern edge of the Akko plain, then this state encompassed only a very small territory (for an attempt to map this territory see Bunimovitz 1989: 139, map 10).

Plotting only the southern sites of the Akko plain in rank-size graph, the settlement system seems to be less well integrated than the northern sites, which form a coherent system around Akko. However, if one assumes that the centre of the southern sites is outside the plain, one

---

2. For Achshaph see Na'aman 1986: 123 (= Tell Keisan) and 126 (on the borders of Galilee, Josh. 11.10), see also 141; Briend 1972: 239-46; Bordreuil 1977: 180; Kallai 1986: 181, 207, 429-31; Lipinski 1991: 158 n. 14 (= Tell an-Nakhl); for references in Egyptian texts Aḥituv 1984: 49.

suddenly finds a better integrated curve (dotted line in Fig. 3.6 with a predicted centre of c. 50–60 dunam). This could be an indication that Achshaph is in fact outside the Akko plain and not to be identified with any of the above mentioned modern sites.

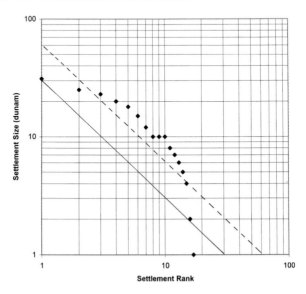

Fig. 3.6. *Rank-size diagram: Late Bronze Age—southern Akko plain*

Apparently, there were two harbours at both edges of the Akko bay, Akko and Tell Abu Hawam. These harbours are specialized sites in the settlement hierarchy of the Akko plain (Soffer and Stern 1986). Since Tell Abu Hawam is situated at the extreme southern edge of the plain, it was probably already outside of the territory of Akko and may have been the harbour of the city state of Achshaph. The harbour may have served especially to supply Megiddo and other sites in the Jezreel valley. This must have had some implications for the role of Achshaph in the area. The special problem of two harbours in one bay recurred also during the Iron Age and the Persian period. Only during the seventh century BCE was there no harbour at Tell Abu Hawam. Apparently, the site was not occupied during most of the Assyrian period. It seems that Akko was the only important harbour during the Assyrian period in the bay. This is surprising since it was assumed that Megiddo was the capital of the Assyrian province of Western Galilee. Tell Abu Hawam would have been the closest and most convenient harbour for Megiddo.

Recent research in the settlement archaeology of Upper Galilee has demonstrated that during the Late Bronze Age the mountain areas were almost empty, and there were only very few settlements during this period (Gal 1988; Frankel 1994; Frankel and Getzov 1997; during 1996 the author together with H.M. Niemann surveyed Upper Galilee for pre-Hellenistic sites, confirming the conclusions of Frankel and Gal; the results of this survey will be published soon).

The Iron Age I settlement pattern was quite different from the Late Bronze Age. According to the excavations at Tell al-Fukhkhar, Akko was still a regional centre during the twelfth century BCE. During Iron Age I, according to the excavator in the eleventh century, the city's importance declined (Dothan 1993). Figure 3.7 with Iron Age I sites illustrates this situation. The settlements in the area of the former city state of Akko are concentrated in Iron Age I on the slopes of the hill country and the mountains. Most of the sites are in the northern part of the research area, in the hinterland of Tell Mimas; there are almost no sites in the southern part of the hill country and only a few in the plain.

Our short and preliminary analysis demonstrates a major break in settlement patterns at the transition from the Late Bronze Age to Iron Age I. The size of the occupied areas, the distribution of the sites, their rank-size and the settlement continuity indicate this development. The old Bronze Age settlements with a size of more than 20 dunam continue to be occupied, but during Iron Age I they were shrinking and unable to develop a hinterland around them. It is questionable to what extent these old Bronze Age cities still had an urban character in Iron Age I. The majority of their citizens were apparently farmers.

In the hill country and on the mountains there are new, small settlements during Iron Age I. Many of them were abandoned at the end of the period. The settlement systems of the plain and in the hill country/ mountains seem to have been independent of each other. Figure 3.6 with the Iron Age I settlements seems to indicate a somewhat neutral zone without sites, a strip running across the middle of the hinterland of Akko between the plain and the hill country. Furthermore, the small villages in the hill country and mountains are situated exactly in the area which one would expect to be the territory of the biblical tribe of Asher (Kallai 1986: 204-24).

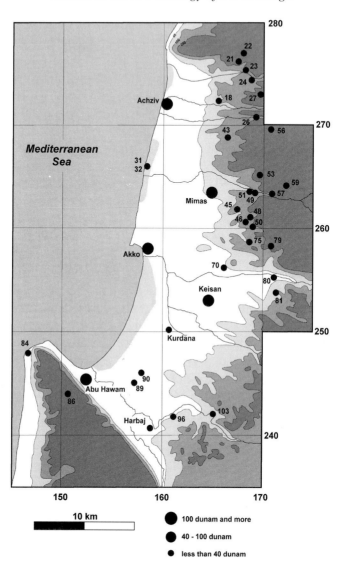

Fig. 3.7. *Iron Age I sites*

However, the identification of these villages with the territory of Asher is far from simple. The historical sources and traditions, especially the Bible, have to be evaluated carefully. Correlating the biblical traditions on early Israel with the archaeological evidence is still one of the major problems of the archaeology in Israel/Palestine. So far one can conclude with Edelman that Egyptian references seem to mention the tribe of Asher in the thirteenth century in Western Galilee (Edelman 1992).

Similarly, the population in the Akko plain in Iron Age I has been seen in the context of the Sea-People phenomenon. It was suggested that they should be identified with the Sherdani (Lemaire 1991: 145; Singer 1994: 297-98) and to attribute to them the monochrome 'Sea-People' pottery mentioned by Singer (1994). Evidence from Akko was repeatedly mentioned by several authors but never published. Both monochrome and bichrome pottery in the area have been recently discussed by Raban (1991). Monochrome pottery was found also in Tel Kabri and in Dor (Lehmann 2001; Stern 1994: 96, Fig. 47). However, the same pottery is once used to identify 'Sikils' and on another occasion 'Sherdani'—a typical case of the 'pots and people' problem. Raban sees both groups mentioned by Ramses III in papyrus Harris I as settled in northern Palestine (Raban 1991: 24-25). He further suggests identifying the activities of Sidon as the leading Phoenician city of the twelfth and early eleventh century with the distribution of the 'Tyrian storage jars' (Finkelstein 1988: 102; Frankel 1994: 27; Stern 1994: 91, Fig. 41 Dor Str. XII). Whether Sikils or Sherdani are involved, we are on safe ground if we assume that all this pottery is connected to a 'Sea-People' phenomenon, that is, the continuing Iron Age I connection of the Palestinian littoral with the Mediterranean.

As for the ethnic situation, Raban suggests that Canaanites, Sea-People and Israelites were living in some kind of symbiosis (Raban 1991: 25). I would generally agree with this view. However, I see the early 'Israelites' (or Proto-Israelites) in Galilee emerging from the 'Canaanites' in the plains. Recent research has demonstrated that the new settlements in the central hill country and mountains of Palestine/ Israel was to some extent the result of a rural population fleeing the increasing burdens imposed by the city-states' elites (Bunimovitz 1994). Such defections during the fourteenth–thirteenth century are illustrated by a number of Ugaritic texts (Heltzer 1976: 60-62). And in a treaty with Duppi-Teshup of Amurru Murshili II demands that the 'fugitives should not go into the mountains' (Klengel 1992: 168). It is tempting to connect these processes with the Khabiru in the Amarna texts and other sources in second millennium Syria and Palestine. The particular variants of storage vessels in upper and western Galilee, 'Galilean' and 'Tyrian' jars as opposed to the 'collared-rim' jars in the central hill country, point to an autonomous development of these early

Iron Age settlers in the Galilean mountains (Finkelstein 1988: 102; Raban 1991: 25 n. 3; Frankel 1994: 27; Stern 1994: 91, Fig. 41). It is in fact an open question when these Galilean tribes were finally considered to be Israelites. I could imagine that this process took place only later in Iron Age II when the Northern Kingdom stabilized its political control over parts of Galilee.

Whoever the people were who were settling in the hill country and in the mountains, Figure 3.7 demonstrates that there was a concentration of settlements, manpower and agriculture in newly founded small villages in these areas north of Akko. It seems as if the hill country north and east of Akko was the main political unit during Iron Age I. Achziv, Akko and Tell Keisan may have formed very small territories. Each of these sites keep some distance from each other. In the south the situation is different. Tell Abu Hawam, Tell al-Harbaj and Tell al-Idham are relatively close to each other, forming a somewhat larger territory. How this territory was connected to the Jezreel valley is still unclear. It may have been the area of Achshaph.

The transition from Iron Age I to Iron Age II witnessed again a fundamental transformation of the settlement pattern (for another such transformation in contemporary Lower Galilee cf. Gal 1992: 94). During Iron Age II Akko is again the largest city and the regional centre of the area, surrounded by sub-centres and small villages (Fig. 3.8). Many of the small villages in the hill country and the mountains which were founded at the beginning of Iron Age I are now abandoned in Iron Age II. Instead, new villages of the same size were founded not far from those Iron Age I sites but on new terrain. The Iron Age II settlement pattern is characterized by one centralized system which dominated both the hill country and the mountain sites from its centres in the plain. However, one has to take into consideration that the Iron Age II period encompassed some 400 years of development and it is difficult to date the archaeological settlement data within this period. Thus, I cannot demonstrate the fluctuations of settlement density in the hinterland of Akko within Iron Age II. Research by Zvi Gal in Lower Galilee indicates that such fluctuations indeed occurred during Iron Age II (Gal 1992: 107). Data available today suggest that the peak of settlement in the hinterland of Akko was reached in the eighth century.

As far as ethnical identifications in this context are concerned, I am less interested in simple statements of Phoenician or Israelite presence. More interesting are the political and economic connections and implications (Rappaport 1992). Stern is suggesting an early Phoenician expansion into Northern Palestine during the second half of the eleventh century, c. 1050–1000 BCE (Stern 1994: 103-104). He bases these assumptions mainly on the occurrence of Phoenician pottery and imports from Cyprus in Dor Str. IX and X-XI (Stern 1990, 1991). This expansion would be reflected with the beginning of Tell Abu Hawam Str. IV and Tell Keisan Niv. 9b (Herrera Gonzalez 1990 and Humbert 1993: 866).

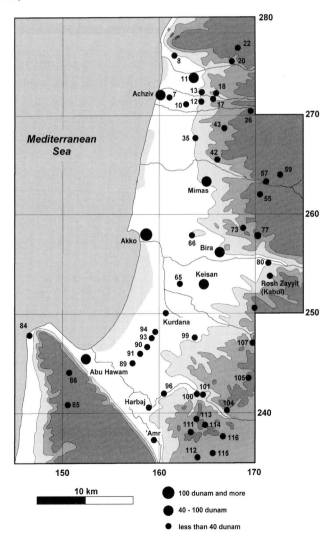

Fig. 3.8. *Iron Age II sites*

The Akko excavations have not been published yet. Dothan mentions a decline in the city's development during the eleventh and tenth centuries (e.g. in Dothan 1993: 21). He also explicitly mentions Phoenician pottery in these levels. In his opinion, Akko again became important only during the ninth century. Since his conclusions are based on unpublished evidence it is difficult to evaluate these statements. They would imply that Akko was not the centre of the plain during the beginning of Iron Age II, the tenth century. The Iron Age II settlement pattern which is presented here in Figure 3.8 would have existed only since Iron Age IIB, after c. 900 BCE. If the identification of Phoenician 'pots' after c. 1050 BCE equals the presence of Phoenician 'people' and their settlement activities in the plain, then the transformation of the Iron Age I settlement system into that of Iron Age II would have lasted for some 150 years. All depends again on the identification of pots and peoples (Stern 1990, 1991).

Zvi Gal identifies the modern site Rosh Zayit (Ras az-Zaytun, Fig. 3.2, no. 58) with biblical Kabul (Gal 1992). In the biblical tradition (1 Kgs 9.11) the area around Kabul, the 'Land of Kabul' was handed over by Solomon to Hiram of Tyre. This text is not contemporary with Hiram or Solomon. We don't even know if the essence of the tradition is authentic. The tradition of the cession of the Land of Kabul was worked over and considerably edited in a later post-Solomonic period. The story in its outline may quite probably reflect a historical event (for a detailed analysis see Donner 1982). However, this depends on the conclusion that the end of verse 1 Kgs 9.11 ('King Solomon then gave Hiram twenty cities in the land of Galilee') is in fact pre-Deuteronomic (Würthwein 1985: 106). If this is correct, in the core of the matter the tradition would have recognized the supremacy of Tyre in Western Galilee. Furthermore, the tradition expressed dependence of Solomon on the Phoenicians of Tyre (Donner 1982; Na'aman 1986: 61-62, Knauf 1991). It was also suggested that the intention of this passage is to express that with Solomon's renunciation the territory of the tribe of Asher was extinguished (Lemaire 1991: 152; Briquel-Chatonnet 1992: 49; Kallai 1986: 77-78).

However, the Bible suggests that the Akko plain was part of David's possessions. The tribe of Asher is situated here and is counted among the twelve tribes, being part of the United Monarchy. The Bible further states that during the reign of Solomon the Land of Kabul was handed over to Tyre. Since the plain with its major sites was never part of

Asher's territory and already in the hands of the Phoenicians (Kallai 1986: 77-78) traditionally the Land of Kabul is identified with the hill country and the mountains in the hinterland of Akko (for the Land of Kabul and the scientific discussion of Solomon's cession see Katzenstein 1997: 103-105).

What really happened is probably impossible to reconstruct. The historicity of the few biblical references to the Akko plain is disputed. With Niemann I tend to believe that if David and Solomon were historical and not only biblical, literary figures, their influence did not reach deep into Lower Galilee, probably not beyond the Jezreel valley, and that Tyre was the actual power in northern Israel (cf. Donner 1982). Finally, Solomon's cession of the Land of Kabul (1 Kgs 9.11-13) may have simply acknowledged the political facts, recognizing the Tyrian supremacy over Western Galilee (cf. Niemann 1997), the cession being an agreement of spheres of influence between Solomon and Hiram, the latter being in the stronger position (Donner 1982). Analysing the political and economic relations between Hiram and Solomon, E.A. Knauf emphasized the dependence of Solomon even further (Knauf 1991: 168-69). He considers 1 Kgs 9.10-14 as postexilic. Similarly, Lipinski assumes that Solomon 'ceded' an area to Hiram, which belonged already to Tyre anyway (Lipinski 1991).

According to A. Alt, the Akko plain was already part of the city state of Tyre in the tenth century BCE (Alt 1953a: 144). Assyrian texts of the late eighth century BCE may confirm this assumption. The annals of Senacherib list places in the Akko plain as part of the Tyrian territory (Luckenbill 1989: II, 239). Thus, at the beginning of Iron Age II the settlement system in the hinterland of Akko would have been transformed by the then leading economic power in the Levant, the city state of Tyre. The early expansion of Tyre during the eleventh and tenth centuries BCE did not direct the Tyrians westward into the Mediterranean, but rather into the nearby territories of western Galilee and southern Cyprus (cf. Aubet 1993).

Independently from the historical sources, the archaeological evidence demonstrates that there was a densely settled area in the hill country north and east of Akko during Iron Age I (maybe this was the Land of Kabul, Fig. 3.7). I have already suggested the possiblity that this area was politically independent during Iron Age I. The transformation of the settlement pattern during Iron Age II has eliminated this political entity, re-integrating the hill and mountain country into the settlement system of the urban centre of Akko.

In this interpretation, the development and transformation of the settlement patterns in the hinterland of Akko was caused by Tyre, the rising city-state under Hiram I which soon became the leading economic power in the Levant. The early expansion of Tyre during the eleventh and tenth century did not lead to colonies in the Western Mediterranean, but to acquisitions in Cyprus and Western Galilee (Aubet 1993). As a reason for this transformation of the settlement patterns in the hinterland of Akko I assume the development of additional agricultural areas for profitable products cultivated for export and the safe investment of profits made in risky sea trade (Aubet 1993: 51-59).

The ability of Tyre's economy to develop what I call 'investment capacities' seems to explain best the changes in the Akko plain during Iron Age II. 'Capital' in the modern sense did exist but only in a rudimentary form in the Iron Age, but it was already possible to 'invest' and secure profits made in the high-risk sea trade in business, which was less risky. One could employ numbers of workers in workshops producing textiles, jewellery or glass. The few less valuable raw materials available to Tyre such as the sand in the bay of Akko was turned into value-added products such as glass. The Tyrian economy was able to 'invest' and to employ experts well versed in the necessary technologies. Tyre was also able to invest in its fleet and to man it with trained sailors. The wood required for building the ships was cut in the mountains of south Lebanon and western Galilee. The sea trade made accessible additional raw materials which were not available in the hinterland of Tyre. These materials formed an integral part of Tyrian industry.

In agriculture the Tyrian wealth permitted the production of cash crops like wine and oil, and the maintenance of the necessary manpower. Again value-added production and expertise are part of the business. Still the Phoenician economy was not 'capitalism'. There was no dynamic investment in the modern sense and the 'financial' system was rather primitive (cf. Finley 1985: especially ch. 5). But the Phoenician trade and landownership certainly aimed at profits (cf. Finley 1985: 188-91).

Tyre was thus able to produce in large quantities and to employ both experts and considerable numbers of less trained workers. As a result, production was also of good quality and profitable. Most significant, however, was that Tyre integrated trade, manufacture and agriculture into one economic system. It is still not clear which role private initiative played in this system and to what extent the state controlled economic activities. In the predominately private economy of Carthage during the Hellenistic period merchants and landowners formed the upper class of the state. Whether these structures developed only late in a Punic context or whether they were already of importance for Iron Age Tyre is not clear. Only further research may answer this question.

Unlike Israel and Judah only the Tyrian economy was thus able to transform the Akko plain politically and economically in the way the archaeological evidence indicates. It is remarkable how the Tyrian 'investment capacity' functioned in the less economically developed areas of Western Galilee, in particular in the hill country and the mountain areas. Tyre profited especially from the exploitation of such 'underdeveloped' areas with rich potential, even more since they were very easily accessible, bordering immediately on the territory of the early city state. Developed technology and 'investment capacity' went together with cheap labour, raw materials and rich agricultural land. This dynamic characterizes the Phoenician interest in the Akko plain.

At the end of the eighth century the successful Assyrian expansion under Tiglat-Pileser III led to the establishment of provinces in Syria and Palestine. Even if Phoenicia was granted a special role in this system with some kind of autonomy it was subject to Assyrian rule. Apparently, this led to conflicts, which are recorded in Assyrian texts (Klengel 1992, Lamprichs 1995). In his reconstruction of Esarhaddon's treaty with Baal of Tyre, Na'aman concludes that Akko was already not part of Baal's territory (Na'aman 1994: 6). He further suggested (*contra* Alt) that Akko became the seat of an Assyrian governor. The fact that during the seventh century BCE Akko was the only important port in the bay, Tell Abu Hawam, the traditional harbour of Megiddo, being abandoned, seems to support this hypothesis. In contrast to this Alt included Akko in the Assyrian province of Megiddo (Alt 1953b: 377-78).

In the excavations at Dor, Tell Keisan and Tel Kabri Assyrianizing pottery was found. Assyrianizing pottery in Palestine was already of considerable interest for a number of scholars (to mention only some: Amiran 1969: 291; Chambon in: Briend and Humbert 1980: 165-66; Mattingly 1980; Hunt 1987: 203; Weippert 1988: 647-48; Pakman 1992; Gilboa 1996; Van Beek *et al.* 2001). Chemical and petrographic analyses of Assyrianizing pottery at Tell Jemmeh have shown that this pottery was produced with local clay (Van Beek *et al.* 2001). From a macroscopic point of view, this may also be the case for the more coarse Assyrianizing vessels in Kabri.

However, the most intriguing question is, what function this class of pottery served and why people started to copy Mesopotamian shapes. An analysis of Syrian and Lebanese pottery shows that Mesopotamian shapes went out of use after the destruction of the Assyrian empire (Lehmann 1996: 93-94). The vessels were prestigious fine tableware (bowls or cups, jugs and krater). They seem to be mainly vessels for the consumption of liquids, probably wine (Stronach 1996). Thus, here at the periphery of the Assyrian empire this pottery apparently served as an object of prestige, copying the life-style of the centre in Assyria.

According to this evidence, Assyrian presence in the Akko plain seems likely. The plain was apparently not in Phoenician, that is, Tyrian, hands during large parts of the seventh century BCE. The territorial transformation of the Akko plain into an Assyrian province began maybe in 701 BCE under Sennacherib (Na'aman 1994: 6). Despite the treaty, conflicts soon arose between Esarhaddon and Baal, and only a few years after their agreement the Assyrian army laid siege to Tyre in 671 BCE.

The Assyrians recognized the strategic importance of the Akko plain. Their presence was intended to control opposition forces at the periphery of their empire to prevent them from forming coalitions against the centre, with Egypt for example. Eventually, such coalitions proved to be a deadly threat to the Assyrian empire at the end of the seventh century BCE (Lamprichs 1995).

The relations between Tyre and Assyria remained tense and conflicts arose over the territory of the Akko plain. In his third campaign Ashurbanipal marched against Tyre in the late 660s BCE (Lamprichs 1995: 173 and Katzenstein 1997: 289, both with more references). Eventually, in one of his last campaigns Ashurbanipal recorded the destruction of Akko, c. 644/643 BCE (Klengel 1992: 230). After the collapse of the Assyrian empire, Tyre seems to have attempted to re-establish its influence over its former territories—only to clash again with the major continental power, the Neo-Babylonian empire (Klengel 1992: 232-34). There are a series of destructions, apparently around 604 BCE in northern Palestine, that is, Tel Kabri, Tell Keisan, Tell Achziv, Tell Dan, Shiqmona and several sites in the Akko Survey such as Tell Da'uq.[3]

---

3.   For references see *NEAEHL*. For Kabri see Lehmann 2001.

The settlement pattern of the Persian period is very similar to that of Iron Age II (see Fig. 3.9). This is particularly important against the background of the fundamental transformation of the settlement patterns in Lower Galilee as a result of the Assyrians campaigns of Tiglat-Pileser III. These campaigns depopulated Lower Galilee to a large extent, the region being resettled only in the sixth century (Gal 1992: 108). In contrast to these developments in Lower Galilee, the analysis of the settlement in the Akko plain demonstrated continuity and a high degree of integration under a central administration. The number of settlements and of the overall occupation area increased a little in the Persian period. Akko still is the regional centre in the area. Larger sub-centres are situated in a circle of some 5–10 km distance around Akko. The small villages of the hill country and the mountains are subordinate to this system.

It is generally assumed, however without clear evidence, that the Akko plain was again part of the Tyrian territory during the Persian period (cf. Stern 1982: 241). The harbour list of Pseudo-Skylax, written probably in the fourth century BCE leaves this question open (cf. discussion in Galling 1938: 79). Lipinski suggested interpreting the list in Josh. 19.25-30 describing the tribal area of Asher as a document of the Persian period, reflecting the settlement situation of the fourth century BCE (Lipinski 1991; cf. Briend 1990; Galling 1938). The Akko plain was of particular strategic importance for the Persian military buildup against Egypt and Phoenicia (Strabo XVI 758, Diodor XV 41, cf. Stern 1982: 241 and Briend 1990: 113). The Achaemenids had similar strategic problems to the Assyrians earlier in the face of possible coalitions at the periphery against the center. Again, eventually these coalitions contributed to the collapse of their empire.

To sum up, a first and preliminary spatial analysis using the data of recent regional surveys was able to demonstrate the transformation of the settlement pattern in the Akko plain between the Late Bronze Age and the Iron Age I. Further research will show whether this transformation may be interpreted as activities of agents such as the tribe of Asher and/or the Sherdani. Another break in the settlement system took place during the transition from Iron Age I to Iron Age II. It seems to be the work of Phoenicians, the city state of Tyre, who expanded into the Akko plain and created a new economic and political system there.

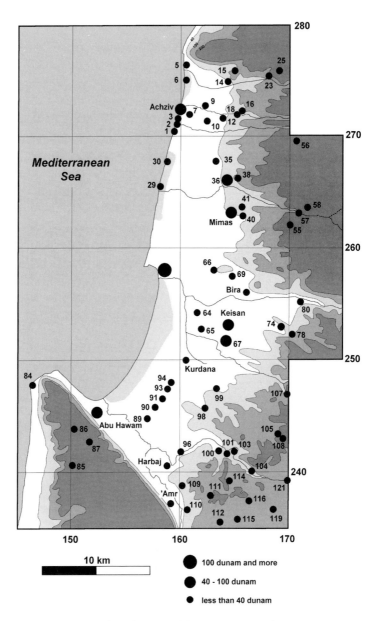

Fig. 3.9. *Sites of the Persian period*

Appendix 3A: *Ancient settlements and selected special sites of the Akko-Survey, 1993–96 conducted by Gunnar Lehmann and Martin Peilstöcker (Fig. 3.1)*

1. Tell Keisan (1645.2531) is the only major site in the survey area which has been excavated and published. A British expedition worked on the tell between 1935-1936, and between 1971 and 1980 a French team excavated. The last field director was J.-B. Humbert from the Ecole Biblique in Jerusalem. Periods: Neolithic, Early Bronze Age, Middle Bronze Age, Late Bronze Age, Iron Age I-II, Persian period, Hellenistic, Byzantine, Mediaeval.

2. and 3. Ḥorvat ‘Uṣa I and II (16485.25760): a large Bronze Age site along the road and a small tell. There were excavations by Amnon Ben Tor 1963 and Nimrod Getzov 1991. Periods: Early Bronze Age, Middle Bronze Age, Late Bronze Age, Persian period, Byzantine, Mediaeval.

4. Tell Da‘uq (1618.2530): tell with mediaeval buildings. Periods: Late Bronze Age, Iron Age, Persian period, Mediaeval.

5. Tell al-Kurdane (Tel Afek, 1605.2500): large tell with springs. Periods: Early Bronze Age, Middle Bronze Age II, Late Bronze Age, Persian period, Roman, Byzantine, Mediaeval, Modern.

6. Tell Bir al-Gharbi (Tel Bira, 1661.2562): large tell excavated by Moshe Prausnitz between 1957 and 1980, Shmuel Yeivin 1959, Yehuda Ben Yosef 1970 and 1979 and Edna Stern 1993. Periods: Middle Bronze Age I, Middle Bronze Age II, Late Bronze Age, Iron Age I-II, Persian period, Hellenistic.

7. Khirbat Tira Tamra (1662.2509): excavations by Alexander On 1988. Periods: Late Bronze Age (? only Saarisalo), Roman, Mediaeval, Modern.

8. Khirbat Kinniya (1659.2528): Periods: Hellenistic.

9. Khirbat et-Tantur (1631.2581): survey by Rafael Frankel. Iron Age, Persian period, Byzantine?, Mediaeval.

10. al-Makr (1633.2597): excavations by Ya’kov Uri 1949, Zvi Safir and Moshe Dothan 1950, Pirhiya Beck 1958, Yehuda Ben Yosef 1964, Vassilius Tzaferis 1977 and Mordekhai Avi’am 1991, survey by Rafael Frankel. Periods: Middle Bronze Age I, Roman, Byzantine, Mediaeval, Modern.

11. Khirbat al-‘Aitawiya (1641.2518): small tell. Periods: Late Bronze Age (? only Saarisalo), Persian period, Mediaeval, Modern.

12. Dabbat al-Khan (16545.25085): remains of a structures on the ancient Roman road, may be a road station.

13. al-Judayda (1650.2592): Periods: Early Bronze Age, Byzantine, Mediaeval, Modern.

14. al-Birwa (1671.2567): Periods: Mediaeval, Modern.

15. Khirbat Bir Tirat Tamra (1660.2515): excavations by Alexander On 1988. Ottoman well building. Periods: Byzantine (?), Mediaeval, Modern.

16. Ard ad-Durma (1688.2586): studied by Mordekhai Avi’am. Period: Hellenistic.

17. ad-Damun (1675.2536): Periods: Late Bronze Age, Byzantine, Mediaeval, Modern.
18. Khirbat al-Waziya (1687.2596): excavations by Mordekhai Avi'am 1989, 1991. Periods: Iron Age I, Hellenistic, Byzantine.
19. Tamra (1695.2506): surveyed by Idan Shaqet. Periods: Early Bronze Age II, Iron Age, Persian period, Hellenistic, Roman, Byzantine, Mediaeval, Modern.
20. Qabr al-Badawiya (1696.2579): Periods: Iron Age II.
21. ar-Ruways (1694.2521): Periods: Roman, Byzantine, Mediaeval, Modern.
22. Ard as-Samarra (16658.25560): also surveyed by Eliezer Stern. Period: Early Bronze Age.
23. Maghar 16816.2562: Mediaeval village.
24. Palestine Grid 16868.25685: rock installations and cisterns.
25. The *Survey of Western Palestine*, map 5, marked here some installations which were not found during the survey.
26. British railway tracks for developing the Government Land in the plain partly built with soil from Tell al-Fukhkhar (Tel Akko).
27. at-Tayyun (16165.2543): dense stray finds, probably soil from Tell al-Fukhkhar (Tel Akko). Periods: Iron Age, Persian period, Byzantine, Modern.
28. Roman milestones (1658.2505).
29. ar-Rujm (1652.2539): remains of a Byzantine building.
30. Bir al-Mughayr (16736.25578): Ottoman well building with settlement remains arround it.
31. Bir Wa'r Mafhara (16808.25627): well of site 23 with dense Mediaeval and Modern stray finds.
32. Palestine Grid 160.255: small Ottoman settlement, marked on map of the Survey of Western Palestine.
33. Palestine Grid 162.258: small Byzantine settlement found by Mordekhai Avi'am and Eliezer Stern.
34. Palestine Grid (16923.25575): flint scatter.
35. al-Hariqa (1629.2518): remains of small Ottoman settlement.
36. Ras 'Arus (1696.2570): Farm of the Byzantine and Mamluke period.
37. Khirbat Ja'ad (1682.2597), remains of a Byzantine building.
38. Palestine Grid 1692.2586, heaps of stones with Byzantine pottery.
39. Ard al-'Uyun (1685.2586), Iron Age and Hellenistic settlement.
40. Bir Asfa (Bir Safa) (1693.2547), Ottoman well building.
41. Ard al-'Ushr (1665.2526), settlement with pottery of the Wadi Rabba culture, nearby rock installations.
42. Kabul (1700.2525), Hellenistic, Roman, Byzantine, Mediaeval and Modern remains.
43. Ard al-'Aymawiya (1656.2513), remains of a small Ottoman hamlet.
44. al-Kurum (16865.2527), Persian period, Byzantine, Mediaeval and Modern pottery.
45. ar-Raba'in (1671.2532), remains of Byzantine buildings, rock installations and tombs.
46. Palestine Grid 16865.25915, remains of a Byzantine building.

47. Palestine Grid 1683.2594, Byzantine settlement with rock installations and tombs.
48. Palestine Grid 1629.2585, discolouration of the soils in the fields with flints finds.
49. Umm as-Surud (1661.2573), Roman and Byzantine installations and settlement remains.

Appendix 3B: *List of sites analysed in this paper (Fig. 3.2)*

	Name	x	y	Periods
1	Nahariya (North)	1593	2707	Persian period
2	Nemal Akhziv South	1595	2714	Persian period
3	Nemal Akhziv North	1596	2718	Persian period
4	Achziv (az-Zib)	1599	2725	Late Bronze Age–Iron Age I–Iron Age II–Persian period
5	al-Mushayrifa	1604	2765	Persian period
6	No name	1605	2753	Persian period
7	Gesher ha-Ziw (ar-Ras)	1607	2722	Late Bronze Age–Iron Age II–Persian period (cemetery)
8	Tell at-Taba'iq (Khirbat al Mushayrifa, Tel Rosh ha-Niqra)	1612	2765	Late Bronze Age–Iron Age II?
9	No name	1622	2728	Persian period
10	Tell Shuqaf (Tel Shaqof)	1625	2715	Iron Age II–Persian period
11	al-Amariya, Kh. (Horvat Kenesiya)	1633	2744	Iron Age II
12	Abu adh-Dhahab	1640	2718	Iron Age II–Persian period
13	Khirbat Humsin (Giv'at ha-Mudot)	1641	2726	Iron Age II
14	'Abbassiya, Kh. ('Ovesh)	1644	2751	Persian period
15	Ma'sub, Kh.	1650	2762	Persian period
16	No name	1652	2723	Persian period
17	No name	1654	2722	Iron Age II
18	Khirbat 'Abda (Tel 'Avdon)	1655	2725	Iron Age I–Iron Age II–Persian period
19	Tell Marad (Mitzpa Hanita)	1668	2774	Late Bronze Age
20	Mugharrat al-'Arus (Me'arrot Eder)	1673	2759	Iron Age II
21	'Ayn Hur	1674	2765	Iron Age I
22	No name	1679	2772	Iron Age I–Iron Age II
23	Mugharrat Mankhir	1682	2756	Iron Age I–Persian period
24	Samah, Kh.	1688	2746	Iron Age I

25	Idmit, Kh.	1691	2761	Persian period
26	al-Ghayyada, Tell	1693	2709	Iron Age I–Iron Age II
27	Khirbat al-Ju'ayla (Horvat 'Edron)	1699	2732	Late Bronze Age–Iron Age I
28	as-Sumayriya (Tell ar-Ras, Giv'at Yasif)	1580	2630	Late Bronze Age–Iron Age
29	Shave Zion	1580	2657	Persian period
30	Nahariya	1580	2670	Late Bronze Age–Persian period
31	No name	1581	2661	Late Bronze Age–Iron Age I
32	No name	1581	2662	Late Bronze Age–Iron Age I
33	Tel Nahali'el	1586	2680	Late Bronze Age
34	Zahr at-Tell	1633	2683	see Kabri: at-Tell
35	Kabri: at-Tell	1634	2680	Late Bronze Age?–Iron Age II–Persian period
36	Khirbat Kafr Buda	1643	2661	Persian period
37	Tell Mimas (Beit ha-'Emeq)	1646	2634	Late Bronze Age–Iron Age I–Iron Age II–Persian period
38	al-Naqar	1653	2663	Persian period
39	at-Tina	1654	2666	Iron Age
40	Beth ha-'Emeq	1657	2630	Persian period
41	al-Murkhan	1657	2639	Persian period
42	'Amqa Tomb	1657	2657	Iron Age II
43	Khirbat ash-Shubayk	1664	2690	Late Bronze Age–Iron Age I–Iron Age II
44	Tell al-Waqiya (Giv'at ha-Meshurim)	1670	2695	Iron Age
45	No name	1674	2620	Iron Age I
46	No name	1682	2607	Iron Age I
47	Khirbat Ga'atun (Khirbat Ja'thun)	1685	2688	Iron Age
48	No name	1686	2611	Iron Age I
49	No name	1687	2637	Iron Age I
50	No name	1688	2603	Iron Age I
51	No name	1691	2635	Iron Age I
52	No name	1693	2663	Iron Age
53	No name	1696	2652	Iron Age I
54	Mugharrat Umm Muhammad	1699	2638	Iron Age
55	Yirka	1702	2622	Iron Age II–Persian period
56	Khirbat Zawinita (Horvat Beit Zeneta)	1708	2698	Iron Age I–Persian period
57	Ras Kalban	1709	2634	Iron Age I–Iron Age II–Persian period
58	Ma'arrat Netifim	1717	2639	Persian period

59	Jatt	1723	2643	Late Bronze Age–Iron Age I–Iron Age II
60	No name	1724	2629	Iron Age
61	Khirbat al-Knissa Ruwayssat (Horvat Knissa)	1725	2673	Iron Age
62	Akko (Tell al-Fukhkhar)	1580	2580	Late Bronze Age–Iron Age I–Iron Age II–Persian period
63	Tell Kurdana (Tel Aphek)	1605	2500	Late Bronze Age–Iron Age I–Iron Age II–Persian period
64	at-Tayyun	1616	2543	Iron Age–Persian period
65	Tell Da'uk	1618	2530	Late Bronze Age?–Iron Age II–Persian period
66	Khirbat at-Tantur (Horvat Turit)	1631	2581	Iron Age II–Persian period
67	Khirbat 'Ayytawiya	1641	2518	Late Bronze Age?–Persian period
68	Tell Keisan	1644	2531	Late Bronze Age–Iron Age I–Iron Age II–Persian period
69	Khirbat 'Ayyadiya (Horvat 'Utza)	1648	2576	Late Bronze Age–Persian period
70	Bir al-Gharbi (Tel Bira)	1661	2562	Late Bronze Age–Iron Age I–Iron Age II–Persian period
71	Khirbat Tirat Tamra	1662	2509	Late Bronze Age?
72	ad-Damun	1675	2536	Late Bronze Age?
73	Ard al-'Uyun	1685	2586	Iron Age II
74	al-Kurum	1686	2527	Persian period
75	Khirbat al-Waziya	1687	2596	Iron Age I
76	Tamra	1695	2506	Iron Age
77	Qabr Badawiya	1696	2579	Iron Age II
78	Kabul	1703	2524	Persian period
79	Qarn Hannawi (Har Gamal)	1707	2583	Iron Age I
80	Khirbat Ya'nin (Horvat Ne'iel)	1711	2553	Iron Age I–Iron Age II–Persian period
81	Ros Zayyit (Ras az-Zaytun)	1713	2538	Iron Age I–Iron Age II
82	Sha'ab (Shaav)	1731	2549	Late Bronze Age–Iron Age
83	al-Mi'ar	1735	2534	Iron Age
84	Tell as-Samak (Tel Shiqmona)	1461	2478	Late Bronze Age–Iron Age I–Iron Age II–Persian period
85	Khirbat al-'Ayn (Horvat Qedem, Khirbat Is'ad al-Yusuf)	1500	2406	Iron Age II–Persian period

86	Khirbat Rushmiya (Horvat Rosh Mayim, Kh. 'Ataysi)	1502	2439	Late Bronze Age–Iron Age I–Iron Age II–Persian period
87	'Iraq az-Zighan	1516	2427	Persian period
88	Tell Abu Hawam	1521	2452	Late Bronze Age–Iron Age I–Iron Age II–Persian period
89	Tell an-Nakhl (Tel Nahal)	1569	2449	Late Bronze Age–Iron Age I–Iron Age II–Persian period
90	Tell al-'Idham	1577	2458	Iron Age I–Iron Age II–Persian period
91	Tell as-Subat (Tell al-Khiyar, Tel Zavat)	1584	2466	Late Bronze Age–Iron Age II–Persian period
92	Tell al-Harbaj (Tel Regev)	1587	2405	Late Bronze Age–Iron Age I–Iron Age II–Persian period
93	Khirbat Jidru (Horvat Gedora)	1589	2475	Iron Age II–Persian period
94	Tell az-Zibda (Tel Zivda)	1592	2481	Late Bronze Age–Iron Age II–Persian period
95	Tell ash-Shumra	1600	2480	Iron Age
96	Tell al-Far (Tel Par)	1601	2418	Late Bronze Age–Iron Age I–Iron Age II–Persian period
97	Khirbat ash-Sharta (Horvat Sirta)	1622	2461	Late Bronze Age–Iron Age
98	Khirbat ash-Shurati	1623	2454	Iron Age–Persian period
99	Khirbat al-Rujm (Gil'am)	1634	2474	Iron Age II–Persian period
100	Khirbat Jibyata (Horvat Govit)	1637	2418	Iron Age II–Persian period
101	Khirbat al-Kasabir (Tel Hali ha-Ma'aravi)	1642	2417	Iron Age II–Persian period
102	Khirbat al-Jahush (Horvat Gahosh)	1645	2494	Late Bronze Age
103	Khirbat Ras 'Ali (Tel 'Alil, Tel Hali ha-Mizrahi)	1649	2419	Late Bronze Age–Iron Age I–Persian period
104	Khirbat Ras al-'Ayn	1667	2401	Iron Age II–Persian period
105	Khirbat at-Tayyiba (Horvat 'Ofrat)	1691	2434	Iron Age II–Persian period
106	Baba al-Hawa	1694	2430	Persian period
107	Khirbat Abu Mudawwar (Tel Mador)	1701	2470	Iron Age II–Iron Age II–Persian period
108	Tell al-'Amr (Tel Geva' Shemen, Tel Ma'amer)	1592	2371	Late Bronze Age–Iron Age II–Persian period
109	Khirbat 'Ajajala (Jabal al-Khirba, Kefar ha-	1601	2387	Persian period?

No'ar ha-Datti)

110	Khirbat al-Harithiya (Sha'ar ha-'Amaqim)	1606	2364	Persian period
111	Khirbat Busayma (Horvat Butzin)	1629	2378	Iron Age II–Persian period
112	Tell Tab'un (Khirbat al-Bir)	1637	2354	Late Bronze Age–Iron Age II–Persian period
113	Khirbat Umm Rashid	1637	2391	Iron Age II
114	Khirbat Qasta (Horvat Qoshet)	1644	2388	Iron Age II–Persian period
115	Khirbat Bir al-Baydar (Horvat Hazin)	1653	2357	Iron Age II–Persian period
116	Umm al-'Amad (Waldheim, Allonei Abba)	1664	2374	Iron Age II–Persian period
117	Khirbat Shabana	1664	2399	Late Bronze Age
118	'Ayn al-Hawwara ('Ein Hevraya)	1676	2365	Late Bronze Age
119	Tell al-Khudayra	1686	2365	Persian period
120	Khirbat al-Mushayrifa (Mitzpa Zevulun)	1697	2390	Late Bronze Age
121	Sur al-Mushayrifa	1699	2391	Late Bronze Age–Iron Age II–Persian period

Bibliography

Aharoni, Y.
 1979 *The Land of the Bible: A Historical Geography* (London: Burns & Oates).
Aḥituv, S.
 1984 *Canaanite Toponyms in Ancient Egyptian Documents* (Jerusalem: Magnes Press).
Alonso, A.M.
 1994 'The Politics of Space, Time and Substance: State Formation, Nationalism, and Ethnicity', *Annual Review of Anthropology* 23: 379-405.
Alt, A.
 1929 'Das Institut im Jahre 1928', *Palästina-Jahrbuch* 25: 5-59.
 1953a 'Das Gottesurteil auf dem Karmel', in *Kleine Schriften zur Geschichte des Volkes Israel* (Munich: Beck), II: 135-49.
 1953b 'Galiläische Probleme: Die assyrische Provinz Megiddo und ihr späteres Schicksal', in *Kleine Schriften zur Geschichte des Volkes Israel* (Munich: Beck), II: 374-84.
Amiran, R.
 1969 *Ancient Pottery of the Holy Land* (Jerusalem: Masada).
Anderson, B.R.O.
 1991 *Imagined Communities: Reflections on the Origin and Spread of Nationalism* (London: Verso and NBL).

Aston, M.
 1985   *Interpreting the Landscape: Landscape Archaeology and Local History* (London: Batsford).
Aubet, M.E.
 1993   *The Phoenicians and the West: Politics, Colonies and Trade* (Cambridge: Cambridge University Press).
Balensi, J.
 1980   'Les fouilles de R.W. Hamilton à Tell Abu Hawam, Niveaux IV et V' (Unpublished Doctorat de 3ème cycle Université des Sciences Humaines, Strasbourg II).
Banks, M.
 1996   *Ethnicity: Anthropological Reconstructions* (London: Routledge).
Ben-Tor, A.
 1966   'Excavations at Horvat 'Utza', *'Atiqot*, Hebrew Edition 3: 1-24, 1*-3* (Hebrew).
Bordreuil, P.
 1977   'De 'Arqa a Akshaph: Notes de toponymie phénicienne', in *La toponymie antique: Actes du colloque de Strasbourg 1975* (Strasbourg: Université des Sciences Humaines de Strasbourg).
Braudel, F.
 1972   *The Mediterranean and the Mediterranean World in the Age of Philip II* (London: Fontana).
Brett, M.G. (ed.)
 1996   *Ethnicity and the Bible* (Leiden: E.J. Brill).
Briend, J.
 1972   'Akshaph et sa localisation à Tell Keisan', *RB* 79: 239-46.
 1990   'L'occupation de la Galilée occidentale à l'époque perse', *Transeuphratène* 2: 109-23.
Briend, J., and J.B. Humbert
 1980   *Tell Keisan (1971–1976): Une cité phénicienne en Galilée* (OBO Series Archaeologica, 1; Freiburg: Universitätsverlag; Göttingen: Vandenhoeck & Ruprecht).
Briquel-Chatonnet, F.
 1992   'Les relations entre les cités de la côte phénicienne et les royaumes d'Israel et de Juda', *Studia Phoenicia* 12.
Bunimovitz, S.
 1989   'The Land of Israel in the Late Bronze Age: A Case Study of Socio-Cultural Change in a Complex Society' (Unpublished PhD thesis; Tel Aviv University (Hebrew).
 1994   'The Problem of the Human Resources in Late Bronze Age Palestine and its Socioeconomic Implications', *UF* 26: 1-20.
 1996   'Philistine and Israelite Pottery: A Comparative Approach to the Question of Pots and People', *Tel Aviv* 23: 88-101.
Burke, P.
 1992   *History and Social Theory* (Cambridge: Polity Press).
Davies, P.R.
 1992   *In Search of 'Ancient Israel'* (JSOTSup, 148: Sheffield: Sheffield Academic Press).

Dever, W.G.
1995 'Ceramics, Ethnicity, and the Question of Israel's Origin', *BA* 58.4: 200-13.

Donner, H.
1982 'The Interdependence of Internal Affairs and Foreign Policy during the Davidic-Solomonic Period (with Special Regard to the Phoenician Coast)', in T. Ishida (ed.), *Studies in the Period of David and Solomon and other Essays* (Winona Lake, IN: Eisenbrauns): 205-14.

Dothan, M.
1993 'Acco', *in New Encyclopedia of Archaeological Excavations in the Holy Land* (Jerusalem: Israel Exploration Society), I: 17-23.

Edelman, D.V.
1992 'Asher', *ABD* 1: 482-83.

Finkelstein, I.
1988 *The Archaeology of the Israelite Settlement* (Jerusalem: Israel Exploration Society).
1993 'Environmental Archaeology and Social History: Demographic and Economic Aspects of the Monarchic Period', *in Biblical Archaeology Today, Proceedings of the Second International Congress on Biblical Archaeology, Jerusalem 1990* (Jerusalem: Israel Exploration Society): 56-66.
1995 'The Date of the Settlement of the Philistines in Canaan', *Tel Aviv* 22.2: 213-39.
1996 'The Archaeology of the United Monarchy: An Alternative View', *Levant* 28: 177-87.
1997 'Pots and People Revisited: Ethnic Boundaries in the Iron Age I', in N. Silberman and D.B. Small (eds.), *The Archaeology of Israel: Constructing the Past/Interpreting the Present* (Sheffield: Sheffield Academic Press): 216-38.

Finkelstein, I., and N. Na'aman (eds.)
1994 *From Nomadism to Monarchy: Archaeological and Historical Aspects of Early Israel* (Jerusalem: Israel Exploration Society).

Finley, M.I.
1985 *The Ancient Economy* (London: Hogarth Press).

Fischer-Elfert, H.W.
1986 *Die satirische Streitschrift des Papyrus Anastasi I* (Ägyptologische Abhandlungen, 44; Wiesbaden: Harrassowitz).

Frankel, R.
1986 'Preliminary Report on the Survey of Western Galilee, 1976–1979', in: M. Yedaya, *The Antiquities of Western Galilee* (Haifa: Defense Ministry/ Regional Council of Asher): 304-17 (Hebrew).
1994 'Upper Galilee in the Late Bronze–Iron I Transition', in Finkelstein and Na'aman (eds.) 1994: 18-34.

Frankel, R., and N. Getzov
1997 *Map of Akhziv (1) / Map of Ḥanita (2)* (Archaeological Survey of Israel; Jerusalem: Israel Antiquities Authority).

Gal, Z.
1988 'The Late Bronze Age in Galilee: A Reassessment', *BASOR* 272: 79-84.

1992   *Lower Galilee during the Iron Age* (Winona Lake, IN: Eisenbrauns).

Galling, K.

1938   'Die syrisch-palästinische Küste nach der Beschreibung bei Pseudo-Skylax', *ZDPV* 61: 66-96.

Getzov, N.

1993   'Horvat 'Uza', *Excavations and Surveys in Israel* 13: 19-21.

Gibson, S.

1995   'Landscape Archaeology and Ancient Agricultural Field Systems in Palestine' (Unpublished PhD thesis; Institute of Archaeology, University College, London).

Gilboa, A.

1996   'Assyrian Type Pottery at Dor and the Status of the Town during the Assyrian Occupation Period', *EI* 25: 122-35, 92*.

Heltzer, M.

1976   *The Rural Community in Ancient Ugarit* (Wiesbaden: Reichert)

Herrera Gonzalez, D.

1990   *Las excavaciones de R.W. Hamilton en Tell Abu Hawam, Haifa: El stratum III: Historia del puerto fenicio durante los siglos X-VIII a. de C* (Universidad de Cantabria, Santander).

Hobsbawm, E., and T. Ranger (eds.)

1983   *The Invention of Tradition* (Cambridge: Cambridge University Press).

Humbert, J.P.

1993   *Tell Keisan: New Encyclopedia of Archaeological Excavations in the Holy Land* (Jerusalem: Israel Exploration Society), I: 862-67.

Hunt, M.

1987   'The Iron Age: The Pottery', in A. Ben-Tor and Y. Potugali (eds.), *Tell Qiri: A Village in the Jezreel Valley* (Qedem, 24; Jerusalem: Hebrew University): 139-223.

Johnson, G.A.

1981   'Monitoring Complex System Integration and Boundary Phenomena with Settlement Size Data', in S.E. van der Leeuw (ed.), *Archaeological Approaches to the Study of Complexity* (Amsterdam: Universiteit van Amsterdam): 144-88.

Jones, S.

1996   *The Archaeology of Ethnicity* (London: Routledge).

Kallai, Z.

1986   *Historical Geography of the Bible: The Tribal Territories of Israel* (Jerusalem: Magnes Press; Leiden: E.J. Brill).

Kamp, K.A., and N. Yoffee

1980   'Ethnicity in Ancient Western Asia during the Early Second Millennium BC: Archaeological Assessments and Ethnoarchaeological Prospectives', *BASOR* 237: 85-104.

Katzenstein, H.J.

1997   *The History of Tyre: From the Beginning of the Second Millennium BCE until the Fall of the Neo-Babylonian Empire in 539 BCE* (2nd rev. edn; Beer Sheva: Ben-Gurion University).

Klengel, H.

    1992   *Syria, 3000 to 300 BC: A Handbook of Political History* (Berlin: Akademie Verlag).

Kloner, A., and Y. Olami

    1980   'The Late Bronze Age and Iron Age Periods', in A. Soffer and B. Kipnis (eds.), *Atlas of Haifa and Mount Carmel* (Haifa: Society of Applied Science, University of Haifa): 36-37.

Knauf, E.A.

    1991   'King Solomon's Copper Supply', in Lipinski (ed.) 1991: 167-86.

Kramer, C.

    1977   'Pots and Peoples', in L.D. Levine and T.C. Young (eds.), *Mountains and Lowlands* (Bibliotheca Mesopotamia, 7; Malibu: Undena Publications): 91-112.

Kuschke, A.

    1971   'Kleine Beiträge zur Siedlungsgeschichte der Stämme Asser und Judah', *HTR* 64: 291-313.

Lamprichs, R.

    1995   *Die Westexpansion des neuassyrischen Reiches: Eine Strukturanalyse* (AOAT, 239; Kevelaer: Butzon & Becker; Neukirchen-Vluyn: Neukirchener Verlag).

Lehmann, G.

    1994a   'Excavations at Kabri: The Iron Age Tell, Area E', in *The 7th and 8th Preliminary Report, 1992–1993 Season* (Tel Aviv: Tel Aviv University).

    1994b   'Hinterland of Akko (Map 20) in S.R. Wolff, *Archaeology in Israel*, *American Journal of Archaeology* 98: 515–16.

    1995   'Survey of Map Aḥihud', *Ḥadashot Arkhiologiyot* 103: 110 (Hebrew).

    1996   *Untersuchungen zur Späten Eisenzeit in Syrien und Libanon: Stratigraphie und Keramikformen zwischen ca. 720 bis 300 v.Chr.* (Altertumskunde des Vorderen Orients, Münster 5; Ugarit-Verlag).

    2001   'Late Bronze and Iron Age Pottery of Area E, Kabri Excavations Seasons 1986, 1989, 1990, 1992, 1993' in *Kabri I* (Tel Aviv Monography; Institute of Archaeology, Tel Aviv University), forthcoming.

Lemaire, A.

    1991   'Asher et le royaume de Tyr', in Lipinski (ed.) 1991: 135-52.

Lemche, N.P.

    1991   *The Canaanites and Their Land: The Traditions of the Canaanites* (JSOTSup, 110: Sheffield: Sheffield Academic Press).

    1998   'Greater Canaan: The Implications of a Correct Reading of EA 151: 49-67', *BASOR* 310: 19-24.

Lipinski, E.

    1991   'The Territory of Tyre and the Tribe of Asher', in Lipinski (ed.) 1991: 153-66.

Lipinski, E. (ed.)

    1991   *Phoenicia and the Bible* (Studia Phoenicia, 11; Leuven: Peeters).

Luckenbill, D.D.

    1989   *Ancient Records of Assyria and Babylonia* (new edn; London: Histories and Mysteries of Man).

Mattingly, G.L.
1980 'Neo Assyrian Influence at Tell Jemmeh', *Near East Archaeological Society Bulletin* 15–16: 33-49.

Mazar (Maisler), B.
1950 'Achshaph', in *Encyclopaedia Miqra'it* (Jerusalem: Bialik), I: 282-83.

Messika, N.
1996 'Persian Period Tombs and Graves near Tell er-Sumeiriya (Lohamé Hageta'ot)', *'Atiqot* 29: 31*-39* (Hebrew).

Moran, W.L.
1992 *The Amarna Letters* (Baltimore: The Johns Hopkins University Press).

Na'aman, N.
1986 *Borders and Districts in Biblical Historiography* (Jerusalem: Simor).
1994 'Esarhaddon's Treaty with Baal and Assyrian Provinces along the Phoenician Coast', *Rivista di Studi Fenici* 22: 3-8.

Niemann, H.M.
1997 'The Socio-Political Shadow Cast by the Biblical Solomon', in L.K. Handy (ed.), *The Age of Solomon: Scholarship at the Turn of the Millennium* (Leiden: E.J. Brill): 252-99.

Ofer, A.
1993a 'The Highland of Judah during the Biblical Period' (Unpublished PhD thesis; Tel Aviv University).
1993b 'Judea: Judean Hills Survey', in *NEAEHL*, 3: 815-16.
1994 ' "All the Hill Country of Judah": From a Settlement Fringe to a Prosperous Monarchy', in Finkelstein and Na'aman (eds.) 1994: 92-121.

Olami, Y.
1974 'Carmel Region: Map of Distribution of Sites in the Israelite Period. Archaeological Survey of Israel', unpublished report, Archives of the Israel Antiquities Authority.
n.d. 'Shefaram Region (Map 24). Archaeological Survey of Israel', unpublished report, Archives of the Israel Antiquities Authority.
n.d. 'Haifa West-Region (Map 22). Archaeological Survey of Israel', unpublished report, Archives of the Israel Antiquities Authority.

Pakman, D.
1992 'Late Iron Age Pottery Vessels at Tel Dan', *EI* 23: 230-40.

Pastor-Borgoñon, H.
1988–90 'Die Phönizier: Eine begriffsgeschichtliche Untersuchung', *Hamburger Beiträge zur Archäologie* 15-17: 37-142.

Portugali, Y.
1982 'A Field Methodology for Regional Archaeology (The Jezreel Valley Survey, 1981)', *Tel Aviv* 9: 170-88.

Prausnitz, M.W.
1973 ''Akhzir and 'Avdon: City Planning of a Harbour and a Fortified City in the Akko Plain', *EI* 11: 219-23 (Hebrew).

Raban, A.
1982 *Archaeological Survey of Israel: Nahalal Map (28) 16–23* (Jerusalem: Israel Antiquities Authority).
1991 'The Philistines in the Western Jezreel Valley', *BASOR* 284: 17-27.

Rainey, A.F.
1996   'Who is a Canaanite? Review of the Textual Evidence', *BASOR* 304: 1-15.

Rappaport, U.
1992   'Phoenicia and Galilee: Economy, Territory and Political Relations', in *Studia Phoenicia 9: Numismatique et histoire économique phéniciennes et puniques* (Publications d'histoire et de l'art et d'archéologie de l'université catholique de Louvain; Louvain-la-Neuve: Université Catholique de Louvain).

Renfrew, C., and P. Bahn
1991   *Archaeology: Theories, Methods, and Practice* (London: Thames and Hudson).

Ronen, A ., and Y. Olami
1983   *Map of Haifa-East (Map 23), 15-24* (Archaeological Survey of Israel; Jerusalem: Israel Antiquities Authority).

Saarisalo, A.
1929   'Topographical Researches in Galilee'. *JPOS* 9: 27-40.

Said, E.
1978   *Orientalism* (New York: Pantheon Books).

Singer, I.
1994   'Egyptians, Canaanites, and Philistines in the Period of the Emergence of Israel', in Finkelstein and Na'aman (eds.) 1994: 282-338.

Soffer, A., and S. Stern
1986   'The Middle East Sea-Port', *Studies in the Geography of Israel* 12: 206-15, xvii (Hebrew).

Stern, E.
1982   *Material Culture of the Land of the Bible in the Persian Period, 538–332 BC* (Warminster: Arris and Phillips).
1990   'New Evidence from Dor for the First Appearance of the Phoenicians Along the Northern Coast of Israel', *BASOR* 279: 27-34.
1991   'Phoenicians, Sikils, and Israelites in the Light of Recent Excavations at Tel Dor', in Lipinski (ed.) 1991: 85-94.
1994   *Dor: Ruler of the Seas* (Jerusalem: Israel Exploration Society).

Stieglitz, R.R.
1990   'The Geopolitics of the Phoenician Littoral in the Early Iron Age', *BASOR* 279: 9-12.

Stronach, D.
1996   'The Imagery of the Wine Bowl: Wine in Assyria in the Early First Millennium BC', in P.E. McGovern, S.J. Fleming and S.H. Katz (eds.), *The Origins and Ancient History of Wine* (Food and Nutrition in History and Anthropology, 11; Amsterdam: Gordon and Beach): 175-95.

Thompson, T.L.
1979   *The Settlement of Palestine in the Bronze Age* (Tübinger Atlas des Vorderen Orients; Beiheft Reihe B Nr. 34; Wiesbaden: Reichert).

Thompson, T.L., F.J. Gonçalves and J.M. van Cangh
1988   *Toponymie palestinienne: Plaine de St Jean d'Acre et corridor de Jérusalem* (Louvain-le-Neuve: Peeters).

Van Beek, G.W., W.G. Melson, D. Stronach and S. Lumsden
    2001   Traveling Pots or Traveling Potters? New Evidence for the Probable Source of the Assyrian Palace Ware found at Tell Jemmeh, Israel (in press).

Weippert, H.
    1988   *Palästina in vorhellenistischer Zeit* (Handbuch der Archäologie, Vorderasien, 2.1: Munich: Beck).

Wilkinson, T.J., and D.J. Tucker
    1995   *Settlement Development in the North Jazirah, Iraq: A Study of the Archaeological Landscape* (Iraq Archaeological Reports, 3; Warminster: British School of Archaeology, Department of Antiquities and Heritage, Baghdad).

Winter, I.J.
    1995   'Homer's Phoenicians: History, Ethnography, or Literary Topos? A Perspective on Early Orientalism', in J.B. Carter and S.P. Morris (eds.), *The Ages of Homer: A Tribute to Emily Townsend Vermeule* (Austin: University of Texas Press): 247-71.

Würthwein, E.
    1985   *Die Bücher der Könige: 1. Könige 1–16* (Das Alte Testament Deutsch, 11,1; Göttingen: Vandenhoeck & Ruprecht).

4

AGRICULTURAL TERRACES AND SETTLEMENT EXPANSION IN THE
HIGHLANDS OF EARLY IRON AGE PALESTINE: IS THERE ANY
CORRELATION BETWEEN THE TWO?

Shimon Gibson

In a recently published book *Mediterranean Peoples in Transition* in
honour of Professor Trude Dothan (Gitin *et al.* 1998), William G.
Dever presents a detailed critique of Finkelstein's views concerning
'pastoral-nomadic' origins for the Israelites. Among his numerous arguments Dever steadfastedly repeats the often made assertion that agricultural terracing was intimately connected with the sudden expansion of
settlements in the highlands in the Iron Age I and that the evidence for
widespread terracing prior to this period is 'extremely weak' (Dever
1998: 227). In this paper I shall be challenging this assumption. Small-
scale terracing, as I hope to demonstrate, was evidently a major feature
of sedentary agriculture in the highlands of Palestine from protohistoric
times and as late as the period of the Israelite monarchy. Widespread
terracing, however, only existed in the highlands from the time of the
divided monarchy, from the eighth century BCE, and not before. This,
of course, has enormous implications for those wishing to reconstruct
the character and mechanisms of settlement patterns and agricultural
territories in this region during the Iron Age I and II.

Agricultural Terraces and Landscape Archaeology

Agricultural terracing is one of the most striking man-made features
dominating the highland landscapes of Palestine. An agricultural terrace
may be defined as an artificially flattened or built-up surface which is
much more horizontal than the land surface which preceded it. The
terrace is constructed to provide additional ground space for the culti-

vation of fruit trees and other crops. Naturally flowing water, whether
from rainwater or by irrigation, spreads across the levelled surface and
provides ground water for the crop or tree growth. The capacity of the
terrace to absorb and conserve moisture depends on the depth of the
terrace fills. Terraces are located on the slopes of hills (known as
'lateral' or 'contour' terraces), on sloping plateau areas (known as 'enclosure' terraces) and across gullies and in valleys (known as 'cross-
channel' terraces or 'check dams').

Terraces on hillslopes in the central highlands were artificially built
over exposed bedrock, or, where possible, over pre-existing pockets or
layers of soil (for the technology of terrace construction, see Gibson
1995) (Fig. 4.1).

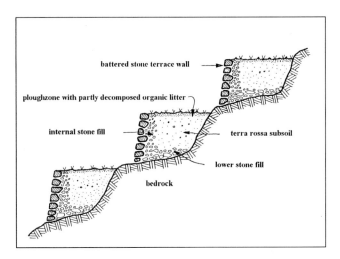

Fig. 4.1. *Schematic section of terrace showing internal fills (drawing S. Gibson)*

Considerable amounts of soil and stone were shifted and redeposited
from the near vicinity or from a distance and used in terraces.
Artificially filled terraces of this kind required an enormous investment
of human energy. It has been estimated, for instance, that 1500 donkey-
loads of material would be required to fill a terrace which is 10 m long
and about 5 m high (Rozenson *et al.* 1994: 71). The time it would take
to build a terrace depended also on environmental and human factors.
The practice of transporting fills over distances is also attested to in
other parts of the world (Spencer and Hale 1961: 20). The deliberate
filling of terraces with soil in Palestine during the Roman period was
clearly referred to in the Mishna (*Sheb.* 3.8). Where pre-existing soils

were to be found, these were incorporated into the terrace fills or cleared and reused as terrace fills elsewhere. The aim was to obtain a sufficient depth of terrace soil which would then absorb and conserve moisture. The topsoil of terraces is usually high in organic matter owing to sedimentation, to manuring practices and to the decomposition of plant debris. While water conservation was important, the quick drainage of excess water was clearly imperative for the stability of the terrace structure and to prevent the lower fills from becoming waterlogged. Therefore, many terraces contained a series of fills of stone. These were laid behind the terrace walls (cf. Spencer and Hale 1961: 16; Gibson and Edelstein 1985: 143-44) and over bedrock, and served to facilitate the efficient drainage of surplus rainwater absorbed by the terrace soils.

Terraces were normally retained by stone walls of dry-built construction founded on bedrock. Mortar appears never to have been used to bind stones together in terracing. The height of terrace walls depended on a number of factors: the angle of the slope, the breadth of the terrace, the availability of stones for the terrace walls, the availability of appropriate soil and stones for the terrace fills, and the skill of the builder. Terrace walls were never vertical but always had an external batter or rearward slope. The general rule is that the higher the wall, the greater the external batter. Stones for the walls came from a variety of sources: fieldstones scattered on the natural slopes, stones from quarries and stones from ruined ancient settlements. Strangely, Ron (1966: 34) has suggested that the terrace wall served as 'a depository for the stones cleared from the terrace surface'. This would only be true if the terrace walls had been erected solely to retain pre-existing soils. However, this was clearly not the case for much of the hills of Judaea and Samaria. Indeed, during periods of extensive terracing, stones sometimes had to be brought from great distances (see the reference to this in *m. Sheb.* 3.9). All terrace construction requires some form of digging, piling and the carrying of earth and stone fills. However, the details of the construction methods of terraces can vary from one sub-region of the highlands of Palestine to another. In some areas where the slopes had a sufficient cover of soil, notably in the Galilee and in the Lebanon (Spencer and Hale 1961: 8-9; cf. Wagstaff 1992), terraces were constructed by backslope digging and foreslope filling. Therefore, care must be taken not to assume that the technology of one set of terraces will necessarily be repeated in other areas, nor that some terraces are superior to others. For example, Golomb and Kedar (1971: 138) have suggested, wrongly we believe, that terracing in the Galilee was 'inferior' to the kind prevalent in the Judaean Hills (see also the comments by Gal 1991b: 108-109 on the terraces of the Galilee). Variations in the construction of terraces can occur even within one system of terraces on the same hillslope, especially where there is evidence indicating continuous use over different periods.

The best method available for the study of terraces is that of landscape archaeology (see the detailed discussion of this method in Gibson 1995). This method is particularly useful for the overall study of agricultural systems and is partly based on existing methods of conventional field surveys, regional surveys and site catchment (or site territory) analysis (see further details in Gibson 1995). Landscape archaeology, however, marks a shift away from the total focus on settlements and their patterns. Each element of a landscape possessing evidence of human activities is sampled and thus is finally given a chance of revealing its archaeology. In this method, the entire landscape is in effect the 'site' and the settlements there are regarded as features contained therein, albeit important features since they represent foci of human habitation activities. Basically, a project of landscape archaeology is carried out by the deconstruction of a cultural landscape into isolated and well-defined categories of apodictic evidence which are recorded as features (e.g. villages, farms, roads, cisterns, tombs, terraces, fields, stone quarries and so forth). Later, the evidence is assembled as reconstructions of specific components of the landscape (clusters of features) within a structured and spatial framework.

Terracing and Israelite Origins: A Review of the Literature

The lining of the slopes of hills with great numbers of terraced fields was a feat that amazed early travellers and pilgrims visiting Palestine prior to the nineteenth century and their construction was generally attributed to ancient peoples and particularly to the Hebrews. This link between Israelites and terracing was also proposed by a number of scholars in the nineteenth century, especially by those studying the geography of the country. C. Ritter, for example, the great compiler of information about the geography of Palestine, wrote of 'Hebrew terrace-culture' (Ritter 1866: II, 21). Warburton commenting on the appearance of terraces near Jerusalem wrote that 'on these steep acclivities, the strenuous labour of the Israelite had formerly grown corn, and wine and oil' (Warburton 1843: 230). Geographers, however, have always suffered from a lack of hard evidence with which they could date terraces. As a result, a certain reticence is displayed by present-day geographers when expressing opinions about the origins of terracing in Palestine. Zvi Ron, who made a major study of terraces in the 1960s, suggested that because there were substantially fewer Bronze Age settlements in the highlands in comparision to those of the subsequent Iron Age (basing himself on archaeological surveys published in Kochavi 1972), 'there can be no doubt that the culture of agricultural terraces developed during the First Temple period and spread considerably thereafter' (Ron 1977: 226). At the same time, Ron expressed caution and conceded that some terracing may even have existed before the Iron Age. Another geographer, Menashe Harel, has made a much more forceful argument for the exclusive invention of terracing by the Israelites. In his booklet, entitled *Dwellers of the Mountain: The Geography of Jewish Habitation of Ancient Judea* (1977), he described terracing as one of the pioneering enterprises unique to the Israelites. Harel wrote that 'with regard to land cultivation, terrace agriculture, unknown to earlier peoples, was the supreme achievement of the Israelites'.

While geographers (excluding Harel) have generally expressed uncertainty over the origins of terracing and are much more circumspect regarding the possible dating of terraces, biblical historians and archaeologists have been much more willing to express an opinion on the subject. As far back as 1942, Nelson Glueck was suggesting, on the basis of his surveys in Jordan, that agricultural terraces were of a much greater antiquity than had previously been thought, with terraces being employed from as early as the Early Bronze Age (1942: 17-18). However, Glueck's views on the early dating of terracing were not accepted at that time by his fellow scholars.

In an important article on terracing, de Geus claimed that during the Iron Age 'large scale terracing of mountain slopes began, followed by new settlements' (de Geus 1975: 69-70; cf. Gottwald 1979: 659-60). While de Geus did not discount the existence of older terraces, 'because every system has its forerunners', he thought it highly unlikely that anything substantial existed prior to the Iron Age (1975: 69). He further questioned whether it was even possible to remove the original vegetation on the hillsides and the preparation of the slopes for agriculture, without the use of iron implements. This led de Geus to suggest, first, that older terraces were initially built in the dry riverbeds because, as he claimed, 'this could be done without the help of iron tools' and, secondly, that primary terracing in the highlands was a significant feature facilitating the subsequent expansion of Iron Age/ Israelite settlement. According to de Geus, the existence of terracing with valuable crops at a distance from the Iron Age settlements, 'presupposes political units of some significance, if not the territorial state of the Iron Age' (de Geus 1975: 69). One should point out that there is no archaeological evidence to support the contention that terraces were being cultivated at great distances from Iron Age settlements, at least not until the time of the divided monarchy (Iron Age II) (see below). Contrary to de Geus's views regarding the significance of iron for deforestation practices, it would appear that the type of bloomery iron (as opposed to steeled iron) in use during the Early Iron Age, at least until the tenth century BCE, was a 'poor substitute for bronze' (according to Maddin, Muhly and Wheeler 1977: 124; cf. Waldbaum 1978). In fact, deforestation in the highlands was probably first undertaken with the use of hafted flint axes in the Early Bronze I and then later with the use of copper axes.

In 1975, Lawrence E. Stager submitted to Harvard University a PhD thesis on Iron Age agriculture in the Buqe'ah Valley in the Judaean Desert. Stager took a major step forward by recognizing the inherent possibilities of undertaking archaeological work on the remains of agricultural terraces, not only in semi-arid regions but also in the central highlands. Basing himself on published surveys previously carried out in the highlands between 1967–68 (cf. Kochavi 1972), Stager hypothesized that the increased number of settlements during Iron Age I (by 82 per cent in comparision to the previous Late Bronze Age) were directly responsible for the decimation of forested and soil-covered hillsides, followed by the transformation of these slopes into terraces, c. 1200 BCE, which were then dry-farmed (1975: 236). Like Aharoni (1979: 239), Stager also interpreted Josh. 17.14-18 as evidence for significant deforestation activities during the Iron Age I in the highlands, but he was also of the opinion that terracing originated before the Iron Age I. In a subsequent publication, Stager showed quite convincingly that the word *šdmt*, which appears in horticultural contexts in Late Bronze Age mythological texts from Ugarit (*CTA* 23.8-11; *CTA* 2.1.43; cf. Stager 1982) as well as in a number of biblical verses (Deut. 32.32; Isa. 16.8;

Hab. 3.17), could be translated as 'terrace'. Stager wrote: 'If my understanding of the Ugaritic evidence is correct, then already by the Late Bronze Age terraced vineyards were a common enough sight in the hills behind Ugarit that bards could evoke their imagery in sustained metaphor without fear of being misunderstood.' (Stager 1982: 116 n. 20). According to Stager, the technology of terracing, which had been in use at least since the Late Bronze Age, was adopted during the Iron Age I and 'dramatically altered the attractiveness of the hill country to the incoming agriculturalists and increased its carrying capacity as never before' (1985: 5).

After conducting a study of settlement patterns in Palestine during the Bronze Age, Thompson reached the conclusion that 'the apparent absence of significant Bronze Age (and especially the LB Age) settlement in the hill country proper, outside of the few scattered agriculturally fertile basins...is in sharp contrast to the extensive settlement of this region during the Iron Age' (1979: 66). This led him to suggest that the failure of the LB occupation in Palestine to renew/expand on the earlier Middle Bronze Age II settlement in the highlands, indicated that there was political instability at that time which made it difficult to settle in the agriculturally marginal highlands. Thompson suggested that Iron Age settlement was facilitated by two essential advances in agricultural technology, namely the storage of water through the use of plaster-lined cisterns and the control of erosion resulting in deforestation through the development of terracing (1979: 66; cf. Albright 1961: 113). There is no supporting archaeological evidence, however, for either one of these so-called 'advances': plaster-lined cisterns existed already in the Middle Bronze Age but only really became frequent in the Iron Age II (see comments and bibliography in Gibson and Jacobson 1996: 225; Tsuk 1998: 25) and terraces were never built with the sole intention of controlling erosion.

Marfoe (1979: 33) described highland terrace farming in Palestine during the Iron Age I as a significant 'unifying ecological feature' among the settling Israelites. The apparent widescale appearance of terracing during this period led Marfoe to infer that 'deforestation had still not progressed very far upslope in Late Bronze II, but by Iron I the gradual degradation of the woodland areas may have reduced many of the arable slopes to a shrubby vegetation' (1979: 32). Interestingly, Marfoe pointed out that terrace agriculture first appeared in the Biqa' Valley in the Lebanon only during the third or second century BCE and apparently not before (1979: 32), results which are now being mirrored in the Modi'in hills of the northern Shephela with the earliest terraces there dating to the Hellenistic period (Gibson and Lass 2001). Marfoe regarded the emergence of the Israelites in the highlands of Palestine as reflecting a withdrawal of peasant groups from the lowlands. He preferred not to regard this as the result of a 'rebellion' but more as 'a basic, alternate strategy in adaptation—one aspect of a constant demographic fluidity' (1979: 33).

During his excavations of the Iron Age I village at 'Ai, Callaway noted similarities between terrace retaining walls and 'barriers built in valleys or *wadi* beds to slow the flow of water and entrap eroded soil'. He believed that because of the similarity of the terraces and barriers in valleys, 'one may conjecture an origin for the villagers in the lowland region west of the hill country' (1976: 29-30; 1980: 250). These views are reminiscent of de Geus's contention (1975: 69) that the older terraces were first built in the dry *wadi* beds (see above).

In April 1984, an International Congress on Biblical Archaeology was held in Jerusalem, one of its central themes being the Israelite settlement in Canaan (Amitai 1985: 29). Terracing and the supposed link with the Israelites were mentioned in a number of lectures. For example, in dealing with the basic factors of Israelite settlement, S. Herrmann questioned the significance of the innovation of agricultural terraces as a convincing element for assuming a new development introduced by new ethnic groups during the early Iron Age (1985: 51). Callaway, one of the respondents at the Congress, mentioned that at the Iron Age I settlements of 'Ai and Raddana, 'steep hillsides which had never before been cultivated were cleared of underbrush and terraced to conserve water from rainfall needed for grain crops and gardens'. Callaway described this terracing as 'an innovative, even revolutionary, new way of wresting a living from the arid, inhospitable hills of central Canaan' (1985a: 73). However, while Callaway regarded terracing as an 'innovation' in the highlands, he did not claim that terracing was invented there. Knowledge of terracing, according to Callaway, was brought to the highlands by farmers fleeing 'from conflict in the lowlands and coastal plain areas to escape more warlike newcomers to those regions' (1985a: 75-76; 1985b: 33, 44). This population movement could be paralleled, or so Callaway believed, by a similar and earlier Late Bronze Age movement of farmers from the coastal region of Ugarit into the mountains of Lebanon where terracing was then subsequently practised (cf. the terracing alluded to in certain Ugaritic texts: Stager 1982). This knowledge of terracing was then passed on by merchants to Canaanite farmers further south in Palestine. Callaway reached the conclusion that in Palestine 'terracing technology would have been known by people in the lowlands and coastal areas before the settlement of the highlands in Iron Age I'. While Callaway's theories are attractive, they do not explain how and why terracing first developed in the mountains above Ugarit during the Late Bronze Age. In any case, our knowledge of the settlement patterns in Lebanon during these periods is still limited (cf. Marfoe's study of the Biqa Valley where terracing could only be dated back to as early as the Hellenistic period: 1979: 32). Nor does it explain why Canaanite merchants should have bothered to transmit knowledge of Lebanese terracing technology to their Canaanite brethren farming in the lowlands of Palestine.

In an article entitled 'Where did the Israelites live?', Ahlström expressed the view that the Iron Age I newcomers in the highlands were an 'indigenous' rather than an 'intrusive' population group (1982: 133-34). He suggested that these indigenous people were responsible for introducing the principle of terrace agriculture into the hill country. According to Ahlström, terracing 'reflects an agricultural background and a level of technology which indicates that they were not "semi-nomads".' In a later publication, Ahlström (1986: 19) described terracing as a land-improvement device designed to increase total agricultural yield in the highlands and that it was the result of the new Iron Age I growth in population. The new settlers, or 'pioneers' as Ahlström calls them, were mainly Canaanites from lowland and coastal areas, fleeing from conflict, harsh taxes and other such problems.

Finkelstein's views on the settlement process are extremely different from those held by Callaway and Ahlström. According to Finkelstein (1985: 81), the Israelite settlers were sedentarized pastoralists who first moved into the northern part of the central highlands, from east to west, and then, eventually, by clearing dense scrub forest and adapting to difficult terrain, practised orchard agriculture. Finkelstein does not believe that terraces were invented by the Israelites or that terracing facilitated the Iron Age I settlement process (1988: 21, 202). Such theories he considers 'bizarre' (1988: 309). The results of his survey in the 'Ephraim' area of the highlands, with a pattern of MBII sites followed by another similar pattern of Iron Age I sites, he claims, completely invalidates the views expressed by Callaway and others. Finkelstein wrote:

> In the western slopes, at least, settlement was obviously impossible without constructing terracing. So it follows that terraces must have been built already during the Middle Bronze period, if not earlier. Further-more, Israelite settlement initially took place in those sectors where cultivation was possible without building terraces, and at that time, there was in fact, relatively little activity in the typical region of terraces (1988: 202).

While Finkelstein's claim (1988: 309) that terracing in the highlands was 'a function of topography and population growth' of greater antiquity than the Iron Age seems entirely reasonable, not all of his other views are sustainable in the same way. First of all, theoretically, agriculture could have been practised without terracing in any one of the sub-regions of the highlands, including the semi-arid, eastern slopes of the highlands. However, such a mismanagement of the soil resources would have led to a rapid and devastating erosion of soils and so undoubtedly some form of terracing, even of an incipient form, would have become necessary from very early on. Secondly, the statement that there was very little settlement 'activity' in the heavily terraced zones of the highlands, appears to be wrong. It is this writer's view that many Iron Age I settlements, which were extremely small, have 'disappeared' under the very extensive terrace systems of later date (similarly, Chalcolithic, EB IV, and MB IIB settlements disappeared beneath later Iron Age to Byzantine-period terraces at Sataf, Masua' in the Rephaim Valley, and at Tel el-Ful). Finally, one must point out that Finkelstein's views on irrigation practices in the highlands appear to be invalid. He claims, without any supporting evidence, that springs and irrigation agriculture were not important for the early Iron Age settlement processes in the central highlands. He states emphatically that 'the practice of irrigation agriculture was, in fact, utterly negligible in the region, and even today has been attempted in only a few villages' (1988: 309). While the percentage of present-day traditional irrigated terraced areas in the highlands is quite small in comparison to the extent of the terraced zones used for dry-farming (Gibson 1995: 86), this picture does not necessarily reflect the situation as it existed during the Iron Age I. There are hundreds of springs in the central highlands and one may assume that Iron Age I settlements existed in the close proximity to each one of these. If this is true, then it would boost the figures we have for Iron Age I settlements in the highlands. There are two reasons, in my opinion, why many settlements next to springs have not been detected hitherto: first, the growth of Roman/Byzantine and Mediaeval to Ottoman terrace systems, including the construction of large-scale water installations, have either destroyed or covered up these settlements. Secondly, very few terrace systems next to springs have been archaeologically investigated and fewer excavated (Sataf is one exception, see below). While it is true that Zertal has shown that Iron Age I settlements especially in the northern hill country tended to be located at some distance from the springs (1987; 1998: 242), this conclusion is surely biased by the factor of archaeological visibility, with the earlier remains at the spring sites probably obscured from the eyes of archaeological surveyors by the later build up of terraces and water systems. This was the case at Sataf where settlement remains of earlier periods were discovered during excavations near springs entombed beneath later terracing (Gibson *et al.* 1991).

In his book *Agriculture in Iron Age Israel* (1987), Borowski, who clearly adheres to the Israelite conquest theory, described the Israelites as having settled in previously uninhabited areas of the highlands which were heavily forested and lacking in suitable agricultural land. According to Borowski (1987: 6), 'for the creation of agricultural land, the Israelites employed terraces, a method heretofore not widely used in Canaan… Near these terraced fields small villages were established and occupied by the clans and families owning and cultivating the land.' Borowski accepted Stager's reading of Ugaritic *šdmt* as 'terrace', and suggested that terracing 'infiltrated Canaan from the north in the Late Bronze Age and was adopted as an agricultural method together with its linguistic label' (Borowski 1988: 10). The Late Bronze Age Jebusite inhabitants of Jerusalem, according to Borowski, were already utilizing agricultural terraces. He believed that Israelite terracing was used not only to facilitate settlement processes in the highlands but also as an economic/military 'power base from which the rest of the country could be overtaken' (Borowski 1988: 9). Runoff farming in the Negev Desert is described by Borowski as 'an offshoot of terracing in the hill-country', dating to the late tenth to early ninth centuries BCE (1987: 18). However, the present evidence would suggest that the use of agricultural terraces in the arid and desert regions of Palestine was preceded by developments in the highlands of the Mediterranean zone and not the other way around (Gibson 1995: 29).

In 1985, D.C. Hopkins published his thesis dealing with agriculture in the Iron Age, entitled *The Highlands of Canaan*. Drawing heavily on ethnographic and anthropological literature, Hopkins was able to provide scholars with a fresh look at old questions. Hopkins very clearly expressed his doubts as to whether any of the so-called 'innovative' technologies, which included terracing, exercised a determining influence on the emergence of Israel during the early Iron Age (1985: 23). Hopkins argued that since early Iron Age sites were located at distances of between 2 and 5 km from each other, there was no real need for highland farmers to make 'great intensifying investments in their lands in order to maintain themselves agriculturally' (1985: 167-68). He suggested, contrary to Stager (see above), that since there was no apparent pressure on the land at this point in time, terracing need no longer be regarded as a technology which supported the establishment of early Iron Age settlements, but that it was instead an evolving agricultural technique connected with the gradual growth of subsequent Iron Age settlement in the highlands. Hopkins does not accept that terracing is the minimum threshold of intensity at which agricultural systems in the highlands must operate, a view which he describes as lacking 'solid foundation' (1985: 180). Rather, he argued that crops could well have been cultivated on slopes without terracing: 'The risks of soil erosion may be perfectly obvious to modern commentators, but examples of short-sightedness among pre-industrial cultivators are numerous' (1985: 180). He claims that 'methods of approximating the time of the origin of terracing either in the highlands themselves or in general have been attempted without reliable results' (1985: 183). In discussing Stager's views regarding the references to terraces in Late Bronze Age Ugaritic poetry (see above), Hopkins wrote:

> It remains to be explained how the occurrences of terraces around the populous city of Ugarit on the Syrian coast can be taken as evidence for their appearance in the highlands centuries later. For this to be true one would be forced to adopt the mistaken view that the art of terracing spread by diffusion because it constituted a 'pull' towards its use in an intensive agricultural system (1985: 184).

While admitting that the date for the introduction of terracing into the highlands remains inconclusive, Hopkins preferred to regard terrace systems 'as the response of a long-tenured, yet developing community to demands for a more stable and dependable productive regime, whatever the form which those demands might have taken' (1985: 186).

In contrast to Hopkins's views, Borowski believes that terracing was an integral part of early Iron Age settlement processes in the highlands, implying that terracing served as a minimum threshold of intensity at which agricultural systems in the highlands operated. His criticisms of Hopkins's views were set forward at a symposium devoted to discussions of Hopkins's book *The Highlands of Canaan*, held in November 1986 at Atlanta, in the United States (LaBianca and Hopkins 1988). Borowski wrote that he found it

> hard to imagine the Israelites constantly moving from site to site in the hill country as soon as their soil resources were depleted. The rocky nature of the terrain would not have permitted it, and it would have been more economical to invest what it takes to build terraces than to have to clear new tracts and build new settlements. Besides, if they were constantly on the move in search of fertile land they could not have achieved the takeover of Canaan (1988: 10-11).

Hopkins's reply to Borowski was that the knowledge of terracing technology cannot have been diffused from an external source; he was willing only to see it as a technology which developed locally. However, while accepting that sporadic terracing in the highlands could go back to as early as the Middle Bronze Age, he did not believe that terracing was adopted on a wide scale before or even during the early Iron Age. According to Hopkins, 'terracing was the key to long-term stability, a key that was turned in the context of a developing community. Terracing must not be depicted as mounting the historical stage as a theatrical god, resolving the subsistence challenges for the resourceful settlers' (LaBianca and Hopkins 1988: 14).

In his book dealing with a suggested theoretical approach to the formation of the state in ancient Israel, Frick wrote that terracing technology was a significant Iron Age I development which 'enabled the intensification of settlement in an area in which the obstacles to productive agriculture were many' (Frick 1985: 130). The risk factors that Frick mentioned include various environmental constraints such as substantial deviations in annual rainfall, devastating soil erosion on steep slopes, the rockiness of highland soils, and problems associated with the maintenance of soil fertility.

Coote and Whitelam (1987) maintained that as a result of a dramatic decline in east Mediterranean trade towards the end of the Late Bronze Age, there was a substantial shift of settlement from the lowlands to the highlands as a scheme of short-term risk reduction. They suggested that lowland Canaanite peasants may originally have managed seasonal settlements in the highlands and that these were also places of refuge at times of instability. Coote and Whitelam suggested that these

> seasonal settlements as part of a general pattern of transhumance could become established agricultural settlements when conditions deteriorated sufficiently to encourage such a shift. Approached from this perspective then, Israel emerged in the Palestinian highlands as a result of a dramatic change in settlement and land use mainly in response to the reduction in east Mediterranean trade which had a seismic effect upon the material prosperity of Palestine (Coote and Whitelam 1987: 129).

Hence, a switch took place from lowland agriculture undertaken under city protection during the thirteenth century BCE, to the expansion of independent highland agriculture in the early Iron Age which was secured with the use of extensive terracing. One could take Coote and Whitelam's extremely hypothetical thesis one step further by suggesting that terracing must originally have been practised in these seasonal agricultural settlements maintained by the Canaanite peasants from the lowlands.

While there are immense problems in identifying the emergence of Israel in the archaeological record of the early Iron Age (see more recently Thompson 1992; Frendo 1992; Kempinsky 1992), all agree that there was a substantial change in the settlement pattern during the Iron Age I in comparsion to the Late Bronze Age, with a proliferation of small settlements established in parts of the highlands which had not been previously settled. However, the ethnic identity of these new high-landers and their place of origin is still debated. It is plausible that some of them were Israelites or, at least, some later *became* Israelites. The new settlements were unfortified, with permanent dwellings in a scat-tered or grouped layout, and with well-planned storage facilities (silos, cisterns and very large pithoi which could also have been used for water storage). This would suggest that the inhabitants came from an agricultural rather than a nomadic background, but this is not conclu-sive. The suggestion that the settlements were inhabited by farmers who withdrew from less marginal agricultural lands in the lowlands, to the west or from the inland valleys, seems reasonable but does not answer all the questions. In support of the theory of indigenous development, there is evidence for some general continuity in the material culture from the Late Bronze Age to the Early Iron Age. The suggestion that the settlements were inhabited by people of a nomadic background who rapidly became sedentarized by adopting a new agricultural lifestyle, is another possiblility but one which is more difficult to prove.

The alternative solution is that there was a much more complex symbiosis of early Iron Age peoples in the highlands, more so than scholars have previously been willing to suppose. These peoples may have come from diverse backgrounds, both agricultural and nomadic, from great distances or from regions in Palestine close by. The gelling together of these diverse peoples within rather harsh and restrictive highland environments may have forced the rapid abandonment of earlier lifestyles and the adoption of a fairly simple way of life based on subsistence agriculture. Such a scenario is admittedly very difficult to prove archaeologically, but it is a reasonable assumption that the Palestinian highland cultures of the early Iron Age were very much more variegated than their material artefacts would suggest them to be.

Gottwald pointed out that 'origins do not tell us everything, but I believe that in seeking them, we will know more' (1985: 93). As we have seen from our review of scholarly opinion, few believe that agricultural terracing was effectively practised in the highlands of Palestine prior to the Iron Age I. There are those who suggest that terracing might have existed in the Late Bronze Age, but only on a very small scale. Others have suggested that terracing was invented elsewhere (the hills above Ugarit in Lebanon are one proposed location) and then imported via the Canaanite lowlands to the Palestine hills as an innovation during the Iron Age I. This idea of diffusion is rejected by those who believe that sporadic terracing activities in the highlands existed from as early as the Middle Bronze Age. However, the general view held by scholars is that terracing was introduced during the Iron Age I by the Canaanites or Israelites, as an adaptation or innovation but not as an invention. Many adhere to the view that terracing played an important role during the Iron Age I either as a technology which facilitated the increase of settlements or as a technology resulting from the successful spread of settlements. Some scholars suggest that terracing was one of a number of local features adopted by the incoming Israelites (Finkelstein 1985). A more radical opinion is that terracing was not a particularly significant technology at all in the highlands of Palestine, at least not until much later during the Iron Age II (Hopkins 1985).

One thing is certain: many of the opinions which have hitherto been proposed are based on very shaky evidence. Indeed, the existing evidence paints a picture of terracing as a constant and integral part of agricultural systems operating in the highlands from the very beginning of permanent agricultural settlement there, from the Early Bronze Age if not from before. This is in total contradiction to the majority of scholars who believe that terracing was an innovation of the Iron Age I. However, while terracing characterized the highlands of Palestine from the protohistoric periods onwards, there can be no doubt that the scale of these terracing activities was relatively small and in direct proportion to the density of settlements. Archaeology can also show that the phenomenon of widespread agricultural terracing in the highlands took place only from the Iron Age II (eighth–sixth centuries BCE) and not before. It thus has to be admitted that the question of the emergence of the nation of Israel and the question bearing on the origins of terracing in the highlands of Palestine, are totally distinct subjects which have no bearing one on the other.

The Archaeological Evidence for Early Terracing

Very little is known about the earliest forms of agricultural terracing in the highlands of Palestine. It seems reasonable to assume that the technology of creating flat areas on hillsides by building walls and levelling fills was invented by various rural groups acting in cooperation at a local level, in different parts of the Levant and at different times. Hence, various centres of origin for terrace construction may have existed, with Palestine being one of them. Incipient forms of terracing, such as soil held in place by logs of wood, by rows of wooden stakes, or piled rocks, would be very difficult to detect in the archaeological record (cf. Spencer and Hale 1961: 3, 15 n. 16), especially when one considers that archaeologists make so very few attempts to excavate terraces. It was probably recognized early on that obstructions placed across a stream channel would eventually help towards stopping the movement of eroded soils and would induce a process of alluviation. Early slope terracing may have taken place initially in the lower parts of hills with newer terraces later being built further up the slopes. Another suggestion which has been made is that the natural step-like appearance of many of the slopes in the highlands, with thin layers of chalky marl interposed between limestone or dolomite strata, may have prompted the first attempts at terracing (Wilson 1906: 200; Dalman 1932: 23; Meshel 1987; Orni and Efrat 1980: 55). However, no evidence supports the assumption made by Spencer and Hale (1961: 180; cf. Ron 1977:

222) that the earliest terraces with stone walls must have been crudely executed, low in height and built on relatively slight slopes. Indeed, one of the terraces unearthed at Sataf, which is believed to be of EB date, was relatively well constructed and was built on a very steep slope (see below). Spencer and Hale (1961: 7 and 14) also suggest that the origins of terracing should be sought in the marginal semi-arid regions of the Near East. They suggest that their 'channel-bottom, weir terrace' type was possibly the earliest form of terrace. However, terracing in semi-arid and desert regions cannot be shown to be older than the Iron Age II (seventh century BCE), particularly in the Judaean Desert, even though the practice of flood-farming itself already existed in the Negev from as early as the Early Bronze Age (Rosen, n.d.). It is interesting to note that Donkin in his study of New World terracing (1979: 131), also reached the conclusion that the earliest terraced sites must have been in the less arid areas first.

Another important point which needs to be taken into account is that the idea of creating levelled areas on hillslopes for agricultural purposes is not dissimilar from the basic technology of architectural terracing or slope stabilization (a subject ignored by Spencer and Hale 1961: 3, but mentioned briefly by Donkin 1979: 131). At settlement sites in Palestine, architectural terracing can be traced back to as early as pre-historic times. A system of four architectural terraces supporting 13 hut dwellings, are known from the Natufian site of Nahal Oren (Stekelis and Yizraeli 1963: 1-12, Fig. 3). These terraces were 24 m in length and 2–5 m in breadth, and their retaining walls were built of field stones. At many Early Bronze Age sites, architectural terraces were built to support houses and other structures on the slopes of hills (contrary to the remarks by Stager 1982: 116 n. 21). Examples of massive EB architectural terraces are known from Tel Yarmut (Miroschedji 1992: 269), Tell el-'Umeiri (Herr 1992: 232) and at sites in the Wadi el-Hasa (Macdonald *et al.* 1983: 318). Architectural terracing has also recently been detected in the Middle Bronze II settlement on the lower eastern slope of Tel el-Ful (unpublished excavations by the author in collaboration with Z. Greenhut). Architectural terracing continued to be used throughout the rest of the Bronze Age. At Jerusalem, a remarkable series of architectural terraces were unearthed by Kenyon on the east slope of the City of David, probably dating from the very beginning of the Iron Age or earlier (Steiner 1993). Since the technology of architectural terracing in Palestine can be traced back to late prehistoric times, it is possible to assume that terracing for agricultural purposes likewise had a similar antiquity in the hilly areas of the country. It would be presumptious for anyone to accept the existence of architectural terracing in earlier periods but not to presuppose the same technological knowledge for agricultural purposes. While it is true that archaeological evidences for very early agricultural terraces are few and far between, the lack of hard evidence is a direct result of the general archaeological disinterest in off-site data. Clearly, until landscape archaeology becomes part of normal archaeological survey and excavation strategies it is unlikely that much more evidence for earlier terracing will become available, especially in the present climate where large tracts of the country with traditional agricultural systems which abound in terrace systems, are being bulldozed into oblivion with scarcely any archaeological attention being given to them .

The earliest agricultural terrace found in Palestine dates from the Early Bronze Age and was unearthed during excavations at Sataf (in Area B) on a hill overlooking the Soreq Valley, west of Jerusalem (for preliminary observations on this terrace, see Gibson *et al.* 1991). It was built across a natural drainage gully high up on the steep slope of the hill above the spring of 'Ein Bikura (Fig. 4.2). Buried beneath this terrace were the earlier remains of a structure, probably used for agricultural storage, dating from the Early Bronze I (Fig. 4.3). The external upper parts of this structure had collapsed down the slope immediately after it had been abandoned. It became clear that the reason the entire structure had not been washed away down the very sheer slope in the drainage gully was because the lower remnants of the structure were subsequently buried and protected from erosion beneath a terrace. Hence, we believe this terrace cannot have been built very long after the actual abandonment of the structure. Moreover, associated with this wall was a fill of brown soil typical of terraces, containing sherds dating exclusively from the Early Bronze Age. The terrace wall consisted of a line of large stones and was preserved to a length of 4 m. The wall had a height of one course, partly resting on bedrock and on earlier buried fills. The terrace appears to have survived for a very long time. The western extension of this terrace was restored in the Early Roman period, following periods of gullying and erosion, and it continued to serve an agricultural function. During the Byzantine period, these earlier terraces were completely buried beneath a new terrace built with a completely different orientation.

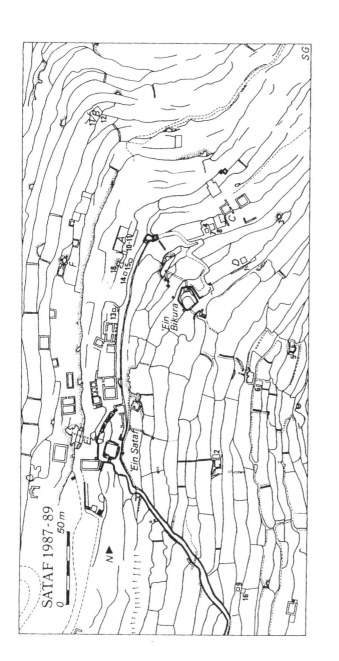

Fig. 4.2. *Map of Sataf (drawing: S. Gibson)*

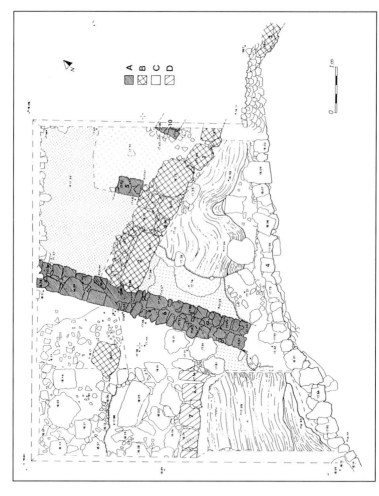

Fig. 4.3. Plan of Early Bronze Age terrace in the gully of Area B at Sataf.
A: EB I structural remains; B: EB terrace; C–D: later terracing activities

In addition to this strong evidence of an EB terrace wall from Sataf, there is also indirect evidence from the site indicating that its very steep slopes must have been terraced at this early period. Excavations revealed the remains of Early Bronze I dwellings scattered up to a distance of 340 m from each other in different parts of the Sataf landscape (in T9, T16, T7, T18 in Area A and T12 and T17 in Area B, see Fig. 4.2). Since there is no evidence to suggest that the entire slope was densely built up during this period, it would appear that the areas between the dwellings were used for cultivation purposes and perhaps also for animal pens. This would imply substantial woodland clearance in the entire area between the structures and the two springs of water at the site. Because of the extreme steepness of the slope, terrace construction must be assumed for the cultivated areas, otherwise the unprotected soils would have been rapidly washed away. We would suggest that the terraces were not necessarily built in a system of serried rows but were probably built as isolated, single fields scattered on the slope between the EB houses (perhaps similar to those described by Spencer and Hale 1961: 9). Some of these terraces may have been hand-irrigated from the nearby springs of water. Woodland clearance and terracing involve a large investment of time and labour, and they are not activities which are usually undertaken by transient semi-pastoralists. This suggests, therefore, a degree of social stability existing at the site during the Early Bronze Age and evidence of a more long-term commitment to the land. One may speculate that such conditions could have led to the onset of territorial demarcations in the landscape. There was clearly an improvement and diversification of agricultural practices during this period (Finkelstein and Gophna 1993).

It is unlikely that the EB terracing activities at Sataf were an isolated phenomenon. Activities of this sort were probably being undertaken in the highlands throughout the Early Bronze Age, as Finkelstein and Gophna (1993: 6) have suggested, and during the Middle Bronze Age as well (Finkelstein 1988: 202; 1993: 64-65). However, much more direct archaeological evidence is needed. An interesting EB site surrounded by terraces was investigated by U. Dinur at Khirbet 'Ein Farah, to the north-east of Jerusalem (Kochavi 1972: 185, Site No. 137; Dinur and Feig 1993: 414-15, Site No. 541). Because of the isolated situation of this one-period site on top of a rocky knoll, it seems fairly reasonable to assume that the terraces must also be of EB date. These terraces should be checked by excavation.

Extensive surveys and excavations to the south-west of Jerusalem have brought to light the remains of numerous agriculturally based Early Bronze IV (Intermediate Bronze Age) and Middle Bronze IIB settlements spread along the length of the Rephaim Valley (Wadi el-Werd, the 'Valley of Roses') on the terraces above 'Ein el-Haniyeh (Gibson and Edelstein 1985: 153), on the slopes of Masu'a (Eisenberg 1993a: 1279–80; 1993b), at Khirbet er-Ras and at Manahat (Edelstein 1993a: 1281–82). Excavations revealed that the wall foundations of the houses of these EB IV/MB IIB settlements had been built directly onto bedrock with only very 'thin' pockets of buried soil preserved here and there. There are indications that the water table during these periods was higher than it is today and a study of phytoliths by A. Rosen (referred to in Edelstein 1993: 1281) from Manahat shows that the immediate vicinity of the site was fairly marshy. It is possible that there were springs there which have now dried up. Edelstein and Milevsky (1994: 20) have suggested that only the soils of the valley bed were cultivated during these periods and that slope terracing was first introduced into this area during the Iron Age I but not before. However, a geomorphological study has not yet been undertaken on the buried soils of the valley bed itself and thus we really do not know how extensive the cultivation surfaces of the valley bed was during these early periods. Clearly substantial deforestation had taken place on the slopes before the settlements were built. However, what is not clear is whether these woodland clearances were restricted solely to the immediate area of the settlements, or whether additional clearances were not also made on nearby slopes for cultivation purposes. Had such areas been cleared for cultivation, then it is likely that they would have been terraced. It is interesting to note that Rosen (1986a: 55) has recorded evidence for large scale flooding episodes during the EB IV with soil stripped from the hillslopes, during her work in Nahal Lachish in the western foothill zone. This is probably indicative of widespread deforestation activities further up in the highlands. Rosen has also pointed out that the gap spanning the MB II to LB was marked by evidence for erosion and wadi incision. This may reflect the abandonment of slope terracing in the highlands further east.

Terraces dating from the Early Iron Age have been excavated at one site and surveyed at a number of others. An Iron Age I terrace was excavated by Callaway (1969: 15-16, Fig. 9) at 'Ai (et-Tell) (Fig. 4.4).

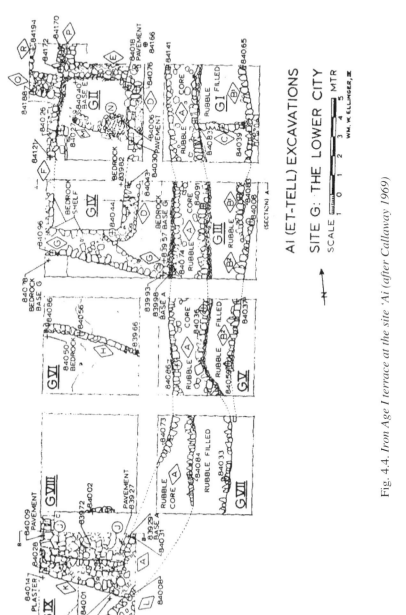

Fig. 4.4. *Iron Age I terrace at the site 'Ai (after Callaway 1969)*

Terraces which may also date from the Early Iron Age were investigated on the steep slopes of Khirbet Raddana (Callaway and Cooley 1971: 14; Stager 1985: Figs. 4–6). On the western slope of this site, a terrace had a wall consisting of one course of large stones built on bedrock and retaining a stony fill of *terra rossa* soil. A second terrace with a wall built of quarried stones was investigated on the southern slope. Scattered on these terrace surfaces was Iron Age I pottery. According to Stager (personal communication, 20 December 1985):

> I was unable to find enough well preserved terrace walls to indicate whether they were part of larger units defined by enclosure walls. Nor did I discover any buildings that could be considered outliers, 'farm houses', or watchtowers. But all of the terrace remnants that I found were on the slopes just below the villages, presumably where the farmers were living.

The suggestion that only cereals were grown on these terraces, based on the discovery of only sickleblades and grinding stones within the Iron I village at Raddana (Stager 1975: 259 n. 3), must be viewed with a certain amount of caution. Another system of Iron Age I terraces was investigated in 1980 by O. Avisar (personal communication) at Mizpeh Har Nof (map ref. 16680 - 13235), in the vicinity of Kefar Shaul, west of Jerusalem (cf. Finkelstein 1988: 51, who claims that Iron Age I sites are not known west of Jerusalem). During a visit that I made to the site with Avisar in 1980, a system of terraces was examined near the summit of the hill, at elevation 808. Scattered on the surfaces of these terraces were sherds dating from the Iron Age I, including fragments of typical 'collar rim' pithoi (cf. Mazar 1990: 134). The site was greatly disturbed by later quarrying and by modern military trenching. Another Iron Age I terrace was sectioned at Khirbet Umm et-Tala, south of Jerusalem (Ofer 1984: 104). According to Gal (1991b: 108-109), terracing in the Lower Galilee during this period was restricted to the *wadis*.

The archaeological evidence which is available suggests that throughout the 2000 years, extending from the Early Bronze Age and until the Iron Age II, all the agricultural terracing activities in the highlands of Palestine were carried out on a fairly limited scale only and that these were focused almost entirely on the immediate vicinity of rural settlements. There is no evidence whatsoever for *widespread* terracing in Palestine at any time preceding the period of the divided monarchy in the Iron Age II. However, this does not mean that such small-scale terracing was 'unsystematic' in any way, as Dever claims in response to the discoveries made at Sataf (Dever 1992: 79). The picture of small-scale terracing from the EB to the early Iron Age reflects a constant strategy of local adaptation which was very specific to the kind of rural settlements that had independent subsistence economies. The typical crops grown on these terraces were the Mediterranean triad: cereals, olives and grapes. Throughout this period gradual deforestation was undertaken in Palestine and throughout the Levant (Rowton 1967: 277; Eckholm 1975: 764-70). The open woodlands in these hills were mainly characterized by the evergreen oak (*Quercus calliprinos*) and, to a lesser extent, by the Atlantic terebinth (*Pistachia atlantica*). Much of the deforestation was undertaken to provide timber and charcoal, but also to open up areas for grazing and expand on existing terraced areas.

Archaeological surveys in the hills of Judaea and Samaria have shown that it was only during the Iron Age II, at a time of stronger organizational authority and economic stability (probably from the late eighth century BCE at the earliest), that widespread terracing activities were first undertaken in the highlands (Dar 1986a: 6; Gibson and Edelstein 1985: 154), with terracing spreading into the climatically marginal lands of the Judaean Desert and the Negev in the seventh century BCE (Finkelstein 1993: 64). These widespread terracing activities in the highlands were matched by a substantial rise in the number of newly founded rural villages/hamlets, towers and farmsteads (cf. Kochavi 1972; Broshi 1993: 15), reflecting a degree of agricultural specialization and organization at this time, perhaps even with an early form of 'plantation production', which went far beyond that of the normal subsistence level of the previous periods (Finkelstein 1993: 62-63). The extensive terracing of this period was the clear outcome of population pressure on the available land and this situation may have been exacerbated by a surplus of labour resulting from an influx of refugees into Judah following the fall of the Northern Kingdom of Israel into the hands of the Assyrians at the end of the eighth century BCE (Broshi 1993: 16-17). The rapid expansion of agricultural areas in the highlands during the course of the Iron Age II may have led to conflicts over land rights and boundaries. Apprehensions which some local farmers may have had over the concentration of agricultural wealth within the hands of an elite, perhaps with the establishing of large estates, appears to be reflected in Isa. 5.8 and Mic. 2.12.

For the first time, there is evidence in the Iron Age II for terrace systems which had been built as predetermined units on the slopes of hills with their boundaries defined by stone-built enclosure walls. An excellent example of a small terraced unit of this kind which dates from the Iron Age II (eighth–sixth centuries BCE), with a number of structures at its centre, at least one of the four-room type, was investigated at Khirbet er-Ras in the Rephaim Valley, to the south-west of Jerusalem (Gibson and Edelstein 1985; see also the comments by Feig 1996: 3, who assumes, incorrectly I believe, that the terracing at the site is entirely post-Iron Age in date) (Figs. 4.5–4.6).

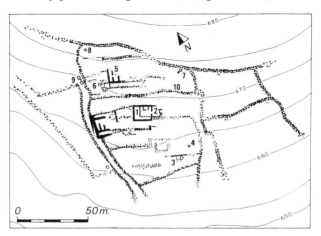

Fig. 4.5. *Khirbet er-Ras: overall plan of site which was in use
from the Iron Age through to the Ottoman period*

Another area of terraces with two structures, one of them of the four-room type, was investigated at the site of Nahal Zimri, to the north-east of Jerusalem (Gibson and Edelstein 1985: 144-45; Meitlis 1992: 9). Additional Iron Age terraces have been investigated at the following sites: Nahal Beit 'Arif, Khirbet Jema'in and at other sites in Samaria (Dar 1986a: 5-6, 37); Jerusalem (Tushingham 1985: 15; Gibson 1987: 87); Ramat Rahel (Aharoni 1965: 15); and Mas'ua (Eisenberg 1993a: 1280). Erosion fills which apparently originated from collapsed Iron Age terraces were investigated by A. Rosen (1986b: 66) in the area of Nahal Lachish in the western foothill zone. An Iron Age terrace has also been investigated at Tell Hesban in Jordan (La Bianca 1990: 151, Wall C.2:49). A system of agricultural terraces associated with a Persian-period farm was surveyed by Zertal (1992: 500, Fig. 468) at El-Quleh on Mount Ebal (for the archaeological evidence relating to the later terracing activities in Palestine, see Gibson 1995: 175-82).

Fig. 4.6. Reconstruction of the 'four-room' structure unearthed at Khirbet er-Ras

Conclusions

The available archaeological evidence, as we have seen, indicates that terracing was introduced into the highlands of Palestine at the beginning of the Early Bronze Age. It is not suprising that the earliest known use of terracing in the highlands should coincide with the introduction of plough agriculture in that area (cf. Sherratt 1981). However, terracing was clearly only practised on a limited scale during the Early Bronze Age and this situation was characteristic of the highlands with very little change until the eighth century BCE. No evidence supports the theory that the early Israelites (or Proto-Israelites) were responsible for inventing or introducing terracing into the highlands c. 1200 BCE. They simply made use of an existing technology without any special adaptations or innovations. This refutes the suggestion made by Dever (1992: 79), without any supporting evidence, that terracing, if it existed prior to the early Iron Age, had to have been 'unsystematic'. Hitherto, it has generally been assumed by archaeologists that the investigation of terraces would yield very little archaeological data. This view can now be shown to be totally incorrect. Moreover, landscape archaeology is a method which may facilitate such research.

Bibliography

Aharoni, Y.
    1965   'The Citadel of Ramat Rahel', *Archaeology* 18: 15-25.
    1979   *The Land of the Bible: A Historical Geography* (2nd rev. edn; London: Burns and Oates).
Ahlström, G.W.
    1982   'Where Did the Israelites Live?', *JNES* 41: 133-38.
    1986   *Who Were the Israelites?* (Winona Lake, IN: Eisenbrauns).
Albright, W.F.
    1961   *The Archaeology of Palestine* (rev. edn; Harmondsworth: Penguin Books).
Amitai, J. (ed.)
    1985   *Biblical Archaeology Today: Proceedings of the International Congress on Biblical Archaeology, Jerusalem, April 1984* (Jerusalem: Israel Exploration Society).
Biran, A., and J. Aviram (eds.)
    1993   *Biblical Archaeology Today, 1990. Proceedings of the Second International Congress on Biblical Archaeology* (Jerusalem: Israel Exploration Society).

Borowski, O.
1987   *Agriculture in Iron Age Israel* (Winona Lake, IN: Eisenbrauns).
1988   'Observations on Terracing, Plowing, Fallowing, etc. in the Early Iron Age', in LaBianca and Hopkins (eds.) 1988: 9-16.

Broshi, M.
1993   'The Population of Iron Age Palestine', in Biran and Aviram (eds.) 1993: 14-18.

Callaway, J.A.
1969   'The 1966 'Ai (Et-Tell) Excavations', *BASOR* 196: 2-16.
1976   'Excavating Ai (Et-Tell): 1964–1972', *BA* 39: 18-30.
1980   *The Early Bronze Age Citadel and Lower City at Ai (Et Tell)*, AASOR.
1985a   'Respondent', in Amitai (ed.) 1985: 72-78.
1985b   'A New Perspective on the Hill Country Settlement of Canaan in Iron Age I', in J.N. Tubb (ed.), *Palestine in the Bronze and Iron Ages: Papers in Honour of Olga Tufnell* (London: Institute of Archaeology): 31-49.

Callaway, J.A., and R.E. Cooley
1971   'A Salvage Excavation at Raddana, in Bireh', *BASOR* 201: 9-19.

Coote, R.B., and K.W. Whitelam
1987   *The Emergence of Early Israel in Historical Perspective* (Sheffield: Almond Press).

Dalman, G.
1932   *Arbeit und Sitte in Palestina* (vol. 2; Gütersloh: Bertelsmann).

Dar, S.
1986a   *Landscape and Pattern: An Archaeological Survey of Samaria, 800 BCE–636 CE* (Bar International Series, 308; Oxford: BAR).
1986b   'Hirbet Jemain: A First Temple Village in Western Samaria', in Dar and Safrai (eds.) 1986: 13-73 (Hebrew).

Dar, S. (ed.)
1992   *New Vistas in the Research of Ancient Agriculture and Economy of Eretz Israel. Proceedings of the 12th Conference Proceedings* (Ramat Gan: University of Bar Ilan) (Hebrew).

Dar, S., and Z. Safrai (eds.)
1986   *Shomron Studies* (Tel Aviv: Hakkibutz Hameuchad) (Hebrew).

Dar, S., Z. Safrai and Y. Tepper
1986   *Um Rihan: A Village of the Mishnah* (Tel Aviv: Hakkibutz Hameuchad) (Hebrew).

Dever, W.G.
1992   'Dever's Reply to Finkelstein, Gottwald and Zertal', in H. Shanks *et al.*, *The Rise of Ancient Israel* (Washington: Biblical Archaeology Society): 79-85.
1998   'Israelite Origins and the "Nomadic Ideal": Can Archaeology Separate Fact from Fiction?', in Gitin *et al.* (eds.) 1998: 220-37.

Dinur, U., and N. Feig
1993   'Eastern Part of the Map of Jerusalem (Sheet 17-13: Sites 429-544)', in I. Finkelstein and Y. Magen (eds.), *Archaeological Survey of the Hill Country of Benjamin* (Jerusalem: Israel Antiquities Authority): 339-427 (Hebrew).

Donkin, R.A.
    1979   *Agricultural Terracing in the Aboriginal New World* (Viking Fund Publications in Anthropology, 56; Tuscon: University of Arizona).

Eckholm, E.P.
    1975   'The Deterioration of Mountain Environments', *Science* 189: 764-70.

Edelstein, G.
    1993   'Nahal Rephaim: The Manahat Excavations', *NEAEHL* 4: 1281-82.

Edelstein, G., and I. Milevski
    1994   'The Rural Settlement of Jerusalem Re-evaluated: Surveys and Excavations in the Reph'aim Valley and Mevasseret Yerushalayim', *PEQ* 126: 2-23.

Edelstein, G., I. Milevski and S. Aurant
    1998   *Villages, Terraces, and Stone Mounds: Excavations at Manahat, Jerusalem, 1987–1989* (Jerusalem: Israel Antiquities Authority).

Eisenberg, E.
    1993a   'Nahal Rephaim', *NEAEHL* 1.4: 1277-80.
    1993b   'Nahal Rephaim: A Bronze Age Village in Southwestern Jerusalem', *Qadmoniot* 26: 82-95 (Hebrew).

Feig, N.
    1996   'New Discoveries in the Rephaim Valley', *PEQ* 128: 3-7.

Finkelstein, I.
    1985   'Respondent', in Amitai (ed.), 1985: 80-83.
    1988   *The Archaeology of the Israelite Settlement* (Jerusalem: Israel Exploration Society).
    1993   'Environmental Archaeology and Social History: Demographic and Economic Aspects of the Monarchic Period', in Biran and Aviram (eds.) 1993: 14-18.

Finkelstein, I., and R. Gophna
    1993   'Settlement, Demographic, and Economic Patterns in the Highlands of Palestine in the Chalcolithic and Early Bronze Periods and the Beginning of Urbanism', *BASOR* 289: 1-22.

Finkelstein, I., and N. Na'aman (eds.)
    1990   *From Nomadism to Monarchy* (Jerusalem: Y. Ben Zvi and the Israel Exploration Society).

Frendo, A.J.
    1992   'Five Recent Books on the Emergence of Ancient Israel: Review Article', *PEQ* 124: 144-51.

Frick, F.S.
    1985   *The Formation of the State in Ancient Israel: A Survey of Models and Theories* (Sheffield: Almond Press).

Gal, Z.
    1991a   *Map of Gazit (46)* (Jerusalem: Israel Antiquities Authority).
    1991b   'The Period of the Israelite Settlement in the Lower Galilee and the Jezreel Valley', *Ma'arav* 7: 101-15.

Geus, C.H.J. de
    1975   'The Importance of Archaeological Research into the Palestinian Agricultural Terraces, with an Excursus on the Hebrew Word *gbi*', *PEQ* 107: 65-74.

Gibson, S.
  1987   'The 1961–67 Excavations in the Armenian Garden', *PEQ* 119: 81-96.
  1995   'Landscape Archaeology and Ancient Agricultural Field Systems in
              Palestine' (PhD thesis, Institute of Archaeology, University College,
              London).
Gibson, S., and G. Edelstein
  1985   'Investigating Jerusalem's Rural Landscape', *Levant* 17: 139-55.
Gibson, S., B. Ibbs and A. Kloner
  1991   'The Sataf Project of Landscape Archaeology in the Judaean Hills: A Pre-
              liminary Report on Four Seasons of Survey and Excavation (1987–89)',
              Levant 23: 29-54.
Gibson, S., and D.M. Jacobson
  1997   *Below the Temple Mount in Jerusalem: A Sourcebook on the Cisterns,*
              Subterranean Chambers and Conduits of the Haram al-Sharif (BAR
              International Series, 637; Oxford: Tempus Reperatum).
Gibson, S., and E. Lass
  2001   *The Modi'in Archaeological Project: Landscape Archaeology in the*
              Northern Shephelah (Jerusalem: Israel Antiquities Authority, forth-
              coming).
Gitin, S., A. Mazar and E. Stern (eds.)
  1998   *Mediterranean Peoples in Transition: Thirteenth to Early Tenth*
              Centuries BCE (Jerusalem: Israel Exploration Society).
Glueck, N.
  1942   'Further Explorations in Eastern Palestine', *BASOR* 86: 14-24.
Golomb, B., and Y. Kedar
  1971   'Ancient Agriculture in the Galilee Mountains', *IEJ* 21: 136-40.
Gottwald, N.K.
  1985   'The Israelite Settlement as a Social Revolutionary Movement', in Amitai
              (ed.) 1985: 34-46.
Harel, M.
  1977   *Dwellers of the Mountain: The Geography of Jewish Habitation of*
              Ancient Judea (Jerusalem: Carta).
Herr, L.G.
  1992   'The Madaba Plains Project', *Syria* LXX: 231-35.
Herrmann, S.
  1985   'Basic Factors of Israelite Settlement in Canaan', in Amitai (ed.) 1985:
              47-53.
Hopkins, D.C.
  1985   *The Highlands of Canaan: Agricultural Life in the Early Iron Age*
              (Sheffield: Almond Press).
Kempinski, A.
  1992   'How Profoundly Canaanized Were the Early Israelites?', *ZDPV* 108: 1-7.
Kochavi, M. (ed.)
  1972   *Judaea, Samaria and the Golan: Archaeological Survey 1967–1968*
              (Jerusalem: ASI) (Hebrew).
LaBianca, O.S.
  1990   *Hesban 1. Sedentarization and Nomadization: Food Cycles at Hesban*
              and Vicinity in Transjordan (Berrien Springs: Andrews University).

LaBianca, O.S., and D.C. Hopkins (eds.)
    1988   *Early Israelite Agriculture: Reviews of David C. Hopkins' Book* The Highland of Canaan (Occasional Papers of the Institute of Archaeology, 1; Berrien Springs: Andrews University).

MacDonald, B., G.O. Rollefson, E.B. Banning, B.F. Byrd and C. D'Annibale
    1983   'The Wadi el Hasa Archaeological Survey 1982: A Preliminary Report', *ADAJ* XXVII: 311-23.

Maddin, R., J.D. Muhly and T.S. Wheeler
    1977   'How the Iron Began', *Scientific American* 237: 122-31.

Marfoe, L.
    1979   'The Integrative Transformation: Patterns of Sociopolitical Organization in Southern Syria', *BASOR* 234: 1-42.

Mazar, A.
    1990   'Jerusalem and its Vicinity in the Iron I', in Finkelstein and Na'aman (eds.) 1990: 70-91.

Meitlis, Y.
    1992   'Agriculture of the Rural Farms Around Jerusalem', in Dar (ed.) 1992: 3-13 (Hebrew).

Meshel, Z.
    1987   'Are Terraces Part of the Natural Landscape?', in Z. Avni (ed.), *Agricultural Terraces in the Judaean Hills. Proceedings of the Jewish National Fund Conference held at Sataf* (Jerusalem: Jewish National Fund) (Hebrew).

Miroschedji, P. de
    1992   'Tel Yarmut, 1992', *IEJ* 42: 265-72.

Ofer, A.
    1984   'Khirbet Umm et-Tala', *Excavations and Surveys in Israel* 3: 104.

Orni, E., and E. Efrat
    1980   *Geography of Israel* (4th rev. edn; Jerusalem: Israel Universities).

Ritter, C.
    1866   *The Comparative Geography of Palestine and the Sinaitic Peninsula* (4 vols.; Edinburgh: T. & T. Clark).

Roberts, B.K.
    1987   'Landscape Archaeology', in Wagstaff (ed.) 1987: 77-95.

Ron, Z.Y.D.
    1966   'Agricultural Terraces in the Judaean Mountains', *IEJ* 16: 33-49, 111-22.
    1977   'The Distribution of Agricultural Terraces in the Hills of Jerusalem', in A. Shmueli *et al.* (eds.), *Judea and Samaria: Studies in Settlement Geography* (Jerusalem: Canaan), I: 210-29 (Hebrew).

Rosen, A.
    1986a   'Environmental Change and Settlement at Tel Lachish, Israel', *BASOR* 263: 55-60.
    1986b   *Cities of Clay: The Geoarchaeology of Tells* (Chicago: University of Chicago).
    n.d.   'The Social Response to Environmental Change in Early Bronze Age Canaan' (Unpublished manuscript, forthcoming).

Rowton, M.B.
    1967   'Woodlands of Ancient Western Asia', *JNES* 26: 261-77.

Rozenson, Y., H. Zoref and G. Bashan
  1994   *A Tour Following the Sources in Sataf and its Vicinity* (Internal publication of the Jewish National Fund) (Hebrew).

Sherratt, A.G.
  1981   'Plough and Pastoralism: Aspects of the Secondary Products Revolution', in I. Hodder *et al.* (eds.), *Patterns of the Past: Studies in Honour of David Clarke* (Cambridge: Cambridge Univesity Press): 261-305.

Spencer, J.E., and G.A. Hale
  1961   'The Origin, Nature and Distribution of Agricultural Terracing', *Pacific Viewpoint* 2: 1-40.

Stager, L.E.
  1975   'Ancient Agriculture in the Judaean Desert: A Case Study of the Buqe'ah Valley in the Iron Age' (PhD thesis, Harvard University).
  1982   'The Archaeology of the East Slope of Jerusalem and the Terraces of the Kidron', *JNES* 41: 111-21.
  1985   'The Archaeology of the Family in Ancient Israel', *BASOR* 260: 1-35.

Steiner, M.
  1993   'The Jebusite Ramp of Jerusalem: The Evidence from the Macalister, Kenyon and Shiloh Excavations', in Biran and Aviram (eds.) 1993: 585-88.

Stekelis, M., and T. Yizraeli
  1963   'Excavations at Nahal Oren: A Preliminary Report', *IEJ* 13: 1-12.

Thompson, T.L.
  1979   *The Settlement of Palestine in the Bronze Age* (Wiesbaden: Verlag).
  1992   *Early History of the Israelite People: From the Written and Archaeological Sources* (Leiden: E.J. Brill).

Tushingham, A.D.
  1985   *Excavations in Jerusalem, 1961–1967* (vol. 1; Toronto: British School of Aarchaeology in Jerusalem).

Tsuk, T.
  1998   'Water Systems in the Middle Bronze Age (2000–1550 BCE)', in S. Gibson and D. Amit (eds.), *Water Installations in Antiquity* (Israel Antiquities Authority Booklet, 1; Jerusalem: Israel Antiquities Authority): 25-31 (Hebrew).

Wagstaff, M.
  1992   'Agricultural Terraces: The Vasilikos Valley, Cyprus', in M. Bell and J. Boardman (eds.), *Past and Present Soil Erosion: Archaeological and Geographical Perspectives* (Oxbow Monographs, 2; Oxford: Oxford University Press).

Wagstaff, M. (ed.)
  1987   *Landscape and Culture: Geographical and Archaeological Perspectives* (Oxford: Basil Blackwell).

Waldbaum, J.C.
  1978   *From Bronze to Iron: The Transition from the Bronze Age to the Iron Age in the Eastern Mediterranean* (Studies in Mediterranean Archaeology, 54; Göteborg: Astroms).

Warburton, E.
    1843   *The Crescent and the Cross, or Romance and Realities of Eastern Travel*
                (London: Hurst and Blackett).
Wilson, C.T.
    1906   *Peasant Life in the Holy Land* (London: Murray).
Zertal, A.
    1987   'The Water Factor During the Settlement Process of the Israelites in
                Canaan', in M. Heltzer and E. Lipinski (eds.), *Society and Economy in the
                Eastern Mediterranean (1500–1000)* (Leuven): 341-52.
    1992   *The Manasseh Hill Country Survey: The Shechem Syncline* (Haifa: The
                University of Haifa Press and the Ministry of Defense) (Hebrew).
    1998   'The Iron Age I Culture in the Hill-country of Canaan: A Manassite Per-
                spective', in Gitin *et al.* (eds.) 1998: 238-50.

Part II

TEMPLES, CULT AND ICONOGRAPHY

5

THE HIGH PLACES OF BIBLICAL DAN

Avraham Biran

The subject of this volume, the archaeology of Israel in the time of the monarchy, is a challenging one in that it links two different disciplines —the Bible and archaeology. Practically all the information about the Israelite monarchy comes from the Bible, while archaeology reveals the physical remains of the period. However, the study of the Bible is governed by its own discipline, and archaeological research is dependent on entirely different principles. A comprehensive picture can only be drawn by developing a dialogue between the two. Thus biblical texts can help interpret archaeological remains and these in turn can serve to illustrate biblical passages.

From 1 Kgs 12.26-29 we learn that a high place existed at Dan in the time of the Monarchy. Jeroboam, for political reasons, sets a golden calf at Dan in the second half of the tenth century BCE. He also 'makes' a *beit bamoth*, a house or shrine of high places and appoints priests who are not of the sons of Levi. No further information is available about the cult at Dan. However, the reference to sacrifices and to 'priests of high places' at Beit El where a golden calf was also set, suggests the same for Dan. This possibility is supported by the mention of Dan in v. 30, 'for the people went before the one unto Dan' which appears to emphasize the centrality of Dan in the cult of northern Israel.

The identification of biblical Dan with Tel Dan, formerly Tel el Qadi, at the source of the river Jordan, was confirmed by a bilingual inscription 'To the God who is in Dan' discovered in the course of the excavations (Biran 1981). The inscription, dated to the Hellenistic period, came to light at the northern end of the site where an elaborate complex of Iron Age structures was found. These include a raised platform, a square enclosure with steps and an altar, a room with an altar, iron shovels and jars containing ashes, two other altars and various other installations. Many objects associated with cult were found—incense stands, seven-wick oil lamps, pithoi with snake decoration, a figurine of a woman, a royal sceptre (Biran 1994: 159-83, 1996: 32-34).

The archaeological discoveries supplement the meagre information in 1 Kings 12 and point to the existence of a major cult centre at Dan in the time of the monarchy in the tenth–eighth centuries BCE. These discoveries serve not only to illustrate the activities taking place at Dan but also their development. These reached their zenith during the reign of Jeroboam II who considerably extended the borders of his kingdom to the north and east. The centrality of the cult at the high place of Dan in the eighth century BCE may have led the prophet Amos—who prophesied in the days of Jeroboam II—to castigate the people for saying 'Thy God, O Dan, liveth' (Amos 8.14).

Important and central as was the high place near the spring, it was not the only one at Dan. Early in the excavation of the Israelite gate complex at the foot of the rampart on the south side of the tel, two structures were uncovered (Biran 1994: 239-41). The row of stones along the east face of the northern gate tower was identified as a bench where the city elders sat, while the decorated bases probably point to a canopied structure for a king or a statue of a deity. The *massebah*, the basalt standing stone at the structure's south-western corner (Fig. 5.1) further suggests the existence of cult. If so, this structure may well represent a high place at the gate such as the one mentioned in 2 Kgs 23.8 (Emerton 1994). The discovery in the following seasons of a 60 cm high well-worked ashlar in front of the outer gate seemed to support this view (Biran 1994: 244-45, 1996: 13).

The renewed excavations in the gate area 20 years later brought to light additional architectural elements which represent installations connected with cult or a high place at the gate. The most significant discovery, after removing the accumulated debris of the Assyrian destruction, were five *masseboth* at the foot of the city wall and a large number of votive vessels (Biran 1994: 244-45). These included incense bowls, seven-wick oil lamps, plates and bowls. Some of these vessels were in a niche next to the *masseboth*. Bones of sheep and goats were also found. The placement of both this niche and the canopied dais in the paved courtyard between the gates is striking (Biran and Naveh 1993: 83).

Fig. 5.1. *Massebah at the canopied structure of the main gate*

Among the remains in the Assyrian destruction level was an especially significant limestone ashlar slab 0.14–16 m thick (Fig. 5.2). Its
upper surface measures 0.72 × 0.52 m. A round, flat-bottomed depression is carved into the face, just a few centimeters from one long edge
and slightly off-centre between the two short edges of the block. The
depression is approximately 0.29 m in diameter, 2–2.25 cm deep
around the edge and reaches a depth of 3.5 cm at the centre. Parallel to
the long edge, a channel extends from either side of the depression to
reach a short edge of the block. The channels are approximately 0.10 m
wide. It is possible that this slab was used in some libation ceremony.
Perhaps a parallel can be found in the carved limestone ashlar found
near the upper gate.

Early in the eighth century BCE an upper gate, with an outer gate and
a paved courtyard between them were built. No doubt the purpose of
the new construction was to strengthen the defences of the city when
the fortifications at the foot of the mound were no longer considered
sufficient (Biran 1994: 249-53). However, the builders did not neglect
ritual needs. To the right of the entrance to the upper gate were four
standing stones and a fifth, fallen, one (Fig. 5.3). The similarity to the
five *masseboth* of the outer gate mentioned above led us to conclude
that also here, by the upper gate, were five *masseboth*. These, together

Fig. 5.2. *Limestone ashlar slab found near the outer gate*

Fig. 5.3. *Masseboth at the entrance to the upper gate*

with the structures at the western edge of the new paved courtyard, appear to constitute another high place at the gate.

Directly opposite the eastern entrance to the courtyard, at its western edge, is a niche 5.00 × 2.50 m with a raised plastered floor and border of small ashlars (Biran 1996: 26). Set into the left corner of the niche is a poorly preserved dais measuring 1.25 m wide and c. 1.60 m from front to back. Its front edge is a single 1.25 × 0.52 × 0.18 m ashlar laid crosswise. A second ashlar extends 0.80 m forward from the back wall forming part of the right edge of the dais and stands 0.45 m higher than the front ashlar (Fig. 5.4). Although there is no direct evidence, it is possible that gaps in the structure may provide space for canopy posts not unlike those at the entrance to the main gate.

Fig. 5.4. *Niche and dias at the upper gate*

Roughly in the centre of the niche area was a limestone ashlar 0.29 m thick, found broken in two and lying upside-down on the floor. Righted and put together, its face measured 0.82 × 0.50 m, while its base was approximately 0.80 × 0.48 m (Fig. 5.5). A rectangular 0.48 × 0.25 m depression is carved into the face 6 cm from one long edge and 0.20 m —slightly off-centre—from one short edge. A 4 cm wide groove, also slightly off-centre, leads from the depression to the second long edge of the stone. The depression and groove are very well-carved: the floor of the depression and the groove slope in an almost clean line, beginning at a depth of 4 cm at the back of the depression and reaching 6.5 cm at the front of the depression and 9 cm at the long front edge of the stone. This configuration strongly suggests the presence of a liquid in conjunction with the use of this stone. A small—c. 5 × 6 cm—'cup' may have been carved into the widest corner of the 'frame' around the depression, near the midpoint of the diagonal between the corner of the stone and the depression. The function of the stone is not clear but perhaps it was a receptacle for offerings or for a libation ceremony connected with the ritual of the high place.

Fig. 5.5. *Limestone ashlar at the upper gate*

If our interpretation of the archaeological remains is correct it would appear that we have at Dan, in addition to the main shrine at the spring, a high place dated to the ninth century BCE between the lower gates, and a high place at the upper gate dated to the eighth century BCE (Fig. 5.6).

More evidence for cultic activities outside the entrance to the city came to light. The flagstone courtyard outside the gates was traced 42 m eastward from the outer gate. Here, at the foot of the city wall at the very eastern end of the excavation, five more *masseboth* were discovered (Biran and Naveh 1995: 6). Indeed, it is evident from yet another discovery that the practice of cult found at the entrance to the city was entrenched in the memory and custom of the people .

On the accumulated debris of the Assyrian conquest a 4.50 × 2.50 m construction surrounding three, possibly four, basalt standing monoliths was found. In front of the largest monolith was a basalt bowl on a carved stone set on a flat base (Biran and Naveh 1995: 2-3). The whole construction is the best example of a *masseboth* shrine or high place discovered at Dan. Dated to the seventh century BCE by the pottery and confirmed by the analysis of the ashes in and near the bowl (Segal and Carmi 1996: 82) it appears that the inhabitants of Dan continued the hallowed practices of their ancestors. In the seventh century BCE, following the Assyrian conquest, the city enjoyed a period of prosperity and its buildings extended to the very edge of the crest of the site. The

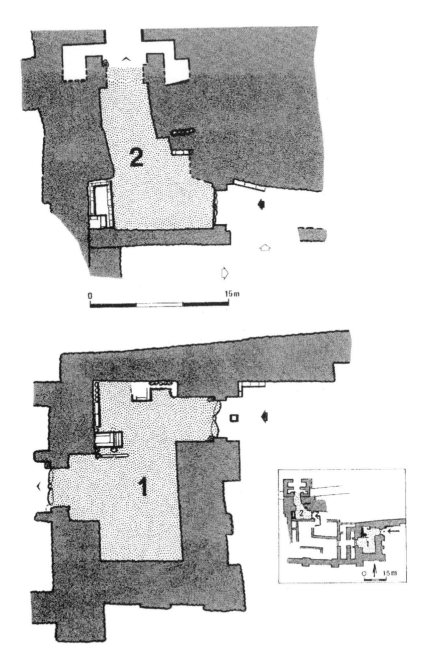

Fig. 5.6. *The high places at the upper and lower gates*

major sanctuary and high place near the spring continued to function, and another one was built at the foot of the mound, near the approach to the city. Whether this *masseboth* shrine or high place was intended for the inhabitants or for the visitors coming to the city cannot be determined, but that the cult at the entrance to the city continued even after the Assyrian conquest seems evident from the archaeological discoveries.

Dan could not possibly be the only site with cult remains at the gates. As more excavations of gates of antiquity continue, other similar elements will probably come to light. The Bible, for reasons of its own, is silent about their existence.

The discussion of the high places at Dan cannot be concluded without calling attention to the Aramaic victory stele which mentions a king of Israel and a king of the House of David (Biran and Naveh 1993, 1995). The smashed fragments of the stele were found on the pavement outside the lower gate and below the post-Assyrian conquest shrine. It is a fair assumption that the original setting of the stele was near where the fragments were found, that is, at the entrance to the city. This would be the natural place for a victorious king to set his stele. The choice of Dan may well have been prompted, in addition to its being the largest city in the region, because of its high places at the gate.

Bibliography

Biran, A.

1981   'To the God who Is in Dan', *Temples and High Places in Biblical Times* (Jerusalem: Nelson Glueck School of Biblical Archaeology, Hebrew Union College-Jewish Institute of Religion.

1994   *Biblical Dan* (Jerusalem: Israel Exploration Society and Hebrew Union College-Jewish Institute of Religion.

1996   *DAN I: A Chronicle of the Excavations, the Pottery Neolithic, the Early Bronze Age and the Middle Bronze Age Tombs* (Jerusalem, Nelson Glueck School of Biblical Archaeology, Hebrew Union College-Jewish Institute of Religion.

Biran, A., and J. Naveh

1993   'An Aramaic Stele Fragment from Tel Dan', *IEJ* 43: 81-98.

1995   'The Tel Dan Inscription: A New Fragment', *IEJ* 45: 1-18.

Emerton, J.A.

1994   'The High Places of the Gates in 2 Kings XXIII 8', *VT* 44.4: 455-67.

Segal, D., and I. Carmi

1996   'Rehovot Radiocarbon Date List V', *Atiqot* 29: 82.

6

THE DATE OF THE TEMPLE AT ARAD:
REASSESSMENT OF THE STRATIGRAPHY AND THE
IMPLICATIONS FOR THE HISTORY OF RELIGION IN JUDAH

Ze'ev Herzog

The temple uncovered at Arad is, as yet, the only such Iron Age structure exposed in Israel. Its excavation over 30 years ago, under the directorship of Y. Aharoni, evoked great interest among archaeologists, historians and Bible scholars. The presence of a temple within a royal fortress in southern Judah bears considerable consequences for the study of the administration of religion in the monarchical period. It allows us to investigate the complex and continuously changing relationship between the archaeological and the biblical records.

Unfortunately Aharoni did not publish the full account of the excavations,before his untimely death in 1976. He was only able to provide a short description of the temple (Y. Aharoni 1968), while more detailed accounts, based on his preliminary observations, were offered by his team members (M. Aharoni 1981; Herzog *et al.* 1984). These accounts were challenged by several scholars who suggested various interpretations of different aspects of the material: of the date of the casemate fortress (Yadin 1965; Nylander 1967); of the date of bowls bearing inscriptions (Cross 1979); and of the basic stratigraphy and dating of the Iron Age Strata (Zimhoni 1985; Mazar and Netzer 1986; Ussishkin 1988).

The conclusions presented here are based on a meticulous re-examination of the complete stratigraphical information conducted by myself and my team in 1995–96.[1] The analysis of every basket, every

1. The research was supported by a grant from Tel Aviv University, Basic Research Foundation. Participants in the team included Linda Meiberg and Rachel

wall segment and every level in the excavation record, never conducted before, has led us to a new and more reliable set of conclusions about the history of the site. It has also provided us with the ability to deal with the criticisms made by different commentators.[2]

Tel Arad is located on the south-eastern edge of the Hebron hills, facing the wilderness of Judah to the east and the Beersheba valley to the south. The site was first occupied in the Chalcolithic period and developed into a large fortified city in the Early Bronze Age (Amiran *et al.* 1978; Amiran and Ilan 1992). After a gap of 1500 years, a gap typical to this marginal zone (Herzog 1994), a small settlement was erected on the eastern hillock of the site during the eleventh century BCE (Stratum 12).[3] A fortress in the Iron Age II soon replaced the settlement, with no sign of violent destruction. The 50 × 50 m large stronghold was destroyed and rebuilt five times throughout this period (Strata 11–6). The site was also utilized sporadically during the Persian, Hellenistic, Roman and early Arab periods.

The most significant findings at Tel Arad are the large assemblages of pottery unearthed in each of the fortress's destruction layers, as well as the large collection of Hebrew (and Aramaic) inscriptions, fully published by Y. Aharoni (1981), and the unique temple which is the focus of this article.

The Stratigraphy of the Temple

The temple consists of a main broad-room hall, with an open niche in the centre of its western long side (analogous to the *debir* in the OT description of the Solomonic temple in Jerusalem). In front of the main hall was a spacious courtyard in which stood a large sacrificial altar. Auxiliary rooms were located on the northern side of the courtyard and apparently on its southern side as well. Once the presence of the temple was recognized at the end of the second season, the temple area was expansively exposed. The early phase of the temple was attributed to Stratum 11 and its second stage to Strata 10 to 8 (or even 7 in the early preliminary reports).

Nahumi (registration and stratigraphy analysis); Lily Avitz-Singer (pottery analysis); and Ora Paran (plans).

2. The full report will include the work of Miriam Aharoni on pottery of selected loci. For an interim report (in Hebrew) of the Arad fortress mound, see Herzog 1997.

3. The date of this settlement is discussed below.

Nonetheless, the information on the stratigraphy of the temple area was limited due to several obstacles. For one, a considerable part of the main hall was demolished when the inner wall of a late casemate fortress was erected through the room. Secondly, the southern side of the courtyard was destroyed when the bedrock layer underneath it collapsed into the water system causing a large section of the temple, by then in ruins, to fall into the depression. Thirdly, the foundations of structures of the Hellenistic and Roman periods were erected on a low level and caused the removal of many of the remains of Iron Age Strata 8–6. In addition, the attempt by the excavators to preserve the walls of the temple prevented the excavations below them (Fig. 6.1). Finally, a strong impact of the 'biblical archaeology' paradigm directed both Yohanan Aharoni (1968, 1976) and his crew members (Herzog *et al*. 1984) to look for a simplistic correlation between the archaeological data and biblical references. This method, now viewed as oversimplified, is considered a most disturbing and misleading approach.

Fig. 6.1. *General view of the temple area: note the later casemate wall on the left and the depression at the bottom of the picture*

All the above factors combined with the discontinuity of the analysis of the excavation material due to Aharoni's involvement in new projects at Lachish and Beersheba, contributed to the misinterpretation put forward in the preliminary accounts. These shortcomings also paved the way for a varied set of proposals of alternative reconstruction of the temple's history and chronology.

My re-examination of the available data, and the new understanding of the complex stratigraphy of the site, relates directly to the association of the temple with the different strata at Arad. Accordingly, these observations required a reassessment of the stratum of the temple's construction, the duration of its use, and finally, the nature and date of its abandonment. This fresh analysis also provided us with the ability to consider the critical discussions and to evaluate their possible acceptance or rejection.

The Debate over the Stratigraphy and the Chronology of the Temple at Arad

The main point of dispute among the critics of the date of the temple at Arad was the assumed relationship between the dismantling of the temple and the erection of the late casemate wall that cut through the main hall of the temple: 'the casemate wall cut through the temple quite deliberately' (Y. Aharoni 1968: 26). Aharoni and his team maintained that the casemate wall dates to Stratum 6, which constitutes the last Iron Age fortress (Aharoni and Amiran 1964; Herzog *et al.* 1984; Herzog 1987; M. Aharoni 1993). This opinion was widely attacked because many dressed ashlar stones of the casemate wall bear the sign of a toothed chisel, believed not to be used before the Persian period (Yadin 1965; Nylander 1967; Laperrousaz 1979; Mazar and Netzer 1986). Renewed examination of the stratigraphical evidence revealed that part of the casemate wall was constructed over the fills that accumulated in the depression formed by the collapse of the bedrock roof of one of the water reservoirs. The fill contained pottery sherds of the Hellenistic period, thus dating the casemate walls to a later phase of this period. Moreover, study of the distribution of stones bearing the combed dressing showed that they were incorporated into walls in a confined area. Ashlar stones were found only in the western and northern sides of the mound. This led me to a conclusion that the casemate walls must belong to the Hellenistic period, as was first claimed by Imanuel Dunayevsky and Y. Yadin in the mid-sixties (Yadin 1965).

Another important new observation suggests that this casemate-fortress had never been completed. Tracing its actual remains reveals that only the western and northern wings were partially erected. At this stage a change in the plan occurred. A solid tower was incorporated into the constructed units and together they formed a rather modest fort. The occasional association of the casemate wall with late Iron Age pottery must have resulted from the construction method of the wall, built into the earlier debris without a foundation trench, as suggested previously by A. Mazar and E. Netzer (1986).

The course of the inner casemate wall through the main hall of the temple is purely accidental. At the same time, however, this late date of the casemate wall must not affect our understanding of history and the phases of use of the temple itself. Now, when no relationship is assumed between the casemate fortress and the temple, the date of the temple must be considered ultimately on the ground of its own floor levels and the finds recorded on them.

Additional critical stratigraphical observation made by Ussishkin led him to a most radical conclusion concerning the chronology of the Arad sanctuary (Ussishkin 1988). He noticed that the water channel that conducted water to the underground system runs under the northern wall of the main hall of the temple. He claims that since the wall of the main hall was constructed over fill layers that covered the channel, the temple must belong to a later period. In addition, he observed in the published pictures of the excavated *debir* a line of destruction debris that he dates to the very end of the fortress's history. He concludes that the temple must have been in use only during the last phase of Arad's fortress, namely during Strata 7 and 6.

Careful examination of all the available data related to this part of the site brought to light entirely different observations. First, it is absolutely clear that the temple was not destroyed by conflagration. The superb state of the white limestone incense altars, as well as all the rest of the temple's interior, show no signs of fire. The diagonal line of fire visible in the pictures of the *debir* clearly cuts into the remains of the temple from above, down into the area south of the *debir*. This diagonal debris definitely resulted from the collapse and burning of the structure located there.

When excavations at this spot were completed during the fourth and fifth seasons, we realized that the burnt layers collapsed into a hollow space. One of the volunteers almost fell down the cavity while digging up the burnt debris. At the bottom of this spot was found the well-built entrance into a secret passage ('postern') leading through the fortress's solid wall. This seems to provide the explanation for the particular stratigraphical situation at this location. The severe fire and the sloping line of debris suggest that the supporting framework of the shaft and the stairs leading down were made out of wood. The structure was set on fire, apparently with the destruction of Stratum 6, and the burnt debris fell into the demolished shaft. This conflagration destroyed the upper part of the southern wall of the debir, and burnt the outer face of the temple's main hall. The diagonal line of debris may not be of any use in dating the period of use of the temple, since at the time of this event, the temple had already been buried under a thick layer of fill for decades (Fig. 6.2).

Fig. 6.2. *The diagonal burnt layer cutting into the shaft from above. The* debir *was not affected by the conflagration*

Secondly, we should consider Ussishkin's critical claim about the stratigraphical relationship between the temple and the water channel that ran under it. He maintained that the temple must have been built in a later period than the water channel. Since Ussishkin considers Strata 10–8 as three phases of a eighth century fortress, the temple, in his view, must be assigned to Strata 7 and 6 dating to seventh–sixth centuries BCE. In this case Ussishkin's basic assumption is erroneous. The level of the bottom of the water channel is over 3 m below the foundations of the temple's wall. Therefore, the narrow channel could have been hewn through the hill's bedrock at such a depth, as a tunnel, disregarding the period of the temple. The more crucial stratigraphical and typological considerations relate to the absolute levels of the floors of the temple in comparison to Strata 7–6. If Ussishkin had this information at hand he would surely have hesitated to assign the temple to Stratum 7 whose floor levels elsewhere in the fortress are about 2.5 m above the temple's floor level. Moreover, the pottery found on the floors of the temple and its immediate neighbouring structures is definitely earlier than Strata 7 or 6.

The final opposition regarding the chronology of the temple relates to the date of two flat bowls bearing a peculiar inscription. The bowls were found on the bench in front of the altar, attributed to Stratum 10. Each of the bowls bore two incised letters. The first sign is clearly the letter *qop*. The second sign was taken by Aharoni to be the symbol for the Hebrew *Qorban* (Y. Aharoni 1981: 181). Cross (1979) suggested that the second sign was the Phoenician *shin* of the seventh century BCE. This view contributed to the chronological confusion regarding the date of the temple (e.g. Dever 1982: n. 11) . But the debate is seemingly solved by the reading by Rainey of the second letter as an archaic *kap*; thus both letters may stand for *qodesh kohanim* (Rainey in Herzog *et al.* 1984: 32).

The Erection of the Temple

One of the most revolutionary observations relates to the attribution of the first phase of the temple to Stratum 11. In this Stratum the first fortress was erected at the site, protected by a casemate wall. The finds in this stratum are attributed to the tenth century BCE and correlated to the time of the Solomonic United Monarchy. The construction of the temple contemporaneously with the Stratum 11 fortress was taken for granted (Y. Aharoni 1968: 18-19; Herzog *et al.* 1984: 6-8). However, a fresh observation of the elements of the temple related to Stratum 11 raised serious doubt as to the validity of this association. Floors and pavements in the main temple and in the courtyard do not provide much assistance since the same levels were considered to be in use in both Strata 11 and 10. Our new observation suggests that the builders of the first temple removed most, if not all, of the floors of Stratum 11.

The basic consideration in ascribing an early phase of the temple to Stratum 11 relied on the interpretation given to a low plastered bench uncovered at the foot of the southern side of the sacrificial altar of

Stratum 10. The bench was assumed to be part of an earlier altar, used in Stratum 11 and dismantled almost completely when the temple was rebuilt in Stratum 10. It was conjectured that a remnant of the supposed altar was incorporated in the new installation, built slightly off the older line and forming a step in front of the Stratum 10 altar. This interpretation was disproved quite accidentally. During long years of neglect of the site the southern side of the altar fell apart. Although regrettable, this incident allowed us to look into the structure of the foundations of the altar at this side. When the spot was cleaned of the collapsed debris (prior to the reconstruction of the altar), we realized that the bench did not continue under the altar but was initially constructed as a step in front of the altar and concurrent with it (Fig. 6.3).

Fig. 6.3. *Excavation under the sacrificial altar of Stratum 10 disproved the alleged presence of an earlier (Stratum 11) altar*

Most of the walls of the main hall in the Arad sanctuary had a single construction phase and were attributed to consecutive Strata. When the walls dated only to Stratum 11 are singled out, a different picture emerges. The wall reconstructed as the northern side of the main hall did not turn to the south but continued westwards to meet the casemate fortifications. Segments of a parallel wall were found to the south, connected by a stone pavement. Another stone pavement was uncovered under the '*debir*' with a segment of a third wall further to the south. These three architectural elements obliterate the basis for reconstruction of the temple in Stratum 11. When all the elements attributed only to

Stratum 11 are drawn the remains of several large structures built of
solid walls are portrayed (Fig. 6.4). The building on the north-western
side of the fortress of Stratum 11 may have served as a managerial unit,
but it was not a temple. The erection of the first temple must be attributed to Stratum 10.

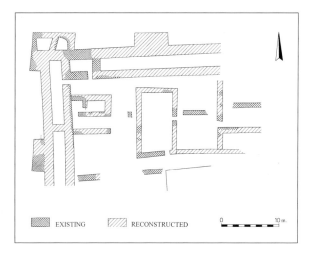

EXISTING   RECONSTRUCTED   0   10 m.

Fig. 6.4. *The north-western corner of the fortress (location of the
later temple) in Stratum 11 according to the new observations*

Utilization of the Temple at Arad

The initial stage of the temple corresponds to the construction of a new
fortress at Arad, assigned as Stratum 10 (Fig. 6.5). In this stage a solid
wall surrounded the stronghold, partly reusing the old casemate
foundation by filling up its rooms with stone rubble. On the eastern side
of the fortress only the inner casemate was incorporated into the solid
wall and a new imposing city gate was erected in the centre of this side.
The construction of the underground water reservoirs (located partly
below the temple's courtyard) and the addition of the earthen glacis
(supported by a low retaining wall) around the fortress are also assigned
to this stratum.

The temple occupied the western quarter of the fortress. The outer
(average) dimensions of the building are 17.50 × 12.00 m with the
debir protruding an additional 1.80 m. The main hall of the sanctuary
measures 10.50 × 2.90 m internally, and the remains of benches made
of stone and mud were observed along its walls. Aharoni looked for

architectural similarity between the building at Arad and the Solomonic temple in Jerusalem (Y. Aharoni 1968: 21-22). However, the basic architectural concept of the two structures is different: the main hall in the Solomonic temple is a long-room while the equivalent unit at Arad is a typical broad-room. It appears that the Arad temple resembles the shape of the common domestic unit of the period, that is, the 'four-room-house' (Herzog 1981).

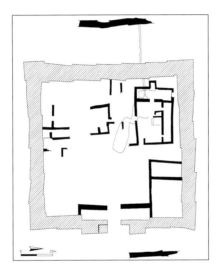

Fig. 6.5. *The fortress of Stratum 10, including the first phase of the temple*

The *debir* niche forms a compartment only 1.80 × 1.10 m, paved with large stone slabs and approached by a single step. A shallow depression in the large stone slab on the right side of the entrance to the *debir* and a recess in the brick wall of the main hall on the opposite (left) side evidently indicate the presence of a wooden door that could close off this small compartment (Fig. 6.6).

The courtyard in front of the sanctuary measures 12.00 × 7.50 m. On the north side of the courtyard stood the sacrificial altar, 2.40 × 2.20 m large and about 1.50 m high. It was built of unhewn fieldstones laid in mud mortar. A large flint stone rested on top of the altar, girdled by plastered shallow channels. Rainey suggested that a metal grill be laid on top of this stone (Rainey 1994: 338). A stone step, or bench, was constructed at the foot of the southern side of the altar. The step was coated with white plaster that was also preserved over the lower part of the eastern side of the altar. A small compartment was built adjacent to the western side of the altar. Red-slipped clay incense-burner made of two parts (a bowl and a stand), and a large oil lamp found inside the room, suggests that this was a storeroom for ceremonial articles.

Fig. 6.6. *The* debir *in Stratum 10. Note the recess in the brick wall on the left*

The second phase of the temple's use corresponds to Stratum 9. In this phase the western wall of the main hall, north of the *debir*, was widened by an inner addition, constructed over an earlier bench. The *debir* was rebuilt with a new stone wall on the northern side and a raised platform made of roughly squared stone slabs was erected at its north-western corner. An oblong stone stelae with rounded corners and remnants of red paint on its short end was found lying to the south of the platform. Two beautifully carved stone incense altars, or offering tables according to alternative interpretation (Haran 1993), were uncovered at the entrance into the *debir*. They had been laid on their sides and were buried under a wall assigned by me to Stratum 8 (Fig. 6.7). The stelae and the incense altars found in the *debir* must have been used in Stratum 9. We may presume that the same or similar apparatus furnished the *debir* in the first stage of the temple in Stratum 10. Two flint stone slabs were found incorporated in the walls of the *debir*. Their crude shape does not support Aharoni's speculation that these were older stelae (Y. Aharoni 1968: 19). Rather, they seem to be simply large construction stones. Consequently these stones may not support a claim that two (or three) deities were simultaneously worshipped in the temple of Arad (Ahlström 1975: 82).

Fig. 6.7. *The* debir *as found in the excavations*

In the courtyard the floor level was raised about 1.20 m so that the sacrificial altar projected only about 40 cm. A stone-lined basin was constructed to the south of the altar; apparently used for ceremonial libation (Fig. 6.8), which considerably diminished the open space available for the worshippers.

Fig. 6.8. *Stone-lined basin in the courtyard of Stratum 9 temple*

Dismantling of the Temple

Aharoni divided the annihilation of the temple at Arad into two stages. According to him, in the first stage the altar was put out of use and totally covered, but the temple was still in use. In the second stage the temple itself had been demolished, mainly by erecting the inner casemate wall across its main hall. These stages seemed to elucidate the two stages of the centralization of worship carried out by Hezekiah and Josiah. Nonetheless, since the date of the casemate wall is proven by our renewed investigations to date to the Hellenistic period, the dismantling of the temple is thus not connected to the construction of the casemate wall.

More significant is the question whether the temple indeed was dismantled in two separate stages. Aharoni himself was puzzled by the possibility that the last temple had no altar for burnt offerings, but maintained the view that 'Arad seems to elucidate the two stages in the centralization of worship carried out by Hezekiah and Josiah, respectively. Its first stage, in the days of Hezekiah, was the prohibition of sacrifice, while only in the second stage, in the days of Josiah, brought about the complete abolition of worship outside Jerusalem' (Y. Aharoni 1968: 26) .

According to my renewed analysis of the floor-levels within the temple, dividing the abandonment of the temple into two stages is unacceptable. The former two-phases assumption poses a functional difficulty. Once the altar was destroyed it was totally covered by an earthen fill. Since, according to the former assumption, the main hall and the *debir* were used at its original level, its floor should have been about 2 m lower than the floor of the courtyard. The absence of any indication of any sort of a wall to retain such a fill, and the absence of stairs which would have descended into the *debir*, disprove this reconstruction. This demonstrates that the main hall and the *debir* could not have been used while the courtyard was filled up to above the level of the sacrificial altar. After all, the view of a pit-like temple looks bizarre and unparalleled in ancient cult places. Consequently, only a single stage of demolishment is evident at the temple of Arad. In Stratum 8 a structure made of thin walls was constructed over the *debir*. The later phases of the Iron Age remains (of Strata 7 and 6) in this location were almost completely removed by the builders of the Hellenistic and Roman periods.

Chronology of the Temple

The current observations of the stratigraphy of the temple at Arad point to a much shorter affiliation than previously conceived. Instead of four or five strata the temple was utilized in only two of the strata, namely Strata 10 and 9. If so, what is the possible date of these strata? This question cannot be answered easily. The dilemma stems from the fact that the pottery assemblages of three Strata, 10, 9 and 8, are quite similar and resemble the typology group of Stratum III at Lachish. This stratum is commonly identified as the city destroyed by Sennacherib in 701 BCE, and thus associated with the late eighth century BCE (Aharoni and Aharoni 1976; Ussishkin 1976). The resemblance of the pottery in Strata 10, 9 and 8 was observed already by Y. Aharoni. Historical correlation led him and his followers to attribute the erection of Stratum 10 to the ninth century (Y. Aharoni 1981: 129; Herzog *et al.* 1984: 8-12). However, M. Aharoni (1985) as well as some of the critics (Zimhoni 1985; Mazar and Netzer 1986; Ussishkin 1988) advocated a date in the eighth century.

The date of the erection of Stratum 10 must also be considered in conjunction with the dates of Strata 12 and 11. Arad became a key site for the discussions on the tenth century since it is mentioned among the cities conquered by pharaoh Shishak. Two strata were suggested as representing the settlement destroyed by Shishak: the fortress of Stratum 11 (Y. Aharoni 1968: 9; Herzog *et al.* 1984: 8) and the settlement of Stratum 12 (Zimhoni 1985: 87; Mazar and Netzer 1986: 89). Finkelstein (1996: 181) also assigned Stratum 12 to the tenth century, but otherwise dated similar assemblages to the ninth century (Mazar 1997: 158). The pottery of Stratum 12 is characterized by the common use of red-slipped and hand-burnished treatment of the face of the vessels. This ware is customary dated to the tenth century, but its earliest appearance is not clarified. A. Mazar indicated the early appearance of this pottery type in Tell Qasile Stratum X (1998), but actually red-slipped and hand-burnished ware is common already in Stratum XI,[4] dated by him to the early eleventh century BCE. Since

---

4.   A careful examination of the captions of the figures in the material from the site in Stratum XI indicates the presence of 18 red-slipped and burnished vessels (Mazar 1985: Figs. 18: 17, 21, 24; 22: 2, 5, 6, 15, 20, 29; 24: 7; 26: 5-6; 27: 3; 28: 9; 29: 1, 9). The burnish is often not marked on the drawings. This is apparently the

several occupational sub-phases are observed in Stratum 12, I see no difficulty in dating the erection of this settlement during the eleventh century BCE.

This conclusion does not exclude, however, the possibility that Stratum 12 terminated in conjunction with the Shishak invasion, in 926 BCE. Interestingly, the last phase of Stratum 12 was not terminated with an overall conflagration. Such a presumption would necessitate inter- preting *hgr* in Shishak's list as an enclosed settlement rather than a fortress, and the understanding that not all the settlements mentioned in the list were violently destroyed.

If Stratum 11 is lowered to the ninth century, then the erection of the Stratum 10 fortress, and the first construction of the temple may be dated to the eighth century BCE. Nevertheless, Strata 10, 9 and 8 at Arad are clearly defined as separate architectural phases, and the temple existed only in the first two.

The construction of the temple within the strong fortress of Stratum 10 may reflect the need for popular ceremonial centres throughout the Kingdom of Judah in the eighth century BCE. The presence of several cultic places in the Northern Kingdom is suggested by the biblical records and so far supported by archaeological evidence at Tel Dan (Biran 1994).

The temple at Arad was not destroyed by conflagration. No signs of fire were noticed in the *debir* or in any other part of the temple. The dismantling of the temple and the complete burial of its holiest parts (the stelae, incense altars and the sacrificial altar) must be considered as an act of religious reform. The dating of the pottery assemblage from Stratum 8 to late eighth century BCE leaves little doubt that this reform should therefore be attributed to King Hezekiah and provides us with one of the neatest correlations between the biblical account and the archaeological record (Rainey 1994; Borowski 1995; *contra* Na'aman 1995).

source for the mistaken figure in Table 7 of only 4 open vessels attributed to Stratum XI. Indeed, the percentage of the total counted sherds (Table 6a) shows that the red-slipped and burnished sherds were similarly common in Strata XI and X: only 0.8% were observed on the sherds in Stratum XII, but 8.0% in Stratum XI and 8.2% in Stratum X. This data further proves that the red-slipped and burnished vessels became popular in Stratum XI of Tell Qasile, which Mazar dates to the first half of the eleventh century BCE.

Stratum 12's Alleged 'High Place'

The interpretation of the remains exposed in Stratum 12 at Tel Arad given by the expedition's team vigorously illustrates the drawbacks of the traditional biblical–archaeology approach. Even before the exposure of the earliest phases of Iron Age occupation, speculation of their ethnic identification and cultic affiliation were offered. Following the exposure of the temple, B. Mazar suggested connecting its construction in the monarchical period by the biblical references, thus relating Arad to the Kenites. Specifically instrumental was the verse in Judg. 1.16 that mentions the settlement of 'the descendants of [LXX adds: Hobab] the Kenite, Moses' father-in-law' in the Negeb of Arad. Mazar concluded from the biblical references that Hobab the Kenite was an eponym of a Kenite tribe, which practised priest-craft and ritual. He speculated that in the middle of their territory, they erected a holy site with an altar and *masseboth* serving the inhabitants of the eastern Negeb for cultic functions.

> And when one of the early Israelite kings constructed a fortress on the site of the earlier unprotected settlement, there was also built, within the holy precinct, a house of God, according to a plan normal for the period in Palestine, including an altar and standing *masseboth*, and the sons of Hobab continued to function within it as priests (Mazar 1965: 303).

Aharoni further developed this theme and claimed that: 'It therefore becomes most likely that this Kenite family, related to Moses through Hobab, occupied important functions in the early Israelite priesthood and worship' (Y. Aharoni 1968: 27). When the domestic remains of the earliest settlement at Arad (Stratum 12) were uncovered below the first fortress, they were immediately interpreted along this line of thinking:

> The early open village of Arad, with its central high-place, apparently represents this famous Kenite establishment. The ancient editors and readers were doubtless well acquainted with the temple of Arad and its tradition. For us, the passage in Judges 1:16 was rather meaningless until the discoveries of the archaeological excavations (Y. Aharoni 1968: 27).

In a later report prepared by Aharoni's team members, we were even more specific, asserting that: 'The round platform and altar base that stood in the centre of the village may reflect in some way the priestly background of this ancient clan' (Herzog *et al.* 1984: 6). We illustrated this opinion by an isometric reconstruction of a cultic 'temenos' with an altar and a round 'high-place' (Fig. 6.9).

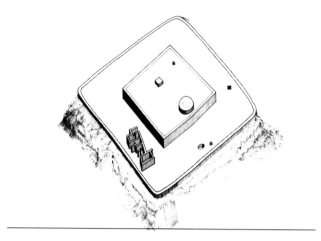

Fig. 6.9. *Former reconstruction of Stratum 12 'High Place'*

When I became more aware of the shortcomings of the direct arch-aeological–biblical analogy I looked at the evidence through different eyes. Freed from the impact of biblical correlation, the remains of the Stratum 12 settlement were explained as resembling the type of 'enclo-sed settlement' occupations observed in several sites across the Beer-sheba valley in the eleventh century BCE (Herzog 1983). The domestic units uncovered west of the later fortress, and under its glacis, were erected over the abandoned ruins of the Early Bronze II city. The settlers of the Iron Age must have found the ruined EB II broad-houses suitable for reuse. They simply rebuilt the fallen walls, attached pillared walls to them and added storage bins in the open space, thus adapting the old remains to their needs. By combining the houses into a peri-pheral belt they provided the settlement with the desired closure. The EB builders constructed a stone fence on the west, near a steep rock cliff, resulting, apparently from a stone quarry used. This fence was erroneously interpreted as a fairly thick fortification wall (Zimhoni 1985).

The remains inside the central open courtyard of the settlement in the vicinity of the later temple were misinterpreted as an altar and a 'high-place'. A more unbiased view of these remains suggests a more con-ventional explanation. The stones of the alleged 'altar' actually belong to a wall segment of Stratum 11 (the stones were reused in Stratum 10 as an edge for a stone pavement in the temple's courtyard). The recon-structed 'high place' was nothing more than an ordinary circular stone granary built in the central courtyard of the 'enclosed settlement' (Fig. 6.10). This type of settlement corresponds to several similar occupations that were typical to the region in the late eleventh century BCE (Herzog 1994).

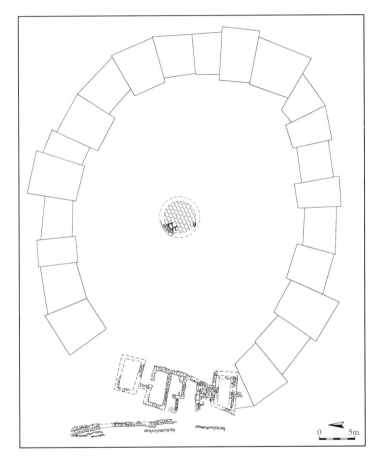

Fig. 6.10. *Reconstruction of Stratum 12 remains as an 'enclosed settlement'*

The reconstruction of the early history of the region based on the renewed archaeological observation calls for fresh conclusions. Eliminating the temple from Stratum 11 and the redating of its first phase to Stratum 10 further disconnects the temple from any pre-monarchical tradition. The attempt to identify the settlement of Stratum 12 at Arad strictly as occupation by the Kenites is also refuted in light of recent understanding of the subject of ethnic identity. The traditional view that considered ethnic groups as collectives pertaining to stable race distinction, such as shared biological ties, common language and territorial continuity, is challenged in the anthropological study (Barth 1969). The alternative opinion views ethnicity along the lines of a constantly changing and variable social phenomenon. Consequently, the settlers of the Beersheba valley may not be identified exclusively as belonging to a positively identified group, such as the Kenites, the Amalekites or the Israelites. I would argue that the new settlements, in a region totally unoccupied for centuries, belong to diverse social groups that were attracted by the prosperous conditions (Herzog 1994: 146-49). Their identity as Judahites was established only a century later, with the founding of the Kingdom of Judah.

Summary

The new stratigraphical and chronological conclusions presented here have drastically modified our understanding of the significance of the Arad temple to the history of religion in Judah. The actual duration of the temple's use was significantly shorter than previously assumed. No evident cult place exited during the first occupational phase of the site in Stratum 12 (eleventh century BCE). Nor was a temple erected within the first fortress of Stratum 11, which was constructed on the site during the tenth century (according to the commonly accepted chronology, see above). Finally, no temple could have been utilized in Stratum 8, which is dated to the late eighth century. This leaves us with only two Strata, namely 10 and 9, during which the temple was operating. In terms of absolute chronology the duration of the temple's use period is less decisive, due to our doubt regarding the date of the construction of Stratum 10. If indeed this fortress was constructed shortly after the destruction of Stratum 11, the erection of the temple may be dated to about 900 BCE. But, if the second option of an occupational gap were favoured, then the temple would have been built only around 800 BCE. This date would also fit the alternative chronology suggested by Finkelstein (1996). The abandonment of the temple seems to corroborate the biblical account on Hezekiah's cultic reform, and thus should be dated to 715 BCE. Accordingly, the temple would have been utilized for about 185 years in the first option, or only about 85 years according to the second option.

The erection of the temple at Arad must be assigned to the period of the kingdom of Judah, during the ninth or early eighth century BCE. It seems significant to note that following the exposure of the Arad temple, during the last 33 years, an indication of the presence of another temple in Judah was found only in neighbouring Beersheba (Y. Aharoni 1974). Were temples not built in other cities or were they more thoroughly destroyed? The beautifully shaped altar blocks found embedded into a later wall and the absence of any concrete remains of the temple at Beersheba (Herzog, Rainey and Moshkovitz 1977), point to the latter option. It is possible that at other sites the order to uproot the temples and demolish the altars was carried out in a more veritable manner.

The changes in the temple's plan, following the destruction of the Stratum 10 fortress, mainly affected the courtyard. The construction of the large basin to the south of the sacrificial altar and the enclosure of a small room on the eastern side considerably diminished the open space in the courtyard. It seems that the entrance to the temple was more limited at this phase than during the initial one. The raising of the floor level also alleviated the approach to the sacrificial platform on top of the altar.

The demolition of the temple in preparation of the construction of the Stratum 8 phase of the Arad fortress seems to present the only direct link with the biblical account. The archaeological material found in the destruction layers of the Stratum 8 fortress is almost identical to the pottery of Lachish Stratum III, and both are considered to be cities destroyed by Sennacherib in 701 (Aharoni and Aharoni 1976). Attributing the abandonment of the temple to Hezekiah would seem quite secure. A. Rainey understood this reform as an outcome of the fall of the Northern Kingdom and the attempt by Hezekiah to unite the northern Israelites around his capital in Jerusalem. This might have generated his decision to destroy cult places in Judah, just as the northerners had to give up their shrines (Rainey in Herzog *et al.* 1984) .

The present reassessment of the history of the temple in Arad negates most of the correlations with the biblical account suggested in previous treatments of the site. Arad is not the location of a Canaanite city whose king prevented the early attempt of the Israelite tribes to invade Canaan from the south (Y. Aharoni 1976); no Kenite sanctuary existed in premonarchical Arad; the temple of Arad is not similar to the Solomonic temple in Jerusalem; the temple at Arad was not rebuilt six times, with every rebuilding of the fortress; and finally the temple was not demolished in two consecutive phases, illustrating the two reforms by Hezekiah and Josiah. The only correlation that appears to remain valid is the intended dismantling of the temple by King Hezekiah.

The previous views undoubtedly were biased by our 'biblical–archaeology' conception. I hope that the present discussion will contribute toward the liberation of the archaeology of Israel from that obstruction.

Bibliography

Aharoni, M.
1981   'Preliminary Ceramic Report on Strata 12-11 at Arad Citadel', *EI* 15: 181-204 (Hebrew).
1993   'Arad: The Israelite Citadels', *NEAEHL* 1: 82-87.
Aharoni, M., and Y. Aharoni
1976   'The Stratification of Judahite Sites in the 8th and 7th Centuries BCE', *BASOR* 224: 73-90.
Aharoni, Y.
1968   'Arad: Its Inscriptions and Temple', *BA* 31: 20-32.
1974   'The Horned Altar of Beer-sheba', *BA* 37: 2-23.
1976   'Nothing Early and Nothing Late: Rewriting Israel's Conquest', *BA* 39: 55-76.
1981   *Arad Inscriptions* (Jerusalem: Israel Exploration Society).
Aharoni, Y., and R. Amiran
1964   'Excavations at Tel Arad: Preliminary Report on the First Season, 1962', *IEJ* 14: 131-47.
Ahlström, G.W.
1975   'Heaven on Earth: At Hazor and Arad', in B.A. Pearson (ed.), *Religious Syncretism in Antiquity: Essays in Conversation with Geo Widengren* (Missoula: Scholars Press): 67-83.
Amiran, R., and O. Ilan
1992   *Arad: eine 5000 Jahre alte Stadt in der wueste Negev, Israel* (Neumuenster: Karl Wachholtz).
Amiran, R., U. Paran, Y. Shiloh, R. Brown, Y. Tsafrir and A. Ben-Tor
1978   *Early Arad: The Chalcolithic Settlement and Early Bronze Age City, I* (Jerusalem: Israel Exploration Society).
Barth, F. (ed.)
1969   *Ethnic Groups and Boundaries: The Social Organization of Cultural Difference* (Boston: Little, Brown).
Biran, A.
1994   *Biblical Dan* (Jerusalem: Israel Exploration Society).
Borowski, O.
1995   'Hezekiah's Reforms and the Revolt against Assyria', *BA* 58: 148-55.
Cross, F.M.
1979   'Two Offering Dishes with Phoenician Inscriptions from the Sanctuary of 'Arad', *BASOR* 235: 75-78.
Dever, W.G.
1982   'Monumental Architecture in Ancient Israel in the Period of the United

Monarchy', in T. Ishida (ed.), *Studies in the Period of David and Solomon and other Essays: Papers Read at the International Symposium for Biblical Studies, Tokyo, 5–7 December 1979* (Winona Lake, IN: Eisenbrauns): 269-307.

Finkelstein, I.

1996   'The Archaeology of the United Monarchy: An Alternative View', *Levant* 28: 177-87.

Haran, M.

1993   ' "Incense Altars": Are They?', in A. Biran and J. Aviram (eds.), *Biblical Archaeology Today, 1990: Proceedings of the Second International Congress on Biblical Archaeology* (Jerusalem: Israel Exploration Society): 237-47.

Herzog, Z.

1981   'Israelite Sanctuaries at Arad and Beer-sheba', in A. Biran (ed.), *Temples and High Places in Biblical* (Jerusalem: Nelson Glueck School of Biblical Archaeology of the Hebrew Union College): 120-22.

1983   'Enclosed Settlements in the Negeb and the Wilderness of Beer-Sheba', *BASOR* 250: 41-49.

1987   'The Stratigraphy of Israelite Arad: A Rejoinder', *BASOR* 267: 77-79.

1994   'The Beer-Sheba Valley: From Nomadism to Monarchy', in I. Finkelstein and N. Na'aman (eds.), *From Nomadism to Monarchy: Archaeological and Historical Aspects of Early Israel* (Jerusalem: Yad Izhak Ben-Zvi): 122-49.

1997   'The Arad Fortresses', in R. Amiran, O. Ilan, M. Sebbane and Z. Herzog (eds.), *Arad* (Tel Aviv: Hakibbutz Hameuchad Publishing House, Israel Exploration Society, Israel Antiquities Authority): 113-292 (Hebrew).

Herzog, Z., M. Aharoni, A.F. Rainey and S. Moshkovitz

1984   'The Israelite Fortress at Arad', *BASOR* 254: 1-34.

Herzog, Z., A.F. Rainey and S. Moshkovitz

1977   'Stratigraphy at Beer-Sheba and the Location of the Sanctuary', *BASOR* 225: 49-58.

Laperrousaz, E.-M.

1979   'Encore "l'Acre des Séleucides", et nouvelles remarques sur les pierres a bossage préhérodiennes de Palestine', *Syria* 56: 123-33, 138-44.

Mazar, A.

1985   *Excavations at Tell Qasile, Part 2, The Philistine Sanctuary: Various Finds, the Pottery, Conclusions, Appendixed* (Qedem, 20; Jerusalem: The Institute of Archaeology, Hebrew University of Jerusalem).

1997   'Iron Age Chronology: A Reply to I. Finkelstein', *Levant* 29: 157-67.

1998   'On the Appearance of Red Slip in the Iron Age I Period in Israel', in S. Gitin, A. Mazar and E. Stern (eds.), *Mediterranean Peoples in Transition: Thirteenth to Early Tenth Centuries BCE* (Jerusalem: Israel Exploration Society): 368-78.

Mazar, A., and E. Netzer

1986   'On the Israelite Fortress at Arad', *BASOR* 263: 87-90.

Mazar, B.

1965   'Arad and the Family of Hobab the Kenite', *JNES* 24: 297-303.

Na'aman, N.

1995   'The Debated Historicity of Hezekiah's Reform in the Light of Historical and Archaeological Research', *ZAW* 107: 179-95.

Nylander, C.

1967   'A Note on the Stonecutting and Masonry of Tel Arad', *IEJ* 17: 56-59.

Rainey, A.F.

1994   'Hezekiah's Reform and the Altars at Beer-Sheba and Arad', in M.D. Coogan, C.J. Exum and L.E. Stager (eds.), *Scripture and other Artifacts: Essays on the Bible and Archaeology in Honor of Philip J. King* (Louisville: Westminster/John Knox Press): 344-54.

Ussishkin, D.

1976   'Royal Judean Storage Jars and Private Seal Impression', *BASOR* 223: 1-13.

1988   'The Date of the Judaean Shrine at Arad', *IEJ* 38: 142-57.

Yadin, Y.

1965   'A Note on the Stratigraphy of Arad', *IEJ* 15: 180.

Zimhoni, O.

1985   'The Iron Age Pottery of Tel 'Eiton and its Relation to the Lachish, Tell Beit Mirsim and Arad Assemblages', *Tel Aviv* 12: 63-90.

7

BETWEEN ARCHAEOLOGY AND THEOLOGY:
THE PILLAR FIGURINES FROM JUDAH AND THE ASHERAH

Raz Kletter

Introduction

The 'pillar figurines' have been discussed many times since their discovery in the nineteenth century CE. Recent discoveries at Kuntillet 'Ajrud and Kh. el Kom, together with a growing interest in the religion of ancient Israel and its material expressions, have led to an overwhelming number of publications that discuss these figurines, from scientific papers and monographs to all kinds of secondary and popular literature. Nowadays, the pillar figurines are usually explained as representations of the biblical Asherah. I will discuss this identification later, but first I wish to deal with archaeological aspects, which have been overlooked in the past (e.g., context, manufacturing and breakage patterns, and the connection between the figurines and the borders of Judah).[1]

A Short History of Research

The fascinating history of research of the pillar figurines (PFs for short, and JPFs for Judaean pillar figurines) can be divided into four distinct phases. Until the first world war, very few figurines were known, but various interpretations were already suggested, especially that these are

1. This paper is a summary of a lecture given at the conference. A monograph on the Judaean pillar figurines has appeared in the meantime (Kletter 1996). I wish to thank Professor N. Na'aman and P. Beck from Tel Aviv University; Professor P.R.S. Moorey and H.G.M. Williamson from Oxford University; The British Council; Professor A. Mazar, Professor M. Geller and all the friends and colleagues who participated in this fruitful and enjoyable conference.

the 'Astartes' of the OT (Clermont-Ganneau 1896: 6-7, 242) and that they were deliberately broken in rituals (Macalister 1905: 270-71). The figurines were often seen as idols of gods (Macalister 1912: 411), but also as a phenomenon of magic (Mackenzie 1912: 76-77). During the second phase, between the two world wars, the numbers of excavations and figurines grew significantly (Tel Beit Mirsim, Lachish, Tel en-Nasbeh, and so on). Pilz (1924) offered the first comprehensive study on figurines from Israel. However, Albright's ideas were more prominent (Albright 1939: 117-20; 1943: 69, 142). I call this phase 'the Astarte phase', as this was the most common explanation for the PFs at that time. Many scholars associated the PFs with magic as well, or even with toys. Kelso and Thorley (1943: 138-41) offered a technical study of manufacture and use. Excavations outside Judah (e.g., at Megiddo, May 1935) started to show regional differences from the assemblage in Judah. The monograph of Pritchard (1943) is a good example for the state of research at the end of this phase. He collected 52 PFs (of which I define today only 12 as JPFs).

The third phase, from World War II until 1975, was long and fruitful. Important assemblages were published from Lachish (Tufnell 1953: 374-78), Jerusalem (Kenyon 1967: 101; Franken and Steiner 1990), Gibeon (Pritchard 1961) and Ramat Rahel (Aharoni 1962, 1964). Major contributions were made, for example, about the OT Asherah (Reed 1949), the borders of Judah (Gophna 1970) and the definition of small fragments (Ciasca 1964). In a popular book, Patai (1967) argued that Asherah was a Hebrew goddess and a consort of Yahweh. He identified her in various naked female figurines, but unfortunately he did not pay attention to basic archaeological aspects and limitation. Ucko offered an important and thorough study of figurines, but not JPFs (1968). The unpublished dissertation of Holland (1975, cf. 1977) marks the end of the third phase. It is a very thorough work in regard to collecting the material and arranging it typologically, without imposing on it external 'theologies'. Its main drawbacks are the lack of analysis, the cumbersome structure and the problematic separation of regional types. Despite these drawbacks, it remains a basic study.

After 1975, the quantity of studies became overwhelming. Typical of many studies is the mixing of data (more correctly, theories) taken from the OT with archaeological aspects. Thus, Engle identified the JPFs with Asherah, but with little discussion (1979: 5-28) and without an understanding of the archaeological factors. The main problem, that occurs again and again, is: what is the basis for identifying the JPFs with Asherah? Engle did contribute to the clear definition of a Judaean type of PF. In a long series of publications, Dever (1982: 38-39; 1984: 28ff; 1990: ch. 4; 1991: 110-12; 1994: 121, etc.) presented time and again his conceptions regarding Israelite religion and the JPFs, but did not prove the assumed identification with Asherah. An interesting school of thought can be termed 'iconographic' (Winter 1983: 106-109; Schroer 1987: 45, 343, 387; Keel and Uehlinger 1992: 369-90). Its basis is rather problematic: the claim that iconography is a more 'direct' source than historical documents is mistaken, as is the treatment of the whole ancient Near East as one cultural unit, regardless of time and space (cf. Lipinski 1986; Van der Toorn 1986; Weippert 1994).

In recent years, almost every archaeologist who has dealt with Iron Age Judah (whether 'new' or 'biblical') had something to say about the JPFs, and theories range from gender studies (Teubal 1984; Gadon 1989; Meyers 1988) to popular religion (Ackerman 1992; cf. Rose 1975: 183-86; in general see Vorlander 1986; Vrijhof and Waardenberg 1979). Other studies were offered by Hubner (1989); Wenning (1991) and Franken (1995). The work of Voigt (1983) is most important as a theoretical study, though she did not discuss the JPFs.

The Typology

I have defined 854 JPFs, excluding at least 100 more figurines of unknown origin. Circa 500 of these JPFs were not included in Holland's work (1975), and many are not yet published. Holland defined 573 PFs, but only 359 are JPFs (following my definitions).

There are clear differences between the JPFs and other PFs from neighbouring areas. The JPFs have solid, hand-made bodies, without legs (Fig. 7.1[1]–[2]). The base of the body is widened and is usually concave. There are two main types of heads. The first is a simple, solid, hand-made head, pinched to form crude eye depressions and protruding nose. There are no incisions and no indication of pupils, but often there are applied hats, 'turbans' or side-locks (Fig. 7.1[1], [3]). The second type of head has a mould-made face, with a hairdress of ridges above the forehead, usually with curls (Fig. 7.1[2], [4]). It has short side-locks, and the ears are never indicated. This type of head always ends in a peg, which is inserted into a cavity in the hand-made body (Fig. 7.1[4]). The body is a stereotype, featuring a standing woman supporting the breasts (the hands are often found a little below, and not in real support, of the breasts). The breasts and hands are applied to the body. There is no indication of fingers, but often bracelets or necklaces are depicted by red or yellow paint.

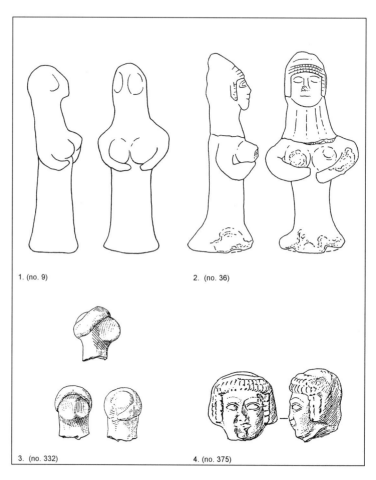

1. (no. 9)   2. (no. 36)

3. (no. 332)   4. (no. 375)

Fig. 7.1. *Judaean pillar figurines (the numbers refer to Kletter 1996: Appendix 2)*

This description clearly defines the dominant type of human figurine in Iron Age Judah. Variant female PFs exist in Judah, but they are few; for example, figurines holding drums (Pritchard 1961: 16, fig. 41, 557; Aharoni 1962: pl. 5; Holland 1975: A.I.G.1); having a hollow, wheel-made base (Tufnell 1953: pl. 28, 10); 'lamp' figurines (Isserlin 1976; cf. Gubel 1991: 134; Beck 1991: 91, nn. 24-26), and even one woman with a child (Albright 1943: pls. 32:1, 54b:4; Holland 1975: A.I.H.2).

There are other Judaean types of figurines, such as male figurines (rare), birds with pillar bases, horse and riders and of course hundreds of animal figurines. The identification of a JPF is often possible, even from a small fragment (Ciasca 1964, versus Engle 1979). True, identification is not always easy, for example, the separation of JPF bases from bird figurines with similar pillar bases, or of JPF hand-made heads from riders' heads.

I have checked the other human figurines of the Iron Age from Israel and Transjordan, altogether some 900 artifacts (there are surely more unpublished examples). It is evident that although female PFs are widespread, the JPFs are distinctive. It is possible to define coastal (Philistine) types, Phoenician types, and Transjordanian types of PFs. Contrary to the JPF, these figurines are usually more realistic in design and elaborately decorated. The coastal types have mould-made heads with exaggerated ears, applied necklaces (often with rosette pendants), and long locks reaching to the shoulders (Fig. 7.2[1]). Coastal hand-made heads are also common, but these have applied disc eyes and incised details (Fig. 7.2[2]). The coastal figurines are often hollow, and the pillar is wheel-made. In Transjordan, the use of black paint is common (Fig. 7.2[3], cf. Amr 1980; Dornemann 1983: 129-37; Gubel 1991: 137; for Edom cf. Beck 1995: 180, 182, 185-87). Phoenician types are also distinctive, for example, pregnant, sitting woman (Fig. 7.2[4]), musicians (Fig. 7.2[5]) and daily life scenes (Fig. 7.2[6]; cf. Culican 1969; 1975–76; Gubel 1991; Meyers 1991).

The Date

Many scholars claimed that pillar-figurines appeared already in the tenth century BCE (Pilz 1924: 140, 161; Pritchard 1943: 57; Albright 1943: 69; Grant and Wright 1939: 155 n. 28; Engle 1979: 20-21; Winter 1983: 107; Aharoni 1975: 16; Bloch-Smith 1992: 219 n. 17). In many cases, these were not JPFs (according to my definition), or the dating was doubtful on archaeological grounds. I have found only few fragments of JPFs, that can be dated to the tenth or ninth centuries BCE, but actually, we cannot define this period well in Judah. There is a growing tendency to lower dates of strata, that were once dated to the tenth century BCE (Jericke 1992: 219 n. 17; Na'aman 1992: 83; Finkelstein 1996, with references). In any case, 'early' dated JPFs are few and their importance is negligible. As a significant phenomenon, the JPFs are evident from the eighth century BCE and later.

Fig. 7.2. *Other types of pillar figurines*
(the numbers refer to Kletter 1996: Appendixes 4–5)

Two heads have been dated to the Persian period, but they are exceptional in many ways, and perhaps not JPFs at all. Continuation in the use of a few JPFs after 586 BCE is possible, since the Babylonian conquests of 586 BCE did not affect each and every artifact in Judah, while the following period (sixth century BCE) is almost a *terra incognita*. A totally different picture emerges during the Persian period: new forms (many of which show Aegean or Persian motifs); a new technique (double-moulding of hollow figurines); different distribution patterns (mainly pits or *favissae* along the coast, Stern 1989; 1992: 159-

74). It would be safe to conclude that the JPFs went out of use before the Persian period, most likely around 586 BCE.

Thus, the JPFs belong to the eighth–early sixth centuries BCE. PFs of neighbouring areas (Phoenicia, Transjordan and Philistia) also belong mostly to the same period. Eighty-four JPFs can be dated to this period tentatively, but the date of other 143 JPFs is secure. Can we separate the eighth and the seventh centuries BCE? It is not an easy task, since only 90 JPFs can be clearly dated to one specific century, mostly to the eighth century BCE. It is clear that the JPFs were very popular by then, unlike the inscribed weights (Kletter 1991). Only 20 JPFs were dated to the seventh century BCE. We can use the evidence of one period sites, that were not settled on a significant scale during the seventh century BCE (e.g., Tel Beit Mirsim, Beth Shemesh, Tel Halif and Tel Beer Sheba), or the eighth century BCE (e.g., Malhata and Tel Masos), but it only helps a little. The small number of well-dated JPFs from the seventh century BCE should not be taken as evidence for a substantial change, nor related in a naive way with biblical 'cult reforms'.

Distribution and Relation with the Borders of Judah

Political borders were a necessity in the ancient Near East, and were defined and maintained for a wide variety of needs (Liverani 1990). Therefore, their study is not a theoretical question.[2] For our specific case, in order to study the relation of the JPFs with the borders of Judah, one must first define these borders independently, with the help of historical sources. These sources are open to various reconstructions, so I had to choose the most likely one (Na'aman 1989). I have also used a conception of 'the heartland of Judah'. This is a minimal definition of Judah, accepted by all scholars, of the area governed by Judah and settled by a Judaean majority. Roughly, it includes the Judaean Mountains and desert, Benjamin, the Negev and the eastern part of the Shephelah (marked by the cities of Beth-Shemeh—Lachish—Azeka in the west).

The definition of the JPF as Judaean relies mainly on their distribution pattern (Fig. 7.3). Of 854 JPFs, 822 (c. 96 per cent) were found in the area defined (above) as the heartland of Judah. Of these, about

2.   Recent archaeological studies focused on prehistory and ethnicity, while political borders are not much discussed. On this, and on the borders of Judah in the late Iron Age according to the historical sources, see Kletter 1999a.

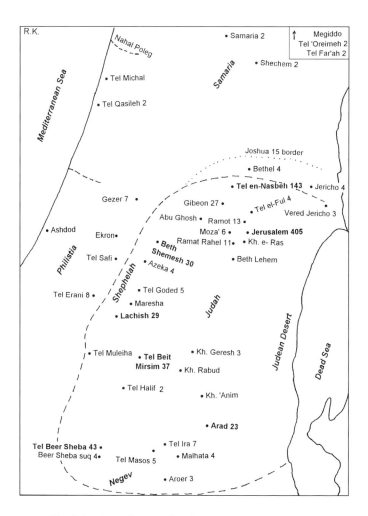

Fig. 7.3. *The Judaean pillar figurines—distribution map*

– – – Judah's border, following Na'aman 1989. The numbers indicate the number of JPFs found at each site (when only one JPF was found the number is omitted). Arrows point in the direction of sites outside the map's limits.

75 per cent (628) were found in the northern Judaean mountains and Benjamin, 15 per cent (126) in the Shephelah and about 10 per cent (89) in the Negev. Only 32 JPFs (3.7 per cent) were found outside the heartland of Judah, but many of these are badly fragmented, and their definition as JPFs is not clear. Four of these 32 figurines are from the coastal plain and seven from northern Israel, that is, very few JPFs that demand no special explanation. Moreover, they are found there as isolated objects among rich assemblages of a local nature. In Ashdod, for example, there is one JPF fragment among about 60 anthropomorphic fragments. The case of Ekron, Gezer and Tell Erani, in the western Shephelah, is somewhat different. In this area, outside 'the heartland of Judah', were found little groups of JPFs: seven in Gezer and eight in Tell Erani (the Ekron finds are not yet fully published). Tell Erani may have belonged to Judah (by the nature of its finds as a whole—such a conclusion cannot be based on the few JPFs found there). The appearance of the JPFs at Gezer and Ekron may be related to a situation before 701 BCE (direct or indirect control of Judah over this area during Hezekiah's revolt, Mittmann 1990). Trade is a possible explanation in regard to the distribution pattern, but is unlikely in view of the religious nature of the JPFs and their crudity. If these figurines were traded, one would have expected a move in the opposite direction, since the coastal figurines are finer than the JPFs, both in manufacture and design.[3] On the whole, the number of JPFs in Ekron or Gezer is not great, and does not in itself prove Judaean political or military control.

Two sites present special problems, Kadesh Barnea and Mesad Hashavyahu (Naveh 1962; Cohen 1983; Reich 1989; Wenning 1989). The material culture of these sites is mixed, but partly Judaean (inscribed weights, JPFs, Hebrew inscriptions and pottery forms). Various explanations can be made for the appearance of Judaean material objects there (Na'aman 1989). But in order to define a border, a group of sites, a 'line', is needed, while Kadesh Barnea and Mesad Hashavyahu are isolated. Thus, they do not imply political control of Judah over their surrounding area (cf. commercial colonies that exhibit foreign material culture within a local assemblage, but do not imply the political control of the foreign culture over the local one. Of course, I bring this as an example only).

---

3.   That the JPFs were not traded does not mean the same for other types of figurines, e.g. the international trade of figurines during later periods in Israel (Linder 1986).

Political borders can block the movement of artifacts to a large extent. The alternating fate of Lachish and Ekron, two cities near each other and in similar environmental conditions, can serve as an example (Kletter, 1999a: 43). The quantity of JPFs is related to other factors as well, for example, the wealth and size of ancient sites, and the nature, extent and publication method of each excavation. The JPFs contribute to the study of site hierarchy in Judah, but I will not discuss these subjects further (see Kletter 1996: ch. 5).

Patterns of Manufacture and Use

Mould-made JPFs are larger than the hand-made ones, both in body and in head size. Hand-made heads vary from between 14–40 mm, excluding a few exceptions; moulded faces vary from between 19–41 mm (excluding hand-made parts of the heads). The measurements are important for the study of the moulds (below) and for the classification of fragments. For example, they can help to separate JPFs' hand-made heads from the smaller horse-and-rider's heads (18 mm in average).

Early scholars believed that the material culture of Israel was impoverished, therefore attributing high-quality artifacts with foreign countries. It was suggested that the moulded JPFs' heads were made in a foreign centre (Albright 1943: 69, 83; Kelso and Thorley 1943: 139-40; Patai 1967: 60 n. 41; Winter 1983: 127; cf. Tufnell 1953: 375). Petrography may help, but very few JPFs were checked. It seems that there was local, regional manufacture, since JPFs from Jerusalem were made from local terra-rossa clay, while JPFs from Tel Ira in the Negev were made from local loess clay (Kletter 1999b: nos. 1, 3; Kletter 1996: Appendix 2, nos. 245, 249; petrography by Y. Goren).

Moorey and Fleming (1984: 77, cf. Spycket 1992: 227 n. 395) suggested that hand-made figurines were made in domestic areas by women. The excavators of Tel en-Nasbeh thought similarly, because of the cheap materials and crude workmanship of the figurines (McCown 1947: 273). This view was adopted carelessly by scholars from the feminist school (Teubal 1990: 43; Meyers 1988: 161-63; Gadon 1989: 177-80, 186), who rely on a pre-conception that female figurines belong to female religion or to female 'house cult'. As far as the JPFs are concerned, there is no archaeological evidence whatsoever for this view. Crude design does not indicate production by women. The figurines did not have to withstand pressures (unlike daily pottery vessels), and this can explain their bad quality. It is unlikely that the JPFs were made by each woman at her own household, because they are very homogeneous in shape and the use of moulds indicates mass manufacture at a rather high technical level.

There are 199 JPFs which show remains of white-wash (probably many more in origin). The white-wash was analysed as $CaCO_3$—a deliberate lime wash. It was probably done in order to give the figurines a smooth finish, stressing the painted decoration. Many JPFs were painted above the white-wash, usually in red (52 figurines). Yellow, brown and black were also used, as well as combinations of red and yellow or red and black. The painting is almost always composed of simple patterns on the face and upper body. In some cases, it is limited to the front, and does not continue to the back (Albright 1943: 138; Pritchard: 1961: 15). This implies that the figurines were supposed to be seen from the front. Further proof for this is found in moulded heads, where the back side is often left crude (Albright 1943: 140; Keel and Uehlinger 1992: 380).

A fascinating aspect is the moulding of the JPFs' heads. Very few moulds of anthropomorphic figurines are known from Iron Age Israel, mostly of plaque figurines (Holland 1975: 314-17 [17 moulds]; Kletter 1996: Appendix 5.VIII [28 moulds]). Only three moulds bear some resemblance to the JPFs (*ibid.*, App. 5.VIII, nos. 1, 2, 14). The lack of moulds forces us to study the moulded heads. This was rarely done (Kelso and Thorley 1943: 138-41). More often, scholars just mentioned the difficulties in this field (e.g., Hubner 1989: 50). With this background in mind, Nicholls's study (1952) on moulded Greek figurines is highly important (cf. also Ammerman 1985). However, it is extremely hard to use Nicholls's work for the JPFs. Not only basic details are missing in reports, but Nicholls had direct access to large assemblages of figurines. This is difficult in our case, since the JPFs are scattered all over the world. At least the questions should be asked: how many moulds were used? How many 'mould-series' came from one mould? Are there regional or temporal variations between the heads, and what does it imply on production, distribution and inter-sites relations? In total, I have studied 183 moulded JPFs' heads, but only 129 are well classified. The minimal number of moulds is 24, being the number of all the sub-types. Taking into consideration differences in heads that belong to the same sub-type and other factors, a cautious estimation of a few dozen moulds for all the JPFs seems likely. This means that we are dealing with a mass-production, of which only a small part has been found.

Scholars agree that the technique of moulding heads, while the bodies are handmade or wheel-made, originated in the Levant. During the eighth century BCE, or even later, it spread to Cyprus, the Aegean world, then to the western Mediterranean (Caubet 1991: 136; Vandenabeele 1986: 352-53, 355; 1989: 266). So far, the exact origin and date of this 'invention' in the Levant are not clear.

The Breaking of the Figurines

Many scholars assumed that the JPFs were deliberately broken (McCown 1947: 145; Franken and Steiner 1990: 128; Hubner 1989: 53; Dothan 1971: 132; Vincent 1907: 163; Holland 1975: 137; Macalister 1905; Barkay 1990: 191). Some scholars even connected the broken JPFs specifically with biblical 'reforms'. They believed that the JPFs represented a foreign, un-Yahwehistic cult, that the reformers took special pains to destroy (Mazar 1979: 152; Nadelman 1989: 123; cf. Dever 1990: 159). These theories are based on the fact that the overwhelming majority of the JPFs were found broken, assuming that such a high percentage of damage cannot be accidental. Yet, there is no decisive archaeological evidence for deliberate mutilation of the JPFs, nor biblical evidence about mutilation of small clay figurines.

I have personally checked about 300 figurines, but found no clear sign of deliberate mutilation. The problem is that almost any point in the JPFs is a weak point, thus it is extremely hard to decide if any part was broken accidentally or on purpose. Ancient figurines were sometimes mutilated, for example, the execration figurines from Egypt, but this is known thanks to their inscriptions (Ritner 1993: 148-55). Another case relates to a stone figurine, where the marks of mutilation are clear (Peltenburg 1988: 292; Ioannides 1992). One possible solution is to find indicative breakage patterns, that is, evidence for a high percentage of broken points, which are not natural weak points. At the moment, such evidence does not exist for the JPFs.

There are many possible ways of deliberately breaking a clay figurine: throwing it forcefully towards a wall or a floor, cutting it with sharp tools, smashing it and so on. On the other hand, only one form is possible for accidental breakage—an accidental fall of the figurines. Possibly, figurines can suffer also from violent destruction of sites, and from secondary damage, for example, when dumped in debris during later building activities. However, if the JPFs were broken accidentally, most of them would have been broken by accidentally falling. This would have occurred from heights of 1.5 m or so (the height of ancient four-room houses). Furthermore, most of the figurines would fall on earth floors (the usual Iron Age floors). By using modern figurines of roughly the same shape and size, results of similar accidental falls can be studied. Some 40 figurines were manufactured from *terra rossa* clay, selected in the vicinity of northern Jerusalem (Fig. 7.4). The figurines were hand-made and fired in low temperatures, c. 600-700°C.[4] These modern figurines do not necessarily resemble the ancient ones in strength or elasticity, but this was not the aim at all. The modern figurines were dropped from heights of 1.5–2 m onto a hard earth surface, and different initial positions were tested. The fragments were then collected and the breaking points registered.

It appears that the position of the figurine at the end of the fall is important. Figurines that hit the base or the head were less damaged. The modern figurines are probably stronger than the ancient ones, being fired in a modern kiln with temperature control (and having good, homogeneous clay). Almost a half remained whole. A comparison group, dropped from 3 m height onto cement floor, shows that the weakest points are first the arms, then the neck, and then the body and the nose. The arms are very vulnerable since they are thin and protruding from the body. The modern figurines sustained fewer neck fractions, but all of them have hand-made heads, which are probably stronger than the ancient moulded necks (because the latter have pegs). Furthermore, the modern figurines have very solid and thick bodies, probably exaggerated in comparison with the JPFs. All the breaks in the modern figurines appear 'new' and are sharp. The JPFs are perhaps worn, maybe because of gradual wear through the years, or due to differences in material and firing.

We cannot apply directly the results of the modern tests to the ancient JPFs, partly because the quantity of the experiments is really too small. I am afraid, though, that my neighbours got the wrong impression about the scientific value of these experiments, as they were conducted in an open-air laboratory (or, to be more exact, backyard).

4.   The clay was selected with the help of Y. Goren and the figurines were manufactured by E. Kamaiski. Some technical aspects of their manufacture are described in Goren, Kamaiski and Kletter 1996.

Fig. 7.4. *A modern replica of a Judaean pillar figurine*

The assumption about deliberate mutilation was common in regard to many other types of figurines, for example, from Susa (Spycket 1992: 235). Spycket did not explain how it fits with the evidence that some figurines were mended by bitumen (1992: 235; cf. Ucko 1968: 419). About 5 per cent of the JPFs remained whole, mostly from tombs, where they were not deliberately mutilated. Is a rate of 5 per cent for whole figurines unusual, indicating deliberate mutilation? Comparison to far away sites, from Ashdod to Susa, provides a clear conclusion: low percentage of whole figurines is not an exception, but rather a norm for small clay figurines. The types matter, for example, a larger percentage of plaque figurines survived whole, probably because of their less vulnerable, 'lump' like form. What really counts is the context. Many whole figurines are found in burials—they are put there cautiously and not disturbed violently (unless by later burials or tomb-robbers). On the other hand, whole figurines are very rare in fills and refuse debris. It is very unlikely that the JPFs were deliberately mutilated during a 'biblical reform', since similar breaking patterns appear elsewhere, in sites that could not have suffered from the hands of 'biblical reformers'.

The JPFs represent favourable figures (the smile, the full face, the breasts which may be portrayed as being offered). If they functioned as 'good' figures, it is hard to assume deliberate mutilation in ritual acts. Mutilation of 'magical' figurines is likely to occur in 'black magic', where the figurines represent enemies or bad spirits. It is also possible in burial contexts, where good figures may be broken as signs of grief. But surely this is not our case (most of the JPFs were found in domestic contexts). Of course, the external form and its appeal to our eyes is not necessarily indicative of the function and meaning in antiquity. I am only saying that one must choose: if the JPFs represented Asherah, who was held to be a good entity by her followers, then it is not logical to suggest that they were mutilated in 'magical' rites (and as for 'biblical reforms', see above).

Another argument against deliberate mutilation is the fact that the faces of many JPFs are well preserved and intact. We know that it was customary to mutilate faces of anthropomorphic figures in many periods and cultures, since they allegedly possessed the powers of those represented. Mutilation of these figures symbolized their 'killing', it denied them the ability to act in the real world. Within this context, the head is especially important, as it enables a person to see, talk, smell, and hear. This is the reason for mutilation of many artifacts in Mesopotamia (Brandes 1980; Nylander 1980), Egypt (Ritner 1993) and elsewhere (Kelley 1994). Such a phenomenon does not appear on JPFs. One can argue that the analogy to the large objects is misleading, and that small clay figurines were considered too trivial for special destruction, but we do have evidence for mutilation of small figurines (Ritner 1993: nn. 671-75). One would rather expect to find at least some mutilated faces if the JPFs were really smashed in the course of 'zealous biblical reforms'.

To sum up, the study of breakage pattern indicates that the JPFs are not fundamentally different from any other assemblage of clay figurines in regard to damage patterns, and there is no real evidence that they were deliberately mutilated. On the contrary, it seems that accidental breakage is a better explanation.

The Context

I have made a thorough survey on the context of the JPF, but this is hardly the place to present detailed statistics. This subject was much neglected, and the only former study worthy of mention is Holladay (1987, but a very limited one). It is important to establish a few guidelines. One must separate whole figurines from fragments, since fragments are small and more likely to be found out of context. Moreover, broken parts indicate usually the place of disposal, rather than the place of use. Even in regard to whole figurines, every case must be studied carefully.

There are 27 whole JPFs, 20 of which come from known contexts. 12 were found in tombs, the rest in various other contexts (water cisterns, pits and a domestic room). The tomb figurines were probably placed carefully, not as special 'grave goods', and they do not prove any religious or 'magic' function of the JPFs.

The many hundreds of fragments were found in a large variety of contexts: cisterns (14), water pools (27), pits (14), caves (16), tombs (8), rooms of houses (49), courts (10), gates (1 or 2), storehouses (7), streets and alleys (8), open areas (9), areas out of the walled cities (12), and so on. Domestic context are by far the most prominent (70 cases, with another 42 in doubt), but JPFs were also found in public places (9, with another 11 in doubt) and burials (20, with another 17 in doubt). Very few fragments are related to religious sites (5 at most), that is, the Arad temple and a room defined as a house shrine at Tel Lahav (Jacobs 1992; Borowski 1995). Part of the problem is how to define a religious site. For example, there is a common view that Jerusalem cave I is a cultic centre (Kenyon 1967; 1974; Franken 1995; Franken and Steiner 1990: 49, 125; for the date cf. Eshel and Prag 1995). This small cave, so full of objects, could hardly function as a centre of rituals. All the JPFs from this cave were broken (the fragments do not join each other), and were deposited—but less likely used—within the cave. Of around 1300 finds from the cave, only three can be termed cultic (two small stone altars and one broken pottery stand, Holland 1977: Fig. 9: 20-23; Franken and Steiner 1990: 44, C270). It seems that the cultic explanation of cave I relies on the pre-conception that the JPFs are related to cult—but this must be proven first. In any case, the JPFs are found in all areas of life, from tombs to domestic loci and public places.

A study of contexts can indicate the existence of groups of figurines. By groups I mean more than one figurine at the same time and place, indicating the use of some JPFs together. It is not a simple task, as this question has never been tested thoroughly. At first glance, many groups of 2–4 JPFs were found together in tombs, pits, cisterns, streets, etc. However, a closer look shows that these are 'mass' loci—places that do not indicate a real relation between the figurines, for example, very long streets, or cisterns into which material was dumped during a long period of time. The same is true for Judaean graves, because these are family graves with multiple burials in each. Thus, 2–4 JPFs from one grave do not form a real group at all. Furthermore, in most cases what we have are fragments of figurines, related to places of disposal rather than places of use. Removal of the doubtful cases leaves so few possible groups, that it is safe to conclude that the JPFs were used singly and not in groups. This may indicate that they represented the same figure and not many individual figures (thus there was no need to group the same figure together, as opposed to figurines of dancers, for example, that appear in groups).

I have also checked the relationship between the JPFs and other finds, such as animal figurines, bird figurines, male figurines, miniature models of furniture, and so on. The data is still very limited, so the results—interesting as they may seem—should be judged cautiously.

Meaning and Function

Four basic attitudes concerning the meaning of the JPFs have been formulated during more than a hundred years of study: (1) toys, used by children; (2) mortal women; (3) goddesses (whether general, e.g., 'mother goddess' or 'fertility goddess', or specific, e.g., Astarte or Asherah); (4) magical figures. Other possible explanations, such as mortuary-figurines (cf. Voigt 1983) were not suggested for the JPFs, but are unlikely and need not be viewed here.

Toys

This explanation was made in the early phases of research, but was never popular. It was often restricted to a few figurines (Albright 1943: 142) or to zoomorphic figurines (e.g., Tufnell 1953: 374; Kenyon 1967: 101; 1974: 142; Burrows 1941: 221). Only a few scholars thought that all the figurines were toys (De Vaux 1958: 82). Fowler (1985: 341-42) mentioned this explanation, but without proving it (cf. Ucko 1968: 422-23). These days, only Hubner (1993: 92-93, Fig. 46) believes in this explanation, but without any new grounds. There are a few reasons why the JPFs are not toys: (1) JPFs were found in public buildings, where we would not expect to find toys (storehouses in Tel Beer Sheba and Tel Ira, the temple area in Arad, the public buildings of Ramat Rahel). (2) The JPFs are very uniform in shape, whereas toys usually exhibit an individual character, either by manufacture, decoration, or through use by children. (3) The crude manufacture and lack of decorations on the back of the JPFs indicate that they were meant to be seen from the front, that is, to stand in a rather static position. This does not fit toys, which are used for playing. (4) The JPFs are very vulnerable, while toys should stand the wear and tear of playing. (5) At present there is no archaeological evidence to connect the JPFs with children, or with children's burials.[5] (6) There is a growing tendency to reject this explanation in regard to other ancient Near Eastern figurines (e.g. Tooley 1991; Gates 1992: 169).

Representations of Mortal Women
This possibility has been almost completely ignored. Pritchard (1943: 86) raised it tentatively. Hachlili suggested that the many variations of shape of figurines from Ashdod imply different women (Dothan 1971: 132). JPFs from Jerusalem cave I were explained as representations of women, who came to the cave to seek help in birth or disease (Franken and Steiner 1990: 128). There are some doubts regarding this explanation: (1) The great physical and technical uniformity (clay, white wash, decoration, position of hands, schematic lower body) seem to imply the lack of any effort in representing individual women. Even the heads are very uniform. (2) The JPFs were probably used separately. This hints that they symbolized the same figure, and not many individual women. (3) The JPFs do not show distinct aspects of 'fertility', such as pregnancy, children and rendering of the pubic area. (4) Understanding the JPFs as mortal women does not solve the problem, for who exactly were these women? Why were they represented in large quantities? How do we explain their wide distribution in various contexts?

It is possible that mortal figures were made without any deep meaning, but for aesthetic reasons only. This explanation was never suggested, perhaps because it is so simple. From an archaeological point of view, it is extremely hard to test such a theory. However, it hardly fits what we know about ancient art, which was a rigid way of expressing (mainly) royal and religious messages. If the JPFs had some symbolic meaning, they had to 'act an action', and this makes them very similar to the so-called magical figures (see below). Seeing the JPFs as mortal

---

5.   When speaking of toys, we mean children's toys by definition. Adults also have 'toys'—only we call these gods or magical figures. Therefore, though the separation of children's toys from adults' toys may not be absolute, it can be used in archaeology and is not artificial.

women is not a full explanation, since it does not clarify what the meaning of such figurines was.

Goddesses
General: Mother Goddess, Fertility Goddess, Nurturing Goddess, Naked Goddess. Many scholars suggested that the JPFs represented female goddesses, but did not identify them with specific goddesses (Hubner 1989: 53; Miller 1986: 245; Barkay 1990: 191). The term 'mother goddess' was most widely used, and often related to fertility (Duncan 1924: 180; May 1935: 27; Burrows 1941: 221; Kenyon 1967: 101; Heaton 1974: 232; Dever 1982: 38; 1990: 137; Keel and Uehlinger 1992: 381; for animal figurines see also Albright 1943: 82; Mazar 1990: 501; McCown 1947: 247; Franken and Steiner 1990: 128). The terms 'nurturing goddess' or 'suckling goddess' were also widely used (McCown 1947: 245; Macalister 1912: 417; Supinska-Løvset 1978: 21-22; Holladay 1987: 278; Wenning 1991: 91; Keel and Uehlinger 1992: 380-81). The term 'naked goddess' was less popular (Watzinger 1933: 117; Tufnell 1953: 374), and adopted mainly within the iconographic school of thought, which also coined the term 'the Syrian goddess' (Winter 1983: 129-31, 192-99; Briend 1992: 27). It seems to me that all these terms are vague and contribute nothing to the understanding of the JPFs.

The notion of a prehistoric 'mother or fertility goddess' was wide-spread at the end of the nineteenth century and the beginning of this century. It was believed that prehistoric figurines represented a goddess, but without written sources this goddess could not be named (Ucko 1968: 409-16). Complex theories were built on the idea of a general 'mother goddess', especially for Europe and the Mediterranean areas. Scholars even reconstructed matriarchal societies ruled by women on the basis of female 'mother goddess' figurines. How absurd this is can be seen from the JPFs; they are all female, but the OT shows that Judaean society was dominated by men. Many scholars criticized sharply such 'mother goddess' theories (Ucko 1968: 417-19; Wiggins 1991: 392; P.L. Day 1992: 181, 185; Walls 1992: 15; Bailey 1994; Lemche 1992: 253 nn. 26-27). Every one of the major known goddesses in the ancient Near East was a 'mother goddess' in that she mixed motherly and divine characteristics, much as every male god is, by definition, a 'father god'. It is a basic idiom in almost any human society. As far as the JPFs are concerned, there is hardly an indication of motherhood (except one unique figurine, Kletter 1996: Appendix 2, 232). A scholar who explains the JPFs as a goddess must try to identify this goddess, but if it cannot be done, then adding 'mother' or 'fertility' to the definition 'goddess' contributes nothing.

Furthermore, during the Iron Age II period, several goddesses are known from Judah and its neighbours (e.g. Astarte, Asherah). Never do we hear about a 'general mother goddess', worshipped by everyone. Is it possible that such major goddess existed in Iron Age II Judah, without being mentioned in any written source? And that the only feature of such a goddess is that she is 'a mother goddess', in other words, without any individuality (but just like any other goddess)? The same is true also for the term fertility: it is a vague term that can be glued to every goddess.[6] Handy (1993: 158) went even further, writing that the mother-goddess is 'a topic, overused since the nineteenth century, which is "in" now, but it is a lazy way to deal with the variety of female deities known from the ancient world'.

The term 'Syrian goddess' is even worse, even if we ignore the mixing of distance sources, periods and places by the iconographic school of thought. What is Syrian in the JPFs? They have no relation with Syria, and this misleading term must be discarded forthwith. The situation is similar for terms such as 'naked goddess' (the JPFs are only partially naked, they have very schematic lower bodies). It is a description, not a real explanation. Behind all these terms lies the assumption that there existed a certain great cosmic goddess or 'general goddess', worshipped by a large number of societies, mainly during prehistoric periods. In my view, this theory cannot be accepted for Iron Age II Judah. There may have been syncretism and influences between different goddesses at different places, or a common origin in some distant past. But, once a population adopts a goddess at a certain time and place, it cannot be a 'general goddess'; it is adopted for specific needs and circumstances of that population, thus becoming unique (at least in some details). The main question, then, is do the JPFs represent a goddess? If not, all these terms are groundless. If they do, one must try to identify a specific goddess. Therefore, all these vague terms are superfluous and we would do much better without them.

---

6. For example, the Greek goddesses: 'almost every single Greek goddess has a fertility aspect of one kind or another' (Hadzisteliou-Price 1978: 3; for fertility cult cf. Bonano 1986).

Specific Goddesses: Astarte, Anat, 'Astarte-Anat-Asherah'. Many scholars identified the JPFs with Astarte (Vincent 1907: 161; Macalister 1912: 412; Driver 1922: 56-59; Pilz 1924: 161, 166). Some scholars used the name Astarte only for convenience sake, without really claiming that they represented Astarte (Barkay 1990: 191; McCown 1947: 245, 273; Albright 1943: 138; Holland 1975: 42, 62, 97; Aharoni 1978: photo 37; Briend and Humbert 1980: 350; Jeremias 1993: 44). Other scholars called the JPFs Astarte on one hand, but explained them as Asherah on the other hand (Ahlström 1963: 53-54; 1984: 138). During the last decades, the Anat/Astarte explanation lost its popularity. These two goddesses are related more with Cana'an, Phoenicia and northern Israel, and not Judah. Anat seems too remote, and is hardly mentioned as a likely candidate for identification with the JPFs today.[7]

Certain scholars combined Astarte-Anat-Asherah into one 'basic' goddess, especially Dever (1982: 39; 1984: 28; 1990: 159-60; 1994: 121-22). This seems doubtful (cf. Reed 1949): the ancient written sources distinguished explicitly between these three goddesses. It is hard to believe that all three could be venerated as one goddess during the later Iron Age period (while the JPFs are so uniform, that they can hardly represent three different goddesses—how would the users know which is which?).

Asherah. This is the most popular explanation today, with variations dependent on the different understandings of the biblical Asherah: a phenomenon of official religion, a forbidden or non-conformist cult, a house-cult or part of popular religion (Patai 1967: 35, 43, 60; Engle 1979: 27-30, 50-52, 80; Dever 1982: 37; Ahlström 1982; 1984: 136; Teubal 1984: 91; Holladay 1987: 278; Gadon 1989: 96, photo, 171; Dever 1990: 158-59; Wenning 1991: 90; Bloch-Smith 1992: 218-19 n. 16; Dever 1994: 120-22). The logic behind the identification with Asherah is that if the JPFs represented a goddess, it must have been Asherah. She is the only likely candidate in later Iron Age Judah, in the light of her dominant position in the Old Testament and her appearance beside Yahweh in the inscriptions from Kh. el-Kom and Kuntillet

7. For Anat see Deem 1978; Smith 1990: 61-64; Walls 1992; P.L. Day 1992; for Astarte see Leclant 1960; Fantar 1973; Delcor 1974; Ammerman 1991: 219-22; P.L. Day 1992; J. Day 1992; Gorg 1993; J. Day 1994: 187; Smith 1994: 205; Lemaire 1994: 129-32. I am using the common English spelling, but when speaking about Judah, the OT term 'Ashtoret' is more appropriate.

'Ajrud (Beck 1982; Lemaire 1994: 134; P.L. Day 1992; Wiggins 1991). In the OT, Asherah is often mentioned as a cultic object made of wood (Exod. 34.13; Deut. 7.5; 12.13). In Judges 6, Asherah may have been an actual tree standing above or near the altar. In a few verses, it seems that Asherah is a goddess or a cult statue of that goddess (Deut. 16.21, 1 Kgs 21.7; 23.6). Asherah was certainly part of the official cult of Judah—she was introduced into the Jerusalem temple by Judaean kings (1 Kgs 15.13, 33; 21.7). It seems that it was not a forbidden cult, nor a foreign one. 2 Kgs 18.19 relates Asherah with Ba'al, but this seems to be a secondary interpolation (while the 'Asherim' of the Chronicler is a late, a-historic form). Whether Asherah was considered as a *paredos* of Yahweh, at least in some circles, is not clear. The amount of recent literature on the Asherah is bewildering (for a basic study see Reed 1949; for the most recent, thorough work see Frevel 1995).[8] For our purpose, the central question is whether indeed the JPFs represent Asherah? This is possible regarding date and distribution. There is no clear evidence for cult in relation to the JPFs, but neither is there for the exact form of veneration of the Asherah (there is also the problem of defining cult and finding it in the archaeological record). The depositing of JPFs as domestic waste into streets and pits may pose a problem if Asherah was a high, venerated goddess. But the status of Asherah is not clear, and there is a great difference between disposal patterns and use-patterns.

Many scholars assumed that the pillar bodies of the JPFs represented a tree-trunk, the assumed form of the OT Asherah, but this has no factual basis. The OT does not provide a specific description of the Asherah. That she was made of wood is common to cult statues (and other objects) in the ancient Near East. Living trees may have been her symbol, or wooden cult objects. However, there is no definite proof that she had a pillar-shaped body. On the other hand, the JPF's body does not seem to represent a tree. Pillar bodies are a widespread solution for

---

8.   A partial bibliography includes Lemaire 1977; Emerton 1982; Winter 1983; Dever 1984; Pettey 1985; Betlyon 1985; Olyan 1985: chs. 2–3; Hadley 1987; Hestrin 1987; Schroer 1987: 21-45; Tigay 1987: 172-73; Koch 1988; North 1989; Dever 1990, ch. 4; Smith 1990: 80-124; Hestrin 1991; Wiggins 1991; J. Day 1992; Dearman 1992: 79; Dietrich and Loretz 1992; Hubner 1992; Whitt 1992; Ikeda 1993; Wiggins 1993; Dever 1994; Dietrich and Klopfenstein 1994; Hadley 1994; Lemaire 1994: 148-49; Smith 1994: 198-206. On the new inscription from Ekron see Gitin 1993: 250-52; 1995: 72.

standing figurines in the Near East. The widened base is necessary for a safe standing. Once a round body with a widening base is used, it is difficult to represent separate legs, except, perhaps, by incisions or stamping on the front part of the round body (this is found very rarely, and looks very awkward, Kletter 1996: Appendix 5.IV.7.19). Legs do 'return' later, in double-moulded figurines, where the whole body is made in a mould. Moreover, some riders of the horse-and-rider figurines have pillar bodies, but they stand on horses and cannot be connected with trees or poles.

Magical Figures
Understanding the JPFs as magical figurines was widespread during early stages of research, when magic was understood as the complete opposite of religion (and gods). Usually, the magic was termed 'sympathetic' or 'apotropaic', and the figurines were regarded as amulets for domestic use, or as 'good luck charms' (McCown 1947: 245, 248; Burrows 1941: 220; Wright 1957: 118; Dothan 1971: 133; Heaton 1974: 232; Franken and Steiner 1990: 128; for an anthropologic discussion of magic see Morris 1987). The date and the distribution may fit a magical explanation of the JPFs. The context is also fitting, as are the (probable) private ownership and cheap material. The disposal as domestic waste (in streets/pits) is possible, or at least less problematic than if the JPFs represented a major goddess. If the JPFs relate to magic, it is probably 'good (white) magic'. They have 'good' outward shape (smile full face, 'offering' the breasts). They were probably not mutilated deliberately, and were very popular in Judah. The lack of overt sexual features suggests that they symbolized 'plenty' rather then 'fertility' (cf. Wenning 1991: 91).

Even so, seeing the JPFs as magical figures is far from simple. There is no archaeological proof that the JPFs are related to any magic rituals. True, one need not suppose complex rituals, of the kind documented from Mesopotamia and Egypt (below), and large parts of such rituals will not be found in the archaeological record. The problem is, however, much more difficult. It relates not only to the question of what is magic (below), but to the fact that defining the JPFs as magical figurines is no real solution. This definition gives a function, but not a meaning: who is this 'magical' figure? Why wasn't it mentioned in the OT, despite its popularity in Judah?

Conclusions: The Figurines and the Asherah[9]

I believe that all the JPFs represented the same figure, and not many, different figures. This is based on the schematic rendering, without any effort to individualize the figurines. The lack of groups of JPFs from the same loci also strengthens this view, as each JPF was meant to be used separately. Following this reasoning, I believe that the JPFs had one meaning only, and represented one figure. Theoretically, the same type of figurine can have more than one meaning, but this is also an easy way of escaping the problem. If the JPFs portrayed the same figure, it is likely that they had one basic function (whatever that may be). Again, one figure may be used for more than one function, but if one considers the majority of the JPFs, I believe that it had one function. It is possible that a few JPFs were used for various other functions, but the burden of proof falls on those who support this possibility.

Two explanations for the JPFs remain probable: magical figure and Asherah. These two explanations are not contradictory, but complementary. Former studies of the JPFs used, to a large extent, a concept of magic based on the work of Frazer (1890), who put magic as the very antithesis of religion. It supposedly deals with natural forces, at the most demons and monsters, coercing them for immediate personal help (while religion deals with supernatural gods, morality and theology). Magic includes rituals, performed by witches or sorcerers (while religion involves cult, prayers and official priests). Magic has no logic (as opposed to science) and is 'primitive', if not totally negative.

As anthropologists and sociologists continued to search for a definition of magic, it seems that the picture became more and more problematic. Weber (1922, ET 1965: 28) defined magic in a similar way to Frazer, but knew that the separation between religion and magic is not absolute: 'the cults we have just called 'religious' practically everywhere contain numerous magical components'. Actually, magic is defined only from an outside point of view. Malinowski (1925: 88) followed Frazer, and saw magic as 'a practical art consisting of acts which are only means to a definite end expected to follow later on'; while religion is 'a body of self-contained acts being themselves the

---

9.   I will not discuss here the problems of 'house cult'; the relations between the JPFs and other types of figurines; and the scarcity of male figurines (Kletter 1996: ch. X).

fulfillment of their purpose'. To make it more simple, 'the belief in magic…is extremely simple. It is always the affirmation of men's power to cause certain definite effects by a definite spell and rite. In religion, on the other hand, we have a whole supernatural world of faith' (Malinowski 1925: 88). Mauss (1950: 18) suggested a social definition of magic (1950: 24), 'A magical rite is *any* rite which does not play a part in organized cults—it is private, secret, mysterious and approaching the limit of a prohibited rite…we do not define magic in terms of the structure of its rites, but by the circumstances in which these rites occur'. However, Mauss returned later to a conception more in line with Frazer's: 'while religion, because of its intellectual character, has a tendency towards metaphysics, magic—which we have shown to be more concerned with the concrete—is concerned with understanding nature'. Skorupski was aware that 'the "opposition" between the two "institutions" of magic and religion does not exist as a general fact' (1976: 127). The problem of demarcating magic from religion is acute: 'we must not expect a neatly exhaustive distinction… between the religious and the magical' (1976: 155). Skorupski con-cluded, though, like Weber: 'what is for us in the end most striking about magical practices is that they require assumptions which in one way or another run counter to the categorical framework within which we (at least officially) interpret the world' (Skorupski 1976: 159).

Magic cannot be separated exactly from religion. Magic is not defined by values, but sociologically: what 'we' do is religion, what 'they' do is magic. Ritner defined magic as 'the religious practices of one group viewed with disdain by another'. In other words, 'Your religion is my Magic' (Ritner 1992: 190; cf. Versnel 1991; Voigt 1983). In ancient Egypt, magic was legal and could be desirable; it was practised in official temples by high-ranking priests, and had no connotation of immorality. Much the same is true for Mesopotamia (Ritner 1992; 1993; Wiggermann 1992).[10] Therefore, the JPFs can represent Asherah, without negating magical aspects or the relation to magical rituals (I follow Ritner's definition of magic here, of course). On the other hand, explaining the JPFs as purely magical figures is not satisfactory, since it relates only to their function, not to their meaning. In order to keep a purely magical explanation, one would have to

10. I had the pleasure of hearing a lecture on early Mesopotamian incantations by M. Cunningham of Cambridge University, England, who has reached (indepen-dently) similar conclusions about magic.

assume that there was a very common magical figure in Judah (the large quantity of JPFs), that was not mentioned in the OT, and is not one of the known goddesses. This is possible, but quite perplexing.

It seems therefore that the JPFs are indeed a representation of the OT Asherah: this is the most logical explanation. On the other hand, the JPFs are not exactly identical with the Asherah. This was the belief of many scholars, who treated the two as equal. The relations between gods and their cult statues have been discussed extensively (Hallo 1983; Jacobsen 1987; for Greece cf. Gladigow 1985–86; Romano 1988; for Mesopotamia see Dietrich and Loretz 1992: 7-38; Matsushima 1993; for Egypt, Ockinga 1984). Most of the large cult statues have disappeared, since they were made of wood and of precious metals (for the burial of statues cf. Hallo 1983: 15-16; Matsushima 1993: 210). Large sculptures are not found in Judah, unlike Ammon (stone sculptures), Cyprus (clay statues, possibly of prayers, Connelly 1989); Phoenicia (Eshmun temple at Sidon: Ganzman *et al.* 1987) and Edom (Qitmit and En-Hazevah: Beck 1995; Cohen and Yisrael 1995). This may strengthen the claim that the OT 'ban of idols' is indeed ancient (Curtis 1984). The relation between small figurines and large cult statues is not always simple. Alroth showed that the two are not necessarily identical in shape, even when depicting the same figure (based on material from Greek temples, Alroth 1989; but the context of the JPFs is mainly domestic). A source from the reign of Nabu-Apla-Iddina (the ninth century BCE) is enlightening. It tells how a model of baked clay of Samas was used to reproduce a cult statue (after the former cult statue was taken by the Sutu). The exact nature of this model is not clear, though: is it a figurine, a tablet of clay, or even a cylinder seal? (Lee 1993; cf. the later story about Herostratos, Atheneaus 16, 675, Ammermann 1991: 223).

The JPFs are small figurines, without special, sacred status and probably not connected with public temples. The sacredness of an object stands in relation to its function (that is, status), its value ('price'), and its form (size). The large cult statue of the Asherah was sacred because it was probably decorated in expensive materials, situated in a public temple and represented the goddess in front of all the population—but especially the higher classes (priests and kings). On the other hand, the JPFs were cheap, everyday objects, representing the goddess in private houses, in front of ordinary people (chiefly, though not only). The JPFs are not evidence of 'popular religion', if by this we mean the opposite to an 'official Yahwistic religion'. The Asherah was part of the Yahwistic religion, though she was probably not as important as he was. The function of the Asherah figurines was possibly as a protecting figure in domestic houses, more likely a figure which bestowed 'plenty', especially in the domain of female lives (but not necessarily used by women only). These figurines have nothing to do with 'black magic' and were not a forbidden cult, at least for most of the time and for most of the population. It seems that they were not broken deliberately. Other than being a symbol for the goddess and what she can bestow, I doubt if the figurines were an object of cult practices. At the most, one can imagine that they were addressed in prayers or wishes, perhaps during times of pressure and need.

It is important to stress that the identification of the JPFs with Asherah seems very probable, but is not proven and should not be taken for granted. This identification is based on the OT sources (together with the Kh. el-Kom and Kuntillet 'Ajrud inscriptions) or, to be more correct, on a certain interpretation of these sources (e.g. in rejecting the 'Asherim' of the Chronicler). It would be unwise to turn the wheel the full way round, and simplistically draw conclusions from the JPFs about the OT Asherah. If this is the case for 854 figurines, the identification of other objects, much more limited in numbers, is hazardous. Varied artifacts were called 'Asherah' in studies (e.g. Pettey 1985), but without any factual basis for their identification with her (cf. already Reed 1949).

Archaeology can, indeed, help us to understand the religion of ancient Israel and Judah, but it is not a totally independent, nor a 'direct' source. Cautious archaeological attitude should be the basis of continuing research, rather than further speculations about meaning and function.

Bibliography

Ackerman, S.
    1992   *Under every Green Tree: Popular Religion in Sixth-Century Judah* (HSM, 46; Atlanta, GA: Scholars Press).
Aharoni, Y.
    1962   *Excavations at Ramat Rahel (Seasons 1959 and 1960)* (Rome: Università di Roma. Centro di Studi Semitici).
    1964   *Excavations at Ramat Rahel (Seasons 1961 and 1962)* (Rome: Università di Roma. Centro di Studi Semitici).

1978   *The Archaeology of the Land of Israel* (trans. A. Rainey; Philadelphia.
            Westminster Press, 1982).

Aharoni, Y. (ed.)
1975   *Investigations at Lachish* (Tel Aviv: Tel Aviv University).

Ahlström, G.W.
1963   *Aspects of Syncretism in Israelite Religion* (Lund: Horae
            Soederblominae).
1982   *Royal Administration and National Religion in Ancient Palestine* (Leiden:
            E.J. Brill).
1984   'An Archaeological Picture of Iron Age Religions in Ancient Palestine',
            Studia Orientalia 55: 117-44.

Albright, W.F.
1939   'Astarte Plaques and Figurines from Tel Beit-Mirsim', in *Mélanges
            Syriens offerts à monsieur René Daussaud* (Paris: Librarie Geuthner):
            107-20.

Albright, W.F. (ed.)
1943   *The Excavation of Tel Beit Mirsim*. III. *The Iron Age* (AASOR 21-22;
            New Haven: American Schools of Oriental Research).

Alroth, B.
1989   *Greek Gods and Figurines: Aspects of Anthropomorphic Dedications*
            (Uppsala: Almquist and Wiksell).

Ammerman, R.M.
1985   'Medma and the Exchange of Votive Terracottas', in C. Molene and S.
            Stoddart (eds.), *Papers in Italian Archaeology IV* (BAR International
            Series, 246; Oxford: BAR): 5-19.
1991   'The Naked Standing Goddess: A Group of Archaic Terracotta Figurines
            from Paestum', *AJA* 95.2: 203-30.

Amr, A.J.
1980   'A Study of Clay Figurines and Zoomorphic Vessels of Transjordan
            during the Iron Age, with special Reference to their Symbolism and
            Function' (PhD thesis, University of London).

Bailey, D.W.
1994   'Reading Prehistoric Figurines as Individuals', *World Archaeology* 25.3:
            321-33.

Barkay, G.
1990   'The Iron Age II–III', in A. Ben-Tor (ed.), *The Archaeology of Ancient
            Israel in the Biblical Period* (The Open University): 77-233 (Hebrew).

Beck, P.
1982   'The Drawings from Horvat Teiman (Kuntillet 'Ajrud)', *TA* 9: 3-86.
1991   'A Figurine from Tel 'Ira', *EI* 21: 87-93 (Hebrew).
1995   'Catalogue of Cult Objects and Study of the Iconography', in I. Beit-
            Arieh (ed.), *Horvat Qitmit: An Edomite Shrine in the Biblical Negev* (Tel
            Aviv University): 27-197.

Betlyon, J.W.
1985   'The Cult of the Asherah/ Elat at Sidon', *JNES* 44: 53-56.

Bloch-Smith, E.M.
1992   'The Cult of the Dead in Judah: Interpreting the Material Remains', *JBL*
            111.2: 213-24.

Bonano, A. (ed.)

1986 'Archaeology and Fertility Cult in the Ancient Mediterranean', Papers presented at the First Conference on Archaeology of the Ancient Mediterranean, Malta 1985 (Amsterdam: Gruner).

Borowski, O.

1995 'Hezekiah's Reforms and the Revolt against Assyria', *BA* 58.3: 148-55.

Brandes, M.

1980 'Destruction et mutilation de statues en Mesopotamie', *Akkadica* 16: 28-40.

Briend, J.

1992 'Bible et Archéologie: dialogue entre deux disciplines', *Le Monde du Bible* 75: 37-41.

Briend, J., and J.P. Humbert (eds.)

1980 *Tell Keisan (1971–1976): Une cité phénicienne en Galilée* (Paris: Gabalda).

Burrows, M.

1941 *What Mean these Stones?* (New Haven: American Schools of Oriental Research).

Caubet, A.

1991 'The Terracottas Workshops of Idalion during the Cypro-archaic Period', in *Acta Cypria 1991/3* (Studies in Mediterranean Archaeology Pocket Book, 120; Jonsered: P. Astrom): 128-49.

Ciasca, A.

1964 'Some Particular Aspects of the Israelite Miniature Statuary at Ramat Rahel', in Aharoni 1964: 95-100.

Clermont-Ganneau, C.

1896 *Archaeological Research in Palestine Vol. I* (repr. 1971; trans. A. Stewart; Jerusalem: Raritas).

Cohen, R.

1983 *Kadesh-Barnea: A Fortress from the Time of the Judean Kingdom* (The Israel Museum Catalogue No. 233; Jerusalem: The Israel Museum).

Cohen, R., and Y. Yisrael

1995 *On the Road to Edom. Discoveries from 'En Hazevah* (The Israel Museum Catalogue No. 370: Jerusalem: The Israel Museum) (Hebrew and English).

Connelly, J.B.

1989 'Standing before one's God: Votive Sculpture and the Cypriote Religious Tradition', *BA* 52.4: 210-18.

Culican, W.

1969 'Dea Tyria Gravida', *Annual of the Japanese Biblical Institute* 1.2: 35-50 (repr. in *Opera Selecta: From Tyre to Tartessos* [Göterborg: P. Astroms, 1986]: 265-80).

Curtis, E.M.

1984 'Man as the Image of God in Genesis in the Light of Ancient Near Eastern Parallels' (PhD dissertation, University of Pennsylvania).

Day, J.

1992 'Asherah, Astarte', *ABD* I: 483-87, 491-94.

1994   'Yahweh and the Gods and Goddesses of Canaan', in Dietrich and
              Klopfenstein (eds.) 1994: 181-96.

Day, P.L.

1992   'Anat: Ugarit's "Mistress of Animals"', *JNES* 51.3: 181-90.

De Vaux, R.

1958   *Les institutions de l'Ancient Testament* (Paris: CERF). English translation
              by J. McHugh, *Ancient Israel, its Life and Institutions* (London: Darton,
              Longman and Todd, 1961).

Dearman, J.A.

1992   *Religion and Culture in Ancient Israel* (Hendrickson: Peabody Museum).

Deem, A.

1978   'The Goddess Anath and some Biblical Hebrew Cruces', *JSS* 23.1: 25-30.

Delcor, M.

1974   'Le Hieros Gamos d'Astarte', *Rivista di Studi Fenici* II (repr. in *Réligion
              d'Israel et Proche Orient Ancient* [Leiden: E.J. Brill, 1976]: 55-71).

Dever, W.G.

1982   'Recent Archaeological Confirmation to the Cult of Asherah in Ancient
              Israel', *Hebrew Studies* 23: 37-43.

1984   'Asherah, Consort of Jahweh? New Evidence from Kuntillet 'Ajrud',
              BASOR 255: 21-37.

1990   *Recent Archaeological Discoveries and Biblical Research* (Seattle:
              University of Washington Press).

1991   'Archaeology, Material Culture and the Early Monarchical Period in
              Israel', in D. Edelman (ed.), *The Fabric of History* (JSOTSup, 127;.
              Sheffield: Sheffield Academic Press): 103-15.

1994   'Ancient Israelite Religion: How to Reconcile the Differing Textual and
              Artifactual Portraits?' in Dietrich and Klopfenstein (eds.) 1994: 105-25.

Dietrich, M., and O. Loretz

1992   *'Jahwe und seine Aschera': Anthropomorphes Kultbild in Mesopotamien,
              Ugarit und Israel* (Das biblische Bildverbot; Münster: Ugarit Verlag).

Dietrich, W., and M.A. Klopfenstein (eds.)

1994   *Ein Gott allein?* (OBO, 139; Freiburg: Universitätsverlag).

Dornemann, R.H.

1983   *The Archaeology of the Transjordan in the Bronze and Iron Ages*
              (Milwaukee: Milwaukee Public Museum).

Dothan, M. (ed.)

1971   'Ashdod II–III: The Second and Third Seasons of Excavations, 1963,
              1965', *'Atiqot* X–IX.

Driver, S.R.

1922   *Modern Research as Illustrating the Bible* (The Schweich Lectures 1908;
              London: Oxford University Press).

Duncan, J.G.

1924   'Fourth Quarterly Report on the Excavation of the Eastern Hill of
              Jerusalem', *PEFQS*: 163-80.

Emerton, J.A.

1982   'New Light on Israelite Religion: The Implications of the Inscriptions
              from Kuntillet 'Ajrud', *ZDPV* 92: 2-20.

Engle, J.R.
1979   'Pillar Figurines of Iron Age Israel and Asherah/Asherim' (PhD thesis, Pittsburgh University).

Eshel, I. and K. Prag (eds.)
1995   *Excavations by K.M. Kenyon in Jerusalem 1961–1967. IV. The Iron Age Cave Deposits on the South-Eastern Hill and Isolated Burials and Cemeteries Elsewhere* (Oxford).

Fantar, M.H.
1973   'A propos d'Astart en Méditerranée Occidentale', *Rivista di Studi Fenici* 1: 19-29.

Finkelstein, I.
1996   'The Archaeology of the United Monarchy', *Levant* XXVIII: 177-87.

Fowler, M.D.
1985   'Excavated Figurines: A Case for Identifying a Site as Sacred?', *ZAW* 97: 333-44.

Franken, H.J.
1995   'Cave 1 at Jerusalem: An Interpretation', in S. Bourke and J.P. Descoeudres (eds.), *Trade, Contact and the Movement of People in the Eastern Mediterranean: Studies in Honour of J.B. Hennessy* (Sydney: University of Sydney).

Franken, H.J., and M.L. Steiner (eds.)
1990   *Jerusalem II: Excavations in Jerusalem 1961–1967. II. The Iron Age Extramural Quarter on the South West Hill* (Oxford: Oxford University Press).

Frazer, J.
1890   *The Golden Bough* (London, abridged from the 3rd edn of 1913, repr.. 1990).

Frevel, C.
1995   *Ascherah und die Ausschlichkeitsanspruch YHWHs: Beitrage zu literarischen, religionsgeschichtlischen und ikonographischen Aspecten der Ascheradiskussion* (Beltz: Athenäum).

Gadon, E.
1989   *The Once and Future Goddess* (Wellingborough: Aquarian Press).

Ganzman, L., H. Van der Meijden and R.A. Stucky
1987   'Das Eschmunheiligtum von Sidon. Die Funde der turkischen Ausgrabungen von 1901 bis 1903 im Archäologischen Museum in Istanbul', *Istanbuler Mitteilungen* 37: 81-130.

Gates, C.
1992   'Art for Children in Mycenaean Greece', in R. Laffineur and J.L. Crouwley (eds.), *eikΩon. Aegean Bronze Age Iconography* (Aegeum, 8; Université de Liège): 161-71.

Gitin, S.
1993   'Seventh Century BCE Cultic Elements at Ekron', in A. Biran and J. Aviram (eds.), *Biblical Archaeology Today II* (Jerusalem: Keter): 248-58.
1995   'Tel Miqne-Ekron in the 7th Century BCE: The Import of Economic Innovation and Foreign Cultural Influences on a Neo Assyrian Vassal City State', in *Recent Excavations in Israel: A View to the West.* (Dubuque, Iowa: Kendall-Hunt): 57-79.

Gladigow, B.
1985–86   'Präsenz der Bilder—Präsenz der Götter', in H.E. Kippenberg *et al.*
           (eds.), *Visible Religion IV–V* (Leiden: E.J. Brill): 114-33.
Gophna, R.
1970   'Some Iron Age II Sites in Southern Philistia', *'Atiqot* VI: 25-30
           (Hebrew).
Goren, Y., E. Kamaiski and R. Kletter
1996   *Appendix C: The Technology and Provenance of the Iron Age Figurines
           in City of David III* (Qedem, 35; Jerusalem: The Hebrew University).
Gorg, M.
1993   'Die "Astarte des Kleinviehs"', *BN* 69: 9-11.
Grant, E., and G.E. Wright
1939   *Ain Shems Excavations Part V* (Haverford: Text).
Gubel, E.
1991   'From Amathus to Zarephtah and Back Again', in F. Vandenabeele and
           R. Laffineur (eds.), *Cypriote Terracottas* (Brussels: Vrije Universiteit):
           131-38.
Hadley, J.M.
1987   'The Khirbet el- Kôm Inscription', *VT* 37: 50-62.
1994   'Yahweh and "His Asherah": Archaeological and Textual Evidence for
           the Cult of the Goddess', in Dietrich and Klopfenstein (eds.) 1994: 235-
           68.
Hadzisteliou-Price, T.
1978   *Kourotrophos: Cults and Representation of the Greek Nursing Deities*
           (Leiden: E.J. Brill).
Hallo, W.W.
1983   'Cult Statue and Divine Image: A Preliminary Study', in W.W. Hallo,
           J.C. Moyer and L.G. Perdue (eds.), *Scripture in Context II* (Winona Lake,
           IN: Eisenbrauns): 1-17.
Handy, L.K.
1993   'Review of Smith, M.S. 1990, "The Early History of God"', *JNES* 52.2:
           157-59.
Heaton, E.W.
1974   *Everyday Life in Old Testament Times* (London: B.T. Batsford).
Hestrin, R.
1987   'The Lachish Ewer and the Asherah', *IEJ* 37: 212-23.
1991   'Understanding Asherah', *BARev* 17: 50-59.
Holladay, J.S.
1987   'Religion in Israel and Judah under the Monarchy: An Explicitly
           Archaeological Approach', in Miller *et al.* (eds.) 1987: 249-99.
Holland, T.A.
1975   'A Typological and Archaeological Study of Human and Animal
           Representations in the Plastic Art of Palestine' (PhD thesis, Oxford
           University).
1977   'A Study of Palestinian Iron Age Baked Clay Figurines with Special
           Reference to Jerusalem: Cave 1', *Levant* 9: 121-55.
Hübner, U.
1989   'Das Fragment einer Tonfigurine von Tell el-Milḥ. Uberlegungen zur

Funkzion der sog. Pfeilerfigurinen in der Israëlitischen Volksreligion',
ZDPV 105: 47-55.

1992   'Der Tanz um die Ascheren', *UF* 24: 121-32.

1993   *Spiele und Spielzeug im Antiken Palästina* (OBO, 121; Freiburg: Univer-
        sitätsverlag).

Ikeda, Y.

1993   'Because their Shade is Good: Ashera in the Early Israelite Religion', in
        E. Matsushima (ed.), *Official Cult and Popular Religion in the Ancient
        Near East* (Heidelberg: Universitätsverlag): 56-80.

Ioannides, G.C.

1992   'Secondary Treatment of Prehistoric Figurines: An Example from
        Chalcolithic Cyprus', in *Studies in Honor of V. Karageorghis* (Nicosia:
        Choregia Hidrumatos Anastasios G. Leventes): 37-40.

Isserlin, B.S.J.

1976   'On Some Figurines of "Lamp Goddess" from Transjordan', *Rivista de la
        Universidado Compultense Hamenaje a Garcia Bellido I* 25: 138-42.

Jacobs, P.

1992   'Iron Age Halif Revisited', *Lahav newsletter* no. 51, September 1992 (ed.
        J. Seger; without page numbers).

Jacobsen, Th.

1987   'The Graven Image', in Miller *et al.* (eds.) 1987: 15-28.

Jeremias, J.

1993   'Thron oder Wagen? Eine aussergewohnliche Terakotte aus der späten
        Eizenzeit in Judah', in W. Zwickel (ed.), *Biblische Welten. Festschrift für
        M. Metzger zu seinem 65 Geburtstag* (Freiburg: Universitätsverlag): 41-
        60.

Jericke, D.

1992   'Tell es-Seba' Stratum V', *ZDPV* 108: 122-48.

Keel, O., and C. Uehlinger

1992   *Göttinen, Götter und Gottessymbole* (Frieburg: Herder Verlag).

Kelley, C.P.

1994   'Who Did the Iconoclasm in the Dura Synagogue?', *BASOR* 295: 57-72.

Kelso, J.L. and J.P. Thorley

1943   'The Potter's Technique at Tell beit Mirsim', in Albright (ed.) 1943: 86-
        143.

Kenyon, K.M.

1967   *Jerusalem: Excavating 3000 Years of History* (London: Thames and
        Hudson).

1974   *Digging up Jerusalem* (New York: Praeger).

Kletter, R.

1991   'The Inscribed Weights of the Kingdom of Judah', *Tel Aviv* 18.1: 121-63.

1996   *The Judean Pillar Figurines and the Archaeology of Asherah* (BAR
        International Series, 636; Oxford: Tempus Reparatum).

1999a   'Pots and Polities': Material Remains of Late Iron Age Judah in Relation
        to its Political Borders', *BASOR* 314: 19-54.

1999b   'Human and Animal Clay Figurines', in I. Beit-Arieh (ed.), *Tel 'Ira: A
        Stronghold in the Biblical Negev* (Institute of Archaeology Monograph
        Series, 15; Tel Aviv: Tel Aviv University): 374-85, 392-94.

Koch, K.
1988   'Aschera als Himmelskönigin in Jerusalem', *UF* 20: 97-120.
Leclant, J.
1960   'Astarte à cheval d'après les representations Egyptiennes', *Syria:* 1-67.
Lee, T.G.
1993   'The Jasper Cylinder Seal of Assurbanipal and Nabonidus' Making of Sin's Statue', *Révue d'Assyriologiques et d'Archéologie Orientale* 87.2: 131-36.
Lemaire, A.
1977   'Les inscriptions de Khirbet el-Qom et l'Asherah de YHWE', *RB* 84: 595-608.
1994   'Déesses et dieux de Syrie-Palestine d'après les inscriptions (c. 1000-500 Av. N. E.)', in Dietrich and Klopfenstein (eds.) 1994: 127-58.
Lemche, N.P.
1992   'The God of Hosea', in E. Ulrich *et al.* (eds.), *Priests, Prophets and Scribes: Essays in Honour of Joseph Blenkinsopp* (JSOTSup, 149; Sheffield: Sheffield Academic Press): 241-57.
Linder, E.
1986   'The Figurines from Shavey Zion: A Re-examination', in M. Yeda'aya (ed.), *The Western Galilee Antiquities* (Haifa) (Hebrew).
Lipinski, E.
1986   'The Syro-Palestinian Iconography of Women and Goddess: Review Article', *IEJ* 36: 87-98.
Liverani, M.
1990   *Prestige and Interset: International Relations in the Near East ca. 1600-1100 BC* (Padova: Sargon SRL).
Macalister, R.A.S.
1905   'Why did Rachel Steal the Teraphim of Laban?', *PEFQS*: 270-71.
1912   *The Excavation of Gezer Vol. II* (London: J. Murray).
Mackenzie, D.
1912–13   'Excavations at Ain Shems (Beth Shemesh)', *PEFA* II.
Malinowski, B.
1925   'Magic, Science and Religion', reprinted in J. Needham (ed.), *Magic, Science and Religion and Other Essays* (Garden City, NY: Doubleday): 17-92.
Matsushima, E.
1993   'Divine Statues in Ancient Mesopotamia: Their Fashioning and Clothing and their Interaction with the Society', in *Official Cult and Popular Religion in the Ancient Near East* (Heidelberg: Universitätsverlag): 209-19.
Mauss, M.
1950   *A General Theory of Magic* (trans. R. Brain; London: Routledge, 1972).
May, J.G.
1935   *Material Remains of the Megiddo Cult* (Oriental Institute Publications, 26; Chicago: University of Chicago Press).
Mazar, A.
1990   *Archaeology of the Land of the Bible* (New York: Doubleday).
Mazar, E.
1979   'Archaeological Evidence for the "Cows of the Bashan Who Are in the

Mountains of Samaria"', in *Festschrift R.R. Hecht* (Haifa: Koren): 151-56 (Hebrew).

McCown, C.
1947   *Tell en Nasbeh I: Archaeological and Historical Results* (Berkeley and New Haven: Pacific Schools of Religion and the AASOR).

Meyers, C.
1988   *Discovering Eve: Ancient Israelite Women in Context* (New York: Oxford University Press).
1991   'Of Drums and Damsels: Women's Performance in Ancient Israel', *BA* 54: 16-27.

Miller, P.D.
1986   'The Absence of the Goddess in Israelite Religion', *HAR* 10: 239-48.

Miller, P.D., P.D. Hanson and S.D. McBride (eds.)
1987   *Ancient Israelite Religion: Essays in Honor of F.M. Cross* (Philadelphia: Fortress Press).

Mittmann, S.
1990   'Hizkia und die Philister', *JNSL* XVI: 91-106.

Moorey, P.R.S., and S. Fleming
1984   'Problems in the Study of the Anthropomorphic Metal Statuary from Syro-Palestine before 330 BC', *Levant* XVI: 67-90.

Morris, B.
1987   *Anthropological Studies of Religion: An Introductory Text* (Cambridge: Cambridge University Press).

Na'aman, N.
1989   'The Kingdom of Judah under Joshia', *Zion* 54: 17-71 (Hebrew; ET [1991] *TA* 18.1: 3-71).
1992b   'Israel, Edom and Egypt in the 10th Century BCE', *TA* 19: 71-93.

Nadelman, Y.
1989   'Iron Age II Clay Fragments from the Excavations: Appendix A', in E. Mazar and B. Mazar (eds.), *Excavations in the South of the Temple* (Qedem, 29; Jerusalem: The Hebrew University): 123-25.

Naveh, J.
1962   'More Hebrew Inscriptions from Mesad Hashavyahu', *IEJ* 12: 27-32.

Nicholls, R.V.
1952   'Type, Group and Series: A Reconsideration of Some Coroplastic Fundamentals', *Annual of the British School at Athens* XLVII: 217-26.

North, R.
1989   'Yahweh's Asherah', in M.P. Horgan and P.J. Kobelski (eds.), *To Touch the Text: Biblical Studies in Honour of J.A. Fitzmyer* (New York: Crossboards).

Nylander, C.
1980   'Earless in Nineveh: Who Mutilated "Sargon's" Head?', *AJA* 84: 329-33.

Ockinga, B.
1984   *Die Göttebenbildlichkeit im Alten Ägypten und im Alten Testament* (Wiesbaden: Harrassowitz).

Olyan, S.M.
1985   'Problems in the History of the Cult and Priesthood in Ancient Israel' (PhD thesis, Harvard University).

Patai, R.
    1967   *The Hebrew Goddess* (New York: Ktav).
Peltenburg, E.J.
    1988   'A Cypriot Model for Prehistoric Ritual', *Antiquity* 62 (235): 289-93.
Pettey, R.J.
    1985   'Asherah: Goddess of Israel?' (PhD thesis, Marquette University, Milwaukee).
Pilz, E.
    1924   'Die weiblischen Göttheiten Kanaans', *ZDPV* 47: 131-68.
Pritchard, J.B.
    1943   *Palestinian Figurines in Relation to Certain Goddesses Known through Literature* (AOS, 24; New Haven).
    1961   *The Water System of Gibeon* (Pennsylvania: University Museum).
Reed, W.L.
    1949   *The Asherah in the Old Testament* (Fort Worth: Texas Christian University Press).
Reich, R.
    1989   'A Third Season of Excavations at Mezad Hashavyahu', *EI* 20: 228-32.
Ritner, R.K.
    1992   'Egyptian Magic: Questions of Legitimacy, Religious Orthodoxy and Social Deviance', in A.B. Lloyd (ed.), *Studies in Pharaonic Religion and Society in Honour of J.G. Griffiths* (Oriental Institute Studies, 54; London: University of Chicago): 189-200.
    1993   *The Mechanics of Ancient Egyptian Magical Practice* (Studies in Ancient Oriental Civilization, 54; Chicago: The Oriental Institute, University of Chicago).
Romano, I.B.
    1988   'Early Greek Cult Images and Cult Practices', in R. Haag, N. Marinatos and G.C. Nordquist (eds.), *Early Greek Cult Practice: Procceedings of the Fifth International Symposium at the Swedish Institute at Athens, 1986* (Stockholm: P. Aströms): 127-33.
Rose, M.
    1975   *Der Ausschliesslichkeitsanspruch Jahwes: Deuteronomische Schultheologie und die Volks-frommigkeit in der späten Königszeit* (BWANT, VI.6; Stuttgart: Verlag W. Kohlhammer).
Schroer, S.
    1987   *In Israel gab es Bilder. Nachrichten von darstellen Kunst im Alten Testament* (Freiburg: Universitätsverlag).
Skorupski, J.
    1976   *Symbol and Theory: A Philosophical Study of Theories of Religion in Social Anthropology* (Cambridge: Cambridge University Press).
Smith, M.S.
    1990   *The Early History of God: Jahweh and the other Deities in Ancient Israel* (San Francisco: Collins).
    1994   'Yahweh and other Deities in Ancient Israel: Observations on Old Problems and Recent Trends', in Dietrich and Klopfenstein (eds.) 1994: 197-234.

Spycket, A.
1992   *Les figurines de Suse*. I. *Les figurines humaines IVe-IIe millénaires Av. J.C.* (Paris: Gabalda).

Stern, E.
1989   'What Happened to the Cult Figurines? Israelite Religion after the Exile', *BARev* 15.4: 22-29, 53-54.
1992   *Dor: The Ruler of the Seas* (Jerusalem: Bialik Institute) (Hebrew).

Supinska-Løvset, I.
1978   *The Ustinov Collection: The Terracottas* (Oslo: Universitatsforlaget).

Teubal, S.
1984   *Sarah the Priestess: The First Matriarch of Genesis* (Chicago: Swallow Press).
1990   *Hagar the Egyptian: The Lost Tradition of the Matriarchs* (San Francisco: Harper).

Tigay, J.H.
1987   'Israelite Religion: The Onomastic and Epigraphic Evidence', in Miller *et al.* (eds.) 1987: 157-94.

Tooley, A.M.J.
1991   'Child's Toys or Ritual Objects?', *Göttinger Miszellen* 123: 101-11.

Tufnell, O. (ed.)
1953   *Lachish III: The Iron Age* (Oxford: Oxford University Press).

Ucko, P.J.
1968   *Anthropomorphic Figurines of Predynastic Egypt and Neolithic Crete, with Compatible Material from the Predynastic Near East and Mainland Greece* (London: Szmilda).

Van der Toorn, K.
1986   'Review of: Winter, U. 1983, "Frau und Gottin" ', *BO* 43: 439-99.

Vandenabeele, F.
1986   'Phoenician Influence on the Cypro Archaic Terracotta Production and Cypriote Influence Abroad', in V. Karageorghis (ed.), *Acts of the International Archaeological Symposium 'Cyprus between the Orient and the Occident' 1985* (Nicosia: Department of Antiquities): 351-60.
1989   'Has Phoenician Influence Modified Cypriot Terracotta Production?', in E. Peltenburg (ed.), *Early Society in Cyprus* (Edinburgh: Edinburgh University): 266-71.

Versnel, H.S.
1991   'Some Reflections on the Relationship Magic–Religion', *Numen* 38.2: 177-97.

Vincent, P.H.
1907   *Canaan d'après l'exploration récente* (Paris: J. Gabalda).

Voigt, M.M.
1983   *Hajji Firuz Tepe, Iran: The Neolithic Settlement* (Hasanlu Excavation Reports, 1; Pennsylvania: The University Museum).

Vorlander, H.
1986   'Aspects of Popular Religion in the Old Testament', in N. Greinacher and N. Mette (eds.), *Popular Religion* (Concilium; Edinburgh: T. & T. Clark): 63-70.

Vrijhof, P.H., and J. Waardenburg (eds.)
1979   *Official and Popular Religion: Analysis of a Theme for Religious Studies* (The Hague: Mouton Publications).

Walls, N.H.
1992   *The Goddess Anat in Ugaritic Myth* (SBLDS, 135; Atlanta: SBL).

Watzinger, C.
1933   *Denkmäler Palästinas: Eine Einführung in die Archäologie des Heiligen Landes, Vol. I* (Leipzig: J.C. Heinrich).

Weber, M.
1922   *Wirtschaft und Gesellschaft* (ET E. Fischoff, *The Sociology of Religion*; London: Methuen, 1965).

Weippert, H.
1994   'Zu Einer neuen ikonographischen Religionsgeschichte Kanaans und Israel', *BZ* 38.1: 1-28.

Wenning, R.
1989   'Meṣad Ḥashavyahu: Ein Stützpunkt des Joyakim', in F.L. Hossfeld (ed.) *Vom Sinai zum Horeb* (Würzburg: Echter Verlag).
1991   'Wer war der Paredos der Aschera? Notizen zu Terrakottastatuetten in eizenzeitlischen Gräbern', *BN* 59: 89-97.

Whitt, W.D.
1992   'The Divorce of Yahweh and Asherah in Hos. 2,4-7.12ff.', *SJOT* 6.1: 31-67.

Wiggermann, F.A.M.
1992   *Mesopotamian Protective Spirits: The Ritual Texts* (Groningen: Styx).

Wiggins, S.A.
1991   'The Myth of Asherah: Lion Lady and Serpent Goddess', *UF* 23: 383-94.
1993   *A Reassessment of 'Asherah': A Study According to the Textual Sources of the First Two Millennia BCE* (AOAT, 235; Neukircher-Vluyn).

Winter, U.
1983   *Frau und Göttin: Exegetische und ikonographische Studien zum weiblichen Göttesbild im Alten Israel und im dessen Umwelt* (Freiburg: Universitätsverlag).

Wright, G.E.
1957   *Biblical Archaeology* (Philadelphia: Westminster Press, 2nd edn, 1962).

8

FIGURINES, FIGURES AND CONTEXTS IN JERUSALEM AND REGIONS
TO THE EAST IN THE SEVENTH AND SIXTH CENTURIES BCE

Kay Prag

As part of the process of preparing the material from Kenyon's excavations in Jerusalem for publication, the small finds register has been put on database. Using this tool, the statistical bases for some of Kenyon's conclusions affecting the Iron Age occupation of Jerusalem are examined. The distribution of Iron Age II figurines, jar stamps and potters' marks from the excavations is reviewed, and levels of occurrence discussed. In general the figures provide support for her conclusions based on primary excavation evidence, but also raise questions concerning intra-site variation. The contexts of the distribution and use of figurines are also briefly discussed, with reference to the south Jordan Valley and central and southern Transjordan.

Kathleen Kenyon's excavations in Jerusalem from 1961 to 1967 produced many notable discoveries, including the first precise evidence for the location and date of the defensive walls of Jerusalem during the Bronze and Iron Ages. The excavations, however, were not conducted to prove or disprove hypotheses concerning Jerusalem, but to achieve as fully as possible, an objective scientific record of the archaeology of the city. Her views on the size and location of the city and its walls were based entirely on the evidence derived from her own work and that of her predecessors. It was unexpected, therefore, to hear recently an archaeologist express his surprise at the immediate willingness of Kenyon to accept the evidence which was excavated later, for a city wall on the western hill in the late eighth or seventh century BCE, as this ran counter to her 'minimalist' position. On the contrary, the emergence of clear evidence would have been a stimulus to her; the surprise was based on the difference in conceptual approaches.

The Kenyon excavations also produced great quantities of much less striking material, all of which was excavated and recorded uniformly for all levels from the surface to bedrock, showing no discrimination or selectivity between periods, whether Ottoman or Bronze Age. No mechanical earth-moving equipment was employed (cf. Ariel 1990: 21, who notes the use of earth-moving equipment in some areas of Shiloh's excavations, which may have affected the recovery and therefore the recorded distribution of amphora stamps). Hence the Kenyon data, gathered by uniform sampling and recording procedures, provides a corpus which is potentially a statistically reliable random sample taken in a number of different locations in the ancient and mediaeval city. Most of the sample, however, comes from wash or tip levels, very rarely from primary contexts.

The Ancient Jerusalem Project of the British School of Archaeology in Jerusalem (now the Council for British Research in the Levant) plans to bring the remaining unallocated material to publication, supported by a generous grant from the Leverhulme Trust. As part of the project, the records, including the small finds register, have been placed on computer which permits quicker and more reliable sorting of the great quantities of data than using the card indexes compiled during the excavation. This conference seemed a suitable occasion not just to explore some of the potential uses of the material, but also to assess some data on which Kenyon's preliminary conclusions concerning the occupation of ancient Jerusalem were based. Following the publication of the fourth volume of reports (Eshel and Prag 1995), with Eshel's analysis of the Iron Age material from Caves I and II, and with the republication of Holland's analysis of the figurines from Cave I, we can consider briefly the evidence derived from the figurines and some contemporary material.

Observations on Finds from Jerusalem in the IA II period

Figurines (Fig. 8.1)

The Iron Age figurines of Palestine were studied in Holland's unpublished doctoral dissertation (1975) which included 2711 examples from Palestine, classified into 16 types. A summary typology and distribution charts for the Palestinian material accompanied his full publication of the figurines from Jerusalem Cave I in 1977. In his study, he suggested that the figurines dated predominantly from the early seventh century

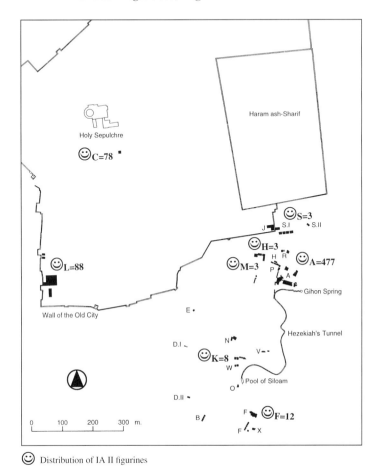

Fig. 8.1. *Distribution of Iron Age II figurines*

(though it is noted here that Kletter in his study of 'Judaean Pillar Figurines' prefers an eighth-century date, with the popularity of the figurines declining through the seventh and sixth centuries [1996: 40-42]). In Holland's study, animal figurines outnumbered human figurines by 3:2. The human figurines are mainly female; those modelling animals are mainly quadrupeds of which a high proportion are identified as horses with or without male riders. The corpus includes birds (like the female figurines, often identified with Asherah/Astarte). In addition there are rattles, furniture, vessels and objects referred to as cult boxes or stands. Many of these objects were originally painted, mainly with a white wash or quite a thick lime paste, but red, ochre, yellow and black painted lines are occasionally noted (cf. Kletter 1996: 50). Current statistics from Kenyon's excavations in Jerusalem, where 672 fragmentary figurines of IA II date were entered in the registers, indicate that at least 187 figurines (or 27.86 per cent) had traces of paint (this figure is undoubtedly too low—the early entries in the register do not mention traces of paint), of which 104 had white paint, 26 had red and white paint, and the remainder unspecified traces of paint or various combinations of two to four colours. It has often been noted that all these figurines are broken, and it has been suggested that this is due to ritual destruction in fulfilment of a votive or magical purpose; this does not, however, explain the very worn condition of the paint, of which it is rare to find more than slight traces surviving. Ritual breakage does not necessarily result in destruction of the paint layer. The latter must be due to the intensive use of objects decorated with paint of poor cohesive quality (as with toys); or the post-use history (destruction of contexts, use in tip levels, pot washing) has caused the damage. The latter processes would account for both breakage and paint loss; but the evidence for loss of paint on what must originally have been quite brightly painted objects, deserves more study.

Of the 672 figurines noted in the Jerusalem registers (cf. 559 counted by Holland), the great majority came from Site A (477), with 88 from Site L, 78 from Site C, and insignificant numbers from five other sites: F(12), H(3), K(8), M(3) and S(3) (see Fig. 8.1).

The figurines are usually thought to represent popular cult or super-stitious beliefs, but their distribution as a normal part of the IA II repertoire is paralleled by two other items, jar stamps and potter's marks. The range of suggested function for the three kinds of objects is varied, but their date in general is grouped between the eighth and sixth centuries, and one might assume that high density distribution is likely to coincide with contemporary settlement. Another common denomina-tor is that all these materials derive from settlement, not burial contexts.

Jar Stamps (Fig. 8.2)

Jar stamps are normally assumed to have a public function connected to the administration, but include a small number of private seals. The latter may belong in the sphere of individual or private activities, although they are usually interpreted as the seals of officials, and as such should probably also be classed in the public domain. A total of

146 examples, mainly of the two-winged scroll type (91 examples, 15 of which are associated with concentric circles), concentric circles without accompanying stamp (20 examples), four-winged scroll type (2 examples) and a small range of other types including private seals, rosette/stars and illegible seals, come mainly from Site A (107 examples), with 27 from Site L, 10 from Site C, and one from each of Sites N and S. (There are in addition three private seals from Site A, which have not been counted with the jar stamps).

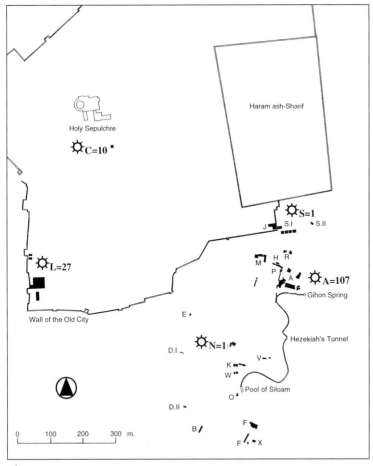

☼ Distribution of IA II jar stamps

Fig. 8.2. *Distribution of Iron Age II jar stamps*

Potter's Marks (Fig. 8.3)

A group of sherds of IA II date have incisions which are described as potter's marks. Potter's marks could be interpreted as indicators of commerce, vessel function, or of public or private activities. The great majority consist of a single cross incised on one handle of a cooking pot, but a limited number of other marks include a double cross or trident, and rarely lines, dots or circles (Prag, in Eshel and Prag 1995, 214-15); these marks are occasionally found on other vessels, twice on the base of bowls, and once inside a lamp. There are 154 examples of these marks, of which 108 come from Site A, 24 from Site L, 16 from Site C, four from site F, and one from each of Sites K and X.

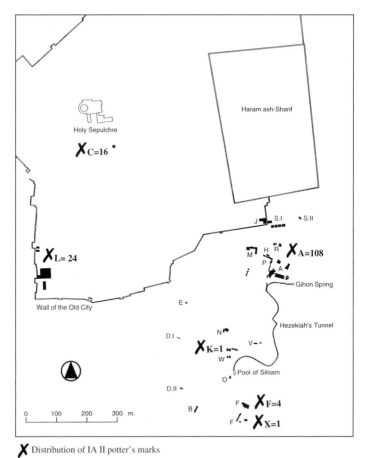

✘ Distribution of IA II potter's marks

Fig. 8.3. *Distribution of Iron Age II potter's marks*

Distribution (Fig. 8.4)

It is not surprising that the distribution of all three classes of objects is dominated by the occurrences in Site A, as this was the sole area excavated by Kenyon with clear evidence for stratified Iron Age building remains; there are fewer occurrences in Sites L and C where no significant building remains were uncovered, but contemporary use of the areas was indicated by quarrying activities, and a series of tips/fills/middens which were uncovered by Kenyon, by Tushingham (his reasoned conclusions are given in 1985: 15-16) and by Lux at the Lutheran Church site adjacent to Site C (Vriezen 1994; see also Magness 1995: 88). In other areas the statistical significance is low.

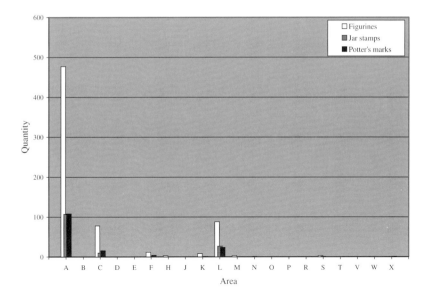

Fig. 8.4. *Comparative distribution of Iron Age II objects by area*

It is notable that on Sites A, L and C the proportional recovery between these three classes of objects is very roughly similar (which at least indicates some sort of statistical uniformity):

	Figurines		Jar stamps		Potters' marks
Site A:	4.7	:	1	:	1
Site L:	4.4	:	1.2	:	1.3
Site C:	7.8	:	1.6	:	1

Soil volume (Fig. 8.5)

Quantification of these items in view of their very rare occurrence in primary contexts is of only general value; and may indeed be governed simply by the soil volume excavated in each area. An accurate assessment of area is readily obtainable, but measurement of volume is less precise. Although the depth of excavation in each trench is measurable from the section drawings, not all areas within the trenches were excavated, and generally a low average measurement of depth has been taken for each trench. The measurement, recorded in units of 10 cubic metres on the chart, is relatively accurate, with currently (2001) a slightly lower degree of reliability for Site F. In all, the Kenyon expedition excavated about 4771.1 sq. m in Jerusalem and moved about 26,367.54 cu. m of debris. The chart shows the relationship of total volume per site for all periods in comparison with finds of the three categories discussed above.

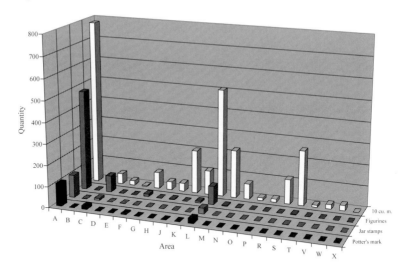

Fig. 8.5. *Distribution of objects and soil volume by area*

Percentage of total finds in three categories from all sites against total volume excavated = 3.6% (1 per 27.12 cu. m)

For Site A percentage of total finds in the three categories against volume excavated = 8.85% (1 per 11.28 cu. m)

For Site L percentage of total finds in the three categories against volume excavated = 2.72% (1 per 36.6 cu. m)

For Site C percentage of total finds in the three categories against volume excavated = 21% (1 per 4.76 cu. m)
For Site F percentage of total finds in the three categories against volume excavated = 2.06% (1 per 48.5 cu. m)
For Site K percentage of total finds in the three categories against volume excavated = 0.78 (1 per 127.33 cu. m)
For Site S percentage of total finds in the three categories against volume excavated = 0.15 (1 per 652 cu. m)
For Site M percentage of total finds in the three categories against volume excavated = 0.13% (1 per 756.5 cu. m)

If the archaeological evidence for Site A in IA II can be taken to represent a general standard for the occurrence of these three classes of objects (8.85 per cent), it can be seen that Site L at 2.72 per cent represents a marked fall (lower than the 'average' 3.6 per cent), which could be statistically relative to the quarry/midden status of the area as proposed by Tushingham. Only 8 to 12 examples actually come from contemporary IA II deposits in Site L, the majority come from the overlying later deposits. Similarly, many figurines were noted in the fill of the Herodian palace platform to the north of Site L (Bahat and Broshi 1972: 172). Other sites show a yet lower ratio: Site F at 2.06 per cent is perhaps more representative of the background noise to be expected in a low-lying area used primarily for water storage, irrigation, cultivation and burial; both rubbish disposal and field manuring could account for the levels of occurrence in Site F. The unexpected statistic, and largest intra-site variation which emerges, however, is for Site C, which has by far the highest ratio of finds to soil volume at 1 per 4.76 cu. m (or 21 per cent). However, none of the Site C material comes from the period of seventh-century quarrying and contemporary IA II deposits; it derives entirely from the many metres of mixed IA II and first century CE material, apparently imported as fill during the construction of Aelia Capitolina in the second century CE (e.g. 32 figurines were found in the lower fill, 39 in the upper fill, and 6 came from later or unstratified contexts [checked against the phasing lists in Franken, 1992]). The concentration of these three categories of objects in the fill is remarkable. The source of the fill is not known. If the fill material was taken from the adjacent areas of IA II occupation on the western hill (as seems most likely), it would be interesting to see comparable distribution figures from the excavation of surviving stratigraphic deposits in the Jewish quarter. It is notable that the proportions of identifiable figurine types making up the total in Site C is 11 human, 61 quadrupeds, possibly 2 birds and 4 unidentifiable fragments. The proportion of animal to human figurines is thus nearly 6:1, much higher than the proportions (3:2) noted by Holland.

It was on the lack of such material in many other areas that Kenyon based her 'minimalist view' of the occupation of the city in the Iron Age. This negative data should still require an explanation when hypotheses advocating much greater settlement patterns are proposed. These explanations may yet be forthcoming—the reasons may be simply the intensity of quarrying in the Roman and Byzantine periods in some areas; but currently some of the evidence remains inconclusive. Shiloh (1989: 98) on the basis of evidence from his Sites E and G in Jerusalem, and his reading of the biblical texts, calculated that the fortified area of the city by the end of the eighth century was 600 dunams. If primary consideration is given to the objectively assessed archaeological evidence, this has still to be proved.

Comparative Data

It has been suggested that during the seventh century Jerusalem became increasingly isolated from the neighbouring kingdoms (Shiloh 1985: 145, 185), though contrary evidence for architectural and other evidence for contact between Judah and the Iron Age kingdoms in Syria, Transjordan and south Arabia has also been noted (Prag 1987: 127). While many aspects of the archaeological assemblages observed in Jerusalem do have a regional aspect, they should nonetheless be understood and assessed in the wider context of contemporary practices.

The popularity of figurines at this time is shown in their wide distribution. To the east, the figurines from contemporary Ammon and Moab are receiving more attention nowadays (e.g. Worschech 1995). The Transjordan distribution also includes Edom, as shown by the recently published group from Tawilan near Petra, with a range of IA II figurines generically comparable to those from Jerusalem (Bennett and Bienkowski 1995: 80, Fig. 9.3; see also the material from Busayra, Bienkowski and Sedman, this volume). Two of the best-known and best-preserved Ammonite figurines of horse and rider were found in the Maqabalain tomb near Amman (Harding 1950: 46-47, pl. XIII, nos. 37 and 38). Here the front of the horse's mane appears to be painted with an item of harness decoration, rather than a sun disk or other cult image; and the riders appear to hold a whip. Karageorghis's volumes on the coroplastic art of Cyprus provide graphic evidence of the popularity of the type in the regions to the west also. Karageorghis illustrates numerous examples of horse and rider figures which appear early in Cyprus (Cypro-Geometric 1), but become frequent by the eighth century and are found through the seventh and sixth centuries; they are particularly popular as votives in the late seventh century at the sanctuary of Apollo Hylates at Kourion; Karageorghis notes both Aegean and Assyrian influences on this figurine tradition in Cyprus. He suggests that the horse itself was a status symbol, and many of the Cypriot riders are depicted as armed warriors; the Cypriot contexts of the figures are both funerary and votive; like many of the Palestinian figurines, they have linear painted decoration, usually in red and black paint (Karageorghis 1995: esp. 61-63 and pl. XLIV). In the Jerusalem context, however, they are often associated with the biblical references to the horses of the sun, though whether a sun disk or a forelock or horse harness decoration is depicted on the head is still debated. There is less to connect the plentiful horse- and rider-figurines from Jerusalem with a biblical description of a cult of the horses of the sun, than there is to connect them with archaeologically attested patterns of use of very similar objects in Cyprus and Transjordan.

As well as the popularity of figurines, and the shared architectural and artistic motifs described previously (Prag 1987), some of the less attractive finds indicate contact between Judah and the eastern regions. David Reese notes many Red Sea shells coming to Jerusalem in the Iron Age and the Roman period. There are 32 Red Sea Shells from Sites A, C and L from the Kenyon excavations in Jerusalem and another 45 from the Shiloh excavations—the source is 270 km from Jerusalem. Their very presence suggests an active trade route or exchange system between Jerusalem and the regions south and east. There are indications of the same patterns of exploitation (of *tridacna*, *lambis* and *turbo* shells in particular) at Tawilan, Busayra, Umm al-Biyara and Jerusalem in the Iron Age, which suggest that the eastern land route was in regular use. Almost all types of Red Sea shells at IA II Tawilan have parallels in IA II Jerusalem (Reese 1995a: 93-96; 1995b: 265).

On a less material note, Keel (1994: 222) notes that seals relating to the moon-cult of Harran were popular in Judah in the seventh century BCE as indeed they were in the kingdoms to the east (e.g. from Ammon, the seal from Maqabalain, Harding 1950: 46, pl. XIII: 2, XV: 9).

Glazier-McDonald's textual study (1995: 27-28, 31) suggests a friendly trading relationship, if not partnership, between Judah and

Edom in the seventh century, a view which may well be supported by
this archaeological material.

   Close analysis of material from Jerusalem cannot be pursued just in
the local and the biblical contexts. The Bible refers to plural societies
and external influences mostly in pejorative terms; this in itself is an
important and much studied subject, but should not govern the primary
analysis of archaeological material.

Decorative Relief Stamps on Pottery

Another variety of figural depiction appears to have a regional
distribution which extends beyond the borders of contemporary
kingdoms or provinces. A pottery fragment from En-gedi (on the
central west shore of the Dead Sea) was published over 30 years ago by
B. Mazar (Mazar and Dunayevsky 1967: 137 and pl. 31: 5; more
recently, Mazar 1993: 402). This was a krater fragment, showing some
wheel-burnishing, with stamped relief motifs. The fragment appears to
show two techniques; in one the wall of the vessel appears to have a
stamp impressed directly; in the other, soft clay was applied to the
surface of the unfired vessel (or perhaps to the stamp), and then
stamped onto the vessel. Three motifs were preserved on the En-gedi
fragment, only one of which was complete. They showed: to the left, a
bearded man, perhaps naked, seated, with right hand on knee, with a
plant/palmette motif in front of the figure: the plant/palmette was
identified by the authors as part of a booth or hut; in the centre, an
animal identified as a ram with projecting horns; and to the right, a
small fragment of a third stamp, suggested as depicting a mask, or a
lion's head, but not clearly identifiable. Stratigraphically, this En-gedi
fragment could date to Stratum V at the end of the Judaean monarchy,
or from the Persian period. Since it was found on bedrock, and had
some burnishing, the earlier date (c. 600 BCE) was preferred by Mazar,
who noted the unique character of the fragment. Holland (1977: 131 n.
6) referred to this piece and quoted T. Dothan who saw analogies to
Phrygian art, and suggested that the type was not indigenous to
Palestine. The fragment was republished with excellent photographs
and detailed comparative discussion by Stern (1978), who proposed
that the artistic derivation was Phoenician; he noted a number of
parallels in stamped, painted or incised Iron Age objects, such as the
painted sherd depicting a seated man from Ramat Rahel, and in

particular the parallels for the stamped technique on pottery from Busayra.

The two sherds found at Busayra in Edom (Bennett 1975: 15, Fig. 8:9 and 10) show a suckling calf and cow on one stamp, and a standing stag on the other; motifs stylistically clearly reflected in Assyrian art. The Busayra sherds are from local fine wares, no. 9 is a bowl rim sherd in very fine ware, with red and black lines painted on the exterior, with an impressed stamp of a stag on the interior; no. 10 is part of a bowl, in very fine ware, with red and black paint on the exterior with a buff reserve panel on which the stamp with a cow and calf, and another with a stag, is impressed. There is no additional applied clay for these stamps—they are impressed directly onto the body of the vessel.

A very fine complete example of the same type of stamped decoration has more recently been found at Nimrin (on the south bank of the Wadi Shu'aib/Nimrin on the northern edge of the 'fields of Moab' in Transjordan) and is published by Dornemann (1995). This krater, standing 33 cm high and 34 cm in diameter, has a frieze of similar motifs 8 cm high running right round the body; in this frieze, several stamps are repeated to make 20 scenes. The ware is similar to the fragment from En-gedi, and the krater is also wheel-burnished. The scenes consist of stags, lions, Bes figures, naked men on either side of an incense altar, and four ithyphallic men carrying boars on their shoulders; the groups are separated by a stamped palm tree. Comparing the animals on the Nimrin vessel to those from En-gedi, it is quite clear that the En-gedi animal in the central stamp is not a ram, but a stag, as already noted by Stern; the stamp could possibly be the same one in both cases, as could that of the lion, which is complete on the Nimrin vessel. The technique, with applied clay, occasionally means that part of the stamp relief is missing, or has become detached from the vessel. The similarities between the two vessels are very close, to an extent that they could well be the product of the same workshop. The seated male figure on the En-gedi fragment is, however, different from the Nimrin standing figures, but like them, also appears to be naked. At both Nimrin and En-gedi a naked man is associated with a plant/palmette, or as noted by Dornemann, possibly 'a decorative space filler...or...some kind of a tree, like a pine', rather than part of a booth, as suggested by Mazar. Unfortunately Dornemann did not know of the En-gedi fragment, and like Mazar, has treated the style as unique. There is also a parallel between the Nimrin krater and the Ramat Rahel painted sherd: the latter has what are presumably the muscles/veins of the arm shown, as in the legs of the Nimrin lions (cf. Stern 1978: pl. II: B; and Dornemann 1995: Fig. 6). The context of the Nimrin krater is eighth–sixth century, and the very eclectic and ancient history of the motifs are explored in detailed, though preliminary, study by Dornemann.

Another such sherd was found during the 1987 season of excavations at Tell Iktanu on the Wadi Hisban, which lies 10 km south-east of Nimrin, on the eastern fringe of the 'fields of Moab'. During the sounding of the later Iron Age and Persian occupation of the tell, the remains of a small fortress were recorded (Prag 1989: 40-44, Fig. 6, 8). In Area D3, on the top of the main tell, a small trench was excavated through the upper levels. The fortress was in use for several phases, from at least the Iron Age II into the Persian period, and showed evidence for complex functions—strategic, storage and industrial. The fragment (Fig. 8.6), of light pink hard ware with cream-pink surface, wheel made, showed a small section of a stamped scene with palmette/ herring-bone motif, and otherwise unidentifiable motifs; there is strong indentation on the interior from finger pressure when the stamp was applied to the exterior (similar to that shown on the Nimrim krater, Dornemann 1995: 621, Fig. 3); a relief groove has indications of per-haps a loose clay pellet or traces of a second stamp. Not enough of the stamp is preserved for identification of the motifs, and as only part of the relief panel is preserved, it is not known whether the vessel was burnished; the closest parallel to the Nimrin and En-gedi stamps is the 'palmette', but assuming that the wiping on the surface of the vessel is also horizontal, the 'palmette' appears to lie horizontally, rather than vertically as on the En-gedi and Nimrin examples, and is linked by impressed lines to a different grouping of impressions. The sherd is tantalizingly fragmentary.

There is evidence for at least two related traditions here: the En-gedi and Nimrin stamps on clay pellets are found on burnished kraters, the Busayra stamps are directly impressed on fine ware painted bowls; the Iktanu stamp, almost certainly of the Persian period, possibly from a krater, is closest to the first group. They share common motifs, and common techniques.

The technique of stamping the wall of a vessel, with a wooden, bone or clay mould (cf. Dornemann 1983: 132-42, Fig. 88), sometimes on a pellet of soft clay added to the surface of the pot, the 'palmette' and stag motifs, suggest that these items all form a coherent group. The

Fig. 8.6. *Stamped sherd from Tell Iktanu, Jordan*

context of the En-gedi piece was stratigraphically the very end of the Iron Age II or the Persian period, but was attributed to the end of the Iron Age largely on the basis of the presence of burnishing. Stern (1982: 93, 133, Fig. 216, 218), however, notes that the use of burnishing continued into the first phase of the Persian period, and notes also the presence of pottery stamped with decorative motifs at this period, the most distinctive of which is also from En-gedi. Dornemann notes that the dating of the Nimrin pottery is still at a preliminary stage, and the Nimrin assemblage overall dates from the tenth to the fourth centuries (Dornemann 1995: 624). The current distribution of the style, on the western shore of the Dead Sea, in the south-east Jordan Valley, and the southern Transjordan plateau, is also coherent and appears to testify not just to local ceramics, but to a very localized set of eclectic art forms which are likely to reflect the stories and cultural milieu of the contemporary population, where perhaps the influences are Syrian/ Assyrian as much as Phoenician. Dornemann (1995: 627), while noting numerous parallels with Assyrian art, considers the Greek preference for depicting the naked body, and other themes found in Greek orientalizing art, which recall T. Dothan's comment about Phrygian parallels noted above. Terracotta plaques stamped from moulds, and bronze shield bands from the Greek world, have features in common (see, e.g., Prag 1985: pl. 1 from Gortyn, dated c. 630–610 BCE; pl. 2a from Olympia, dated to the second quarter of the sixth century BCE). Attic black-glazed pottery of the fifth century was imported to Tell

Iktanu. However, palm trees, lions, stags, cattle are all attested in the region at this period, and wild-boar hunting continues into modern times along the Jordan river. There seems no reason to look further afield for the origin of this style than in tracing the broader aspects of a very eclectic art history—whether Assyrian, Phoenician, Egyptian, Phrygian or Greek, and to note the reinforcement of these cultural affiliations across the contemporary political boundaries.

Acknowledgments

I am grateful to Leonie Sedman and Piotr Bienkowski for illustrations of the Busayra stamp impressions and the Maqabalain figurines; and to Amihai Mazar and E. Stern for the reference to Stern's article on the En-gedi sherd.

Bibliography

Ariel, D.T.
    1990   *Excavations at the City of David 1978–1985*. II. *Imported Stamped Amphora Handles, Coins, Worked Bone and Ivory, Glass* (Qedem, 30: Jerusalem: Hebrew University).
Bahat, D., and M. Broshi
    1972   'Jerusalem, Old City, the Armenian Garden', *IEJ* 22: 171-72.
Bennett, C.-M.
    1975   'Excavations at Buseirah, Southern Jordan, 1973: Third Preliminary Report', *Levant* VII: 1-19.
Bennett, C.-M., and P. Bienkowski
    1995   *Excavations at Tawilan in Southern Jordan*. With contributions by Khaireh 'Amr, Stephanie Dalley, Stephen Hart, Ilse Köhler-Rollefson, Jack Ogden, Dani Petocz and David S. Reese (British Academy Monographs in Archaeology, 8; British Institute at Amman for Archaeology and History; Oxford: Oxford University Press).
Dornemann, R.H.
    1983   *The Archaeology of the Transjordan in the Bronze and Iron Ages* (Milwaukee, WI: Milwaukee Public Museum).
    1995   'Preliminary Thoughts on the Tall Nimrin Krater', *Studies in the History and Archaeology of Jordan* V: 621-28.
Eshel, I., and K. Prag (ed.)
    1995   *Excavations by K.M. Kenyon in Jerusalem 1961–1967*. IV. *The Iron Age Cave Deposits on the South-east Hill and Isolated Burials and Cemeteries Elsewhere* (British Academy Monographs in Archaeology, 6; British School of Archaeology in Jerusalem; Oxford: Oxford University Press).
Franken, H.J.
    1992   'Excavations of the British School of Archaeology in Jerusalem',

Unpublished report on Site C in the Muristan. Manuscript in the British School of Archaeology in Jerusalem Archive, The Manchester Museum.

Glazier-McDonald, B.

1995 'Edom in the Prophetical Corpus', in D.V. Edelman (ed.), *You Shall Not Abhor an Edomite for He Is Your Brother: Edom and Seir in History and Tradition* (Archaeology and Biblical Studies, 3; Atlanta, GA: Scholars Press): 23-32.

Harding, G.L.

1950 'An Iron-Age Tomb at Meqabelein', *Quarterly of the Department of Antiquities of Palestine* 14: 44-48, pls. XIII-XVII.

Holland, T.A.

1975 *A Typological and Archaeological Study of Human and Animal Representations in the Plastic Art of Palestine during the Iron Age* (2 vols.; unpublished DPhil thesis submitted to the Faculty of Anthropology and Geography of the University of Oxford: Bodleian Library, Oxford).

1977 'A Study of Palestinian Iron Age Clay Figurines with Special Reference to Jerusalem Cave I', *Levant* IX: 131-55.

Karageorghis, V.

1995 *The Coroplastic Art of Ancient Cyprus. IV. The Cypro-Archaic Period: Small Male Figurines* (Nicosia: A.G. Leventis Foundation and University of Cyprus).

Keel, O.

1994 *Studien zu den Stempelsiegeln aus Palästina/Israel, Vol. IV* (OBO, 135; Freiburg: Universitätsverlag; Göttingen: Vandenhoeck & Ruprecht.

Kletter, R.

1996 *The Judean Pillar-figurines and the Archaeology of Asherah* (BAR International Series, 636; Oxford: Tempus Reparatum).

Magness, J.

1995 'Review of Vriezen 1994', *BASOR* 298: 85-87.

Mazar, B.

1993 'En-gedi', *NEAEHL* II, 399-405.

Mazar, B., and I. Dunayevsky

1967 'En-gedi: The Fourth and Fifth Seasons of Excavations. Preliminary Report', *IEJ* 17.3: 133-43.

Prag, A.J.N.W.

1985 *The Oresteia: Iconographic and Narrative Tradition* (Chicago: Bolchazy-Carducci).

Prag, K.

1987 'Decorative Architecture in Ammon, Moab and Judah', *Levant* 19: 121-27.

1989 'Preliminary Report on the Excavations at Tell Iktanu, Jordan, 1987', *Levant* 21: 33-45.

Reese, D.

1995a 'Marine Invertebrates and Fossils', in Bennett and Bienkowski 1995: 93-96.

1995b 'Marine Invertebrates and Other Shells from Jerusalem (Sites A, C and L)', in Eshel and Prag 1995: 265-78.

Shiloh, Y.
  1985   'The Material Culture of Judah and Jerusalem in Iron Age II: Origins and
          Influences', *Orientalia Lovaniensia Analecta* 19: 113-46.
  1989   'Judah and Jerusalem in the Eighth-Sixth Centuries BCE', in S. Gitin and
          W.G. Dever (eds.), *Recent Excavations in Israel: Studies in Iron Age
          Archaeology* (AASOR, 49; Winona Lake, IN: Eisenbrauns): 97-105.
Stern, E.
  1978   'New Types of Phoenician Style Decorated Pottery Vases from
          Palestine', *PEQ* 110: 11-21.
  1982   *Material Culture of the Land of the Bible in the Persian Period* (Qedem,
          9; Jerusalem: Hebrew University).
Tushingham, A.D.
  1985   *Excavations in Jerusalem 1961–1967, Vol. 1* (Toronto: Royal Ontario
          Museum).
Vriezen, K.J.H.
  1994   *Die Ausgrabungen unter der Erlöserkirche im Muristan, Jerusalem
          (1970–1974)* (Abhandlungen des Deutschen Palästinavereins, 19;
          Wiesbaden: Harrassowitz).
Worshech, U.
  1995   'Figurinen aus *el-Bālū'* (Jordanien)', *ZDPV* 111: 185-92.

9

IŠTAR AS DEPICTED ON FINDS FROM ISRAEL*

Tallay Ornan

Figures and symbols that appear on seals may serve as criteria for chronology and as a means for offering some insight into the beliefs of their ancient owners. One group of seals found in Israel, dated to the eighth–seventh centuries BCE, the period of the Assyrian conquest of Israel, consists of seals considered to reflect Assyrian iconography. Of these, some depict a goddess within a circle, who is known in first-millennium Assyrian imagery, mainly in glyptic art, and is identified as Ištar. My aim here is to focus on the depictions of this goddess dated to the period of the Assyrian conquest found in Israel. Some of these representations reveal a blend of Assyrian and local traits and thus imply local manufacture inspired by Assyrian imagery. This Assyrian inspiration may add iconographical considerations to the debate with regard to the identification of the biblical Queen of Heaven.

The goddess shown within a circle is found on six seals found in Israel: two cylinder seals (Figs. 9.1 and 9.2),[1] three stamp seals (Figs.

*   The text of this paper is an enlarged version of the one presented at the Institute of Jewish Studies, University College, London, 1996. I am grateful to M. Geller and A. Mazar for inviting me to take part in that conference. I wish to thank Amnon Ben-Tor and Gary Beckman for reading the manuscript and for their useful suggestions and remarks.

1.   Fig. 9.1 is a drawing of a cylinder seal from Shechem, found in 1928 in the debris above the north-west temple. It is made of hard black stone speckled with white spots, h. 2.5 cm, d. 1 cm, Israel Antiquity Authority (IAA) I.744. (Parker 1949: 7, no. 6; Keel and Uehlinger 1992: 334, Fig. 287). Fig. 9.2 is a drawing of an unpublished carnelian cylinder seal kept in the Israel Museum 70.32.20, acquired in the vicinity of Shechem.

9.3–9.5),[2] and one barrel-shaped seal (Fig. 9.6).[3] Two of these seals were discovered in controlled excavations at Shechem and at Tel Dor (Figs. 9.1 and 9.6); two were surface finds, from Nahal Issachar in the lower Galilee and from the vicinity of Beth-She'an (Figs. 9.3 and 9.4). The other two seals were bought in the antiquities market and their attribution to Israel is thus somewhat conjectural (Figs. 9.2 and 9.5). To this group one should add a silver pendant that was discovered in Tel Miqne-Ekron, on which a portrayal of the same goddess in a more detailed presentation is depicted (Fig. 9.7).[4]

Fig. 9.1. *Cylinder seal from Shechem (Keel and Uehlinger 1992: Fig. 287)*

2.   Fig. 9.3 is a drawing of a scaraboid seal made of green stone, h. 0.8 cm, w. 1.8, l. 2.5, IAA 80-5. It was found on the surface of Nahal Issachar and could perhaps be connected to finds from Tel Rechesh, north of Nahal Issachar, which include an Assyrionized pottery bowl (Hestrin and Stern 1973). Fig. 9.4 is a drawing of a conoid stamp seal, made of limestone, which was found in the vicinity of Beth She'an, kept in a private collection (Keel and Uehlinger 1992: 334, Fig. 288b). Fig. 9.5 is a drawing of a stamp seal formerly belonging to the collection of H.E. Clark, vice-consul of the United States in Jerusalem in 1912. Its present whereabouts is unknown (Keel and Uehlinger 1992: 331, Fig. 288a).

3.   Fig. 9.6 is a drawing of a somewhat flattened barrel-shaped seal, made of reddish-brown hard stone, h. 3 cm, w. 1.8 cm. It was found in area B2 on the eastern part of Tel Dor, below a Roman pavement together with finds dated from the Persian to the Roman periods. I wish to thank E. Stern for providing me with these details (Stern 1994a: 140-42, Fig. 80). In contrast to Stern's opinion, however, the worshipper cannot represent an Assyrian king as he lacks the typical Assyrian headgear and the deity is not to be identified with the god Aššur as apparently he is not known to be depicted in Assyrian art surrounded by a circle.

4.   Gitin 1997: 93, Fig. 21.

Fig. 9.2. *Unprovenanced cylinder seal, Israel Museum 70.32.20 (drawing by Noga Z'evi)*

Fig. 9.3. *Stamp seal from Nahal Issachar, surface find, Israel Antiquities Authority 80-5 (drawing by Noga Z'evi)*

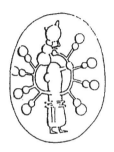

Fig. 9.4. *Stamp seal from the vicinity of Beth Sh'ean (Keel and Uehlinger 1992: Fig. 288b)*

Fig. 9.5. *Unprovenanced stamp seal (Keel and Uehlinger 1992: Fig. 288a)*

Fig. 9.6. *Barrel-shaped seal from Tel Dor (Keel and Uehlinger 1992: Fig. 288c)*

Fig. 9.7. *Silver pendant from Tel Miqne*
(drawing by Noga Z'evi after BARev 19.1 (1993): 34)

Identification of Encircled Ištar

Depictions of Ištar on Near Eastern first-millennium monumental works of art are rather uncommon. She is portrayed on the stele of Šamaš-reš-uṣur dated to the first third of the eighth century, found in Babylon where it was taken as war booty from Suḫu on the middle Euphrates. Ištar is shown on the far left on Fig. 9.8, behind the image of Adad, who is facing Šamaš-reš-uṣur. Part of a figure of a third deity is shown behind Šamaš-reš-uṣur.

The identification of Ištar on this stele is confirmed by a small label seen next to her and by the star she holds above her bow.[5] On Sennacherib's rock relief from Maltai, Ištar is depicted twice mounted on her sacred beast, the lion: the second seated figure identified with Ninlil, who is Ištar of Nineveh, and the last figure, identified with Ištar of Arbela.[6] She is probably also represented on a fragment from Uruk, dated to the ninth–seventh centuries BCE.[7]

---

5. Cavigneaux and Ismail 1990: 324, 401, Fig. 3. For the identification of the star see n. 9 below (the two other deities are also identified by small labels).

6. Börker-Klähn 1982: 210-11, no. 210-207 (and bibliography there). For the identification of Ninlil (Mullissu) with Ištar of Nineveh see Menzel 1981: 64 and Livingstone 1989: 18-19.

7. Becker 1993: 61, pl. 50: 795. The authenticity of the relief, allegedly from Babylon, mentioned by Oates (1986: 125, Fig. 84) is dubious (Börker-Klähn 1982: 232, no. 270).

Fig. 9.8. *Stele of Šamaš-reš-uṣur (after Cavigneaux and Ismail 1990: 401, Fig. 3)*

Mesopotamian literature refers to the multifaceted Ištar with different epithets, most of which relate to her various cult centres, as for example Ištar of Nineveh, or Ištar of Aššur. Her various epithets indicate that, alongside features commonly shared by the different representations of the goddess—her warlike character, for example—each figure had its own peculiarities. Nevertheless, it is usually hard to determine which of her various textual manifestations are represented in her visual depictions. Thus, for example, some scholars believe that Ištar of Nineveh was shown naked (Wiggermann 1994: 232), whereas others suggest that she was shown fully dressed, as can be seen in her appearance on the Maltai rock relief. As a rule the records concerning the exact qualities that characterize each figure and the visual details that may identify the various manifestations of Ištar are insufficient for our purposes.

As the known anthropomorphic representations of Ištar found in Israel depict her only within a circle,[8] I wish to elaborate on the difficulties in identifying this specific visual portrayal of the goddess. Encircled Ištar appears on a wall relief from the North Palace of Aššurbanipal where she decorates a chariot pole (Fig. 9.9). Usually, however, Ištar is mainly depicted on minor works of art, usually seals and jewels, in the ninth–seventh centuries and not in Assyrian monumental art. The identification of the encircled goddess with Ištar is

---

8.   The figure depicted on a stamp seal from Shechem (Keel and Uehlinger 1992: Fig. 286) cannot with certainty be identified with Ištar, as it lacks specific attributes that may confirm such identification.

based on representations in which stars, regarded as her emblems,[9] are depicted together with the circle (e.g. Figs. 9.5, 9.15 and 9.18), and on the features of light and radiance that are attributed to the goddess in written sources.[10] Those cases in which the goddess is surrounded by a circle of stars may imply that she can also be identified with Ištar when she is surrounded by a circle without stars (Figs. 9.1–9.4, 9.6, 9.7, 9.9, 9.13, 9.14 and 9.17). The same identification may even be applied to those examples in which the circle does not surround her completely, and is seen mainly on the goddess's back (Figs. 9.7 and 9.14).

Fig. 9.9. *Decoration on a chariot pole, wall relief from the North Palace of Aššurbanipal, Nineveh (drawing by Noga Z'evi after Reade 1977: pl. 3:b)*

Encircled Ištar is identified sometimes with Ištar of Arbela (Wilcke 1976–80: 82; Seidl 1976–80: 88; Herbordt 1992: 110 n. 331). This identification was first suggested by the excavators of Til Barsib with regard to the depiction of Ištar on a stele, found out of context and dated to the first half of the eighth century (Fig. 9.10). It was based on an interpretation of the 'half circle' seen on the back of the goddess as a circle of fire, envisioned in a dream of a priest, in a seventh-century text (Thureau-Dangin and Dunand 1936: 156-57). As the stele from Til

9. The star is an age-old symbol that became common as an independent emblem already at the end of the fourth millennium BCE. It can be identified as the emblem of Ištar on the Šamaš-reš-uṣur stele and on the Til Barsib stele where it is depicted above the goddess's headdress (Figs. 9.8 and 9.10). The labels accompanying these two portrayals confirm the identification with Ištar in both cases. See also the stelea of Bel-Ḫarān-bel-uṣur, of Sargon from Larnaka, of Sennacherib from Bavian and the Sippar tablet (Seidl 1989: 100 n. 12; van Buren 1945: 85-82).

10. Porada 1948: 84; Winter 1994: 123 (and bibliography there).

Barsib was accompanied by a dedication inscription of Aššur-dûr-pânia, the governor of Kar-Shalmaneser (Til Barsib) to Ištar of Arbela, it was deduced that the encircled Ištar is to be identified with the goddess who dwelt in Arbela. However, the curving-out curling line seen on the back of the goddess seems to depict the upper part of a composite bow (Yadin 1963: 7-8, 295), that she carries on her back, and is neither part of a *melammu*, an awe-inspiring aura, nor a circle of fire surrounding her. The short lines radiating from the bow may represent the bright sparkling that accompanies the divine weapon, as is seen also on weapons held by other deities.[11]

Fig. 9.10. *Stele from Til Barsib (after Parrot, A. 1961,*
Nineveh and Babylon, *London: Thames and Hudson, Fig. 85)*

As suggested by Barrelet (1955: 259), through a probable misinterpretation in antiquity, the bow on Ištar's back on the Til Barsib stele was perhaps associated with the circle in Ištar's other portrayals. Nonetheless, even if this explanation is accepted, one cannot ultimately identify the encircled Ištar with the goddess from Arbela. Additional details concerning the visual appearance of Ištar of Arbela cannot even be deduced from a bronze statuette inscribed with a dedication to Ištar

11. See, for example, the stars on the bow of the god (Ninurta?) shooting at a lion-griffin (Porada 1948: no. 689) and compare the stars that are seen at the ends of Ištar's quivers and the row of dots that adorn her sickle sword (Fig. 9.12).

of Arbela, as it portrays the figure of the worshipper who dedicated it, and not that of the goddess.[12] Thus relating the representations in which Ištar is shown within a circle specifically to Ištar of Arbela is rather difficult. The only conclusion one may draw from the juxtaposition of legend and picture on the stele of Til Barsib with regard to the imagery of Ištar from Arbela concerns her warrior aspects which are highly emphasized in written sources (Pongratz-Leisten 1994: 81). One is tempted to distinguish between the warrior Ištar from Arbela depicted in the Til Barsib stele mounted on her lion, and the encircled goddess, who probably represents Ištar in her role as an astral deity, as suggested by Teissier (1984: 37). However, such a suggestion is disproved by pictorial depictions in which the goddess within the circle also wears a long sword and is sometimes mounted on a lion (e.g. Figs. 9.7 and 9.15).

A figure of a goddess, who is depicted with 'half circles' hanging from her back in a manner similar to the depiction on the Til Barsib stele, is seen on an unprovenanced eighth–sixth century bronze axe, which is regarded as a Phoenician product (Fig. 9.11).[13] Other figures, depicting divine (?) male warriors, carrying similar elements on their backs, can be seen on the Aramaic inscribed seal of Ṣuri, and on a bronze bowl from Nimrud, both reflecting Phoenician imagery.[14] These examples imply that the depiction of Ištar on the Til Barsib stele could have been inspired by visual traditions prevailing in North Syria and probably in the Phoenician coast, which were intertwined with those of Assyria and Babylonia. The find spot of the stele of Til Barsib in Northern Syria may in itself strengthen the suggestion that the hanging bow on the goddess's back was in fact a trait native to Syria. Dependence on Syrian iconography may be traced also in the mounting of the goddess on a lion on the stele from Til Barsib. Although deities mounted on animals are known already on Assyrian cylinder seals from the end of the ninth century,[15] in Neo-Assyrian monumental art they appear a result of Syrian inspiration only on monuments dating from the reign of Sennacherib, as shown by Winter (1982: 6). It seems there-

---

12. Thureau-Dangin 1907: 133-34 (photo in *Reallexikon der Assyriologie*, I, pl. 8).

13. Barnett 1969: 7, pl. 8 A-B; Seeden 1980: 145, pl. 131:11.

14. Avigad and Sass 1997: 314, no. 840; Barnett 1969: Fig. 1.

15. Herbordt 1992: 193, 196 nos. 88, 97, pls. 1:1, 21:6. Mounting deity on a lion is already attested to in late Middle Assyrian glyptic (Moortgat 1942: Fig. 36).

fore, that mounting the goddess on her sacred beast on the earlier stele of Til Barsib can be regarded as a continuation of second millennium Syrian traditions that were inspired by Hittite and, perhaps, Hurrian traditions.[16]

Fig. 9.11. *Goddess depicted on a Phoenician bronze axe (Winter 1983: Fig. 211)*

Encircled Ištar on Seals from Israel

As a sole element on the seal, encircled Ištar appears only on stamp seals (Figs. 9.3–9.5), that can be dated by comparisons to seals and sealings from Nimrud and Tell Halaf, to the last quarter of the eighth and the seventh centuries BCE.[17] Encircled Ištar is shown together with a worshipper and a high cultic stand on the cylinder seal from Shechem, on the cylinder seal attributed to the Shechem vicinity, and on the pend-

16. Menzel 1981: 6 (and bibliography there).

17. Herbordt 1992: pl. 15: 9, 11. The fish, seen on the back of the Nahal Issachar seal (Fig. 9.3b) can be regarded, because of its proximity here to Ištar, as a benevolent emblem. However, in contrast to the divine figure, here it does not necessarily reflect Assyrian influence, as it is depicted on contemporary Hebrew seals (Sass 1993: 218). Compare Buchanan and Moorey 1988: no. 362 and see Hrouda 1990: 111-13.

ant from Tel Miqne where the circle, though, is hardly visible (see below and Figs. 9.1, 9.2 and 9.7). On the barrel-shaped seal from Dor the goddess is seen together with a worshipper but with no cultic stand (Fig. 9.6).

In spite of the fact that the cylinder seals from Shechem and its vicinity were made of hard stones, they were engraved mainly through linear incisions and not, as was usual in Mesopotamian glyptic of hard stones, by drilling. The application of linear techniques on hard stones implies that these two cylinder seals represent local variants inspired by two different Assyrian prototypes depicting encircled Ištar. The first Assyrian prototype was composed of drilled style seals made of hard stones, which omit a stand between the deity and the worshipper. The second group is constituted by seals made of softer material (e.g. sintered quartz or limestone) that were worked in chip carving technique (*kerbschnitt*), on which a stand is to be seen between the goddess and the worshipper. Based on these Assyrian prototypes, we may date the two cylinder seals from Israel to the end of the ninth century and the eighth century BCE.[18] However, a cultic stand above which there are traces of flames, depicted on a wall-relief of Sennacherib, may allow us to narrow the date of these seals to the end of the eighth century (Russell 1991: 207, Fig. 113).

The third seal from Israel, which depicts a worshipper standing in front of encircled Ištar, is the one from Tel Dor (Fig. 9.6). This seal is unique in its barrel shape as well as in its depiction, which shows a female worshipper standing in front of the goddess. Female worshippers are not very common in Neo-Assyrian art. Nevertheless, they are shown gesturing in front of Ištar on an elaborate eighth-century cylinder seal, kept in the British Museum (Fig. 9.12) and on a Babylonian cylinder seal inscribed with a South-Semitic legend (Collon 1987: no. 773; Sass 1991: 51-53). A female worshipper, probably Sennacherib's spouse, is seen together with the king in front of encircled Ištar mounted on a lion, on seal impressions from Aššur and Nineveh (Fig. 9.13).[19] A female worshipper is shown on a silver pendant from Zinjirli (Fig. 9.14), and women worshippers are represented on Urartian metal medallions (von Luschan 1943: pl. 46a; Merhav 1991: 175, Fig. 1).

---

18. Herbordt 1992: 74. Teissier 1984: nos. 210-14 compare Porada 1948: nos. 679-82 and Moortgat 1940: nos. 598-99.

19. Reade 1987; Herbordt 1992: 112, 137; Klengel-Brandt 1994.

Fig. 9.12. *Neo-Assyrian cylinder seal (Winter 1983: Fig. 504)*

Fig. 9.13. *Seal impression of Sennacherib (Klengel-Brandt 1994: Fig. 1)*

Fig. 9.14. *Silver pendant from Zinjirli (Winter 1983: Fig. 503)*

Fig. 9.15. *Neo-Assyrian cylinder seal (Black and Green 1992: Fig. 87 bottom (= Moortgat 1940: no. 598)*

These Neo-Assyrian portrayals indicate that the depictions of female worshippers should not be seen as an exclusive trait of Middle Assyrian glyptic, as was suggested by Porada (1978: 77 and n. 4), but rather as an element of continuity between the two periods. The fact that the women on these Neo-Assyrian examples and on the seal from Tel Dor are shown together with Ištar may corroborate the goddess's special role with regard to the cult carried out by women, as is suggested by both Mesopotamian literature and the Bible with regard to the worship of the Queen of Heaven (Ackerman 1989: 116). As the seal from Dor was found in a late post-Assyrian phase, it can be dated only by typological comparisons. Its modelled style and the appearance of the female worshipper, which finds a securely dated parallel only in Sennacherib's bullae, suggest dating it to the end of the eighth–seventh centuries. Another unique element of the Dor seal is the object held by the worshipper, which may be interpreted as a bowl.[20] Neo-Assyrian worshippers are not, as a rule, depicted carrying bowls, except the king when represented as a priest or in banquet scenes.[21] Thus the appearance of the bowl may suggest a non-Assyrian production of the seal from Dor. A woman holding a bowl portrayed on a decorated scapula found at Dor, which presumably depicts a cultic scene (Stern 1994b: 11, Figs. 8 and 12), may strengthen our suggestion and imply a local production of the seal from Dor.

The Pendant from Tel Miqne

The only depiction of Ištar from Israel known thus far, other than on seals, is her portrayal on the silver pendant found at Tel Miqne (Fig. 9.7).[22] This representation of the deity, although somewhat worn, is the most complete one among her manifestations from Israel. She is standing on a lion, holding its leash with her left arm, while raising her

20. Stern 1994a: 140. See also the above-mentioned inscribed South Semitic seal, in which the female worshipper carries a goblet and a stand (Sass 1991, *idem*).

21. Magen 1986: 67-68; Moortgat 1940: nos. 665, 668, 670; Porada 1948: 664-672. See also Winter 1986.

22. Gitin 1995: 93, Fig. 21. It was discovered as part of a silver hoard that contained other silver fragments, in Stratum B1, in the upper city, which was presumably destroyed during the Babylonian conquest in 603. In its upper end the pendant has a loop, in which traces of different material, perhaps unglazed sintered quartz, were found. Two of the *Sebettu* 'circles' are hidden by the loop and imply that it was folded after the pattern was completed.

right arm in a blessing gesture. The long, somewhat slanting line seen above the goddess's left arm, and ending behind her body, stands for the long sword she is carrying. Behind the goddess's back are three triangles terminating in small circles. Another one can be observed in front of her, below the lion's leash. By comparisons with other portrayals of Ištar these triangles can be understood as part of an incomplete circle surrounding her (compare Fig. 9.14). In front of the goddess is a worshipper, extending both his arms toward the deity in a gesture of prayer or entreaty. Between the worshipper and the lion there is a cultic stand decorated with horizontal lines, probably imitating similar painted vessels discovered in Tel Miqne (Gitin 1997: Fig. 12:20). The lion holds his mouth open as if roaring, and its tail, terminating in a bulb, is erect. Above and between the goddess and the devotee there are seven small circles, which represent the *Sebettu*, the Pleiades, and a winged disc above a crescent.

As was indicated by Gitin, the nearest parallels to the pendant are silver pendants from Zinjirli in Northern Syria (Fig. 9.14).[23] However, the pendants from Zinjirli differ from the Tel Miqne piece in details, style and workmanship. The winged disc is not depicted on the pendants from Zinjirli, on which only the crescent and the Pleiades are shown. The cultic stand is shown only on the Tel Miqne pendant. The divine headdresses of the Zinjirli pendants are depicted like the Assyrian ones, while the crown of the goddess from Tel Miqne, consisting of five vertical lines and two horizontals, may imitate the Babylonian feather crown, seen also on the seal from Nahal Issachar and on the stele from Til Barsib (Figs. 9.3a, 9.10). The encounter between the mortal and the deity on the Zinjirli examples takes place above a scale pattern, which symbolizes mountains in Mesopotamian iconography, while on the Tel Miqne pendant, the meeting is shown above a net-like pattern, known on Phoenician seals.[24] On the pendant from Tel Miqne the supplicant raises both hands with his palms open toward the goddess, similar to a praying gesture common in Phoenician iconography, which is different from both Assyrian and Babylonian gestures.[25] The

23. Gitin 1997: 93 n. 58 (von Luschan 1943: pl. 46:a-d).

24. Wiggermann 1994: 236, 242; Avigad and Sass 1997: nos. 725, 728, 745; Keel and Uehlinger 1992: Figs. 361b, 363a, 363d, 364-66 (though some of these last examples are later than the pendant from Miqne).

25. Compare the Babylonian gesture depicted in Fig. 9.14 and the Assyrian one depicted in Figs. 9.12 and 9.15.

components of the Zinjirli compositions are well organized and balanced, and their proportions are harmonious, whereas those of the Tel
Miqne pendant are distorted. The arm of the goddess is much too thin
compared with her palm, and the heads of both figures and that of the
lion are too big in relation to their bodies. In addition, the deity's chin
and nose are too heavy and protruding when compared with the depictions from Zinjirli. The negligent workmanship of the design is evident
by a contrast between deeply incised lines and very thin ones, hardly
visible, that often extend from the contour lines of the various elements.
It is manifested also by the uncompleted circles of the Pleiades, by the
rendition of the winged disc with two wings combined with an unclear
element, by the rendering of the divine headdress, and by depicting the
worshipper 'hovering' above the ground line as opposed to the lion,
which stands on it.

The rendering of Ištar mounted on a lion on the Til Barsib stele, on
the cylinder seal of the eunuch Nabu-uṣalla, dated to the reign of
Sargon (Fig. 9.16) and on the impressions from the reign of Sennacherib (Fig. 9.13), may imply an eighth-century dating for the pendant.
However, the attribution of the Zinjirli pendants to Stratum IV, which
probably was destroyed shortly before 670–671 BCE (Lehmann 1994:
117-18) confirms a seventh-century or perhaps late eighth-century date
for the pendant from Tel Miqne.

Fig. 9.16. *Seal of Nabu-uṣalla (Watanabe 1992: Fig. 1)*

The degenerate style and workmanship, the careless imitation of
Assyro-Babylonian motifs, and the addition of local features (e.g. hand
gestures, net-like patterns and hatched clothing[26]) imply that it was

---

26. For the clothing see Keel and Uehlinger 1992: Figs. 299a-304, 346.

made locally with a clear dependence on Assyrian iconography. The resemblance to the Zinjirli pendants may hint that the Assyrian theme conveyed on the pendant was transferred to Israel via the Assyrian provinces of Syria.

The Goddess on the Lachish Seal

Having established the role of encircled Ištar in local finds from Israel, I wish to focus now on a depiction seen on a stamp seal found on the surface at Lachish (Fig. 9.17; Tufnell 1953: 365, pl. 44:124; Keel and Uehlinger 1992: 377, Fig. 323). The divine identification of the central figure on this seal is established, as indicated by Uehlinger, by the gesturing worshipper who accompanies the goddess, and by the crown on her head (Keel and Uehlinger 1992: 377). Her association with abundance and fertility can be assumed from the positioning of her hands on her breasts.

Fig. 9.17. *Stamp seal from Lachish (Keel and Uehlinger 1992: Fig. 323)*

Although the representation of this seal differs from the Assyrian depictions in which Ištar is shown, some of its details disclose Assyrian inspiration, mixed with local features. The most conspicuous among these is the worshipper's pose, revealing one foot, which is close to Neo-Assyrian prototypes. His position on a small podium, although not common, is also known in Neo-Assyrian art (Börker-Klähn 1982: Fig. 237). However, it is the branch seen behind the deity, which appears both in Assyrian and in local finds, that may attest to the connections between the two visual traditions. The branch is a very common element in local representations, in which it sometimes appears alongside

a worshipper or with a star.[27] A branch behind a worshipper is seen on
the back of a seal from the city of Aššur (Fig. 9.18b). On the other side
of that seal is a depiction of encircled Ištar (Fig. 9.18a), and therefore
the worshipper is probably gesturing towards her. The use of the branch
on the seal from Lachish and on the one from Aššur hints that the
figures on both seals may represent the same deity, or else two deities
who share common characteristics.

Fig. 9.18. *Stamp seal from the city of Aššur, Jakob-Rost 1975: no. 199*
(drawing by Noga Z'evi)

Although many of the portrayals of Ištar depict her as a war-like
goddess, a portrayal which does not fit her proposed identification on
the Lachish seal, there are other renderings in which she appears with
no weapons, and thus other characteristics, such as fertility, could be
assigned to her. Such iconography may be implied from her appearance
on the impressions from the reign of Sennacherib (Fig. 9.13), in which
the goddess has no weapon. Moreover, the scorpion seen between the
goddess and the worshippers on these impressions may confirm her fertility aspects, as it stands for the goddess Išhara, who is sometimes
identified with Ištar/Innana in her non-warrior manifestation (Seidl
1989: 157; Black and Green: 1992, 160). Corroboration for the
abundance or fertility aspects of Ištar can also be found in prophetic
documents dating to the reign of Aššurbanipal, in which she is
described as the goddess with four breasts, who is the good wet nurse

27. Reisner *et al.* 1924: 377, AII no.11, pl. 57a:2 (Samaria); Keel and Uehlinger
1992: Fig. 312a, (Acco); and on inscribed seals: Avigad and Sass 1997: nos. 994,
1079. On the relationship between a branch (or a tree) and a female deity on local
second-millennium iconography see Keel and Uehlinger 1992: 378.

of the king (Livingstone 1989: 34). The selection of the frontal position and emphasis on the breasts on the seal from Lachish, fit the local Judahite tradition of portraying abundance and fertility by means of female figures, as attested by the pillar-shaped figurines (Kletter 1996). The varying motifs depicted on the Lachish seal thus represent a mixture of local and Assyrian traits, which imply Assyrian inspiration on the local Judahite iconography.

Conclusions

The portrayal of Ištar on the pendant from Tel Miqne and on the cylinder and stamp seals discussed here constitutes the most common depiction of a human-shaped Assyrian deity on local finds from Israel dating to the period of the Assyrian conquest. The popularity of this Assyrian goddess during the period of the Mesopotamian rule on Israel can be corroborated by other manifestations of Ištar in which she is represented only by her symbol, the star, on contemporary stamp seals found in Israel.[28] The locally made products that depict Ištar, and the use of Assyrian traits exemplified here by the seal from Lachish, suggest adaptation of Assyrian imagery by local artisans and imply penetration of the worship of Ištar into local cult.

This conclusion with regard to Assyrian penetration into local iconography and the prominent role of the goddess Ištar as reflected on finds from Israel, may have some bearing on the identification of the biblical Queen of Heaven. The epithet, mentioned with regard to a cult carried out both in Judah and in Egypt, among Judahite exiles (Jer. 7.18; 44.17-19, 25), can be associated with several principal goddesses known in ancient Near Eastern literature.[29] Among these goddesses Astarte and Ištar are probably the two most plausible candidates for identification with the biblical Queen of Heaven (Olyan 1987: 174; Ackerman 1989: 110-16). Hadley (1997: 117-78) has suggested that the epithet replaced the name of the specific goddess whose cult is described, but was forgotten at the period of the compiling of the book of Jeremiah. Even if one accepts this suggestion, the use of the *kawwanim,* cognate to the

28. Keel 1997: 694, no. 140 (Ashkalon), 520, no. 1232 (Ajjul); Reisner *et al.* 1924: 377, pl. 57a:d (Samaria); Lamon and Shipton 1939: pls. 67, 68, no. 9 (Megiddo); Petrie 1928: 11, pl. 20:17 (Tell Jemmeh) and see above, n. 9.

29. *ABD* 6: 586-88; van der Toorn, Becking and van der Horst 1995: 1279 and bibliography there.

Assyrian *kamanu,* which appears in association with the Queen of Heaven and is as yet known only with regard to Ištar, emphasizes the similarity of the worship of Queen of Heaven to that of Ištar.[30] The manifestations of Ištar on locally made finds from Israel strengthen the notion of the Assyrian inspiration on the image of the Queen of Heaven and the resemblance of her cult to that of Ištar.

Bibliography

Ackerman, S.
  1989   'And the Women Knead Dough': The Worship of The Queen of Heaven in Sixth-Century Judah', in P.L. Day (ed.), *Gender and Difference in Ancient Israel* (Minneapolis: Fortress Press): 109-202.

Avigad, N., and B. Sass
  1997   *Corpus of West Semitic Stamp Seals* (Jerusalem: The Israel Academy of Sciences and Humanities, The Israel Exploration Society and the Hebrew University).

Barnett, R.D.
  1969   'Anat, Ba'al and Pasargade', *Mélanges de l'Univesité Saint-Joseph* 45: 407-22.

Barrelet, M.-Th.
  1955   'Les Déesses armées et ailées', *Syria* 32: 222-60.

Becker, A.
  1993   'Uruk, Kleinfunde I. Stein', in R.M. Boehmer (ed.), *Ausgrabungen in Uruk-Warka – Endberichte* 6 (Mainz: Philipp von Zabern).

Black, J. and A. Green
  1992   *Gods, Demons and Symbols of Ancient Mesopotamia: An Illustrated Dictionary* (London: British Museum Press).

Börker-Klähn, J.
  1982   *Altvorderasiatische Bildstelen und vergleichbare Felsreliefs* (Mainz: Philipp von Zabern).

Buchanan, B., and P.R.S. Moorey
  1988   *Catalogue of Ancient Near Eastern Seals in the Ashmolean Museum.* III. *The Iron Age Stamp Seals* (Oxford: Clarendon Press).

Cavigneaux, A., and B.K. Ismail
  1990   'Die Statthalter von Suḫu und Mari im 8. Jh. v. Chr.', *Baghdader Mitteilungen* 21: 321-456.

Collon, D.
  1987   *First Impressions: Cylinder Seals in the Ancient Near East* (London: British Museum Press).

Gitin, S.
  1995   'Tel Miqne-Ekron in the 7th Century BCE: The Impact of Economic Innovation and Foreign Cultural Influences on a Neo-Assyrian Vassal City-State', in S. Gitin (ed.), *Recent Excavations in Israel: A View to the*

---

30.   In contrast to Olyan 1987: 173 and see Weinfeld 1972: 150 and n. 137.

West, Reports on Kabri, Nami, Miqne-Ekron, Dor and Ashkelon (Archaeological Institute of America, Colloquia and Conference Papers, 1; Dubuque, Iowa: Archeological Institute of America): 61-79.

1997 'The Neo-Assyrian Empire and Its Western Periphery: The Levant, with a Focus on Philistine Ekron', in S. Parpola and R.M. Whiting (eds.), *Assyria 1995* (Helsinki: The Neo-Assyrian Text Corpus Project): 77-103.

Hadley, J.M.

1997 'Chasing Shadows? The Quest for the Historical Goddess', in J.A. Emerton (ed.), *Congress Volume, Cambridge 1995* (VTSup, 66; Leiden: E.J. Brill): 169-84.

Herbordt, S.

1992 *Neuassyrische Glyptik des 8.-7. Jh. v. Chr. unter besonderer Berücksichtigung der Siegelungen auf Tafeln und Tonverschlossen* (Helsinki: The Neo-Assyrian Text Corpus Project).

Hestrin, R., and E. Stern

1973 'Two "Assyrian" Bowls from Israel', *IEJ* 23: 152-55.

Hrouda, B.

1990 'Zur Bedeutung des Fisches in der "späthethitischen" Kunst: Religise oder nur Profane Darstellung?', in P. Matthiae, M. Van Loom and H. Weiss (eds.), *Resurrecting the Past: A Joint Tribute to Adnan Bounni* (Istanbul: Nederlands historisch archaeologisch Instituute te Istanbul): 109-15.

Jakob-Rost, L.

1975 *Die Stempelsiegel im Vorderasiatischen Museum* (Berlin: Akademie-verlag).

Keel, O.

1997 *Corpus der Stempelsiegel-Amulette aus Palstina/Israel, Von den Anfngen bis zur Perserzeit, Katalog* Band I: *Von Tell Abu Farağ bis 'Atlit* (OBO.SA, 13; Freibourg: Universitätsverlag; Göttingen: Vandenhoeck & Ruprecht).

Keel, O., and C. Uehlinger

1992 *Göttinnen, Götter und Gottessymbole, Neue Erkenntnisse zur Religionsgeschichte Kanaans und Israels aufgrund bislang unerschlossener ikonographischer Quellen* (Freiburg in Breisgau, Basle and Vienna: Herder).

Klengel-Brandt, E.

1994 'Ein königliches Siegel aus Assur', in P. Calmeyer *et al.* (eds.), *Beiträge zur Altorientalischen Archäologie und Altertumskunde, Festschrift für Barthel Hrouda zum 65. Geburstag* (Wiesbaden: Harrassowitz): 147-49.

Kletter, R.

1996 *The Judaean Pillar-Figurines and the Archaeology of Asherah* (BAR International Series, 636; Oxford: Tempus Reparatum).

Lamon, R.S., and G.M. Shipton

1939 *Megiddo. I. Seasons of 1925–34, Strata I–IV* (Chicago: University of Chicago Press).

Lehmann, G.

1994 'Zu den Zerstrungen in Zincirli whrend des frhen 7. Jahrhunderts v.Chr.', *Mitteilungen der Deutschen Orient-Gesellschaft* 126: 105-22.

Livingstone, A.
    1989   *Court Poetry and Literary Miscellanea* (SAA III) (Helsinki: Helsinki University Press).

Magen, U.
    1986   *Assyrische Knigsdarstellungen—Aspekte der Herrschaft, eine Typologie* (Mainz: Philipp von Zabern).

Menzel, B.
    1981   *Assyrische Tempel: Untersuchungen zu Kult, Administration und Personal*, I, II (Rome: Biblical Institute Press).

Merhav, R. (ed.)
    1991   *Urartu: A Metalworking Center in the First Millennium BCE* (Jerusalem: The Israel Museum).

Moortgat, A.
    1940   *Vorderasiatische Rollsiegel: Ein Beitrg zur Geschichte der Steinschneidekunst* (Berlin: Gebr. Mann verlag).
    1942   'Assyrische Glyptik des 13. Jahrhunderts', *Zeitschrift für Assyriologie* 13: 50-88.

Oates, J.
    1986   *Babylon* (rev. edn; New York: Thames and Hudson).

Olyan, S.M.
    1987   'Some Observation Concerning the Identity of the Queen of Heaven', *UF* 19: 161-74.

Parker, B.
    1949   'Cylinder Seals from Palestine', *Iraq* 11: 1-43.

Petrie, W.M. Flinders
    1928   *Gerar* (London: British School of Archaeology in Egypt).

Pongratz-Leisten, B.
    1994   *Ina ulmi irub, Die kulttopographische und ideologische Programmatik der akitu-Prozession in Babylonien und Assyrien in I. Jahrtausend v. Chr.* (Mainz: Philipp von Zabern).

Porada, E.
    1948   *Corpus of Near Eastern Seals in North American Collections*. I. *The Pierpont Morgan Library* (Washington: Pantheon Books).
    1978   'Appendix A. The Cylinder Seal', in P. Bikai, *The Pottery of Tyre*, (Warminster: Aris and Phillips): 77-82.

Reade, J.E.
    1977   'Shikaft-i Gulgul: Its Date and Symbolism', *Iranica Antiqua* 12: 33-44.
    1987   'Was Sennacherib a Feminist?', in J.-M. Durand (ed.), *La femme dans le Proche-Orient antique, compte rendu de la XXXIIIeme rencontre assyriologique internationale (Paris, 7–10 Juillet 1986)* (Paris: Editions recherche sur les civilisations): 139-45.

Reisner, G.A. C.S. Fisher and D.G. Lyon
    1924   *Harvard Excavations in Samaria, 1908–1910* (2 vols.; Cambridge, MA: Harvard University Press).

Russell, J.M.
    1991   *Sennacherib's Palace Without Rival at Nineveh* (Chicago: University of Chicago Press).

Sass, B.

1991   *Studia Alphabetica: On the Origin and Early History of the Northwest Semitic, South Semitic and Greek Alphabets* (OBO, 102; Freibourg: Universitätsverlag; Göttingen: Vandenhoeck & Ruprecht).

1993   'The Pre-Exilic Hebrew Seals: Iconism vs. Aniconism', in B. Sass and C. Uehlinger (eds.), *Studies in the Iconography of North Semitic Inscribed Seals* (OBO, 125; Freibourg: University Press; Göttingen: Vandenhoeck & Ruprecht).

Seeden, H.

1980   *Standing Armed Figurines in the Levant* (Munich: C.H. Beck).

Seidl, U.

1976–80   'Inanna/Ištar (Mesopotamien), B. In der Bildkunst', *Reallexikon der Assyriologie* 5: 87-89.

1989   *Die babylonischen Kudurru-Reliefs* (OBO, 87; Freibourg: Universitätsverlag; Göttingen: Vandenhoeck & Ruprecht).

Stern, E.

1994a   *Dor, Ruler of the Seas: Twelve Years of Excavations at the Israelite-Phoenician Harbour Town on the Carmel Coast* (Jerusalem: Israel Exploration Society).

1994b   'A Phoenician-Cypriote Votive Scapula from Tel Dor: A Maritime Scene', *IEJ* 21: 1-12.

Teissier, B.

1984   *Ancient Near Eastern Cylinder Seals from the Marcopoli Collection* (Berkeley: University of California Press).

Thureau-Dangin, F.

1907   'Inscriptions diverses du Louvre', *Revue d'Assyriologie* 6: 133-38.

Thureau-Dangin, F., and M. Dunand

1936   *Til-Barsib* (Paris: P. Geuthner).

Tufnell, O.

1953   *Lachish. III. The Iron Age* (Oxford: Oxford University Press).

van Buren, E.D.

1945   *Symbols of the Gods in Mesopotamian Art* (AnOr, 23; Rome: Pontificum institutum biblicum).

van der Toorn, K., B. Becking and P.W. van der Horst (eds.)

1995   *Dictionary of Deities and Demons in the Bible* (Leiden: E.J. Brill).

von Luschan, F.

1943   *Ausgrabungen in Sendschirli. V. Die Kleinfunde von Sendschirli* (Berlin: W. de Gruyter).

Watanabe, K.

1992   'Nabu-uṣalla, Statthalter Sargons II in Tam(a)nuna', *Baghdader Mitteilungen* 23: 357-69.

Wiggermann, F.A.M.

1994   'Mischwesen A', *Reallexikon der Assyriologie* 8: 222-44.

Weinfeld, M.

1972   'The Worship of Molech and of the Queen of Heaven', *UF* 4: 133-54.

Wilcke, C.

1976–80   'Inanna/Ishtar (Mesopotamien) A. Philologisch', *Reallexikon der Assyriologie* 5: 74-87.

Winter, I.J.
1982   'Art as Evidence for Interaction: Relations between the Assyrian Empire and North Syria', in H.-J. Nissen and J. Renger, (eds.), *Mesopotamien und seine Nachbarn, Politische und kulturelle Wechselbeziehungen im Alten Vorderasien vom 4. bis 1. Jahrtausend v. Chr.* (Berlin: Dietrich Reimer): 355-82.
1986   'The King and the Cup: Iconography of the Royal Presentation Scene on Ur III Seals', in M. Kelly-Buccellati *et al.* (eds.), *Insight Through Images, Studies in Honor of Edith Porada* (Bibliotheca Mesopotamica, 21; Malibu: Udenda Publications): 253-68.
1994   'Radiance as an Aesthetic Value in the Art of Mesopotamia (with some Indian Parallels)', in B.N. Saraswati, S.C. Malik and M. Khanna (eds.), *Art—The Integral Vision: A Volume of Essays in Felicitation of Kapila Vatsyayan* (New Delhi: D.K. Printworld): 123-32.

Winter, U.
1983   *Frau und Göttin* (OBO, 53; Freibourg: Universitätsverlag; Göttingen: Vandenhoeck & Ruprecht).

Yadin, Y.
1963   *The Art of Warfare in Biblical Lands in the Light of Archaeological Study* (Jerusalem: International Publishing).

10

A Room with a View: Images from Room V at Khorsabad, Samaria, Nubians, The Brook of Egypt and Ashdod[*]

Norma Franklin

The Historical Setting

Samaria and the Samarians

The last king of Israel, Hosea, rebelled in c. 724 BCE, and Samaria was subdued once, twice, perhaps even four times (Tadmor 1958; Na'aman 1990; Hayes and Kuan 1991; Becking 1992). However, upon Shalmaneser's demise, Samaria rebelled at least once more (Na'aman 1990: 213). The final conquest and deportations were major events, to judge by the central place they occupy in Sargon's annals (1990: 208). In an attempt to further extol Sargon's name, the annals glorify the final defeat of Samaria which took place soon after Sargon's accession to the throne in 720 BCE (Tadmor 1958: 31).

The inscriptions state that 27,290 inhabitants of Samaria were deported by Sargon, among them a unit of 50 charioteers (Luckenbill 1927: 4, 55), including top equestrian officers who subsequently served as an elite charioteer force in the Assyrian army, retaining its own name. Hence, it can be proven that Samaria had deployed charioteers (Dalley 1985: 32, 38). Further, according to the texts, the best chariot horses were of the 'Kush' breed from Nubia, and there is evidence for a particular 'Kushite' way of harnessing them (1985: 43, 44). They were apparently traded from Nubia to Samaria, via Nubians who may have been resident in Samaria (Anderson 1996: 64-65).

---

[*]   This paper is a revised and updated version of N. Franklin, 'The Room V Reliefs at Dur-Sharrukin and Sargon II's Western Campaigns', *Tel Aviv* 21 (1994): 255-75. All the illustrations are after Botta and Flandin 1849.

According to 2 Kgs 17.4 Hosea formed an alliance with So', king of Egypt. The identity of King So' has intrigued many scholars (Yeivin 1952; Baer 1973; Spalinger 1973; Kitchen 1983; Christensen 1989; Na'aman 1990; Green 1993). The riddle has finally been solved by Na'aman (1990) and Green (1993). They identify King So' with Pihanky, the brother of Shabako, the Nubian founder of the Egyptian 25th Dynasty. In fact the Nubians tended to mimic the Egyptians and often a noted Egyptian presence is in reality Nubian or Cushite (Anderson 1996: 68). Hosea depended on King So' (Pihanky King of Nubia) as an ally, perhaps because of their existing trade relationship.

Deportations

The ninth century BCE witnessed the beginning of 'enforced urbaniza-tion' in Assyria, relocated deportees being routinely used as building labourers by Ashurbanipal II and Shalmaneser III, setting the pattern for larger scale deportations under Tiglath-Pileser III and Sargon II (Tadmor 1975: 40). Sargon deported thousands of local inhabitants between the years 720–708 BCE from the regions of Samaria and the Philistine coast (Na'aman 1993: 111). The main movement of deportees was to Assyria proper, the principal cities of Ashur, Calah, Nineveh and Dur-Sharrukin receiving 85 per cent of all recorded deportees during the period of the empire (Oded 1979: 28). Men were deported with their families, not only reducing their chance of escaping, but improving their prospects of settling down in their new environment. Furthermore, families were not separated from the members of their communities, and homogeneous groups were settled together (Oded 1979: 24-25).[1]

It is related in 2 Kgs 17.6 and 18.12 that 'Israel was carried into Ashur and resettled in Halah, Habor, and the River of Gozan'. The Nimrud Prism confirms that Samarians were deported to Halah in central Assyria. The deportations occurred in 715 BCE, five years after the final conquest of Samaria (Na'aman 1993: 107-109), and two years after the foundations of Dur-Sharrukin were laid in Halah.

---

1.   See Room V, Reliefs 8-L and 9-L, where men, women, and children travel calmly with their possessions. These captives were ostensibly the property of the king (Oded 1979: 40). To emphasize this, they are shown filing past the king immediately after the conquest of their city on Relief 2-L(O).

King Hanunu of Gaza, the Brook of Egypt and Raphia
In 722/721 BCE, Hanunu of Gaza allied himself with the Syro-Palestinian coalition headed by Yaubi'idi, King of Hamath (Tadmor 1966: 91), which included the Kings of Hamath, Arpad, Hatrika, Simirra, Damascus and Samaria. Sargon defeated this coalition at Qarqar, then continued south in pursuit of Hanunu, who had fled to Raphia, situated south of Nahal Besor. Na'aman (1979: 74, 77) has identified Nahal Besor with the Brook of Egypt. According to his annals, Sargon destroyed Raphia in 720 BCE (Tadmor 1966: 92), taking Hanunu to Ashur in chains together with 9033 people and their possessions (Luckenbill 1927: 5). The defeat of Raphia is also mentioned in the Pavement Inscription (Type 4) (Luckenbill 1927: 99).[2]

Gibbethon
Gibbethon is referred to in 1 Kgs 16.15 as a Philistine border settlement. It was identified with Tel Melat by von Rad (1933: 38-39), whose equation is acknowledged by Aharoni (1979), but recently questioned by von Schmitt (1989). Tel Melat has been only partially excavated (Shavit 1993: 45), and the identification is still inconclusive.[3]

Philistia
Philistia was especially important to Assyria, as the Assyrians did not want to upset the precarious trade relations that they had with Egypt by way of Philistia. Therefore the Assyrians were cautious not to disrupt the delicate social fabric by deportations (Epha'al 1979: 286, 287). Tiglath-Pileser III's first campaign to Philistia is recorded in Inscription ND 400, after which the Assyrians effectively ruled Philistia until 630 BCE (Tadmor 1966: 86; Mattingly 1979: 55). However, in 720, 716, 713 and 712 BCE Sargon undertook four campaigns to Philistia (Na'aman 1979: 85) to subdue the area and promote trade. Among the facilitators of trade in northern Sinai were the Nubians or Cushites (Elat 1983: 11-12). The campaign of 716 BCE was of an exceptionally commercial character (Mattingly 1981: 47). Many key sites were devastated including Arad, Tel Malhata, Tel Beersheba, and Tel Sera, while others were created as mercantile centres, for example, Tel

2.   Hanunu appears on Reliefs 1–4 in Room VIII (Wafler 1975).
3.   Gibbethon is depicted and named on Relief 5-L in Room V (Fig. 10.5).

Jemma (Arza), Tel Abu-Seleimeh (Anthedon) and Tel Sera (Na'aman 1979: 82-85).[4]

Ashdod

There may have been a minor campaign to Ashdod in 713 BCE when Azuri of Ashdod withheld his tribute, and whom the Assyrians then replaced with his brother Ahimitu. However, the locals rebelled and chose Yamani, a Philistine, as their leader. The main campaign which followed was led by Sargon's Turtanu in 712 BCE (Isa. 20.1-6). Sargon did not lead the campaign personally, perhaps due to his attention being required by the construction of Dur-Sharrukin (Tadmor 1958: 79 n. 208). In Prism Fragment S 2022 this campaign is known as the ninth, and in the annals as the tenth (Tadmor 1958: 79). The 'Pavement Inscriptions' (Type 4) mention that Sargon carried off the spoils from Ashdod (Luckenbill 1927: 99), and a further reference is contained in the 'Summary Inscription'.

The peoples of Ashdod, Gath and Ashdod-Yam were taken captive together with their belongings (Luckenbill 1927: 62). Yamani, the locally elected king, escaped, fleeing over the border into Egypt (1927: 79) and was then, perhaps surprisingly, handed over to Assyria by the King of Kush (1927: 63). However, if Shabako, the founder of the 25th Egyptian Dynasty, was the king of Kush (Spalinger 1973: 95), Yamani, who as the protégé of Bakenranef of the 24th Dynasty (Kapera 1981– 84: 291), was no friend of Shabako. As a reward, the Nubians were granted lower Egypt by the Assyrians (Hallo 1960), which, along with the death of Bakenranef, coincided with the establishment of the 25th Dynasty, dated by Spalinger (1973: 99) to 712 BCE.

The earliest account of Sargon's campaign against Ashdod is contained in Prism A from Nineveh, composed in 710 BCE (Kapera 1987: 29-39). Three fragments of a basalt stele, excavated in Ashdod in 1963, relate to Sargon's annexation of Ashdod (Dothan 1964: 87). The stele had been broken in antiquity, possibly as early as 705 BCE, when a new anti-Assyrian coalition was organized by Hezekiah of Judah (Kapera 1976: 89, 92).[5]

---

4.   Philistines are shown on Reliefs 7–10 of Room IV (Wafler 1975).
5.   The fate of Yamani of Ashdod appears on Reliefs 5-8 in Room VIII (Wafler 1975).

Ekron

Ekron is identified with Khirbet Muqqanna (Naveh 1958; Aharoni 1979). It was transformed into a vassal state by Sargon. Later, during the rebellions that broke out upon the accession of Sennacherib, Padi, the vassal king of Ekron, was deposed and handed over to Hezekiah of Judah, who also looked to the then king of Kush for assistance (Luckenbill 1927: 311). Sennacherib is also known to have fought Nubian forces nearby. Haak (1996: 250-51) has recently proposed that 'Cushites' had migrated to areas bordering on southern Judah. The Nubian presence which is now known to have existed from the time of Sargon onwards supports this theory.[6]

Khorsabad: Dur-Sharrukin

Dur-Sharrukin, the 'Palace of the True King', Sargon II, was a massive corpus of personal propaganda (Reade 1979b: 331). To build his new capital, Sargon purchased the town of Magganubba, situated in central Assyria, the region of Halah at the foot of Mount Musri (Luckenbill 1927: 119). The foundations were laid in 717 BCE, the gods entered their temples in 707 BCE, and the city was inaugurated on the sixth of Iyyar, 706 BCE (Tadmor 1958). According to the texts, a great festival was attended by 'kings from (foreign) lands; the governors of my land; the overseers, commanders, nobles, high officials, and elders of Assyria' (Luckenbill 1927: 74). Among the foreign kings were 'princes of the four quarters (of the world), who had submitted to the yoke of my rule, whose lives I had spared' (Luckenbill 1927: 98).

Wall Reliefs

The reliefs decorating the walls of Dur-Sharrukin were carved on slabs of Mosul marble, 2–3 m high. The carving was carried out once the slabs were placed in position (Reade 1979a: 17). Scenes are consecutive, suggesting a cartoon effect (Reade 1980: 85). Since few people were literate the reliefs had to be self-explanatory, the participants and location easily recognizable. The visual narrative is independent of the annals (Reade 1976: 97), yet also served as propaganda.

However, instead of paralleling one another, the texts and images are often complementary (Marcus 1987: 98). Text and visual image would have shared some common sources, but other factors, such as the

6.   Ekron is depicted and named on Relief 10-L in Room V (Fig. 10.8).

anticipated audience, governed the selection of material (Russell 1991: 30). Scenes of warfare are depicted in areas of the palace frequented by visiting dignitaries, such as Room V, while others depict court scenes or religious themes (Saggs 1955: 149).

The slabs from Room V were removed so that they could be displayed in European museums, but unfortunately, the ship carrying them sunk in the Chatt-el-Arab waterway in 1855. The only record of their content is preserved in the on-site sketches by M. Flandin and the notes compiled by P.E. Botta.

The Ekallu *and its Inscriptions*
The main feature of the suite or *Ekallu* that incorporated Room V (Fig. 10.1) is the three parallel communicating rooms that project from the main body of the palace onto a level terrace. This style of *Ekallu* was catalogued as a Type F suite by Turner (1970). Designed for ceremonies involving visiting dignitaries (Reade 1979b: 338), it is the only part of the palace with reliefs on the external, as well as internal, walls (Loud *et al.* 1936: 72).

The *Ekallu* is accessed from the main palace through connecting Corridor X. The main room is Room VIII, the throne room, which contains single-register reliefs depicting rebels. Room V is a centrally placed antechamber, which contains two-register reliefs displaying the western campaigns. The third long reception room, Room II, displays two-register reliefs of the eastern campaigns and feasting scenes. Room I, a small entrance room, also displays reliefs from the eastern campaigns. From Room I access is gained to Room III, a similarly decorated bathroom. Room IV is a reception or banquet room with single-register reliefs, in which the punishment meted out to the rebels whose uprisings brought about the campaigns depicted in Rooms I, II, III and V is shown. Room IV grants access to Room VII, a small banquet room, containing hunting and banqueting scenes.

Rooms IV, VII, VIII and Corridor X are inscribed with the 'Summary Inscription', which followed a clear geographical or associative, rather than chronological, sequence (Tadmor 1958: 36; Na'aman 1979: 68 n. 2). Rooms II, V, XIII and XIV are inscribed with the 'Annals', a militaristic narrative which also serves as a band dividing the two registers.

Twenty-nine 'Pavement Inscriptions' of five different types are inscribed on thresholds within the *Ekallu*, 21 of which have been published (Russell 1991: 17). 'Pavement Inscriptions' Types 3, 4, 5 relate that, 'with the (labour) of the enemy peoples my hands had captured, I built a city...and called its name Dur-Sharrukin' (Luckenbill 1927: 98, 99, 102). Dur-Sharrukin was not unique in being built by captive exiles. Calah, the previous capital, had been built thus in the ninth century BCE. Sennacherib later employed 200,000 Chaldaeans and Judaeans in his work force (Tadmor 1975: 40-41), a fact confirmed by Russell (1991: 167) in his analysis of captive foreign labour. All the inscriptions inscribed in the *Ekallu* and its adjacent ancillary rooms date to 707 BCE, the fifteenth year of Sargon's reign, although the last preserved date is 709 BCE (Tadmor 1958: 36).

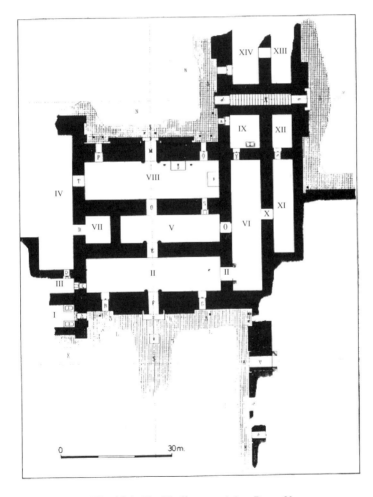

Fig. 10.1. *The* Ekallu *containing Room V*

A Geographic Sequence

The 'Summary Inscriptions' are organized according to geographical locale (Marcus 1987: 81). Likewise, the reliefs, regardless of whether they portray battles from a single campaign or a series of related campaigns, often follow a geographical sequence (Gunter 1982: 104). Reade (1976: 95) also noted that when displayed in their true sequence, as if in a cartoon strip, the reliefs can reveal geographical or historical information. In addition (Reade 1980: 85) military narratives are restricted to one geographical region per room. In fact, art functioned as a visual validation for the acquisition of territory. For example, Assurnasirpal II's throne room is divided into two distinct geographical areas; the south-west, west and north compose one area, and the south-east, east and south another. A geographical sequence is also employed on Shalmaneser III (Marcus 1987: 84) and Sargon II's throne bases (Winter 1983: 24-27) and the principal source for Sargon's annals is the Nimrud Prism that also follows a geographical order (Tadmor 1958: 36).

The Arrangement of the Room V Reliefs

Botta numbered the slabs in Room V from 1 to 25 (Fig. 10.2), in accord with the annals serving to divide the upper and lower registers. The reliefs will be henceforth referred to as 1-U and 1-L, and so on, for the upper and lower registers, respectively. Entranceway O was never

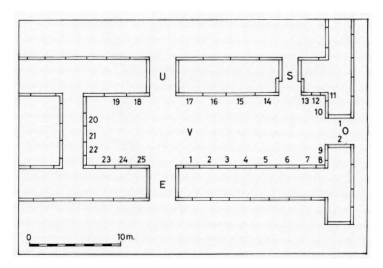

Fig. 10.2. *Room V, the doorways and the numbered slabs*

closed by a fixed door—there are no pivot sockets—so the entranceway reliefs form an integral part of Room V. Therefore its upper and lower registers will be referred to as 1-U(O) and 1-L(O).

The numbering system begins at Door E, on the 'main axis-way'. This axis-way starts at Door M near Court III, then leads by way of Doors U, E and F to Monument X. The route continues through throne Room VIII (rebels), Room V (western war) and Room II (eastern war and feasting), ending at the steps of Monument X. If viewed from the south, the numbering system runs in an anti-clockwise direction. The annals, which divide the slabs into two registers, begin on slab 25, and must be read in a clockwise direction, finishing on slab 1. Entranceway O, situated between slabs 9 and 10, disrupts Botta's numbering system.

The Campaigns Depicted in Room V
The Room V reliefs were attributed by El-Amin to a single campaign, that of 720 BCE (1953: 35-40), but Tadmor dated the scenes to 712 BCE (1958: 83 n. 243). Guterbock (1957: 68) disagreed with the supposition that only one campaign is depicted in each room. Reade (1976), although not concurring with all of El-Amin's arguments, attempted to impose a chronological order on the reliefs, which he believed belonged to 720 BCE. However, the campaigns against the east, depicted in Room II, are variously ascribed to 715 BCE and 714 BCE (Albenda 1986). Therefore, it is reasonable to presume that the Room V reliefs, when contemplated jointly with their diverse inscriptions and the mix of campaigns in Room II, also encapsulate a series of events that took place between Sargon II's first western campaign in 720 BCE and Dur-Sharrukin's completion in 707 BCE, or more correctly, 709 BCE, the date proposed for the compilation of the various inscriptions.

The Upper Registers
Ten of the 27 reliefs were discovered completely ruined, and the remainder were badly damaged. None have previously been dealt with in depth, though Reade (1976: 99) did ascertain that they represent the battles of 720 BCE against the Hamath coalition. The reliefs in the upper register appear to consist of one long battle beginning on Relief 25-U, which is situated on the north side of Door E, the main axis door, and runs in a clockwise direction, as do the annals. There is no apparent break in the narrative flow. Reliefs 25-U, 24-U, 22-U and 21-U portray Assyrian war chariots chasing and trampling a foe armed with easily distinguishable elliptical shields.

Reliefs 20-U to 14-U on the north side of Door S were very poorly preserved. Botta (Botta and Flandin 1849: 145) observed that in 16-U there appears to be a *fortress*, the siege of which is depicted in 17-U. However, no sketch was made because of its fragmentary condition. Following 17-U, the direction of battle remains constant, and the narrative apparently continued. The unrecorded reliefs are situated midway along the long wall of Room V, upon which it is conceivable that another siege scene, or even two, might have existed.

Reliefs 13-U to 9-U (Figs. 10.7–10.8) contain additional Assyrian charioteers and cavalrymen pursuing the same foe depicted in Reliefs 20-U to 14-U, but armed with spears and curved swords as well as the elliptical shield. There is no break in the narrative at Entranceway O. The chase continues on 1-U(O) and 2-U(O), ending on Relief 8-U (Fig. 10.7), where two defenders are hemmed against a tower, apparently part of a city wall. The city in its entirety is missing, as Slab 7 is not preserved in its upper register. However, another tower, situated on the far side of the missing city, is discernible on Relief 6-U (Fig. 10.6). The missing city of Relief 7-U was strategically placed facing Door S, which led from Room VIII, and the immediate area of the throne base. Important city scenes or royal figures are often situated opposite entranceways (Guralnick 1976: 7). Therefore, this large city, its depiction extending over more than one slab, must have been a significant site. Next to the tower in Relief 6-U, a captive is dispatched by an Assyrian. Reliefs 5-U to 2-U (Figs. 10.3–10.5) show a review of the spoils brought before Sargon by the Assyrian troops. The stationary chariot just perceptible in Relief 2-U is the royal chariot (Fig. 10.3). Slab 1 was not preserved, but it would have been out of sight behind the door of Doorway E, and therefore it is improbable that it contained significant data. This epic saga is then concluded.

In the upper registers (unlike the scenes in the lower registers) chariots are portrayed. Chariots were deployed against chariots, and would have been unnecessary in a stationary siege. According to the texts, Samaria in particular had a remarkable chariot force (Dalley 1985). The curved swords used by the defenders are quite unique, paralleled only by the curved swords taken from Judaean Lachish as booty by Sennacherib in 701 BCE (Ussishkin 1982: 84-85, pl. 69, 105-109). It is thus conceivable that the significant city once portrayed on Relief 7-U was Samaria. Further, the booty carried off by the Assyrians (Fig. 10.4) is seemingly the Samarian booty, not detailed in the inscriptions.

Fig. 10.3. *Slab 2. Upper register (2-U): Sargon's stationary chariot; lower register (2-L): Raphia, defended by the Nubian soldiers of King So'/Pihanky*

The Lower Registers

Four slabs from the lower registers were destroyed, while 22 Reliefs survived to be published. They contain a number of independent 'narratives'.

1) An uninterrupted narrative runs from Slab 1 to the centre of Relief 5-L. As mentioned above, Slab 1 was situated next to Door E, which when open would have hidden the reliefs, indicating that Slab 1 would have been of little consequence.

The enemy shown on Reliefs 2-L to 5-L (Figs. 10.3–10.5) consists of ambidextrous Nubians, each warrior being armed with two long spears. Botta and Flandin (1849: 137) first noted the African countenance of the enemy. Now, with the decipherment of the texts and an improved understanding of the politics of the period, we can positively confirm their identity. They are the warriors of King So'/Pihanky of the 25th Nubian-Egyptian Dynasty. The city which they defend is situated on a rocky hill (Fig. 10.3) and is portrayed quite differently from western Syro-Palestinian cities. For example, there are neither crenellations along the top of the walls nor towers, but rather features which are characteristic of Egyptian cities depicted elsewhere (Albenda 1982: 13-14), and which distinguish it from other cities portrayed in Room V.

Fig. 10.4. *Slab 4. Upper register (4-U): Assyrian soldiers carrying the booty from Samaria; lower register (4-L): the Brook of Egypt, Nahal Besor, and the continuing battle between the Nubian soldiers of King So'/Pihanky and the Assyrians*

The city in Relief 5-L (Fig. 10.5), is named Gabbtunu, identified by El-Amin (1953) as Philistine Gibbethon. The defenders of Gibbethon are also ambidextrous African spearmen, that is Nubians, who also engage the Assyrians in Relief 4-L (Fig. 10.4). The city, situated on a small hill, has the typical Syro-Palestinian crenellated towers and walls and is separated from the city referred to in the previous paragraph by a river denoted by its spirals. Sea water is shown by wavy lines while river and marsh scenes are portrayed by wavy lines concluding in spirals (Linder 1986: 280). The only reasonable candidate for the river, which was important to the narrative as it was expressly shown separating the two cities, is Nahal Besor, the Brook of Egypt. This identification, together with the presence of Nubians, also raises the question regarding the identification of 'from beyond the river of Cush' in Zeph. 3.10. Haak (1996: 244-46) has recently proposed the eastern irrigation canal of the Nile delta. El-Amin (1953) identified these targets of the 720 BCE campaign as Raphia and Gibbethon, respectively. He mistakenly identified Raphia due to its proximity to the 'sea', because of his misinterpretation of the Assyrian iconography for a river. Only now can the city be identified securely with Raphia. We also know that Raphia was ruled by the Nubian-Egyptian King Pihanky, and the defending warriors are Nubians. The city's appearance is not Syro-Palestinian, but rather resembles the cities portrayed in the reliefs of Ashurbanipal's Egyptian campaigns.

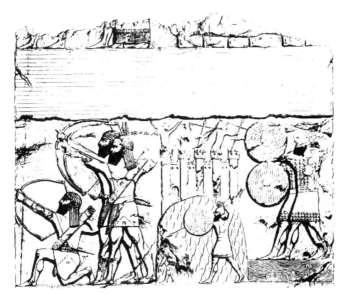

Fig. 10.5. *Slab 5. Upper register (5-U): the closing scene of the battle for Samaria and the beginning of the removal of the booty from Samaria; lower register (5-L): Gibbethon defended by the Nubian soldiers of King So'/Pihanky*

The prevailing action is from south to north. Perhaps, based on strategic considerations, Sargon first attacked Raphia, defeating the Nubians and taking Hanunu of Gaza prisoner, thus effectively cutting off the Nubian forces deployed to the north. Alternatively, after depicting the southernmost city reached in Sargon's western campaigns, Raphia, the Dur-Sharrukin artist merely reversed the flow of the narrative. The geographical sequence in the upper registers runs from north to south, and that in the lower registers from south to north.

2) The second narrative runs from midway in Relief 5-L through
Relief 9-L (Figs. 10.5–10.7) and ends on Relief 2-L(O). Troops attack a
city from two sides; it has a lower city wall, one side of which is being
demolished by two battering rams (Fig. 10.6).

Fig. 10.6. *Slab 6. Upper register (6-U): one of the towers of Samaria and an*
Assyrian soldier killing a defeated Samarian; lower register (6-L): Ashdod
defended by hooded bowman. The acropolis and lower city are clearly shown

A separate fortified acropolis and a small tower are shown, separated by a non-fruit bearing palm tree, possibly to emphasize these features (Bleibtreu 1980: 99). The crenellated towers and walls are defended by hooded bowmen. The scene changes as the story continues from Relief 7-L to Reliefs 8-L, 9-L and Relief 2-L(O), in which the same men, accompanied by their wives and children, are taken captive, and to conclude the narrative, paraded before Sargon II (Fig. 10.7).

Fig. 10.7. *Slabs 8 and 9. Upper register (8-U and 9-U): another tower of Samaria, defended by Samarian warriors with curved swords; lower register (8-L and 9-L): hooded Ashdodites, deported in family groups*

Though the city was identified by El-Amin (1953) as Gaza, a sea is nowhere depicted, and it cannot be identified with Arza/Tell Jemma, as no river is represented. It is, however, listed in the inscriptions as a city from which deportees were taken for resettlement. There are also architectural similarities between this city and the other Syro-Palestinian cities depicted on the Room V reliefs. The depiction of a city with a separate acropolis corresponds with the excavated remains of Ashdod, where Dothan (1993: 98-100) excavated sections of the lower city, including a massive wall and a six-chambered gate, as well as a fortified acropolis. The Assyrian inscriptions record that Yamani reinforced Ashdod with a siege wall and a moat. This similarity, together with the prominence given to the deportees, points to the identification of this city with Philistine Ashdod, and the campaign as that of 712 BCE.

3) The third narrative begins on Relief 1-L(O) and continues into Room V proper, where it runs through Reliefs 10-L to 13-L. A city named Amqarruna in the reliefs was identified as Ekron by El-Amin (1953). It is shown attacked on both sides by Assyrians and defended by bonneted bowmen (Fig. 10.8). The city stands on a podium, has crenellated towers and walls and shows clear architectural similarities with the previously mentioned cities of Gibbethon and Ashdod. The captured defenders, males only and therefore prisoners, not deportees, are brought before Sargon II, thus concluding the narrative.

Fig. 10.8. *Slabs 10 and 11. Upper register (10-U and 11-U): part of the chariot battle against the Hamath coalition; lower register (10-L and 11-L): Ekron defended by bonneted bowmen*

4) A new narrative begins on Reliefs 14-L and 15-L. Assyrian archers, assisted by a team with a battering ram, are besieging a double-walled city named Bailgazara, identified by El-Amin (1953) as a Phoenician city. The city is defended by bowmen and it is depicted, like the other Syro-Palestinian cities, with crenellated towers. Relief 17-L, poorly preserved, is probably part of the same narrative and depicts a city named Sinnu, also identified by El-Amin (1953) as a Phoenician city, probably the Siannu near Ugarit mentioned in the annals of Tiglath-Pileser III, and which he defeated in 734 BCE. It is possible that this narrative continues on the wall north of Door U, since a remnant of a city is visible on Relief 18-L, and there is no clear conclusion to the narrative.

5) On the short northern wall there are two reliefs, 21-L and 22-L, with faintly visible remains. In a siege scene, Assyrian bowmen and spearmen are depicted scaling a city on a hill. The actual city and its defenders are not discernible. The narrative may continue into the next group of reliefs, 24-L and 25-L, which shows Assyrian bowmen and spearmen besieging and scaling a city, perched on a hill, with crenellated walls and towers and defended by bonneted bowmen. The two cities have much in common with the other cities depicted on the lower registers and presumably portray Phoenician cities.

Conclusion

The Room V reliefs, as previous scholars have recognized, deal exclusively with Sargon II's western campaigns. The emphasis here is on the plural. There is no need to try to identify a single campaign. The depictions in both the upper or lower registers are arranged according to their geographical location. These reliefs show, in step with the Annals, Summary Inscriptions, and the Pavement Inscriptions, a synopsis of all Sargon's western campaigns, c. 722–709 BCE.

The upper register deals with the inland-highland sites belonging to the Hamath coalition. The chariot battles, typical of these cities, progress from north to south. The last depicted city, partially preserved, is therefore the most southerly of this coalition—Samaria. Furthermore, the booty carried off from this last depicted city by the Assyrians, when considered together with the distinctive curved swords wielded by the defenders (similar to those used 20 years later at Judaean Lachish), strengthens this identification. Samaria occupies a prime place among the reliefs of Room V. The prominent position given to the Samarian reliefs was an explicit message to those early inhabitants of Dur-Sharrukin in Halah who were deportees from Samaria. They would have been continually confronted with a graphic and powerful reminder of the defeat of their city. The use of wall reliefs to convey such messages are used elsewhere in Sargon's palace (Russell 1991: 226).

The lower register deals with the coastal-lowland sites of the western campaigns—the allies of Hosea, the Nubian warriors of King So'/ Pihanky, fight the Assyrians on both sides of the Egyptian border.

The scenes progress northwards, depicting the defeat of Ashdod[7] and the deportation of its population in 712 BCE. The siege of Ekron is difficult to date, possibly relating either to the campaign of 720 BCE or to that of 712 BCE. Ekron is situated to the north of Ashdod, which is to be expected in any geographical sequence. The final cities are Phoenician sites.

Thus aided by the geographic sequence and a deeper understanding of the historical background, Samaria, Nubians, the Brook of Egypt and Ashdod, become newly revealed images from the past.

Bibliography

Aharoni, A.
    1979   *The Land of the Bible* (2nd edn; Philadelphia: Westminster Press).
Albenda, P.
    1982   'Observations on Egyptians in Assyrian Reliefs', *Bulletin of the Egyptological Seminar* 4: 5-23.
    1983   'A Mediterranean Seascape from Khorsabad', *Assur* 3.3: 1-34.
    1986   *The Palace of Sargon King of Assyria* (Synthesis, 22; Paris: Editions Recherche sur les Civilisations).
Anderson, R.W. Jr.
    1996   'Zephania ben Cushi and Cushi of Benjamin: Traces of Cushite Presence in Syria-Palestine', in Holloway and Handy (eds.) 1996: 45-70.
Baer, K.
    1973   'The Libyan and Nubian Kings of Egypt: Notes on the Chronology of Dynasties XXII–XXVI', *JNES* 32: 4-25.

7.   If Tel Melat is Gibbethon (an identification which has been challenged by von Schmitt 1989), then it is slightly too far to the north of Ashdod to maintain a true north-south geographic order. The map coordinates for Ashdod are 117 129, and for Tel Melat 137 140 (Aharoni 1979: 431, 435). Yet if Gibbethon was situated 011 minutes to the north of Ashdod, it is unlikely that this detail would have been noticed by the Assyrians, especially as it was also situated 020 minutes to the east.

Becking, B.
    1992   *The Fall of Samaria: An Historical and Archaeological Study* (Leiden: E.J. Brill).

Bleibtreu, E.
    1980   *Die Flora der neuassyrischen Reliefs* (Vienna: Verlag des Institutes für Orientalistik der Universität Wien).

Botta, P.E., and M.E. Flandin
    1849   *Monument de Ninive* (Paris: Imprimerie nationale).

Christensen, D.L.
    1989   'The Identity of "King So" in Egypt (2 Kings ii)', *VT* 39: 140-53.

Dalley, S.
    1985   'Foreign Chariotry and Cavalry in the Armies of Tiglath-Pileser III and Sargon II', *Iraq* 47: 31-48.

Dothan, M.
    1964   'Ashdod: Preliminary Report on the Excavations in Seasons 1962–1963', *IEJ* 14: 79-95.
    1993   'Ashdod', *New Encyclopedia of Archaeological Excavations* I: 93-102.

El-Amin, M.
    1953   'Die Reliefsmit Beischriften von Sargon II in Dur-Sharrukin', *Sumer* 9: 35-59, 214-28.

Elat, M.
    1983   'Assyrian Imperialism and International Trade', a paper presented at the 30th Rencontre Assyriologique Internationale, Leiden, 4–8 July 1983.

Epha'al, I.
    1979   'The Assyrian Domination of Palestine', in A. Malamat (ed.), *The Age of the Monarchies: Political History* (The World History of the Jewish People; Jerusalem: Massada): 276-89.

Green, A.R.W.
    1993   'The Identity of King So of Egypt: An Alternative Interpretation', *JNES* 52.2: 99-108.

Gunter, A.
    1982   'Representation of Urartian and Western Iranian Fortress Architecture in the Assyrian Reliefs', *Iran* 20: 103-12.

Guralnick, E.
    1976   'Composition of Some Narrative Reliefs from Khorsabad', *Assur* 1.5: 1-23.

Guterbock, H.G.
    1957   'Narration in Anatolian, Syrian and Assyrian Art', *AJA* 61: 62-71.

Haak, R.D.
    1996   ' "Cush" in Zephania', in Holloway and Handy (eds.) 1996: 238-51.

Hallo, W.W.
    1960   'From Qarqarto Carchemish: Assyria and Israel in the Light of New Discoveries', *BA* 23: 34-61.

Hayes, J.H., and J.K. Kuan
    1991   'The Final Years of Samaria (730–720 BC)', *Biblica* 72: 153-81.

Holloway, S.W., and L.K. Handy (eds.)
    1996   *The Pitcher Is Broken. Memorial Essays for Gosta W. Ahlström* (JSOTSup, 190; Sheffield: Sheffield Academic Press).

Kapera, Z.J.

1976 'The Ashdod Stele of Sargon II', *Folia Orientalia* 17: 87-99.

1981–84 'Biblical Reflections of the Struggle for Philistia at the End of the Eighth Century BC: Analysis of Chapter XX of the Book of Isaiah. Judgement on the Neighbouring Countries (Zechariah 9, 1-8)', *Folia Orientalia* 22: II, 277-93; III, 295-307.

1987 'The Oldest Account of Sargon II's Campaign against Ashdod', *Folia Orientalia* 24: 29-39.

Kitchen, K.A.

1983 'Egypt, Levant and Assyria in 701 BC', in M. Gorg (ed.), *Fontes Atque Pontes: Eine Festgabe für Hellmut Bruner* (Agypten und Altes Testament, 5; Wiesbaden: In Kommission Bei O. Harrassowitz).

Linder, E.

1986 'The Khorsabad Wall Relief: A Mediterranean Seascape or River Transport of Timbers?', *JAOS* 106: 273-81.

Loud, G., H. Frankfort and T. Jacobsen

1936 *Khorsabad I* (Oriental Institute Publication, 38; Chicago: University of Chicago Press).

Loud, G., and C.B. Altman

1938 *Khorsabad II* (Oriental Institute Publication, 40; Chicago: University of Chicago Press).

Luckenbill, D.D.

1927 *Ancient Records of Assyria and Babylon. II. Historical Records of Assyria from Sargon to the End* (Chicago: Chicago University Press).

Marcus, M.I.

1987 'Geography as an Organising Principle in the Imperial Art of Shalmaneser III', *Iraq* 49: 77-90.

Mattingly, G.L.

1979 'The Role of Philistine Autonomy in Neo-Assyrian Foreign Policy', *Near Eastern Archaeological Society Bulletin* 14: 49-57.

1981 'An Archaeological Analysis of Sargon's 712 Campaign Against Ashdod', *Near Eastern Archaeological Society Bulletin* 17: 47-64.

Na'aman, N.

1979 'The Brook of Egypt and Assyrian Policy on the Border of Egypt', *Tel Aviv* 6: 68-90.

1990 'The Historical Background of the Conquest of Samaria (720 BC)', *Biblica* 71: 207-25.

1991 'Forced Participation in Alliances in the Course of the Assyrian Campaigns to the West', in M. Cogan and I. Eph'al (eds.), *Ah, Assyria... Studies in Assyrian History and Ancient Near Eastern Historiography Presented to Hayim Tadmor* (Scripta Hierosolymitana, 33; Jerusalem: Magnes Press, Hebrew University): 80-89.

1993 'Population Changes in Palestine Following Assyrian Deportations', *Tel Aviv* 20: 104-24.

Naveh, J.

1958 'Khirbet al-Muqanna—Ekron: An Archaeological Survey', *IEJ* 8: 87-100, 165-70.

Oded, B.
    1979   *Mass Deportation and Deportees in the Neo-Assyrian Empire* (Wiesbaden: L. Reichert).

Rad, G. von
    1933   'Das Reich Israel und Die Philister', *PJ* 29: 30-42.

Reade, J.E.
    1976   'Sargon's Campaigns of 720, 716, and 715 BC: Evidence from the Sculptures', *JNES* 35: 95-104.
    1979a   'Assyrian Architectural Decoration: Techniques and Subject Matter', *Baghdader Mitteilungen* 10: 17-49.
    1979b   'Ideology and Propoganda in Assyrian Art', in M.T. Larsen (ed.), *Power and Propoganda* (Copenhagen: Akademisk forlag).
    1980   'The Architectural Context of Assyrian Sculpture', *Baghdader Mitteilungen* 11: 75-87.

Russell, J.M.
    1991   *Sennacherib's Palace without Rival at Nineveh* (Chicago: University of Chicago Press).

Saggs, H.W.F.
    1955   'Assyrian Warfare in the Sargonid Period', *Iraq* 17, 145-54.

Schmitt, G. von
    1989   'Gabbutunu', *ZDPV* 105: 56-69.

Shavit, A.
    1993   'Tel Malot', *Hadashot Arkheologiot* 99: 45 (Hebrew).

Spalinger, A.
    1973   'The Year 712 BC and its Implications for Egyptian History', *Journal of the American Research Center in Egypt* 10: 95-101.

Tadmor, H.
    1958   'The Campaigns of Sargon II of Assur: A Chronological Historical Study', *Journal of Cuneiform Studies* 12: 22-40, 77-100.
    1966   'Philistia under Assyrian Rule', *BA* 29: 86-102.
    1975   'Assyria and the West: The Ninth Century and its Aftermath', in H. Goedicke and J.J.M. Roberts (eds.), *Unity and Diversity* (Baltimore: The Johns Hopkins University Press): 36-47.

Turner, G.
    1970   'The State Apartments of Late Assyrian Palaces', *Iraq* 32: 177-213.

Ussishkin, D.
    1982   *The Conquest of Lachish by Sennacherib* (Tel Aviv: Tel Aviv University, Institute of Archaeology).

Wafler, M.
    1975   *Nicht-Assyrer neuassyrischer Darstellungen* (AOAT, 126; Kevelaer: Butzon & Bercker).

Winter, I.
    1983   'The Program of the Throne-room of Assurnasirpal II', in P. Harper and H. Pittman (eds.), *Essays in Near Eastern Art and Architecture in Honour of Charles K. Wilkinson* (New York: The Metropolitan Museum of Art): 15-32.

Yeivin, S.
    1952   'Who was So', the King of Egypt?', *VT* 2: 164-68.

Part III

ASPECTS OF MATERIAL CULTURE

11

JERUSALEM IN THE TENTH AND SEVENTH CENTURIES BCE:
FROM ADMINISTRATIVE TOWN TO COMMERCIAL CITY

Margreet Steiner

The position of Jerusalem in the time of the Monarchy has been the subject of many books in the past. It has also been extensively treated in some recent studies that have aroused great interest: the studies of David Jamieson-Drake (1991) and Thomas Thompson (1992). Thompson sketches a picture of Jerusalem through the ages, largely based on the study of Jamieson-Drake, who uses archaeological data in what he calls a socio-archaeological approach.

According to Thompson Jerusalem had throughout the Late Bronze Age and Early Iron Age functioned as a politically dominant centre of commerce and trade for the small agricultural settlements nearby. During the tenth and ninth centuries BCE it still was a small provincial town, a market centre for the immediate region only. It was only in the eighth and seventh centuries that the site was transformed into the capital of a regional state, with a stratified society, a dominant urban elite, a state bureaucracy, and perhaps a temple supporting a state cult (Thompson 1992: 333). This would also be the first period that we can expect the formation of scribal schools. Thompson asserts that Samaria, the capital of Israel, had a completely different background: this was not an agriculturally based market town (as Jerusalem was before the eighth century), but what he calls a capital city with dominant public structures (1992: 408).

Both authors rightly complain about the lack of archaeological data available because of the dearth of publication of excavations at Jerusalem. I am in the lucky position to have access to some of these data. In Leiden a team consisting of Professor Franken and myself has been working on the publication of a large part of Kathleen Kenyon's excavations in Jerusalem, that took place in 1961–67. The main part of the material we are working on consists of the Bronze and Iron Age finds from her site A, which was the large trench and surrounding squares on the eastern slope of the south-eastern hill, also called the City of David nowadays. In this area R.A.S. Macalister conducted large-scale excavations in the 1920s (Macalister and Duncan 1926) and the ill-fated expedition of Charles Parker took place there as well (Vincent 1911). From 1979 onwards the late Yigal Shiloh excavated in the same area (Shiloh 1984; Ariel 1990; De Groot and Ariel 1992). This means that material from several excavations over a large area is available now for analysis. I have been able to use not only the unpublished material from Kenyon's excavations, but also the published material from the older and later excavations, as well as some unpublished data from Professor Shiloh's dig, that have kindly been made available to me by the excavator.

It is on the basis of an analysis of this archaeological material that it is possible to correct and supplement the picture of Jerusalem painted above. It seems that in the tenth/ninth century BCE Jerusalem was an administrative centre of at least regional importance, and that in the seventh century it became an urban centre of exceptional dimensions.

The dates used are based, as usual, on the excavated pottery. Unfortunately tenth-century pottery is notoriously difficult to date (Finkelstein 1990; Wightman 1990). Finkelstein has recently argued that the conventional dates of the buildings in Megiddo, Hazor and Gezer, commonly assigned to the tenth century, should be lowered to the ninth century BCE (Finkelstein 1996), and the same is proposed by Woodhead (personal communication). The pottery found in Jerusalem cannot be of help here. In Kenyon's excavation squares very little pottery from this period was found, and most of it came from unstratified deposits. This pottery was frequently irregularly burnished, but only one sherd had a dark red slip, and most vessels were simply not slipped at all. Because of the burnishing and because the forms were certainly earlier than the late ninth century pottery already studied (Franken and Steiner 1990), this pottery was assigned to the tenth century, but a date in the early ninth century is equally possible. Thus building constructions in Jerusalem may have been built later than generally assumed.

Tenth/Ninth Century BCE

Several public structures from the tenth/ninth century BCE have been found. Most conspicuous is what is commonly called the stepped stone structure. Elements of it were already discovered by Macalister who called it the Jebusite Ramp. Other parts have been found by Kenyon and Shiloh. It consists of a mantle of stones and some adjoining terraces, laid out over the pre-existing buildings and debris on the slope of the hill. Originally it must have been at least 27 m high and 40 m wide at the top, which makes it by far the largest and most impressive structure of this kind (Steiner 1993). It had a defensive function. Linked with this structure is a casemate wall, of which a very small part has been discovered on top of the hill. This wall probably ran north (Kenyon 1974: 114-15, pl. 37).

Building elements normally used for public buildings were found by Kenyon, such as a large number of fine ashlar blocks and a very large proto-aeolic capital, found in destruction debris near the stepped stone structure (Kenyon 1967: 59, pl. 20). The capital was dated by Shiloh to the ninth century BCE (1979: 21). A fragment of a wall made of fine ashlar masonry was found in Kenyon's site SII (Kenyon 1974: 115, pl. 38) and subsequently published by Mazar and Mazar (1989: 9-12, photo 13). Some luxury items came from Shiloh's dig: a bronze fist, that must have belonged to the statue of a god (Baal?), and part of a large pottery stand portraying a bearded man (Shiloh 1984: 17, pl. 29).

These finds indicate the existence of defensive walls, fortifications and public buildings, maybe even a temple (for Baal) in the settlement. What is lacking in the archaeological record are houses. Compared to the finds from the Middle Bronze Age and the seventh century BCE the difference is striking. In those periods a city wall was built lower down the slope of the hill to protect a residential quarter there (Steiner 1986, 1988; Franken and Steiner 1990: 50-56; Shiloh 1984: 26-29). Apparently the top of the hill did not offer enough space for the inhabitants of the town and they had to use the slope. Not so, however, in the tenth century. The slope was partly covered by the stepped stone structure, but no town wall was discovered there, and no houses at all. It seems the building area was restricted to the top of the hill. The town was apparently fortified (if at all) by walls along this top. The above-mentioned casemate wall may have functioned to connect this built-up area with another quarter more to the north, of which no trace has been discovered. Excavations on the Ophel hill by Benjamin and Eilat Mazar have shown that the earliest buildings there date from the ninth century BCE at the earliest (1989: 58-60).

Based on the archaeological evidence Jerusalem of the tenth/ninth century BCE can be described as a small town, occupied mainly by public buildings. Its size will not have exceeded 12 hectares and it may have housed up to 2000 inhabitants. What is more significant: this centre was a new foundation. There had not been, in the centuries before the tenth/ninth, a town there at all. In the second half of the Middle Bronze Age and the whole of the Late Bronze Age no settlement had existed in Jerusalem. No trace has ever been found of any city that could have been the Urusalim of the Amarna letters. It is only in the twelfth century that building began again. Then a fortification was constructed on top of the hill, above the spring of Gihon—the large earth-filled terraces that Kenyon and Shiloh have excavated belong to that period (Steiner 1994). But more than a fortress it was not, and certainly not a town.[1]

This means that in the tenth or, more likely, the ninth century BCE a new town was founded, a town with impressive public buildings, but without large residential quarters, indicating that it functioned as a regional administrative centre or as the capital of a small, newly established state. As such its function will not have differed much from that of Samaria. Surveys in the hill country of Judah have confirmed this picture of Jerusalem as the centre for the region in Iron IIA (Ofer 1994).

It seems, however, unlikely that this Jerusalem was the capital of a large state, the capital of the United Monarchy of biblical history. Compared to other towns of the tenth and ninth centuries, Jerusalem was not very different. Megiddo, Hazor, Gezer and Lachish were all small towns showing the same characteristics: large fortifications, ashlar masonry, public buildings and hardly any ordinary houses. Based on the archaeological record alone, one could assume that these were the seats of the governments of several small regional states that only later fused into the historically attested states of Israel and Judah. We simply cannot assume that the United Monarchy is a historical fact (Gelinas 1995), and much more research has to be done on the political and economic situation in the tenth and ninth centuries BCE.

---

1. So Thompson's centre for commerce and trade during the Late Bronze and Early Iron Ages simply did not exist, at least not in Jerusalem. Neither was Jerusalem the centre of a polymorphous chiefdom during the Middle Bronze II period and the Late Bronze Age (Finkelstein 1992), nor the centre of a city state in the Late Bronze Age (Bunimovitz 1995).

Seventh Century BCE

In the seventh century the situation was completely different. In the intervening period Jerusalem had slowly grown, but it was only after the destruction of the country by the Assyrians that the city took its central position. Jamieson-Drake has given an accurate, although incomplete description of the city (1991). The destruction of the city by the Babylonians in 597 BCE resulted in massive debris layers, yielding an enormous amount of architecture and objects. This makes it possible to reconstruct life in the city in the second half of the seventh century, just before its tragic end. Jerusalem was then about 50 hectares in extent, and was fortified by 5–7 m wide city walls, which had been built at the end of the eighth century (Steiner 1986; Shiloh 1984: 28; Avigad 1983: 46). Water was being supplied by several technically sophisticated undergound systems (Amiran 1976). The area inside the city walls was taken up, at least on the southeast hill, by residential units only. None of the many excavations here or in other parts of Jerusalem has revealed the remains of public buildings that were constructed during the seventh century.

What has been excavated are houses, belonging to what may be called the elite of Jerusalem: artisans and traders, and wealthy ones at that. A residential quarter was laid out on top of the stepped stone structure, whose defensive function had been overtaken by the new city wall. Streets, 2 m wide and at right angles with each other, gave access to houses, one or two storeys high (Steiner 2001; Shiloh 1984: 28-29). In one house, excavated by Kenyon, a bronze workshop was discovered, with stone implements, pieces of bronze and iron, and many stone weights (Scott 1985; Steiner 2001). The famous bullae house yielded 51 bullae, the remains of an archive. Shiloh interpreted this as a state archive, but the bullae were found amid broken household pottery (cooking pots) and other small objects indicating family life: an iron knife, a bronze earring, a stone pestle—thus an interpretation as a private archive seems more plausible (Shiloh 1986). On one of the streets more than 100 loom weights were excavated, attesting to commercial weaving activities (Steiner 2001). Three complete ostraca discovered by Kenyon under the floors of the bronze workshop are of an administrative nature and mention jars of grain and olive oil, both important export products (Lemaire 1978).

Imports were of luxury goods. Excavations in and around the city have revealed the following imports: wooden furniture from North Syria (Shiloh 1984: 19), ivory from Syria or Mesopotamia (Ariel 1990: 119-48), decorative shells from the Red Sea (Mienis 1992; Reese 1995), wine jars from Greece or Cyprus (Steiner 2001), fine pottery bowls from Assyria from Shiloh's excavation (not yet published), and scarabs from Egypt (Steiner 2001), while bronze must have come from either Cyprus or Transjordan.

To put Jerusalem's size in perspective it is necessary to compare it with other towns.[2] In Judah itself in the seventh century there seem to have been no other towns. Excavation reports of sites such as Beersheba, Tell en Nasbeh, Tell Beit Mirsim and Beth Shemes show that after the Assyrian attack many towns did not restore their demolished city walls, while occupation on the tells was either absent or on a much smaller scale. Lachish was given new fortifications after a while, but occupation inside the walls was poor, and the administrative centre seems not to have been used again. Although some old towns seem thus to have been reoccupied, their urban functions were negligible. The complex and differentiated settlement system of the eighth century, with its many specialized towns, was never restored. New settlements were built in the second half of the seventh century: agricultural and industrial villages, fortresses, and palaces, but no towns have yet been discovered. This left Jerusalem as the only centre, in terms of people, and thus in terms of economy, politics and, probably, religion.

Not only in Judah, but also in the rest of Palestine, no comparable city has been found. Ekron on the coastal plain was the second largest city of the country, with its 20 ha against Jerusalem's 50. The other towns did not exceed 5–7 ha.

Jerusalem had become what urban geographers call a primate city, a city very much larger than other settlements, where all economic, political and social power is centralized—one could say: an extreme city (Carter 1983). It must have had complete economic control over the countryside. An interesting question is: who exercised this control? Was it the royal court, supported by a large bureaucracy, or was it rather the urban elite of traders and artisans? The archaeological record does not show many signs of a centralized administration, except for the *lmlk*-seals, already out of use in the second half of the seventh

2.   Information from *NEAEHL*.

century, and maybe the gauging of stone weights used by traders. The large public works for defence and water supply had all been built in the previous century.

Compared to the tenth century, however, the layout of the city shows a definite change from a purely administrative centre with public buildings only, to a city composed of residential quarters without large official buildings. This could mean that the urban elite had gained much more economic and probably political power than in earlier centuries. The social implications of this relegation of power are still to be analysed, as are the consequences of Jerusalem's supreme position in the religious notions of the inhabitants, as possibly expressed in the Old Testament.

Bibliography

Amiran, R.

  1976   'The Water Supply of Israelite Jerusalem', in Y. Yadin (ed.), *Jerusalem Revealed* (Jerusalem: The Israel Exploration Society): 75-78.

Ariel, D.T.

  1990   *Excavations at the City of David 1978–1985*. II. *Imported Stamped Amphora Handles, Coins, Worked Bone and Ivory, and Glass* (Qedem 30; Jerusalem: The Institute of Archaeology, Hebrew University).

Avigad, N.

  1983   *Discovering Jerusalem* (Nashville: Thomas Nelson).

Bunimovitz, S.

  1995   'On the Edge of Empires: Late Bronze Age (1500–1200 BCE)', in T.E. Levy (ed.), *The Archaeology of Society* (London: Leicester University Press): 320-29.

Carter, H.

  1983   *An Introduction to Urban Historical Geography* (London: Edward Arnold).

Finkelstein, I.

  1990   'On Archaeological Methods and Historical Considerations: Iron Age II Gezer and Samaria', *BASOR* 277/278: 109-20.

  1992   'Middle Bronze Age "Fortifications": A Reflection on Social Organization and Political Formations', *Tel Aviv* 19: 201-20.

  1996   'The Archaeology of the United Monarchy: An Alternative View', *Levant* XXVIII: 177-87.

Franken H.L., and M.L. Steiner

  1990   *Excavations in Jerusalem 1961–1967*. II. *The Iron Age Extramural Quarter on the South-east Hill* (British Academy Monographs on Archaeology, 2; Oxford: Oxford University Press).

Gelinas, M.M.

  1995   'United Monarchy—Divided Monarchy: Fact or Fiction', in S.W. Holloway and L.K. Handy (eds.), *The Pitcher Is Broken; Memorial*

Essays for Gösta W. Ahlström (JSOTSup, 190; Sheffield: Sheffield Academic Press): 227-37.

Groot, A. de, and D.T. Ariel (eds.)

1992   *Excavations at the City of David 1978–1985*. III. *Stratigraphical, Environmental, and Other Reports* (Qedem, 33; Jerusalem: Institute of Archaeology, Hebrew University).

Jamieson-Drake, D.

1991   *The Scribes and Schools in Monarchic Judah; A Socio-Archaeological Approach* (The Social World of Biblical Antiquity Series, 9; JSOTSup, 109; Sheffield: Almond Press).

Kenyon, K.M.

1967   *Jerusalem: Excavating 3000 Years of History* (London: Thames and Hudson).

1974   *Digging Up Jerusalem* (London: Ernest Benn).

Lemaire, A.

1978   'Les Ostraca Paléo-Hébreux des Fouilles de l'Ophel', *Levant* X: 156-60.

Macalister, R.A.S., and J. Garrow Duncan

1926   *Excavations on the Hill of Ophel, Jerusalem, 1923–1925* (PEFA, 4; London).

Mazar, E., and B. Mazar

1989   *Excavations in the South of the Temple Mount: The Ophel of Biblical Jerusalem* (Qedem, 29; Jerusalem: Institute of Archaeology, Hebrew University).

Mienis, H.K.

1992   'Molluscs', in de Groot and Ariel (1992): 122-30.

Ofer, A.

1994   '"All the Hill Country of Judah": From Settlement Fringe to a Prosperous Monarchy', in I. Finkelstein and N. Na'aman (eds.), *From Nomadism to Monarchy: Archaeological and Historical Aspects of Early Israel* (Jerusalem: Yad Izhak Ben-Zvi): 92-121.

Reese, D.S.

1995   'Marine Invertebrates and Other Shells from Jerusalem (Sites A, C and L)', in I. Eshel and K. Prag (eds.), *Excavations by K.M. Kenyon in Jerusalem 1961–1967*. IV. *The Iron Age Cave Deposits on the South-east Hill and Isolated Burials and Cemetaries Elsewhere* (Oxford: Oxford University Press): 265-78.

Scott, R.B.Y.

1985   'Weights from the 1961–1967 Excavations', in A.D. Tushingham, *Excavations in Jerusalem 1961–1967* (Toronto: Royal Ontario Museum): I, 197-212.

Shiloh, Y.

1979   *The Proto-Aeolic Capital and Israelite Ashlar Masonry* (Qedem, 11; Jerusalem: Institute of Archaeology, Hebrew University).

1984   *Excavations at the City of David I, 1978–1982* (Qedem, 19; Jerusalem: Institute of Archaeology, Hebrew University).

1986   'A Group of Hebrew Bullae from the City of David', *IEJ* 36: 16-38.

Steiner, M.L.
   1986   'A Note on the Iron Age Defence Wall on the Ophel Hill of Jerusalem',
                 PEQ 118: 27-32.
   1988   'The Earliest City Wall of Jerusalem', *IEJ* 38: 203-204.
   1993   'The Jebusite Ramp of Jerusalem: The Evidence from the Macalister,
                 Kenyon and Shiloh Excavations', in *Biblical Archaeology Today 1990,*
                 Proceedings of the Second International Congress on Biblical Archaeol-
                 ogy, Jerusalem, June 1990 (Jerusalem: The Israel Exploration Society,
                 The Israel Academy of Sciences and Humanities): 585-88.
   1994   'Redating the Terraces of Jerusalem', *IEJ* 44: 13-20.
   2001   *Excavation in Jerusalem 1961–1967.* III. *The Settlement in the Bronze*
                 and Iron Ages (Sheffield: Sheffield Academic Press).
Thompson, T.
   1992   *Early History of the Israelite People, from the Written and*
                 Archaeological Sources (Leiden: E.J. Brill).
Vincent L.-H.
   1911   *Jerusalem sous Terre: les récentes fouilles d'Ophel* (London: Horace
                 Cox).
Wightman, G.J.
   1990   'The Myth of Solomon', *BASOR* 277/278: 5-22.

12

BETH SHEAN DURING THE IRON AGE II:
STRATIGRAPHY, CHRONOLOGY AND HEBREW OSTRACA

Amihai Mazar

The Hebrew University excavations at Tel Beth Shean, conducted between 1989–96 enabled us to clarify the Iron Age stratigraphic sequence of the tel and investigate some features of the Iron Age town plan.[1] The dates of the strata under discussion are framed by two chronological boundaries: the upper one is the termination of Egyptian rule in Canaan late in the twentieth dynasty, and the lower one is the conquest of the northern part of the Kingdom of Israel by the Assyrians during the reign of Tiglath Pileser III (732 BCE). In the first part of this paper I present the main conclusions stemming from our excavation concerning the Iron Age II, while the second part presents ostraca written on storage jar sherds dating to the Iron Age II.

Beth Shean in the Iron Age II

The University Museum of the University of Pennsylvania conducted excavations at Tel Beth Shean during the 1920s and unearthed various remains of the Iron Age II (Strata V–IV). However, the interpretation of these excavations has remained difficult and disputable. The architectural plans are schematic and abound with numerous incomprehensible details. Despite W.F. James's meticulous efforts to publish these strata

---

1.   The excavations at Tell Beth Shean between the years 1989–96 were directed by the author on behalf of the Institute of Archaeology of the Hebrew University of Jerusalem in the framework of the Beth Shean Archaeological Expedition, which is sponsored by the Israel Antiquities Authority and the Beth Shean Tourist Development Authority.

(James 1966), many questions have remained open and the reconstruction of the site's history during the Iron Age II remained problematic.

One of our main goals in the renewed excavations at Tel Beth Shean was to attempt to clarify the situation pertaining to this important period. However, we faced many objective obstacles: in the area excavated by the University of Pennsylvania on the summit of the mound the Iron Age II layers had been virtually removed. Only in Area S, located on the south-eastern part of the summit (Fig. 12.1), were we able to locate isolated remains of monumental structures which can be dated to the tenth century BCE (Mazar 1993: 224-26). In order to examine the stratigraphic sequence, however, as well as the scope and nature of the Iron Age II occupation on the mound, we had to open new excavation areas which had been untouched by our predecessors. The two areas opened for this purpose were Area L, located in the centre of the mound at the foot of the summit, and Area P, located to the west of Area L, adjoining the western slope of the mound (Fig. 12.1).

To our surprise, we discovered that the occupation history of these two areas differed from one another to a large extent, despite the short distance of 45 m between them and their similar elevations. In Area L thick occupation levels of the Early Islamic and the Byzantine periods covered scattered remains of Middle Bronze Age burials and an occupation level of the Early Bronze Age, while no Iron Age II remains were found whatsoever. In contrast, Area P contained massive remains dating to the Iron Age II covered by thick occupation layers dating to the Hellenistic, Byzantine and Islamic periods.

These results lead to important conclusions as to the extent of the occupation on the mound between the Middle Bronze and the Iron Age II periods. It appears that during these periods the settlement was limited to the summit of the mound. South of Area L, there is a steep step in the topography of the mound, which is visible in aerial photos taken prior to the excavations of 1921. This step traverses the mound from east to west. While Area L was located outside the limits of this area, Area P was located in the north-west corner of the perimeter of the settled area. The steep step most probably indicates the edge of the thick occupation debris of the second and first millennia BCE, excavated to the south of this line. This indicates that during the Middle Bronze, Late Bronze and Iron Ages the settlement on Beth Shean was only 1.4 hectares in area.

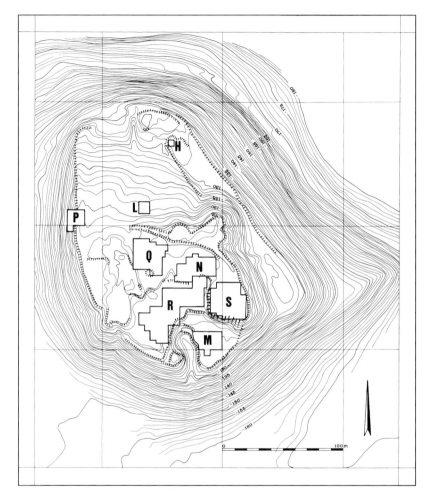

Fig. 12.1. *Topographic map of Tel Beth Shean showing the
excavation areas of the Hebrew University expedition*

This is a surprising conclusion in light of the strategic location of the
mound and the status of Beth Shean as an Egyptian administrative
centre during the New Kingdom. It now appears that this New Kingdom Egyptian administrative centre was a relatively small and unfortified site, composed mainly of administrative buildings, a temple and a
dwelling quarter. The Canaanite settlement which preceded the
Egyptian administrative centre, as well as that which followed its
demise, and the Israelite town of the Period of the Monarchy, all

occupied only this limited area. Essentially, it appears that Bronze Age and Iron Age Beth Shean had never been a major city of central importance. Such a city in the Beth Shean Valley was Rehov (Tel Rehov, Arabic Tel eṣ-Ṣarem), located just 5 km south of Beth Shean. Our recent excavations at this impressive site indicate that it covered an area of c. 12 hectares during the Late Bronze and Iron Age I-IIA and c. 3–4 hectares during the Iron Age IIB. Rehov was probably the main Canaanite city state in the Beth Shean valley during the second millennium BCE.

The combination of data from Area S at Tel Beth Shean, where our excavations began at the level of the tenth-century BCE occupation layer, and from Area P, where the tenth-century BCE level was reached at the bottom of a small probe, enabled us to reconstruct the stratigraphic and chronological sequence of the Iron Age II at this site. The following brief summary presents the main results of the excavations concerning this period. Table 12.1 summarizes the stratigraphic sequence in Areas S and P.

Table 12.1. *Stratigraphic sequence in Areas S and P*

Date	University Museum	Area S	Area P
Late 8th century BCE [?]		—	P6: poor remains
8th century until 732 BCE	'Stratum IV'[?]	University of Pennsylvania Strata V-IV	P7: large building; destruction by heavy fire
9th–early 8th centuries BCE	Parts of Level V (?)	University of Pennsylvania Strata V-IV	P8a-b: two phases of occupation
9th century BCE	Parts of 'Stratum V'	University of Pennsylvania Strata V-IV	P9: surface in small probe
10th century BCE	Parts of Level V	S1: remains of 3 massive buildings; destruction by fire	P10: surface in small probe
11th century BCE	Temples of Level V and structures of Level VI Upper	S2: occupation level	—
12th century BCE (20th dynasty)	Level VI	S3: Egyptian garrison town	—

Area S: Twelfth–Tenth Centuries BCE

The stratigraphic-chronological starting point in the extensively excavated Area S is Stratum S3, which is equivalent to Level VI of the
University of Pennsylvania (James 1966) and Stratum 4 of Yadin and
Geva (1986). This Egyptian garrison town was destroyed in a fierce
conflagration which can be related to the termination of the Egyptian
presence at Beth Shean during the late twentieth dynasty. Stratum S2,
found on top of S3, is equivalent to Stratum Late VI of the American
expedition. Some of the mudbrick walls of this stratum were in fact a
rebuilding of earlier mudbrick walls, stumps of which remained from
the previous stratum. It appears that the builders of the new town were
well aware of the remains left by their predecessors so that in parts of
the excavation area, architectural continuity is demonstrated by the
rehabilitation of destroyed buildings and the continued use of the street
system. At the same time, in other parts of the area, new structures were
erected which altered the previous town plan.

Since most of the construction in the area under discussion was of
mudbricks, it appears that only a short time elapsed between the two
strata, since a longer gap would have resulted in the collapse and
deterioration of the brick walls of the last Egyptian occupation. The
pottery assemblage also indicates the short time separating the two
strata: the S2 repertoire includes vessels in the Canaanite tradition, both
in shape and decoration, while the Egyptian forms which were so
ubiquitous in the previous stratum were virtually non-existent in S2
(Mazar 1993: 220: Fig. 14). The two factors detailed above contradict
Finkelstein's claim (1996b) that Stratum S2 at Beth Shean dates to the
tenth century BCE, and that a chronological gap of close to 100 years
separated S3 from S2. Since there is a close affinity in the material
culture of S2 and Stratum VIA at Megiddo, this would also rule out
Finkelstein's proposal that Megiddo VIA dates to the second half of the
tenth century BCE. Both Beth Shean S2 and Megiddo VIA should be
ascribed to the eleventh century BCE, in line with the traditional
chronology of the Iron Age I (see also Peleg-Zarzeki 1997).

In Stratum S1, a major change took place in both the town planning
and pottery production at Tel Beth Shean. Fragments of three large
structures which had been destroyed in a violent fire were uncovered in
Area S (Fig. 12.2). Two of these (Building A and Building B) must
have been parts of monumental public buildings. The three are built of
similar constructional techniques: wooden beams were laid on basalt

stone foundations, on top of which a brick superstructure was built. Some of the stones in the basalt foundations of Buildings A and B are exceptionally large. The fierce conflagration which ravaged the three structures resulted in bricks of the preserved superstructure becoming vitrified to the consistency of ceramic, fired to a reddish colour. In many cases, the heat of the fire melted the brick superstructure above the wooden beams to a powdery, white amorphous substance.

Building A is part of a massive structure located in the south-eastern corner of the mound, in a lofty spot which commanded the view of the valley below to the east and to the south. It appears that the fragmentary remains found by us had been part of a citadel several stories high, as indicated by the width of the walls which was up to 2.5 m. One room in this building (the south-western room) had been excavated by the University of Pennsylvania (Room 1551 in Square S8 in their excavation, see James 1966: Fig. 75). Three additional rooms in this building were uncovered by our excavation. Building B had been damaged by later pits; the foundations of a large rectangular hall were uncovered, its inner dimensions are 10.3 × 4.2 m, its walls c. 1.2 m wide.

The walls of Building C are of more modest dimensions, and only two small rooms remained in our excavation area. It is possible, however, that this structure was part of a well planned architectural complex uncovered by the University of Pennsylvania expedition, which they attributed to Stratum V (James 1966: Fig. 75, the block of buildings north of the 'Northern Temple'; our Building C is located at the western edge of Square S7 in this plan).

In one of the rooms of Building A, a group of storage jars was found, all belonging to the 'Hippo' type which was characteristic of the tenth–ninth centuries BCE. Similar jars were found at other sites destroyed by fire in the Beth Shean and Jezreel Valleys, such as Tell el-Hamma, Tel Amal, Tel Rehov, Megiddo Stratum VA–IVB and Hurvat Rosh Zayit (Alexandre 1995). Small amounts of other pottery types were found as well; though they are for the most part fragmentary, they resemble the pottery from the above-mentioned sites as well. The appearance of red slip and irregular hand burnish in this stratum demonstrates a break from the previous Canaanite tradition of painted pottery, which lasted until the late eleventh century BCE. Carbon 14 dating of an olive tree beam used in one of the buildings yielded a date range of 1018–920 BCE (100 per cent certainty). This date fits the dating of Stratum S1 in the tenth century BCE, however it should be taken with caution since olive tree timber could survive for a long time. Short-lived botanical samples were not available for radiometric dating (on the chronological controversy concerning this period see Finkelstein 1996a; Mazar 1997; Finkelstein 1998; Ben-Tor and Ben-Ami 1998).

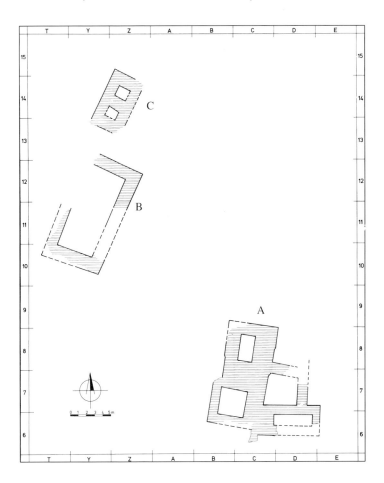

Fig. 12.2. *Schematic plan of Stratum S1 structures in Area S (tenth century BCE)*

The extremely violent destruction by fire of Stratum S1 is similar to that found in other sites in this region, cf. Tell el Hamma and Tel Amal. It seems probable that these devastations were caused by the military campaign of Shishak, the Egyptian Pharaoh of the twenty-second dynasty, whose army passed through the Beth Shean valley between 930 to 925 BCE (for the latest discussion with full literature see

Na'aman 1998). It appears that sites in the western Jezreel Valley such as Megiddo IVB–VA and Taanach IIB were probably also destroyed during the same invasion (note, however, that Na'aman 1998 denies wide-scale destructions as a result of this invasion).

Yet this conclusion (presented in the 1996 lecture on which this paper is based) has to be revised now in light of the excavations at Jezreel and at Tel Rehov. At Jezreel, the pottery assemblage found in the destruction layer of the royal citadel of Ahab is very similar to that found in the destruction layers of the sites mentioned above, and traditionally dated to the tenth century BCE. At Tel Rehov, similar pottery was found in three successive strata (VI–IV in the final strata numbers, corresponding to C1a, C1b and C2 in the preliminary report). While Finkelstein (1996) concluded on the basis of the finds from Jezreel that the entire tenth-century assemblage should be moved to the ninth century BCE, I prefer to claim that the same assemblage contined to be in use throughout much of the tenth and ninth centuries, from c. 980 to c. 830 BCE (for detailed discussion and references see Mazar 1999: 37-42).

Area P: Ninth–Eighth Centuries BCE
The ninth–eighth century stratigraphic sequence at Tel Beth Shean was determined in Area P, where the following occupation strata were identified.

Stratum P10. This stratum is known from only one rather small probe. An earth layer was found which contained sherds similar to those found in Stratum S1 in Area S. This determines a stratigraphic correlation between these two excavation areas.

Stratum P9–8. These are two phases of one stratum which was exposed in probes under the floors of a large dwelling belonging to the subsequent stratum. The finds include segments of brick walls, an oven, various installations and beaten earth floors with accumulations of pottery sherds. The ceramic-rich assemblage include red slipped bowls of the 'Samarian' type as well as several vessel types which indicate a date in the ninth or early eighth centuries BCE. Despite the proximity to the slope of the mound, no evidence of fortifications was found.

Stratum P7: A large dwelling was erected in Area P in this stratum. The location and orientation of its walls point to a major departure from the previous stratum in the town plan. The walls of the building were built of mudbricks without stone foundations; their average width was 1 m, and their foundations reached c. 0.8 m beneath the floor level inside the house. The basic plan of the building follows the 'four room house', though the stone pillars or wooden columns so characteristic of Iron Age II dwellings were lacking (Fig. 12.3).

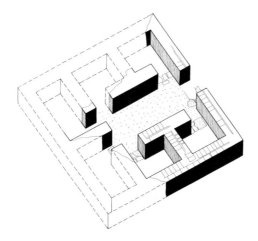

Fig. 12.3. *Isometric drawing of the dwelling house in Area P,*
Stratum P7 (eighth century BCE).

The external dimensions of the building are 14 × 14 m, and it includes a central rectangular space (internal dimensions 4 × 8.1 m), and six square rooms: two on each of the three sides of a central rectangular hall (eastern, western and southern). The entrance to the house was from a street to its north, leading directly into the central hall, which most likely was roofed. The thresholds were made of mudbricks, and the walls, which were preserved in certain places to a height of over 1.5 m, were covered with a thick mud plaster. The two western rooms of the house as well as the western inner room were constructed on the line of the western slope of the mound, and they were almost entirely destroyed as a result of erosion, as well as by the foundations of a massive Byzantine wall which penetrated deep into the Iron Age levels. The south-eastern room was located outside the border of the excavation area, and only its entrance was exposed. The south-western room was also located beyond the limits of the excavation area, but a narrow probe excavated along the slope of the mound uncovered part of this room and its southern wall. This is one of the most massive dwellings of the Iron Age in the Land of Israel. Though its basic plan accords with the tenets of domestic house plans of this period, it is difficult to find an exact parallel to the particular layout of the rooms in this building. It appears that this had been a particularly large and well-planned residency of an affluent tenant.

The building was destroyed by a fierce fire which caused the collapse of the ceiling and brick walls into the rooms. This violent destruction was most probably caused by the Assyrian conquest of Beth Shean, apparently in 732 BCE. The destruction layer contained many finds, including more than 100 restorable pottery vessels and other objects typical of the eighth century BCE (Fig. 12.4). Remains of a loom with more than 120 clay loom-weights were found near one of the walls of the central hall. Most of the pottery vessels were found along the walls of the central hall and in the entrances to the southern rooms. The southernmost of the two rooms to the east of the main hall yielded numerous vessels which had been crushed by the thick destruction debris. Among the objects found *in situ* was a pithos similar in shape to the pithoi from Kuntillat 'Ajrud which bore Hebrew inscriptions and paintings. The northernmost of the two rooms to the east of the central hall served as a silo during the final occupation phase of the house. Its entrance was found blocked and the room contained a large amount of grain. This room had been especially badly burned and its brick walls were fired to the consistency of ceramics. The rich and homogenous assemblage of pottery vessels found on the floors of this building is typical of the eighth century BCE. Considerable differences may be discerned between the vessels of this stratum and those of the previous stratum dating to the ninth or the beginning of the eighth century BCE.

To the north of the building was an open area which was probably a wide street. To the east of the house were building fragments which can be divided into two phases. On the eastern edge of the excavation area, part of a paved street was found on a level considerably higher than that of the floors inside the house. This is evidence that the town had been built on a series of terraces which descended to the north-west, following the natural slope of the tel. One of the reasons which prompted the choice of this area for excavation was the quest for the Iron Age fortifications. However, the location of the western rooms of this dwelling on the slope of the mound does not leave any room for a fortification system. The fact that the University Museum expedition did not find any trace of Iron Age fortifications either, though they excavated along the edge of the site in the south and east, leads to the conclusion that the Iron Age II town remained unfortified. This is an exceptional phenomenon during this period, when most of the towns in the kingdoms of Judah and Israel were surrounded by walls.

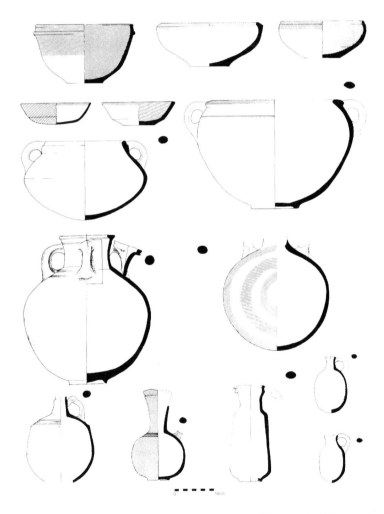

Fig. 12.4. *Pottery types found in the destruction of Stratum P7 (732 BCE)*

Stratum P6: Several fragments of brick walls were found above the ruins of the Stratum P7 dwelling, representing a short interlude following the destruction. No floors were found and the finds from this stratum are negligible.

Correlating the above stratigraphic sequence with that of the University of Pennsylvania is not an easy task since the data we possess concerning the older excavation is wanting. It seems that the northern block of buildings attributed to Lower Level V (using the terminology of James 1966) can be dated to the tenth century BCE as James suggested, though perhaps the double temple complex ('the Northern Temple' and the 'Southern Temple') should be separated from this block of building (to which they don't have any direct connection) and should be dated to the eleventh century BCE (Mazar 1993: 221-23). Upper Level V, whose architectural components are not clear, may be contemporary with our Stratum P9–P8 (ninth–early eighth centuries BCE). Level IV included indeterminate remains of structures and pottery which is partially similar to that of P7 in our excavation, though some forms date to later. In a discussion of these strata, Geva (1979) attempted to determine that Level V was destroyed by the Assyrian conquest, while Level IV post-dates this event. However, the pottery on which she based her suggestion was mainly unstratified. Thus it is possible that most of the Level IV structures belong to the period prior to the Assyrian conquest, and only some are contemporary with our Stratum P6, which post-dates the Assyrian conquest.

Ostraca from Tel Beth Shean

During the first days of our second season at Tel Beth Shean (October 1990) we began to expand the excavation of Area S on the summit of the tell. All remains of Iron Age II (Stratum IV and parts of Stratum V) had been removed by the University of Pennsylvania expedition, so that we began our excavation at an occupation level of the eleventh century BCE (Stratum S2); basalt stone wall foundations of the tenth century BCE (Stratum S1) had been dug into this level. To our surprise, several centimetres below topsoil, several sherds of a storage jar base were found which bore Paleo-Hebrew ink inscriptions, apparently dating to the eighth century BCE. The sherds were found in Locus 78801 in Square Y-8, and were most likely lying at the bottom of an Iron Age II pit which had penetrated into the earlier Iron Age I occupation levels.

The upper part of this pit was probably removed by the University of Pennsylvania expedition, and apparently we excavated the bottom of it.[2]

Four inscribed sherds (some composed of several joining sherds) were found, all of which originally had been part of the same storage jar or large jug. This is apparent from the identical fabric of the sherds: brown clay with a grey core, numerous black inclusions and traces of wet smoothing outside. It appears that the entire inscription had been written on the base of the jar (possibly after it had been broken), with the base held upwards; it thus appears that the inscription is unrelated to the original use of the jar, and was probably written on the base of this jar after it was broken. The fragmentary inscriptions on the sherds may be understood as broken parts of one inscription, which may be defined as an ostracon. The inscription was written in black ink, in large letters (0.7–1.0 cm). It was read with the help of Dr Ada Yardeni who also prepared the drawing and transliteration. In the discussion and interpretation of the inscription, I consulted Professor F.M. Cross.

The following is the reading of the four sherds.

Sherd No. 1 (Reg. No. 788033)

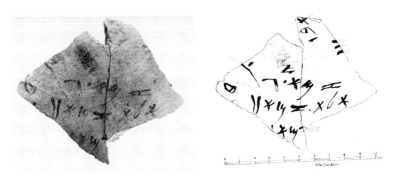

Fig. 12.5. *Sherd No. 1*

2. The inscriptions were found in Area S, supervised by Nava Panitz-Cohen. For a preliminary report on the excavations in this area see Mazar 1993. I am grateful to Mrs Ada Yardeni who prepared the illustrations and transcription and made important suggestions concerning the reading of the inscriptions, and to Professor F.M. Cross who discussed the inscriptions with me in the Spring of 1991 and also made some valuable suggestions.

This is the largest fragment, measuring 9 × 10 cm and 1.5 cm thick (it is actually composed of two joined sherds). The fragment is part of the base of a storage jar, with the inscription written around the base while it was held upside down. It appears that only part of the inscription remained, and that the inscription was written on the entire circumference of the bottom of a broken jar and thus was originally much longer. Since the inscription had been written on a convex surface, the lines are not straight; some of the words on the margins which were poorly preserved were written almost perpendicular to the rest of the inscription.

Line 1:	. zm' . ⌐
Line 2:	'lt . zm' t ||
Line 3:	[z]m' ⸌
Side letters:	
	] 'b |
	|||
Translation:	
	Zema 5
	Elath (or: Ela son of) Zema 2
	Zema 1(?)
Side:	]ab 1
	3(?)

Comments. Line 1: The name *Zma* is followed by a separation dot and the hieratic numeral 'five'.

Line 2: The combination *'lt zm'* is curious. It may be translated as 'goddess of *Zema*' but it could also be a combined private name with the components *'lt* and *zm'* in construct state. An alternative is to read the last letter in the first word as *'aleph*; in that case, the first word will be *'l'*, which is the name Ela, known once in the Bible (1 Kgs 4.18). In such a case, we have a composed name: 'Zema [son of] Ela'. Lines 1 and 3 can be reconstructed as also having names before the name *Zema*, and thus the three lines may have contained three names of brothers (?), sons of Zema (this was suggested to me by F.M. Cross). However, the preferred reading of the last letter in the first word is *taw*, and thus the first interpretation is preferred. The name is followed by two vertical lines which could be the numeral 'two'; yet in other cases (line 1 in this inscription and line 3 in inscription no. 2) there is a separation dot between the name and the numeral, while here no such dot exists. After a break, the letter *ṭet* appears, perhaps a beginning of a new word or name.

Line 3: The name *zm'* is reconstructed here on the basis of two letters *m'*; of the supposed *zayin* only a small line was preserved. The name is followed by a vertical line before a break in the sherd; this line is probably part of a numeral.

The name *zm'*, which perhaps should be read Zema or Zoma, appears three times in this inscription. It is unique in West Semitic inscriptions, except on three arrowheads from Lebanon, probably of the eleventh century BCE: *ḥs yt' bn zm'* (Cross 1992: 25* No. 10 and Cross 1996: 14* No. 9); *ḥs špt bn zm'* (Cross 1996: 15*; the latter, however, is defined as 'spurious' by Cross); *ḥẓ zm' bn 'lṣ'l* (Deutsch and Heltzer 1994: 18-19, inscription no. 5). The appearance of the name *zm'* three times is curious. It is very rare that the same name appears several times in the same list.

At the right top edge of the inscription the combination *'b* is followed by a vertical line which is the numeral 'one'. *'b* is probably the ending of a private name, like Eliab for example. Yet it should be noted that the *'aleph* is very pale; its transcription, suggested by Ada Yardeni, is not secure. The three broken lines at the right edge of the sherd stand for the number 'three', though they could also be the upper part of a broken *shin*. The diagonal line above the *ṭet* in the left upper part of the inscription is probably meaningless.

Sherd No. 2. (Registration Number 788042/2)

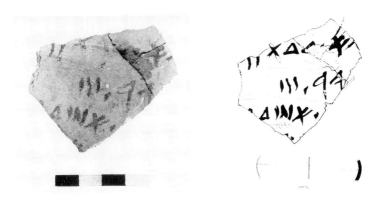

Fig. 12.6. *Sherd No. 2*

A fragment composed of three sherds that fitted together, probably belonging to the same jar as No. 1, since it is made of similar clay. However, the sherd is much thinner (0.8 cm) and is angular; it probably belonged to the shoulder of the jar. The size of the sherd is 6 × 6 cm, but it is broken on all its sides unintentionally.

Reading:

Line 1:   ]

Line 2:   ]ţ' . ddt ǀǀ

Line 3:   ]yr . ǀǀǀ

Line 4:   ] . 'šd [

Line 5:   ] . [

Comments. Line 1: only one foot of a long letter was preserved. It might be *nun, mem* or *kaf*.

Line 2 is reconstructed from three sherds; a break which chipped the surface of two of these sherds makes the reading of the second letter difficult. It is also not very clear whether there is a separation dot after the first *'aleph*. If indeed the second letter is *dalet* (as transcribed) then the reading might be *'ddt*. Yet if there is a separation dot after the first *'aleph*, then we should read ' . *ddt* followed by the number 'two'.

Line 3: only the ending *yr* was preserved, followed by a separation dot and the number 'three'. The name might be Yair or the like.

Line 4: After the letters *'šd* one can see the top of a triangle. Professor Cross suggested to me that this is part of another *dalet*, and thus the reading: *'šdd* 'Ashdod' or 'Ashdodite' occurs. Yet this is a very insecure reading.

Sherd No. 3. (Registration No. 788042/1)

Fig. 12.7. *Sherd No. 3*

No. 3 is a fragment composed of three sherds that fitted together, size 4 × 7 cm, thickness 0.7 cm. The sherd is very chipped on all sides. The sherd probably belongs to the same jar as Nos. 1 and 2, though the colour of its surface is more gray than brown; inside the clay looks very much like that of the other sherds.

Reading:
Line 1:   ]b˙ [
Line 2:   . b' . 'z'[
Line 3:   y(?) . hḋ[
Line 4:   ] . '[

Comments. The very fragmentary state of preservation of this inscription does not permit secure interpretation.

Line 1: the *bet* is clear, while the second letter is poorly preserved. Perhaps it was a *ṭet*.

Line 2: the first letter is obscure. *ṣade, waw* and *qof* were suggested, but in any case the form is exceptional and appear to be an error by the scribe. If he intended to write a *ṣade*, then the word can be read as *ṣava* (army). The second word can be read '*z'*, though the '*ayin* is somewhat problematic: a faint line (seen in the photograph) may be a leg of a letter like *bet*. If the reading '*Uza* is accepted, then it is a well-known private name, known from several biblical references (2 Sam. 6.6; 2 Kgs 21.26; 1 Chron. 8.7; 1 Chron. 13.7, 9-11; Ezra 2.49; Neh. 7.51). It is a shortened form of the theophoric name '*Uziah*. The form '*Uza* is known also in one case on the Samaria Ostraca (No I, Gibson 1971: 8; Renz 1995: I, 89); on several Hebrew, Ammonite and Aramaean seals (Avigad and Zass 1997: 521) and on an Aramaean ostracon from Nimrud dated to the eighth century BCE (Albright 1958: 33; Aḥituv 1971: 112-13). The two words may be in the construct state and thus be translated as 'the army of '*Uza*'.

Line 3: the two letters *hd[* can be reconstructed as part of the name Hadad, or a composite name with the component Hadad.

Line 4: only one letter, '*aleph*, was preserved in this line.

Sherd No. 4 (Registration No. 788042/4)
This is a small sherd (2.5 × 3 cm, thickness 0.8 cm). Though the clay is more gritty than the other sherds, its colour and texture show that it may belong to the same jar as Nos. 1-3.

Fig. 12.8. *Sherd No. 4*

Reading:
Line 1:   bʿlẏ[
Line 2:   yh

Comments. Line 1: Following the first two clear letters *bet* and *ʿayin*, there is very faint letter. The reading *lamed*, suggested by Mrs Yardeni, may show that this word was a theophoric name with the component *Baal*. The last letter, probably belonging to the same name, is perhaps *yod* or *ṣade*.

Line 2: the two letters *yod* and *he* can be part of a theophoric name with the component *Yah*, yet this is very hypothetical. If correct, it would be interesting to have this component in the Northern Kingdom of Israel, where the more common ending is *yo*.

Paleographically, the letters in our inscriptions are very similar to those of the bulk of the Samaria Ostraca (compare with the table in Renz 1995: Band III Tf. 6). Most of these ostraca are dated to the first half of the eighth century. This date fits our ostraca as well. The numerals 1, 2, 3, 4 which appear in the inscriptions are in the hieratic forms, as in Judaean weights and Hebrew ostraca, including the Samaria Ostraca which are the closest to ours both spatially and temporally. The use of dots as dividers between the words is also common in the Samaria Ostraca.

Significance
As can be seen, the inscriptions are very fragmentary, and it is difficult to read some of the letters. It appears that these inscriptions are a small part of a longer list of names with numbers next to them, signifying quantities of merchandise, payment or the like. Lists of this type are well known among the ostraca of the Iron Age II in the Land of Israel, such as at Arad (Aharoni 1981, Inscriptions Nos. 31, 36, 49, 72). These are simple daily lists, written on cheap material like a bottom of a

broken jar. The private name Zema (or Zoma?) which appears several times in the inscriptions deserves special attention. It is possible that the list mentions several members of the same family. Another noteworthy point is the element *yah* in sherd No. 4 which may have been part of the Judaean theophoric component *yahu*, though this reading is not at all certain.

These inscriptions from Beth Shean are the only ink ostraca found in the Kingdom of Israel apart from the Samaria Ostraca (for a comprehensive catalog of inscriptions from the Iron Age II see Renz 1995) . This may be a consequence of the chances of discovery, yet it serves to emphasize the rarity of such inscriptions in the Northern Kingdom of Israel. It can be assumed that these were inscriptions of routine daily use, which were dumped into a refuse pit some time in the eighth century BCE, most probably before the conquest of the region by Tiglath Pileser III in 732 BCE.

Conclusions

The combination of the data from the excavation in Areas P and S enables us to reconstruct the stratigraphic sequence of the Iron Age II at Tel Beth Shean, as well as the extent of the town of this period. It appears that during the Iron Age only the upper part of the mound had been settled and the entire occupied area was no more than 1.4 hectares. Based on the evidence from Area P, and the finds of the previous excavations, it appears that the town remained unfortified. Three settlement strata dating to the period between the tenth and eighth centuries BCE were identified, two of which had sub-phases. Clear trends in the development of the pottery between these strata may be discerned. It appears that these three strata represent, respectively, the tenth, ninth and eighth centuries BCE. The city was destroyed during the Assyrian invasion in 732 BCE. Following this conquest, the site was only sparsely settled for a short period of time, after which there was an occupation gap until the Hellenistic period. The Hebrew inscriptions from Beth Shean, dating to the eighth century BCE, belong to the type of administrative-economic documents typical of the Iron Age. They are the only inscriptions of their kind to be found in the Kingdom of Israel aside from the Samaria Ostraca.

Bibliography

Aharoni, Y.
 1981   *Arad Inscriptions* (Jerusalem: The Bialik Institute and the Israel
           Exploration Society).
Ahituv, S.
 1971   'z'. *Encyclopaedia Biblica* (Jerusalem: The Bialik Institute), Vol. VI (in
           Hebrew).
Albright, W.F.
 1958   'An Ostracon from Calah and the North-Israelite Diaspora', *BASOR* 149:
           33-36.
Alexandre, Y.
 1995   'The "Hippo" Jar and Other Storage Jars at Hurvat Rosh Zayit', *Tel Aviv*
           22: 77-88.
Avigad, N., and B. Zass
 1997   *Corpus of West Semitic Stamp Seals* (Jerusalem: The Israel Academy of
           Sciences and Humanities, The Israel Exploration Society and the Institute
           of Archaeology of the Hebrew University).
Ben Tor, A., and D. Ben-Ami
 1998   'Hazor and the Archaeology of the Tenth Century BCE', *IEJ* 48: 1-37.
Braemer, F.
 1982   *L'Architecture Domestique du Levant à L'Age du Fer* (Paris: Editions
           Recherche sur les civilisations).
Chambon, A.
 1984   *Tell el Far'ah 1, L'Age du Fer* (Paris: Editions Recherche sur les
           civilisations).
Cross, F.M.
 1992   'An Inscribed Arrowhead of the Eleventh Century BCE in the Bible
           Lands Museum in Jerusalem', *EI* 23: 21*-35*.
 1996   'The Arrow of Suwar, Retainer of 'Abday', *EI* 25: 9*-17*.
Deutsch, R., and M. Heltzer
 1994   *Forty New Ancient West Semitic Inscriptions* (Tel Aviv: Archaeological
           Center Publications).
Finkelstein, I.
 1996a   'The Archaeology of the United Monarchy: An Alternative View', *Levant*
           28: 177-87.
 1996b   'The Stratigraphy and Chronology of Megiddo and Beth-Shean in the
           12th–11th Centuries BCE', *Tel Aviv* 23: 170-84.
 1998   'Bible Archaeology or Archaeology of Palestine in the Iron Age?', *Levant*
           30: 167-73.
Geva, S.
 1979   'A Reassessment of the Chronology of Beth Shean Strata V and IV', *IEJ*
           29: 6-10.
Gibson, J.C.L.
 1971   *Textbook of Syrian Semitic Inscriptions*. I. *Hebrew and Moabite
           Inscriptions* (Oxford: Clarendon Press).

James, W.F.

    1966   *The Iron Age at Beth Shean* (Philadelphia: University Museum).

Mazar, A.

    1993   'Beth Shean in the Iron Age: Preliminary Report and Conclusions of the 1990–1991 Excavations', *IEJ* 43: 201-29.

    1997   'Iron Age Chronology: A Reply to I. Finkelstein', *Levant* 29: 157-67.

    1999   'The 1997–1998 Excavations at Tel Rehov: Preliminary Report', *IEJ* 49: 1-42.

Na'aman, N.

    1998   'Shishak's Invasion of the Land of Israel in Light of the Egyptian Inscriptions, the Biblical Sources and the Archaeological Finds', *Zion* 63: 247-76 (in Hebrew).

Peleg-Zarzeki, A.

    1997   'Hazor, Jokneam and Megiddo in the Tenth Century BCE', *Tel Aviv* 24: 258-88.

Renz, J.

    1995   *Die Althebraischen Inschriften. Band I and Band III* (Darmstadt: Wissenschaftliche Buchgesellschaft).

Yadin, Y., and S. Geva

    1986   *Investigations at Beth Shean: The Early Iron Age Strata* (Qedem, 23; Jerusalem: Hebrew University).

13

BUSAYRA AND JUDAH:
STYLISTIC PARALLELS IN THE MATERIAL CULTURE

Piotr Bienkowski and Leonie Sedman

Introduction (Piotr Bienkowski)

The purpose of this paper is essentially to present some of the Iron Age small finds from the excavations at Busayra in Jordan, and to compare them with material from sites in Judah, particularly material from the so-called 'Edomite' sites of Horvat Qitmit and 'En Haseva. The discussion will attempt to sum up what the parallels signify, and in particular will address—again—the question of what is 'Edomite'.

The modern site of Busayra is located about 10 km south of Tafila and 45 km north of Petra in Jordan (Bennett 1983). The ancient site, to the north of the present-day town, is on a spur about 3200 sq. m in area. It is surrounded on three sides by deep ravines and is connected to the main land mass only to the south.

Busayra was first identified with biblical Bozrah by Ulrich Jasper Seetzen following his trip to the southern end of the Dead Sea in 1806 (Seetzen 1854–59). There is no inscriptional evidence to confirm or deny this equation. Bozrah as a city of Edom appears five times in the Old Testament. Scholars sometimes refer to it as Edom's capital, but nowhere is this explicitly stated—the closest is the reference in Amos 1.12, referring to the destruction of 'the palaces of Bozrah' which was to be symbolic of the defeat of Edom.

Nelson Glueck was the first to survey Busayra—it is interesting to recall that originally he thought the site was small and mostly Nabataean, and he preferred to identify Tawilan near Petra with biblical Bozrah (Glueck 1934: 14). Later, though, he changed his mind and accepted the equation of Busayra with Bozrah, an identification that is accepted today (Glueck 1935: 83).

Crystal Bennett excavated Busayra from 1971 to 1974 and in 1980 (Bennett 1983). She excavated four main areas; of particular interest were Areas A and C with monumental buildings, probably to be identified as a temple and palace, the one in Area C having a bathhouse. The material dates to the Late Iron II/Persian period possibly extending into the Early Hellenistic period (late eighth century BCE to c. 300/200 BCE) and there are some Nabataean/Roman remains. There has been a debate about whether there is any pre eighth-century material, but that is not relevant to the present paper (Bienkowski 1992b).

Bennett published preliminary reports on her excavations (Bennett 1973, 1974, 1975, 1977), but died in 1987 before starting work on a final report. Stephen Hart published a report on Busayra Area D and its pottery (Hart 1995), although that was taken more or less unchanged from his doctoral dissertation (Hart 1989), and it does not quite constitute a final report on that area. The final report on Bennett's excavations is currently being prepared by the writer (PB).

One of the authors (LS) is preparing the small finds from Busayra for publication in the final report (Sedman 2000). The Busayra material is the largest corpus of small finds so far excavated in Edom. One of the questions set when beginning her work was to see what, if anything, might be characteristic of this material and might allow us to talk about a recognizable 'Edomite' material culture. It has been particularly useful that so much good comparative material has recently been discovered and published from sites in Judah. The final report on Horvat Qitmit in the Negev has been published (Beit-Arieh 1995a), and material is beginning to be published on 'En Haṣeva, about 45 km to the south-east of Qitmit (Cohen 1994; Cohen and Yisrael 1995a, b). Both have been labelled 'Edomite shrines' or 'cult places' by their excavators. This makes it all the more worthwhile to start—or even to continue—asking questions about what is characteristically Edomite, and whether, in fact, 'Edomite' has any meaning in terms of material culture.

Parallels from Busayra (Leonie Sedman)

The excavations at Busayra produced a number of female figurines. They are without exception naked and pregnant, with both hands held to the breasts. None of the examples from Busayra is holding a baby or tambourine, and none has outstretched arms. At the time of writing, no specific identity can be attributed with confidence to these figurines. The preliminary impressions in this report are presented in the hope of promoting discussion regarding the relationship between Transjordan and Judah in Iron II.

The Busayra figurines are similar in form and size to many others from Iron Age sites all over the southern Levant. However, apart from those from Tawilan, which in some cases were nearly identical to the Busayra examples, there were no exact parallels at the time of their excavation. Although the figurines depicting a female, often pregnant, with her hands over her breasts were probably intended to represent the same subject, they do not appear to have come from the same artistic 'school'.

The publication of the finds from Horvat Qitmit has provided the first really close parallels to the Busayra material. The Busayra figurines already published in a preliminary report (Bennett 1973: pl. VIIIa) are cited as parallels in the Qitmit report; but there are additional unpublished objects from Busayra which provide interesting parallels to the finds from both Qitmit and 'En Haseva.

Comparing Figure 13.1 (centre, bottom) with Beit-Arieh (1995a: Fig. 3.69a), the horizontal double-row necklace is not absolutely identical, but seems to come from the same artistic 'genre'. A figurine head from Busayra (Fig. 13.2) compares well with Beit-Arieh (1995a: Fig. 3.75, 114-16), especially in the way the wig or headdress comes forward to frame the face, and the striking similarity of the representations. Although the details of the three examples from Qitmit seem to vary considerably, they are thought to have been possibly cast from the same mould, then finished with different incised or applied decoration.

A male head from Busayra (Fig. 13.3) seems to have a family resemblance to the 'kneeling man' from Qitmit (Beit-Arieh 1995a: 111, Fig. 3.80, 119) in its general appearance and the applied knobs for eyes. However, Pirhiya Beck (personal communication) noted that in fact the 'kneeling man' has a flattened appearance when viewed from the front which is not obvious from the published illustration. This emphasizes the pitfalls of attempting to compare objects known only from published illustrations but not actually seen and handled.[1]

1.   See also the bearded man from Qitmit (Beit-Arieh 1995a: 72, Fig. 3.44a, b), although this figure is hollow, unlike the Busayra example.

Fig. 13.1. *Four figurine heads from Busayra*

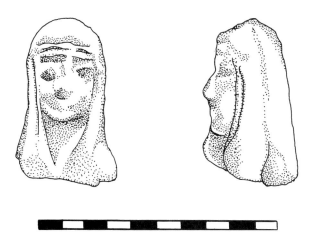

Fig. 13.2. *Figurine head from Busayra*

Fig. 13.3. *Bearded male figurine head from Busayra*

Beck also suggested that another head from Busayra (Fig. 13.4) may have broken away from the body in a particular way due to a method of manufacture whereby the head was made separately and joined to the body by a plug or dowel-like wedge at the neck. Examination of the figurine, however, indicated that, as with the other female figurines from Busayra, this example was manufactured in one piece in a deep mould.

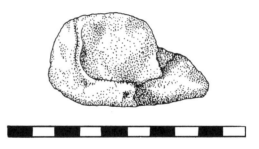

Fig. 13.4. *Figurine head from Busayra*

Some of the most beautiful objects from Busayra are the spouted zoomorphic vessels[2] (Fig. 13.5), the examples illustrated here all with applied trappings, paralleled by a less ornate example from Qitmit (Beit-Arieh 1995a: Fig. 3.93). It is possible to see where the bridle broke off, and it has a flat, fin-like mane, similar to one of the illustrated Busayra examples. The Qitmit fragment is identified as bovine (Beit-Arieh 1995a: 139), while some of the Busayra examples were originally registered as camels. The present writer prefers to identify them as horses, but of course horse and camel heads can appear very similar in isolation. Unfortunately there are no complete examples from Busayra, only heads without bodies and vice-versa, with none matching. None of the existing bodies appears to have been intended as a camel.

Fig. 13.5. *Two spouted zoomorphic vessels from Busayra*

The finds from 'En Haseva have not been published in full, but preliminary publications yield two strong parallels. A fragment of decorated pottery from Busayra (Fig. 13.6) and a large cult vessel from 'En Haseva (Cohen and Yisrael 1995a: 226; 1995b: 9) share the same indentation across the top and the same applied knob decorating the centre of the top. They both share a parallel from Megiddo (Schumacher 1908: pl. XXXIX) although that appears to be a decorative handle rather than a purely decorative element in itself.

---

2 . These appear to be vessels, since the heads and mouths (which is all that survives) are hollow.

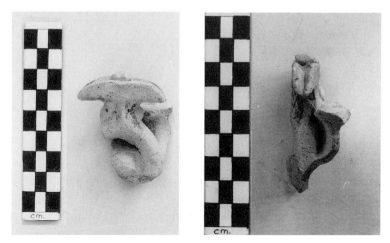

Fig. 13.6. *Fragment of decorated pottery from Busayra*

The hollow male figurine head from Busayra (Fig. 13.7, first published in Bennett 1973: pl. VIII), although much smaller in size, bears a close stylistic similarity to some of the large anthropomorphic stands from 'En Haṣeva (Cohen and Yisrael 1995a: 226; 1995b: 24, 33).[3] Both Qitmit and 'En Haṣeva produced decorative models of pomegranates (Beit-Arieh 1995a: 158, Fig. 3.107:187; Cohen and Yisrael 1995a: 227). P. Beck suggested (personal communication) that certain fragments from Busayra (Fig. 13.8) might possibly be pieces of a pottery pomegranate, but sufficient fragments do not remain for a positive identification. The largest Busayra fragment has bulbous projections, pushed out from the inside, which bear some similarity to pomegranate fragments (also pushed out from the inside) from Qitmit (Beit-Arieh 1995a: 156-57). However, the Busayra example appears to be more extreme in shape (leading to an initial identification as the breasts of a broken female figure). This is another example of the difficulties caused by not comparing objects directly, but relying solely on illustrations. Kletter (1999: 376) has also compared this Busayra example with a fragment from Tel 'Ira (Kletter 1999: Figs. 7.1:7, 7.2:6), although the Tel 'Ira fragment retains less of the surrounding area than the Busayra example.

3.   The Busayra head also has similarities to a fragment from Qitmit (Beit-Arieh 1995a: 50-51, Fig. 3.24:25a), especially the large flat nose and the bulbous eyes.

Fig. 13.7. *Hollow male figurine head from Busayra*

Fig. 13.8. *Pottery fragments from Busayra: part of pomegranate?*

There are parallels between the Qitmit and 'En Haseva cult vessels and finds from other Iron II sites in Transjordan (e.g. Tell el-Kheleifeh, Pratico 1993: 138, pl. 29:12), but these are not considered here. To date, the finds from Horvat Qitmit and 'En Haseva have provided some of the closest parallels yet for certain aspects of Busayra's material culture.

Discussion (Piotr Bienkowski)

The material presented shows that there are some close parallels between the finds from Busayra, a major centre in Edom, and Horvat Qitmit in particular, but also 'En Haseva, both in Judah. The excavators of Qitmit and 'En Haseva, Itzhaq Beit-Arieh (Qitmit) and Rudolph Cohen and Yigal Yisrael ('En Haseva), clearly think that this is significant. They have characterized both sites as Edomite shrines (Beit-Arieh 1995a: 306-10; Cohen and Yisrael 1995a: 224-28).

There is no problem with the identification of Horvat Qitmit as a shrine, which seems reasonable. It should be noted, however, that the 'cultic' material from 'En Haseva all came from a *favissa*, and the excavators' reconstruction of the shrine is hypothetical. Furthermore, the *favissa* assemblage as a whole is clearly not Edomite: there are very few parallels with material from Edom proper, and characteristic material of Edomite assemblages is missing. It is more likely that the *favissa* cultic assemblage is material characteristic of the Negev itself, and there is no need to look for outside influences. A distinction must be made between the assemblage from the *favissa*, which is not Edomite, and seventh-century BCE material from other contexts at 'En Haseva, some of which does have parallels in Edom.

Both Israel Finkelstein and the present writer have argued against the unrigorous use of the label 'Edomite' (Finkelstein 1992; 1995: 139-44; Bienkowski 1995a: 139). The reason for repeating these arguments is that the identifications as 'Edomite' shrines are being widely accepted, uncritically, and used as solid, unquestionable evidence for the movement of Edomites across the Wadi Arabah in the seventh or sixth centuries BCE, into the area which later became Idumaea (but see now Bartlett 1999). Indeed, Beit-Arieh has specifically argued that the finds at Qitmit indicate that Edom invaded and conquered parts of Judah (1995a: 314-15).

Apart from the iconographic parallels, there are three elements at Qitmit which have been labelled as 'Edomite': the pottery, the use of the name 'Qos', and the script. Beit-Arieh claims that the script and the occurrence of the name 'Qos' are 'strong culture-identifying elements', and that therefore the link between the material culture and ethnicity seems to be obvious (1995a: 316). Looked at rigorously, this link is not beyond dispute.

The root of the problem is the use and meaning of the word 'Edom'. It was variously used in antiquity to denote a geographical area, then a political state, and an ethnic group (Edelman 1995). Qitmit had a mixture of Palestinian Iron Age pottery and so-called 'Edomite' pottery, although analysis showed that none of the latter came from Edom proper but was probably locally made (Beit-Arieh 1995a: 285). By 'Edomite' pottery is meant painted pottery characteristic of Busayra and other sites in Edom, but it is also found at sites in the north-western Negev. Interestingly, it is not found at *all* sites in Edom: the mountain-top sites around Petra have little or no painted pottery (Zeitler 1992), so it is misleading to call it *characteristically* Edomite. Just because this pottery has been labelled 'Edomite', does not mean that wherever we find it, it was made and used by Edomites. There is *nothing* to indicate that this pottery was of necessity confined to any ethnic group, rather than being the standard Iron II/Persian painted pottery of an area extending beyond Edom proper, indeed, not even extending over all of Edom.

Beit-Arieh does not accept my labelling of this pottery as 'Busayra Painted Ware' (Bienkowski 1992a: 7), on the grounds that 'the diffusion of such pottery in the Negev does not support its definition as a local phenomenon' (Beit-Arieh 1995a: 303 n. 1). He misunderstands my purpose. I merely wish to avoid labelling this pottery with such a misleading term as 'Edomite', a term which changes its meaning depending on circumstances but which to most scholars implies a causal link between a political entity and one aspect of material culture that has not been adequately demonstrated. The label 'Busayra Painted Ware' is not meant to imply a phenomenon local to Busayra, but that this is the place where such pottery is most frequent and best known. Analogies might be Jemdat Nasr pottery in Mesopotamia, named after the site where it was discovered but a chronological indicator for the latest Uruk period over a wide area; or the proposal to rename 'Midianite' pottery—another misleading term—as 'Qurayyah Painted Ware', although it is distributed a long way from the site of Qurayyah itself (Parr 1988: 74).

The theophoric name Qos has been found in two inscriptions at Qitmit (Beit-Arieh 1995a: 259-60). However, the presence of the name 'Qos' is not by itself compelling evidence. We actually know very little about Qos. The name is found in Edom, the Negev and later in the Hejaz. Evidence for its use is still fairly sparse and uncertain, and we cannot automatically conclude that its use indisputably indicates an Edomite, nor that its mere presence at a shrine makes the shrine itself 'Edomite' (Bartlett 1989: 200-204; Dearman 1995).

The same argument holds for the 'Edomite' script, which is even less well known (Vanderhooft 1995). For all we know, its usage may be geographical rather than ethnic, and it too cannot automatically be used as an argument for the presence of Edomites. We may call it 'Edomite', but there is no clear evidence that it is specifically, characteristically and exclusively Edomite.

Beit-Arieh has stated that Edomite presence in the eastern Negev is an 'objective fact' (1995b: 38). There are actually very few objective facts in archaeology! What we have here is no more than conjecture and interpretation. Horvat Qitmit was a shrine, but we cannot prove that it was an Edomite shrine. 'En Haseva was *not* an Edomite shrine, but material from elsewhere at the site shows evidence of use by different groups. Beck's study of the iconographic material from Qitmit also concludes that there was a mixture of Transjordanian, Phoenician and general Levantine elements, and there is much that is not paralleled at all at Busayra or anywhere else in Edom proper (Beck 1995: 189-90). In addition, no shrine comparable to that at Horvat Qitmit has been found in Edom proper—indeed, no Iron Age shrine of any kind has been excavated in Edom, although the Area A building at Busayra might be identified as a temple. At this stage of our knowledge, it is simply misleading to use this material as indisputable proof for Edomite movement across the Wadi Arabah, let alone invasion and conquest (see Bartlett 1999).

During the discussion following this paper at the conference, I was accused of destroying the 'Edomite invasion and conquest' model and challenged to replace it with my own hypothesis. This I was not prepared to do at that time: we really know very little for certain about the Edomites, their chronology and their culture (Bienkowski 1995b: 61), and until we know more I felt strongly that we should eschew hypotheses in favour of keeping an open mind about the possibilities. As new evidence comes to light, we can then more easily ascertain which of the various possibilities is the more likely (see now Bienkowski 2000; Bienkowski and van der Steen 2001). There are several alternative possibilities for interpreting the finds from Qitmit and Haṣeva and their relationship with Edom, each with its own problems, and all subject to change and challenge from new evidence:

1) Finkelstein has interpreted Qitmit as a wayside cult place used by pastoral nomads. Among the deities worshipped was the Edomite god Qos (1995: 149). Beit-Arieh has criticized this hypothesis on the basis that the only 'foreign' pottery is Edomite and that he sees no connection with nomads (1995a: 310 n. 9). As argued above, the pottery is likely to have been locally produced, and I am unhappy about automatically concluding that any occurrence of the name Qos always denotes an Edomite connection. The little evidence we have does indicate that the Edomites worshipped Qos, but there is certainly insufficient evidence at present to make this conclusion absolute, that is, that the Edomites worshipped *only* Qos or that *only* the Edomites worshipped Qos.

2) The 'Edomite' elements at Qitmit and Haṣeva may not have involved people from Edom at all, but were merely aspects of a material culture shared between southern Transjordan and parts of the Negev and southern Judah. The *favissa* at Haṣeva was originally judged to be concurrent with the Stratum 4 fortress, which the excavators suggested was constructed by Josiah in the second half of the seventh century BCE (Cohen and Yisrael 1995a: 223). The excavators concluded that 'En Haṣeva was a high place dedicated to the worship of

one of the 'abominations' (1995a: 225). If they are correct,[4] and if this shrine was associated with an official Judahite fortress and had evidence of the worship of unsanctioned idols, then there is absolutely no reason to conclude that ethnic Edomites were ever present there or, consequently, at Qitmit. The implication is, surely, that it was *Judahites* worshipping Qos here, who would have been one of the pagan, foreign gods later suppressed. This option disassociates the material culture from the question of ethnicity and leaves it to future evidence to prove—or disprove—a direct link between this material and ethnic Edomites. However, the excavators' current (unpublished) view is that the seventh-century BCE materials from the 'fort' area at 'En Haseva all came from later fills, and that there are no *in situ* deposits contemporary with the *favissa* (Y. Yisrael, personal communication).

3) Qitmit and Haseva might be evidence of the movement of Edomites across the Wadi Arabah, but this would be a peaceful infiltration, perhaps by independent (pastoralist?) tribal groups, rather than a state-sponsored invasion and conquest. Everything we know about Edom as a state suggests that centralized control was weak (Knauf 1992: 52) and that its structure was tribal (LaBianca and Younker 1995). Lily Singer-Avitz persuasively interprets the westward distribution of 'Edomite' pottery as reflecting the route of the Arabian trade running through Edom via 'En Haseva, Qitmit and Beersheba to the Mediterranean coast (Singer-Avitz 1999). It is likely that such trade was conducted by pastoralist tribal groups, who were partially settled but continued to move and interacted with other similar groups from Arabia, the Negev and the west (Bienkowski 2000; Bienkowski and van der Steen 2001).

---

4.   Beit-Arieh (1995a: 310) speculates that the 'En Haseva Stratum 4 fortress might be Edomite, thus fitting into his invasion-conquest model. However, one of the excavators, Yigal Yisrael (personal communication), now disassociates this structure from the 'Edomite' pottery found within the fort area, and no longer dates it to the seventh-century BCE, preferring a Roman-period date.

Bibliography

Bartlett, J.R.
    1989   *Edom and the Edomites* (Sheffield: JSOT Press).
    1999   'Edomites and Idumaeans', *PEQ* 131: 102-44.
Beck, P.
    1995   'Catalogue of Cult Objects and Study of the Iconography', in Beit-Arieh (1995a): 27-208.
Beit-Arieh, I. (ed.)
    1995a   *Horvat Qitmit: An Edomite Shrine in the Biblical Negev* (Tel Aviv: Sonia and Marco Nadler Institute of Archaeology).
Beit-Arieh, I.
    1995b   'The Edomites in Cisjordan', in Edelman (ed.) 1995: 33-40.
Bennett, C-M.
    1973   'Excavations at Buseirah, Southern Jordan, 1971: A Preliminary Report', *Levant* 5: 1-11.
    1974   'Excavations at Buseirah, Southern Jordan 1972: Preliminary Report', *Levant* 6: 1-24.
    1975   'Excavations at Buseirah, Southern Jordan, 1973: Third Preliminary Report', *Levant* 7: 1-19.
    1977   'Excavations at Buseirah, Southern Jordan, 1974: Fourth Preliminary Report', *Levant* 9: 1-10.
    1983   'Excavations at Buseirah (Biblical Bozrah)', in J.F.A. Sawyer and D.J.A. Clines (eds.), *Midian, Moab and Edom: The History and Archaeology of Late Bronze and Iron Age Jordan and North-West Arabia* (Sheffield: JSOT Press): 9-17.
Bienkowski, P.
    1992a   'The Beginning of the Iron Age in Southern Jordan: A Framework', in Bienkowski (ed.) 1992: 1-12.
    1992b   'The Date of Sedentary Occupation in Edom: Evidence from Umm el-Biyara, Tawilan and Buseirah', in Bienkowski (ed.) 1992: 99-112.
    1995a   'The Architecture of Edom', *Studies in the History and Archaeology of Jordan* 5: 135-43.
    1995b   'The Edomites: The Archaeological Evidence from Transjordan', in Edelman (ed.) 1995: 41-92.
    2000   'Southern Jordan and the Negev in the Iron Age: Developing a New Model', *ASOR Newsletter* 50.3: 7-8.
Bienkowski, P. (ed.)
    1992   *Early Edom and Moab: The Beginning of the Iron Age in Southern Jordan* (Sheffield: J.R. Collis).
Bienkowski, P. and E. van der Steen
    2001   'Tribes, Trade and Towns: A New Framework for the Late Iron Age in Southern Jordan and the Negev', *BASOR* 323, in press.
Cohen, R.
    1994   'The Fortresses at 'En Haseva', *BA* 57: 203-14.
Cohen, R., and Y. Yisrael
    1995a   'The Iron Age Fortresses at 'En Haseva', *BA* 58: 223-35.

1995b   *On the Road to Edom: Discoveries from 'En Haseva* (Jerusalem: Israel
             Museum).

Dearman, J.A.
1995   'Edomite Religion: A Survey and an Examination of Some Recent
             Contributions', in Edelman (ed.) 1995: 119-36.

Edelman, D.V.
1995   'Edom: A Historical Geography', in Edelman (ed.) 1995: 1-11.

Edelman, D.V. (ed.)
1995   *You Shall Not Abhor an Edomite for He is Your Brother: Edom and Seir
             in History and Tradition* (Atlanta: Scholars Press).

Finkelstein, I.
1992   'Horvat Qitmit and the Southern Trade in the Late Iron Age II', *ZDPV*
             108: 156-70.
1995   *Living on the Fringe: The Archaeology and History of the Negev, Sinai
             and Neighbouring Regions in the Bronze and Iron Ages* (Sheffield:
             Sheffield Academic Press).

Glueck, N.
1934   'Explorations in Eastern Palestine and the Negeb', *BASOR* 55: 3-21.
1935   *Explorations in Eastern Palestine II* (AASOR, 15).

Hart, S.
1989   The Archaeology of the Land of Edom (unpublished doctoral dissertation,
             Macquarie University).
1995   'Area D at Buseirah and Edomite Chronology', in S. Bourke and J-P.
             Descoeudres (eds.), *Trade, Contact, and the Movement of Peoples in the
             Eastern Mediterranean* (Sydney: Meditarch): 241-64.

Kletter, R.
1999   'Human and Animal Clay Figurines', in I. Beit-Arieh (ed.), *Tel 'Ira: A
             Stronghold in the Biblical Negev* (Tel Aviv: Sonia and Marco Nadler
             Institute of Archaeology).

Knauf, E.A.
1992   'The Cultural Impact of Secondary State Formation: The Cases of the
             Edomites and Moabites', in Bienkowski (ed.) 1992: 47-54.

LaBianca, Ø.S., and R.W. Younker
1995   'The Kingdoms of Ammon, Moab and Edom: The Archaeology of
             Society in Late Bronze/Iron Age Transjordan (ca. 1400–500 BCE)', in
             T.E. Levy (ed.), *The Archaeology of Society in the Holy Land* (London:
             Leicester University Press).

Parr, P.J.
1988   'Pottery of the Late Second Millennium BC from North West Arabia and
             its Historical Implications', in D.T. Potts (ed.), *Araby the Blest: Studies in
             Arabian Archaeology* (Copenhagen: Museum Tusculanum Press): 73-89.

Pratico, G.D.
1993   *Nelson Glueck's 1938–1940 Excavations at Tell el-Kheleifeh: A
             Reappraisal* (Atlanta: Scholars Press).

Schumacher, G.
1908   *Tell el-Mutesellim I* (Leipzig: Rudolf Haupt).

Sedman, L.

    2000   The Busayra Small Finds: An Edomite Assemblage? (unpublished MPhil dissertation, University of Liverpool).

Seetzen, U.J.

    1854–59   *Reisen durch Syrien, Palästina, Phönicien, Transjordan-Länder, Arabia Petraea und Unter-Aegypten* (Berlin: G. Reimer).

Singer-Avitz, L.

    1999   'Beersheba: A Gateway Community in Southern Arabian Long-Distance Trade in the Eighth Century BCE', *Tel Aviv* 26.1: 3-74.

Vanderhooft, D.S.

    1995   'The Edomite Dialect and Script: A Review of the Evidence', in Edelman (ed.) 1995: 137-57.

Zeitler, J.P.

    1992   '"Edomite" Pottery from the Petra Region', in Bienkowski (ed.), 1992: 167-76.

INDEX OF AUTHORS

INDEX OF PLACE NAMES

JOURNAL FOR THE STUDY OF THE OLD TESTAMENT
SUPPLEMENT SERIES